W9-CZZ-532

DAT

Marx and the Ancients

Marx and the Ancients
Classical Ethics, Social Justice, and
Nineteenth-Century Political Economy

George E. McCarthy

Rowman & Littlefield Publishers, Inc.

ROWMAN & LITTLEFIELD PUBLISHERS, INC.

Published in the United States of America
by Rowman & Littlefield Publishers, Inc.
8705 Bollman Place, Savage, Maryland 20763

British Cataloging in Publication Information Available

Library of Congress Cataloging-in-Publication Data

McCarthy, George E.
Marx and the ancients : classical ethics, social justice, and
nineteenth-century political economy / George E. McCarthy.
p.   cm.
Includes bibliographical references and index.
1. Marx, Karl, 1818-1883.   2. Philosophy, Ancient.
3. Social ethics—History.   4. Social justice—History.
5. Economics—History—19th century.   I. Title.
B3305.M74M3915   1990   193—dc20   90–36564 CIP

ISBN 0-8476-7641-2 (alk. paper)

5   4   3   2   1

Printed in the United States of America

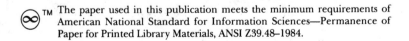 The paper used in this publication meets the minimum requirements of
American National Standard for Information Sciences—Permanence of
Paper for Printed Library Materials, ANSI Z39.48–1984.

For my son and daughter,
Devin and Alexa McCarthy,
with love

Contents

Acknowledgments

I would like to thank the Geschwister-Scholl-Institut für Politische Wissenschaft at the University of Munich for the use of their facilities in writing this work. Mention should be made of the encouragement and support by Professors Thomas Blakeley of Boston College and Royal Rhodes of Kenyon College. I would also like to recognize the research help received from Carol Marshall and Alan Bosch of Kenyon College's library staff. And a special thanks to Pat McCarthy who made a difficult transition easier.

Parts of Chapter Two appeared previously as "German Social Ethics and the Return to Greek Philosophy," *Studies in Soviet Thought* 31 (1986), and parts of Chapter Three appeared as "Marx's Social Ethics and the Critique of Traditional Morality," *Studies in Soviet Thought* 29 (1985). Permission for their use in this book has been given by Kluwer Academic Publishers.

A man of Greece was the first to raise mortal eyes in defiance, first to stand erect and brave the challenge. Fables of the gods did not crush him, nor the lightning flash and growling menace of the sky. . . . Therefore religion in its turn lies crushed beneath his feet, and we by his triumph are lifted level with the skies.

Marx quoting from Lucretius,
Doctoral Dissertation, 1841

Freedom, the feeling of man's dignity, will have to be awakened again in these men. Only this feeling, which disappeared with the Greeks and with Christianity vanished into the blue mist of heaven, can again transform society into a community of men to achieve their highest purposes, a democratic state.

Marx's Letter to Ruge,
May 1843

The criticism of religion ends with the doctrine that *man* is *the highest being for man,* hence with the *categorical imperative to overthrow all conditions* in which man is a degraded, enslaved, neglected, contemptible being.

Marx's *Contribution to the Critique of Hegel's Philosophy of Law: An Introduction,* 1843

In bourgeois economics . . . this complete working-out of the human content appears as a complete emptying-out, this universal objectification as total alienation, and the tearing-down of all limited, one-sided aims as sacrifice of the human end-in-itself to an entirely external end. This is why the childish world of antiquity appears on one side as loftier.

Marx in the
Grundrisse, 1858

Introduction

From his earliest days in the gymnasium to the completion of his university studies, Karl Marx was steeped in the culture and philosophy of the Ancients. From his earliest interests in Greek and Roman history and mythology to the completion of his dissertation on the physics of Epicurus and Democritus, ancient philosophy formed a central focus of his intellectual life. The purpose of this book is to examine some of the aspects of these interests with special attention to the philosophy of Aristotle and Epicurus. It will be shown how the values and ideals of the Greeks influenced the later development of his ideas of social justice, participatory democracy, and even his theory of economics. In fact, it will be argued that a true understanding of Marx's theory of value, his economic crisis theory, and his critique of political economy ultimately rests on his vision of social justice grounded in the ideals of the Greek polis. Without an appreciation for Epicurus's theories of happiness and nature or Aristotle's theory of universal and particular justice, the purpose of Marx's later analyses of the classical political economy of Ricardo, Smith, and Malthus would be lost. As unusual as it may sound, Marx's analysis of Ricardo's *Principles of Political Economy and Taxation* makes sense only within the context of Aristotle's *Nicomachean Ethics*. Within this context, too, Marx's ethics and theory of social justice will be closely examined.

In the past few years, the topic of Marx and ethics has been a popular one in North America. New works have produced a flood of analyses over whether Marx has a theory of ethics or a theory of social justice. One problem with many of them is that these questions have been asked within a cultural vacuum. Though they have been characterized by close exegetical scholarship, they have failed to

1

investigate the philosophical contexts and traditions on which the development of Marx's ideas were based. This has resulted in a study of Marx's words, but a loss of the underlying spirit that gives them meaning and relevance. This work will examine the deep structures and traditions on which his ideas were founded, through an examination of the classical ethics of Greek philosophy and the German Enlightenment. Karl Marx was caught between the two worlds of the Ancients and Moderns as he tried to integrate his critique of the structures and values of modern political economy with the ideals and norms of the Ancients. In the *Grundrisse* and *Capital* he analyzed the development of the structures of modern political economy, the workplace, the crisis of the economic system, and the institutional forms of liberalism. But what interested him in particular was the dialectic between these structures of industrial capitalism, and the formation of modern consciousness—the very possibilities of rationality, self-consciousness, and freedom within modern society.

Beginning with his Ph.D. dissertation on the Epicurean philosophy of nature and its critique of Democritus and Aristotle and extending into his later historical writings, Marx incorporates the ethical ideals and values of Greek social life into his understanding and evaluation of modern industrial society. Marx stood midway between the modernization of the workplace and the formation of new class institutions and forms of abstract labor, on the one hand, and the classical demands for equality, community, and social justice, on the other. These latter values were, in turn, not simply accepted as given, but were integrated and transformed by the ideals of individual freedom and the protection of human rights stimulated by eighteenth-century political philosophy and the French Revolution.

A closer investigation into the Ancients will unlock some of the secrets of Marx's views on materialism, science, ethics, and social praxis. Certainly an interpretation of these categories will be different if they are filtered through the classical traditions, rather than through the mechanical and deterministic materialism of the French Enlightenment and the ahistorical positivism and science of British political economy. By integrating Epicurus's materialism and philosophy of nature with Aristotle's critique of ethics as science *(episteme)* and his theory of social justice, Marx develops economic theory in an entirely new direction. The Ancients offer the reader of Marx a distinctly different picture of his approach than that of the more ordinary interpretation of reading him through the materialism and methods of Descartes, Holbach, Hobbes, Locke, Smith, and Ricardo.

By expanding the foundations of Marxism to include the Ancients, a broader and more fully developed understanding of some very perplexing issues comes about. Some of these issues include: (1) the richness of Marx's view of democracy, individual freedom, human rights, and personal development; (2) a more profound understanding of his critique of liberalism and modernity; (3) an historical and ethical reading of his law of value that differs greatly from the labor theory of value of Smith and Ricardo; (4) an integration of science and ethics (Epicurus); (5) the development of an alternative view of knowledge based on a critique of science and positivism that develops from Hume, Kant, and Hegel, but goes back to Epicurus and Aristotle; (6) the application of "theory and practice" as Marx's epistemological response to the "dilemma of objective validity" and his critique of science, epistemology, and foundationalism; (7) a broadening of our understanding of Marx's use of "praxis" to include not only theory, work, and art (Hegel), but also political and ethical activity in a democratic state (Aristotle); (8) a return to a materialist consensus theory of truth based on democracy and political economy (Aristotle and Rousseau); and (9) the reintegration of economics, politics, and moral philosophy into a social ethics as appeared in the Ancients.

Much of the contemporary U.S. literature on Marx and ethics has centered around a very narrow definition of moral philosophy by reducing it to questions about individual moral decision-making. This corresponds to the prejudices of the modern philosophical and religious traditions. It thereby eliminates from consideration almost immediately the nonmodern ethical perspectives, which included both the substantive content and ideals of classical ethics and the social theory and political economy of its metaethics. Marx—by this definition—has no moral philosophy, since he relied on a different perspective than that of the modern traditions. When this is joined to his critique of bourgeois morality and ideology, there is no place left for any moral theory. The final blow is administered by the general acceptance of the interpretations of his later historical materialism and economic theory as being scientific and positivistic. This precludes the acceptance of nonscientific criteria of evaluation. It is very difficult to make a case for an ethical theory in his works once these ideas are established and accepted.

Even among those who are more subtle in their interpretations and do not reduce Marx to a vulgar materialist, there is still a general acceptance of a split between his earlier philosophical writings and his later scientific ones. Critical theorists would prefer to stress the dialectical and philosophical approach, rather than his economic and scientific perspective. But this surrenders to modernity more than Marx himself was willing to accept. A narrow definition of both morality and science leads to a fundamental error in the study and evaluation of Marx. By seeing him in the tradition of Aristotle and Epicurus, morality is joined to social ethics, political economy, and political philosophy. Fresh air breaks through the rigidity and reified perspectives of modernity. This new view offers us a substantive break and transcendence of the morality of modernity, and broadens the horizons of our understanding of the nature of ethics and the applicability of classical ethics to the modern context, while at the same time expanding our appreciation of Marx's own social analysis.

In a previous work on Marx's critique of epistemology and science, I attempted to show that he was incapable and unwilling to apply the metaphysics of modern science to a critique of political economy.[1] By examining three different levels of concept and theory formation in his political economy, the positivistic interpretations of Marx were shown to be inadequate and inappropriate. The *methodological, ontological,* and *temporal* dimensions of a critical and historical science as found in *Capital* reveal a different set of priorities, methods, and purposes than those needed for a positivistic science. In fact, *Capital* does not have a concept of a predictable future (time), a deterministic and mechanical materialism (ontology), or a copy theory of reality (method), but—instead—a method based on historical analysis and dialectical critique. There is no split between his earlier and later works, since there is no split between philosophy and science; in fact, it is philosophy as "critique" that informs us as to the exact nature of Marx's understanding and use of the term "science."[2] While writing his later economic works, Marx was well aware of the epistemological problems associated with the formation and justification of modern science—what is called the "dilemma of objective validity." This is the problem of relating concepts to reality—theory to history—and the philosophical justification of the correspondence between them. What is at stake in social theory is the nature of the relationship between theory and ontology and the finding of a privileged form of discourse, through either empirical reality or deductive concepts, which will allow the justification of truth claims about our experience and knowledge of the world. The privileged access to truth and its epistemological justification through either empiricism or rationalism was called into question by Hume's critique of science and then by Hegel's later critique of the possibility of epistemology itself.

Once the rejection of the positivistic reading of Marx is established through a detailed investigation of the epistemology and methods used in *Capital* and the *Grundrisse,* the stage is set for the major question. If Marx was not applying a positivistic method in either work, then what was he doing? If *Capital* was not designed to explain economic crises, predict social breakdowns, or determine the particular costs and profits of commodities, then what was the purpose of its critique of political economy? When the writings of Marx are interpreted within the framework of the eighteenth- and nineteenth-century critique of science and foundationalism, then his dialectical method takes on new meaning. When access to truth was blocked due to the rejection of any privileged representation resulting from inductive or deductive logic, both Hegel and Marx turned to the concrete universal and social totality. "The being of a thing is the entire dynamic of its becoming something else and unifying itself with its other. Something can be known only by knowing its development—history. It is this movement or force which constitutes the reality of an entity."[3] The dialectical method is used to uncover the structures of historical reality, their internal ethical contradictions, and the organic interrelationship among their social institutions.

The later works of Marx are products of his understanding of history and social relations, which establish the material basis for his theory of ethics and social justice.[4] The critique of positivism clears away any hindrances to seeing these works in a new light and to recognizing the philosophical importance of the Ancients. The latter takes on real importance only when the scientific status of Marx's writings is undermined. When the German critique of positivism is united with the Greek and German theories and ideals of social justice, then ethics is fused with science in a new way that requires a careful exegesis of Marx's later political economy. With the critique of epistemology and science and the search for new methods to justify knowledge and truth claims, the traditional interpretations of the radical differences between Marx's and Aristotle's view of epistemology, praxis, and politics must be rethought. It is almost a truism in German social theory that Aristotle's view of praxis is antithetical to that of Marx's. This, too, is open to serious questioning.

With the critique of modern science and the reincorporation of the Ancients into modern social theory, a rethinking of Marx's theory of value, his views on human rights, democracy, and individual freedom, and—finally—the relations between politics and epistemology can also occur. The result is that the later economic and historical writings represent a synthesis of an historical critique of political economy within an overall ethical critique of capitalism. Though there is a normative critique throughout the *Grundrisse,* it is in *Capital* that ethics is united to a critique of the internal contradictions of the capitalist social system. Rather than being a work on the labor theory of value; rather than being a work on the prediction of economic breakdown; and rather than being a work on a theory of price determination, this work represents an historical analysis and dialectical presentation of the underlying structures of modernity, which are insurmountable barriers to the self-realization of the individual within society.

The purpose of Marx's critical method has never changed from his earlier works. "The criticism of religion ends with the doctrine that *man* is *the highest being for man,* hence with the *categorical imperative to overthrow all conditions* in which man is a degraded, enslaved, neglected, contemptible being."[5] The study of the social relations of production, the application of science and technology to material production, the class organization and nature of alienated work, and the macroeconomic features of an economy based on abstract labor and surplus value that tend toward overproduction, underconsumption, disproportionality, and a falling rate of profit are all part of a general theory of ethics and social justice. The latter lies deep within the structures of Marx's own thought. The critique of political economy supplies him with the social component within which the categorical imperative loses its abstraction from social reality and begins to take on a concrete historical form. Marx gives a materialist basis for furthering Hegel's critique of Kantian abstractionism. Morality has meaning for individual action only within the context of social institutions. If these institutions hinder or undermine the possibilities of rational self-conscious action, then morality itself becomes impossible. For Marx the social relations of an oppressive economy hinder the development of individual freedom and rational action.

Though Hegel's critique of Kant is the most immediate form of this perspective, the ethical foundations for both the substance and method of Marx's critique of capitalism lie in the Ancients. The real problem is that Marx never articulates this theory in a traditionally philosophical manner. His ethics is also too closely tied to his political economy and social theory to make much sense for contemporary philosophers unaccustomed to viewing them together. The difficulty is increased by the fact that with each new writing in his later period there is a new method used. Even within *Capital* alone, there are seven distinct levels and meanings of "critique": normative critique, immanent critique, fetishism critique, critique of political economy, dialectical critique, historical critique, and critique as crisis theory. They are all interwoven in his theory, and they are all based on different methodological and ethical traditions—some on liberalism, socialism, Aristotelian ethics, and so forth. The method peculiar to *Capital* places both social ethics and political economy within the context of the structural contradictions (dialectical method) of capitalism. In this fashion, the concept of alienation used in Marx's early writings (normative critique) is joined with his analysis of exploitation in the workplace and the irrationality of a crisis-ridden economic system. It begins with the contradiction between the social relations of production and the productive forces, and concludes with the crisis of the tendential fall in the rate of profit. The dialectical method transforms the analysis of political economy into a critique of the historical development and social organization of modernity. This is the real transformation that occurs in the law of value.

Marx criticized capitalism because it distorts human development and crushes individual potentialities (Aristotle); it creates a transcendent world of natural laws and economic divinities over which the individual human being has no control (Epicurus); it turns historical and human productions (objectification and externalization) into idolatrous objects of blind fate and blinder devotion (the Epicurean and Hebrew traditions); it undermines human rationality, moral autonomy, and self-determination (Rousseau and Kant); and it leads to distorted self-development and false consciousness (Hegel). These are some of the threads of the substantive ethics that run throughout Marx's writings. *Capital* is thus a sociological and logical critique of capitalism based on his unique appropriation of the three major traditions of classical social ethics: the ideals of the Greek polis, the Hebrew prophets, and late eighteenth- and early nineteenth-century German Idealism.[6] The integration of these traditions provides the ethical framework on which the evaluative and moral critique of capitalism rests. Rather than being a science of political economy, the later works of Marx provide us with an ethical critique of capital along with a concomitant moral imperative for social change.

Most clearly, the bulk of his writing is not on ethics, but rather on metaethics. Much of the substance of Marx's ethical theory assumes these philosophical traditions, while he spends his time and effort on clarifying the structures of social domination in the economic realm.

If an economy cannot realize its own normative ideals of freedom, equality, and social justice; if it cannot result in economic rationality and social prosperity; if its science and technology are utilized as mechanisms for intensification of the production of surplus value and further social control, then the system is not rational even by its own standards (immanent critique). This book will analytically break down the different intellectual traditions and their contributions to Marx's ethical theory and, in the final chapter, reintegrate them into a comprehensive social theory of justice. The book is divided into three main parts detailing the Ancients, the Moderns, and their synthesis in Marx's social theory. This synthesis provides us with insights into his postmodern critiques.

OUTLINE OF THE WORK

Part I: The Ancients

Chapter One examines Marx's dissertation written at the University of Berlin, but submitted to the University of Jena. It represents the culmination of years of academic study and personal interest in the aesthetics and politics of ancient Greece precipitated by the works of Winckelmann, Goethe, Schiller, Hegel, and Bauer. Marx's dissertation analyzes the metaphysical and natural theories of Epicurus and Democritus. Particular emphasis is placed on Epicurus's theory of the atom and meteors; the freedom, nonmechanical, and rational movement of the atom; Marx's distinction between *Naturphilosophie* and *Naturwissenschaften;* and his critique of positivism and heavenly bodies. The sense of harmony, rational integration, and beauty that marked nineteenth-century German neohumanism was to remain forever an ideal and political goal of Marx's life. What attracted him to this topic in the first place was Epicurus's integration of science and ethics and his attack on Aristotle's whole system—prefiguring Marx's later critique of Hegelian metaphysics. The quest for knowledge was to serve the quest for happiness *(ataraxy)*, and theories that undermined happiness were to be rejected. The natural theories of physics and astronomy were to serve the interests of ethical values and goals.

Chapter Two centers on epistemology, praxis, and the polis. It begins by outlining Aristotle's theory of social justice and its particular forms: distributive, corrective, and reciprocal justice. These different components present the structural foundations of a society within which ethics is defined as living in virtuous community interaction and prudential deliberation. Since it cannot be the result of a priori theoretical reasoning, ethics must arise out of the fragility of human experience and happiness in the good life. Because social and political norms cannot be determined outside the community, deliberation and political action become the defining characteristics of ethics. Human activity creates the framework within which the world is experienced and norms created and justified. Though working out of an entirely different set of epistemological assumptions, Marx—by responding to the debates surrounding the dilemma of modern science since Hume—comes to a conclusion about the nature of objectivity, truth, and social consensus that is similar to Aristotle's. Questions about the nature of knowledge are transformed into issues of praxis. Theory cannot provide the answers to questions raised by itself or by epistemology, but instead requires a social foundation for its truths—economic and political justice, a community of equals, political participation within a democracy, and the development of individual potentials. "Marx with Hegel before him, was profoundly influenced by the classical ideal of the citizen. The classical ideal of political freedom had to do with the freedom to be a full and participating member of the polis."[7]

Part II: The Moderns

Chapter Three deals with the rise of German Idealism. The central focus here is on Hegel's critique of Kant's practical reason and categorical imperative. Pressing the move from abstract moral philosophy with its emphasis on the alienated individual, Hegel attempts to reintegrate the individual back into the community and—in the process—moves from an ethics of *Moralität* (morality) to *Sittlichkeit* (social ethics). The ties between Hegel's political philosophy and his vision of the ideals of the Greek polis from his *Early Theological Writings* and *System of Ethical Life* to his later *Phenomenology of Spirit* and *Philosophy of Right* are examined. At this point the reader has a vantage point from which to view the full scope of the history of social ethics in these classical traditions, with their synthesis of ethics and political economy. In this chapter, there is also an analysis of Hegel's reaction to the violent extremes of the French Revolution, and the connection in his mind between the Terror and the abstract morality and subjectivism of Kantian moral philosophy. This becomes

the basis for Marx's criticism of abstract self-consciousness and morality in general, from his dissertation to his later writings.

Marx transforms the modern tradition's questions about moral
issues of right and wrong (Kantianism), good and bad (Protestantism
and Jansenism), and the nature of the good life and material happiness (utilitarianism)—along with questions about the nature of knowledge, truth claims, and the formation of consciousness—into inquiries
about the structure of modern social institutions—that is, into political
economy. The content and form within which moral and epistemological issues are decided, the personality developed, and various
claims to truth justified are made within historically specific social
relationships. Social class, power relations, property ownership, and
the social relations of production become the backdrop within which
traditional moral questions are to be answered. Philosophy has raised
these questions, but any hope of answering them requires social
theory and political economy.

Chapter Four reflects on Marx's more developed and expansive
theories of human rights and democracy, to show how they incorporate and then radicalize the liberal tradition and its defense of civil
rights and individual freedoms. The reasons for his critique of
liberalism are clearly outlined; rather than seeing his political theory
as a rejection of liberalism, it would be more appropriate to see it as a
radicalization *(Aufhebung)* of the social ideals of the French Revolution
within the philosophical parameters set by the classics. What Marx
especially rejects in liberalism are its philosophy of man and its
economic imperative to private accumulation and worker alienation,
which lies at the heart of the modern society. Of special interest is the
development of his theory of democracy from its early liberal stage in
the 1843 critique of Hegel's *Philosophy of Right* to his later socialist
views in the study of the Paris Commune of 1871. Within the context
of Marx's theory of democracy, his theory of human rights will be
further developed by comparing and analyzing his statements in
regard to the 1793 French "Declaration of the Rights of Man and
Citizen." Not enough time has been spent on Marx's distinction
between the ethical foundations of the rights of citizens in the state as
opposed to the rights of individuals in civil society. Generally, Marx's
defense of the former—human rights—has been overlooked, while
his critique of the latter has been interpreted as a critique of all
individual rights and personal freedoms. This comparison will help

to clarify further the developments and novelties in Marx's theory of human rights and his transcendence of the ideals of liberal democracy. The analysis of these ideas of his political philosophy will be tied to Marx's reliance on the Ancients. Also considered will be the reasons for these developments and their relation to his economic theory. This chapter will offer a critique of the whole of liberalism in its various forms including its epistemological and scientific assumptions, its political and social philosophy (natural rights theory and utilitarianism), its psychology of man from the state-of-nature arguments, and—finally—its economic doctrine found in classical political economy. While Marx may accept some of the social institutions and advances of liberalism, having one foot in the ancient traditions means that he cannot accept the limited perspective of modern individualism as manifested in its psychological, economic, and political forms of alienation. Modern individualism will not lead to self-determination, moral autonomy, and individual development. In fact, it will only ensure their failure.

Part III: The Synthesis of the Ancient and Modern in Marx

Now that the ethical traditions and their integration into Marx's social theory have been analyzed, I will turn to an investigation of the labor theory of value. This theory provides the historical and structural content to Marx's ethical theory; without it, there would be no ethics. Arguing against liberal political theory and political economy, Marx radically changes the theory of value from an ontology of labor and price determination to an historical and transcendental law of the development of modern industrial capitalism. It is no longer a political or economic theory, but an historical analysis and evaluation of those institutions and structures that were the necessary structural prerequisites for the evolution of modern society. This is just another implication of the meaning of his term "critique of political economy." Marx develops a law of value *(Wertgesetz)* that is not a law of price determination *(Wertrechnung)*, but an historical and sociological analysis of the social preconditions for capital accumulation, profit realization, and continued economic development. Beginning with an analysis of the structures necessary for abstract labor and surplus value production in the *Grundrisse* and volume 1 of *Capital*, Marx shows the connection between these man-made historical institutions and the chronic economic crises of modernity in volume 3 of *Capital*.

Throughout this analysis, the connections are made between history and ethics, the development of modern social institutions and the failure of species- and self-realization. In his historical structuralism, the law of value is transformed into a social critique—that is, an ethical condemnation of exploitation, alienation, the lost possibilities of human development, and the irrationalities and barbarism of the "anarchy of production." The original integration of science and ethics that Marx saw in Epicurus's physics and astronomy is recapitulated in his own later writings.

Chapter Six—the final chapter here—pulls this material together to form a comprehensive theory of ethics and social justice by integrating Marx's theory of the needs of species being (social eudaimonism), human rights, political and human emancipation, democracy, and the critique of political economy (as covered in Chapters Three, Four, and Five) with the substantive ethical ideals of the Ancients (discussed in Chapters One and Two). In the last analysis, social justice for both the Ancients and Marx deals with the nature of social relationships, the integrity of the community, the development of the communal nature of human beings, and self-realization. At the turn of the twentieth century, the Marburg School of neo-Kantians attempted the synthesis of Kantian ethics and Marxian political economy in order to rectify what they perceived as the weaknesses of the asocial and ahistorical moral philosophy of Kant and the historical materialism without ethics of Marx. At the end of the century, the "Tucker–Wood Thesis" now contends that Marx did not develop a moral theory or a theory of justice, because his scientific methodology and critique of ideology precluded him from doing so.

There are many variations on these themes. Some social philosophers accept the view that Marx does have an ethical critique based on such categories as economic exploitation, freedom, self-realization, and so forth; but they, too, conclude that he has no theory of justice. The two sides of the debate over the existence or nonexistence of a theory of ethics and social justice are clearly outlined and juxtaposed for easy comparison. As they have appeared up until now, both sides must be rejected as having a too narrow understanding of the nature of ethics, since they mainly limit Marx's concept to a discussion of the distribution or exchange of social wealth and do not focus on the structure of society as a whole. Nor do they—for the most part— attempt an integration of his economic perspectives with the classical ethics of German Idealism and the Ancients, with his own historical critique and social theory of value, or with his critique of science and positivism. Marx must be rethought—from his materialist epistemology to his materialist ethics.

This chapter will then proceed to define the use of such categories as justice, morality, social ethics, and metaethics and will show their relation to social theory and political economy. Much of Marx's social theory simply does not make sense within the context of Anglo-American definitions of morality and justice, because they have consistently separated ethics from metaethics, morality from political economy. This becomes immediately clear when compared to the methods of the classical traditions. These traditions are juxtaposed to the U.S. analytical perspective to see what insights may be gained for a reading of Marx. The analysis begins not with a predefined and prejudged interpretation of morality, but with the actual traditions that laid the foundations for Marx's own analysis. Ethics comes from within Marx's political economy and is not imposed from without. We must see Marx as he dialogues with the Ancients and draws his normative support and critique from them.

The last two sections of Chapter Six develop the radical implications of the previous studies on epistemology and ethics by summarizing Marx's ethical and metaethical theory and its three crucial components: (1) a theory of social justice; (2) a materialist consensus theory of truth based on his ethical epistemology; and (3) a democratic theory of political economy. These ideas are further developed by a comparison of Marx's ethics and theory of democratic consensus with Habermas's theory of ethics and discursive rationality. Habermas—by reducing Marx's dialectical science to positivism, praxis to *techne,* political activity to instrumental activity, and reflective knowledge *(Reflexionswissen)* to productive knowledge *(Produktionswissen)*—also misinterprets his views of praxis and political activity, democratic consensus, and the integration of ethics and political economy. Habermas has failed to recognize that there is a rich intellectual tradition of consensus theory based on both materialism and political economy, running from Aristotle to Marx.

In these sections, the main thesis of the work is finally presented in its full form. If the objects of experience are constituted in human activity—if social reality is not an empirical fact or a deduced idea, but the creation of the social organization of reality in history (historical materialism)—then there is no privileged access to truth or transparency of nature through either empiricism or rationalism. The correspondence between thought and reality is severed, and with it an epistemological theory for the justification of truth claims based on a privileged access to truth.[8] Without a privileged form of discourse, then, what are the standards of judgment or criteria of ethical evaluation in Marx's critique of modernity? How are they to be justified? How are they to be applied in practical activity? And what are the epistemological foundations and justifications for Marx's ethics and theory of social justice? The substructure of Marx's later writings corresponds to Aristotle's *Nicomachean Ethics* and *Politics* as he responds to the crisis of epistemology and science and the dilemma of ethical objectivity arising out of the writings of Hume, Kant, and Hegel. The modern crisis of epistemology and science, along with his own ethical ideals, drives Marx back to the Greeks. Marx responds to the epistemological critiques of Hume, Kant, and Hegel—on the one hand—and Ricardo's labor theory of value—on the other—by return-ing to Aristotle for inspiration and guidance.[9]

Aristotle was faced with similar problems in defining the nature of universal ethics, justice, equality, and the correct political order. He, too, found the process of determining the normative truth of ethical judgments and political theory and the nature of the future good society impossible to decide scientifically. He reached the conclusion that ethics and the good life develop from political interaction and public deliberation. Neither Aristotle nor Marx would define justice, happiness, or the good society; neither of them outline or describe in any detailed way their social ideals or the institutional frameworks that would give them meaning. Both recognize the impossibility of an a priori determination of truth, and both critique pure theory isolated from practical activity. And finally, both recognize this dilemma of epistemology and turn to democratic consensus to solve it.

Rejecting the traditional approaches to Marx's view of theory and praxis, it will be argued here that practical activity for both Marx and Aristotle includes both *praxis* (practical action) and *phronesis* (political wisdom). Marx's theory of praxis cannot be limited to simply an economic category of work. History and political economy give social and ethical content to practical activity, and it is through public participation and accumulated political experience that the truth of ethics is finally determined. Aristotle and Marx replace dogmatic epistemology with the polis and universal ethics with political dialogue as the quest for certainty becomes transformed into the search for political wisdom through public deliberation and democratic consen-sus in the polity. The Ancients have been incorporated into the Moderns. However, neither Aristotle nor Marx have a pure consensus theory of truth, since both also incorporate theories of happiness and self-realization into their social ethics. The connections between these elements will be worked out in the course of the next few early chapters.

And finally, Chapter Six attempts to make a statement regarding Marx's comprehensive theory of ethics and social justice. His theory integrates his philosophy and dialectical science, his early and later works, and his views on modernity and the Ancients into one complete picture. The theory may be outlined as follows:

Ethics: Moral Values and Abstract Ideals of Classical Ethics

1. individual freedom and moral autonomy (Epicurus and Kant); see Chapters One and Three
2. self-realization of human possibilities within the community (Aristotle and Hegel); see Chapters Two and Three
3. critique of alienation, exploitation, and fetishism (German Idealism); see Chapter Two
4. distributive justice, human rights, and self-determination in a participatory democracy; see Chapter Four

Metaethics: Structures of Modern Political Economy and Social Justice

1. analysis of the *past* through an historical critique based on the application of a transcendental logic; theory of value and abstract labor; history of capitalism *(Grundrisse);* see Chapter Five
2. analysis of the *present* potentialities through an immanent critique based on a dialectical logic; social contradictions and economic crisis theory; logic of capital *(Capital);* see Chapter Five
3. deliberation about the *future* based on a critique of epistemology and a materialist consensus theory of truth; ideals cannot be determined by pure theory, but are formed through practical action (praxis); theory of economic democracy and "theory and praxis" *(Theses on Feuerbach* and the *Civil War in France: The Paris Commune);* see Chapter Six

Marx's theory is composed of an ethical and metaethical component in a manner similar to Aristotle's ethical and political theory. There is a dialectical relationship between the two. This integration of ethics and political economy expresses the novelty of his analysis of morality and ethics in the nineteenth century. Ethics provides the substantive moral content of social critique (moral and social philosophy) and the abstract political ideals for a future society (political theory), while metaethics provides the analysis of the broader social structures within which these values and ideals can or cannot be realized (political economy). The historical and dialectical critiques of metaethics show how a social system built on the law of value and abstract labor and the contradictions between use value and exchange value cannot possibly realize the ideals of classical ethics and social justice. A social system founded on an historical system of social alienation and economic exploitation—whose future is clouded by economic stagnation, class struggle, and social discontent—cannot actualize the potentialities inherent in the ideals and technology of liberalism. Metaethics is thus the social frame within which the ethical values are made concrete and real. It provides an analysis of the structures of political economy that overcomes Marx's criticism of the abstract metaphysics and subjective morality found in Epicurus, Kant, the French Socialists, and the Left-Hegelians. The result is a theory of social justice.

Metaethics integrates not only the temporal dimensions of the past, present, and future in its analysis of capitalism, but also the different types of critical analyses appropriate to each dimension found in Marx's writings. Each type is necessitated by the material under investigation—whether that be the history of capitalism or the logic of capital. From the list above, we can see that the balance between modernity and the Ancients is reflected in the relationships between Kant and Hegel, and Epicurus and Aristotle. Both pairs express the dialectic between individual freedom and the common good. Their relationships in Marx's thought are mediated by the law of value and the structures of modernity.

Part I

The Ancients

Chapter One

Post-Aristotelian Greek Philosophy of Nature: Marx and Epicurus

INTRODUCTION

A cursory review of Marx's educational background reveals an extensive training in Greek and Roman language, philosophy, and history. At the Trier Gymnasium he steeped himself in the works of Cicero, Tacitus, Horace, Plato, Thucydides, Homer, and Sophocles. Here Marx's favorite subjects were Greek, Latin, German, and history. During his early university days in Bonn, Marx centered his studies around Greek and Roman poets and philosophers. In the house of his father-in-law Baron von Westphalen (to whom his dissertation was dedicated), he was inundated with the works of the Romantic School, especially Voltaire and Racine along with Homer and Shakespeare. At the University of Bonn he continued his interests in the Romantic School through attendance at the literary lectures of A. W. von Schlegel entitled "Questions about Homer" and "Elegies of Propertius" and in F. G. Welcker's course "Mythology of the Greeks and Romans."[1] At this time Marx belonged to a group of "Bonner Poets" (which included Karl Grün and Emanuel Geibel), whose interests were in a rebirth of the Greek aesthetic ideal, especially the ideals of beauty and harmony.

As Rolf Sannwald states in his important work on Marx and the Greeks, these individuals were searching for the beautiful, for happiness, and for peace led by their prophets Goethe and Heine. Marx

19

absorbed everything new written about the Ancients, especially by Lessing and Winckelmann, and continued his research and translations of some of the major classical texts: Tacitus's *Germania,* parts of Aristotle's *Rhetoric* and *De anima,* and the *Libri tristium* from Ovid. At the University of Berlin, Marx continued to discuss these works and their implications with Bruno Bauer, Köppen, Feuerbach, and the other members of the famous *Doktorklub.*[2] Both Bauer and Köppen had an interest in post-Aristotelian Greek philosophy, and Bauer was also a scholar of the Old Testament. While working on his dissertation material at the university, Marx took a course taught by Bauer on the Old Testament prophet Isaiah. Marx also was interested in the contemporary historical conflict between the ideal picture of Greece and the reality of German research about the Ancients in the works of Boeckh, Sismondi, Dureau de la Malle, Mommsen, Niebuhr, and Garnier, along with the original sources about Greek society from Aristotle and Xenophon. When Marx's personal library was catalogued toward the end of his life, there were more than 90 works by Greek and Roman authors—two-thirds of which were in the original language.

It is clear that, from his early days in the gymnasium through his studies at the universities of Bonn and Berlin, Marx had intensified his interest in the Ancients, who provided him with the wellspring for many of his dreams and hopes for the future and for a picture of mankind on which he would later build his critique of political economy. They provided him with an anthropological insight into the integrated and harmonious human being, which would be incorporated into his *Economic and Philosophical Manuscripts of 1844* (also known as the *Paris Manuscripts*) and also lay behind much of the political economy in the *Grundrisse* and *Capital.*[3] All these works draw heavily from the elegiac spirit and the aesthetic radicalism of his early university days. Trying to understand Marx without Aeschylus or Homer is the same as attempting to understand Marx without Smith or Ricardo. The Greeks were at the intellectual and emotional heart of Marx's critiques of modernity, science and positivism, and the false objectivity of the capitalist social relations that undermine possibilities for individual freedom and self-consciousness. It is for this reason that his choice of dissertation topic was so important.

Marx had paid special attention to Epicurus not only because he seemed to have led Greek philosophy to its conclusions with its important consequences, in which he freed the individual from the last conditions, and because the modern promethean pathos receives its impetus from his work, but because Hegel had not found a correct relationship to Epicurus as the ancient philosopher of self-consciousness. The atheistic follower was convinced to work on the solution of a not yet solved problem from the history of Greek philosophy. Hegel's judgement on atomic physicists and Epicurus in particular is the take-off point for Marx's analysis.[4]

For Sannwald, Epicurus represents the inevitable consequence of Greek philosophy as it leads to its logical conclusions. Epicurean thinking recapitulates theoretically the development of the Greek spirit, with its central emphasis on one major philosophical subject: the development of the self-conscious individual from the substance of the social world of the Greek polis. Out of the social forms comes the free individual, as manifested in the development of Epicurean philosophy out of and in reaction to the Aristotelian system and the religious tradition and values of Greece.

> Marx placed Epicurus, the greatest of the Greek Enlightenment, in the line with Prometheus, the opponent of Zeus. It is the battle against the gods and the faith in the autonomy of human self-consciousness, which unites both. Also Marx's atheism lives genuinely from the ideal of the completely independent man, who at last wants no other master but himself.[5]

For Marx, both Epicurus and Prometheus personify opposition to all forms of externally imposed authority, whether it come from the religious mystification of the Greek myths or the myths of the phenomenology of the Spirit. Through the praxis of theoretical critique, the objectivity and reality of human-created myths are exposed; and behind them is revealed only the subject itself. This reintegration of the subject and object—of essence and appearance—is the Hegelian imperative, which Marx carries through by means of his analysis of post-Aristotelian Greek philosophy and the critique of both Aristotle and Hegel.

MARX'S DOCTORAL DISSERTATION

The Greek polis, the substance of the Greek spirit, and Aristotle—in particular—offered Marx the classical ideal from which he drew much insight and vision for development of his notion of the commonwealth and common being of man *(Gemeinwesen).*[6] The further development of his thought and its relation to Hegel's metaphysical system is revealed in his dissertation, *Difference between the Democritean and Epicurean Philosophy of Nature* (1840–41)—of which only parts remain—and in the equally important preparatory notebooks filled with intellectual raw material on which the dissertation was based: *Notebooks on Epicurean Philosophy* (1838–40).[7] The dissertation is divided into two main parts and a two-part appendix. The first part, which contains only three of the original five chapters, examines the epistemological and methodological differences between Democritus's and Epicurus's theories of the atom. The second part deals with Epicurus's theory of the movement and properties of atoms and the ethical primacy of self-consciousness over the physical laws of nature. The appendix constitutes the third section and is entitled "Critique of Plutarch's Polemic against the Theology of Epicurus." It contains only a three-page fragment; and some have speculated that it originally contained a synthesis of Epicurus's views on science, materialism, and atheism. From the table of contents, it appears that, through his analysis of Epicurus, Marx had begun to develop a theory of religion. Marx intended to use both the *Doctoral Dissertation,* the *Notebooks,* and the two sections of this appendix as the basis for an expanded version that would examine the whole of post-Aristotelian philosophy including Epicureanism, Stoicism, and Skepticism. This new book was intended to satisfy the second dissertation requirement for teaching at a German university.[8]

The *Notebooks* helped prepare for the dissertation by examining the history of philosophy for its various critical responses to Epicurus's atomism. It draws mainly from the works and interpretations of Diogenes Laertius, Sextus Empiricus, Eusebius, Simplicius, Stobaeus, Aristotle, Plutarch, Lucretius, Seneca, and Cicero and contains an impressive number of quotations from the classical Greek and Roman authors. Both the *Notebooks* and the *Dissertation* are extremely important in that they prefigure some of the central ideas of Marx's later social theory and have been generally overlooked as helpful material in recreating Marx's later methodological concerns in his critique of political economy. We also see an explicit combination of ideas such as ethics and science in these early works. Though the combination of ethics and science appears contradictory to the modern consciousness, it forms the methodological foundation for Marx's later political economy in *Capital*—where, however, it is never explicitly articulated. This failure to articulate the issue of ethics has led—as we shall see in

Chapters Five and Six—to much confusion and contradictory statements regarding Marx's methodological intentions and the exact
nature and scope of his critique of bourgeois political economy.
Though explicit correlations between his *Dissertation* and his later
works can be made only carefully—due to the intellectual distance
between the two periods, methods, and orientations—the former does
offer us insight into a clarification of the direction and justification of
his later works.[9]

Some of these ideas centering around Epicurus's epistemology,
theory of science, ontology, and social ethics that continue to be
important later for Marx's intellectual development of his economic
theory include: (1) the importance of the contradictions between
essence and existence, principle and foundation, and concept and
reality in his theory of atomic physics (alienation); (2) the centrality
of chance, abstract possibility, and *ataraxy* (happiness) in his theory of
atomic declination or swerving; (3) the methodological issues and
problematic status of scientific explanation, and the relationships
between experience (sensuous perception) and reflection (abstract
reason); (4) the nature of science, its truth claims, and the ontological
status of its concepts and theories; (5) the critique of positivism and
natural science in his analysis of Democritean materialism, which
forms the basis for distinctions between the different methodological
views of science in Greek philosophy: *Naturwissenschaften* (Democritus)
and *Naturphilosophie* (Epicurus); (6) the initial development of the
relationships among epistemology, philosophy of nature, and ethics
and the synthesis of materialism and ethics—of science and ethics—
in Epicurus's *Naturphilosophie;* (7) Epicurus's critique of mystification,
religion, and false consciousness in his meteor theory; (8) the primacy
of subjectivity, self-consciousness, and freedom over natural laws and
determinism in his physics; (9) the critique of the notions of destiny
in Stoicism and necessity in Democritus—the atom being viewed as
abstract self-consciousness; (10) Epicurus's critique of the totality of
Aristotle's philosophical system—which forms the basis for Marx's
critique of Hegel's abstract system; (11) the development of the theory
of the atom from substance (Democritus) to subject (Epicurus) as
representing the theoretical expression of the very dynamics of Greek
society, as subjective freedom breaks with the restrictions of Greek
ethos and law; Greek philosophy expresses the social consciousness
and contradictions of social life in Greek society; (12) examination of
the debate between two German theories of science—Kant *(Verstand)*
and Hegel *(Vernunft)*—as prefigured in the relationships between

Democritus's natural science and Epicurus's philosophy of nature; (13) comparison between two views of Greek materialism: the empiricism of Democritus and the idealism of Epicurus; (14) the centrality of physical movement and activity (swerving and repulsion) and theoretical praxis as the basis of science and the being of man—man as a *Vernunftswesen* in nature; (15) the examination of positivism and science as a process of mystification (forerunner of ideology) and a distortion of the relationship between objectivity (substance, matter, and nature) and subjectivity (individuality and self-consciousness); (16) the importance and centrality of Schelling's philosophy of nature and his critique of mechanical and deterministic natural science, which will frame the whole body of Marx's works, from his analysis of Epicurus's theory of atomic motion to his later economic analysis of Ricardo's theory of value; and finally (17) a clearer appreciation of an alternative view of materialism that develops from Aristotle, Epicurus, and Schelling to Marx and represents a rejection of the Cartesian view of materialism.[10]

In the contemporary history of philosophy, various authors have attempted to attribute one major cause behind Marx's interest in the classical materialism of post-Aristotelian Greece. Cornu, Mehring, Lukács, Sannwald, Hülsewede, and Hillmann have attributed one or more of the above points as the major reason for his interest.[11] Whether one cause or many, it is clear that Marx's contact with and dependency on the intellectual wellsprings of Greek philosophy provided crucial inspiration, which—while transformed—was never forgotten in his later writings. "His lifelong confrontation with Greek philosophy, especially with Aristotle, decidedly influenced and formed his whole work, not only his economic theory."[12]

Though Hegel had correctly related the general aspects of Epicurean, Stoic, and Skeptic philosophy in his *History of Philosophy*—according to Marx in the foreword to his *Dissertation*—he was unable to understand the real importance of these three schools of Greek thought and their relevance for the history of philosophy.[13] For Marx this was due to the abstractness of Hegel's thinking. In fact, Hegel was extremely critical of Epicureanism, whose epistemology, metaphysics, and philosophy of nature he characterized as trivial, superficial, arbitrary, and boring; while Marx characterizes Epicurus as the greatest of the Greek Enlightenment. Baronovitch argues that Marx is critical of Hegel's thinking on this issue, especially the idea that Epicurus's theory of the atom is "devoid of both thought and a general moving principle."[14] However, Baronovitch also recognizes that Marx is reconstructing the origins of theoretical self-consciousness of which Hegel's theory of the Absolute Spirit is the historical apex.

A superficial reading of Epicurus, which has been—unfortunately for Marx—the legacy of Western philosophy, would indicate that many of the former's key concepts were taken from Democritus's theory of the atom. However, on closer examination, a real profound difference between the two arises within the philosophical context in which these categories are developed. Marx sees in Epicurus a radical critique and a break with traditional Greek philosophy—and with Aristotle, in particular. Hillmann argues that it was in this very break from Aristotle and the development of an alternative understanding of *Naturphilosophie*, praxis, and subjectivity, that Marx hoped to sharpen his own critique and break with Hegel.[15]

Epicurus provided the philosophical and psychological strength Marx needed to make his own personal and philosophical break with the towering figure of the former Berlin professor, who had died in 1831. Marx would accept Köppen's statement that "Epicureanism, Stoicism, and Skepticism are the nerves, muscles, and intestinal system of the ancient organism, whose immediate natural unity conditioned the beauty and customs of the ancient Greeks and which by whose death conditioned the same breakup."[16] The Epicurean system was the more highly valued by Marx because—as the nerve system of Greek thought—it connected the organism to the external world, acted on that world, and mediated all connections between subjectivity and objectivity. Marx makes clear in the foreword that his positive appreciation of Epicurus rests on the centrality given to freedom, self-consciousness, and the critique of all forms of alien objectivity.

> Philosophy makes no secret of it. The confession of Prometheus: I hate the pack of gods, is its own confession, its own aphorism against all heavenly and earthly gods who do not acknowledge human self-consciousness as the highest divinity. It will have none other beside.[17]

This is also the battle cry of German neoclassical humanism, which will form the foundation stone for Marx's analyses of alienation and commodity fetishism, and his theory of value. The priority of the individual and freedom is expressed in the critique of all externally enforced social and cultural values that undermine the possibilities of the development of rational self-consciousness. Thus, the major theme in Marx's *Dissertation* is an analysis of traditional Greek philos-

ophy and alienated self-consciousness in the Aristotelian and Democritean philosophy of nature.

EPICURUS'S CRITIQUE OF POSITIVISM

Though the evidence from the history of philosophy, especially the
works of Cicero and Plutarch, reveals little difference between Democritean and Epicurean physics, Marx sees crucial distinctions in
the areas of their definitions of knowledge and science, their differing
truth claims and scientific methodologies, their different forms of
explanation of the physical phenomena (metaphysics), and—perhaps
most important of all—their different interpretations of the relationships between concepts and reality, theory and being, and epistemology and ontology.[18] "They stand diametrically opposed in all that
concerns truth, certainty, application of this science, and all that
refers to the relationship between thought and reality in general."[19]
These discussions are found in the first part of the extant *Dissertation*.

Democritus makes a sharp distinction between the opinions *(Schein)*
of the senses (subjective semblances) and the reality of the atoms and
the void perceived through reason. The distinction is so strong that
the principle of the atom does not enter into the appearances; it does
not attain existence or reality. And therefore—almost as if by de-
fault—the "world of sensation" takes on ontological priority. It is this
reality that has importance, and Democritus relies on empirical observation (positivism) as the basis for knowledge. The theory of the atom
is never developed and is used more as a deus ex machina.

The principles of atomic physics do not enter into the world of
appearance, and thus the world of sensation is perceived as the real.
Since atoms are not part of the sensuous world, they do not have
"objective appearance but subjective semblance *(Schein)*."[20] Though
the principle is the real, it never enters into the world of perception,
leaving the senses as the only guide to knowledge. The world becomes
its own criterion divorced from the principles of physics. This separation, in turn, produces a skepticism about the knowability of the
real world and the adequacy and relevance of knowledge about the
empirical one. Democritus distinguishes between the subjective semblance of perception (mere opinion) and the reality of the principle.
It is this contradiction between semblance and reality that is never
overcome in his thought. The senses reveal only subjective opinions
and feelings, while only the atoms and the void are real—but never

theoretically explained. As a result of these contradictions, the sensuous reality becomes merely a subjective semblance and never the basis for true knowledge about nature.

Here Marx is using the Hegelian notion of semblance *(Schein)*[21] to characterize the relationship between Democritus's ideas of reality as atoms and the void and his idea about the objects of experience. The latter are not a reflection or appearance through which the essence appears. Rather, the phenomenal world is a mere semblance, an apparent being; it is naturally deceptive, as the knower mistakes it for being one thing when it is in fact something else. It is nothing more than mere opinion. But because of the radical separation between the principles of theory and experience, the opinions become ontologically real themselves, further creating the illusion of an independent reality. This is a twist of philosophical fate in Democritus's thinking and his turn to science. The confusion is solved by Democritus in his unreserved call for empirical knowledge. His skepticism about the relation between the real and the experienced throws him into the method of empiricism and positivism. His metaphysics is transformed by its own inherent contradictions—according to Marx—when the world turns into the only thing that truly can be known. "The knowledge which he considers true is without content, the knowledge that gives him content is without truth."[22] This is similar to the position taken by Hegel in his critique of Kant's moral philosophy and the abstractionism of the categorical imperative.[23] Just as the categorical imperative was a moral command without content, Democritus's principles of science are without content, while the empirical content is itself not real. In the end, it is the empirical that asserts itself in both Kant's moral philosophy (see Chapter Three) and Democritus's science.

Epicurus—on the other hand—grounds his view of knowledge in an acceptance of the reality of the phenomenal world and in a materialist epistemology that is critical of positivism and Democritean empiricism. In fact, he is very distrustful of science and its causal and deterministic laws of nature. In one extant piece, Epicurus writes, "I would rather serve the gods than be a slave to the destiny of the physicists."[24] It is for this reason that Epicurus is accused of being an "enemy of science, a scorner of grammar," and an individual who has "contempt for the positive sciences."[25] In reference to Epicurus's understanding of the phenomenal world, Marx uses the term "objective appearance." The sensuous reality is not an illusion or merely opinion, but a manifestation of the laws of self-consciousness; its reality is given to it by both self-consciousness and experience. In the beginning the sensations are the ultimate criteria of truth, but then there appears a contradiction in Epicurus's philosophy between thinking and reality, self-consciousness and experience, the material world and the essence (Concept). Though experience is the criteria of knowledge, Epicurus turns to the realm of the creative imagination as the basis for the essential principles of the laws of physics. "The phenomenal world, therefore, is explained in terms of the subjectivity which is its foundations."[26]

Peter Fenves writes that "Marx's *Thesis* is, in the strictest sense of the word, an experiment which tests the validity of Hegel's central philosophical claim."[27] Does science examine the empirical appearances with the abstract causal laws of understanding *(Verstand)?* Or is science concerned with the logical and dialectical development of all the historical and theoretical categories of experience *(Vernunft)*— with the dialectic of the *Begriff* (Concept)? Marx decides in favor of Hegel. Throughout his *Dissertation,* Marx stresses the categories of necessity and possibility; and the connections he sees between Epicurus's view of science and that of Hegel's are clear. In both cases, there is a critique of the immediacy of experience and a material world uninformed by the priority of thought. It is a world of constantly evolving possibilities and interpretations. Both Epicurus and Hegel direct their criticisms against the determinism, simple causality, and immediate facts of positivism. Hegel's critique of Kant's distinction between the appearances and thing-in-itself is foreshadowed by Epicurus's critique of the physical laws of positivist science in physics and astronomy; this also forms the foundation for the latter's rejection of religion. With both Epicurus and Hegel, the priority is on the individual self-conscious knower over the demands and dictates of external objectivity (the empirical world of the senses). Regarding Hegel's critique of Kant's epistemology, Herbert Marcuse writes:

> Since, then, we know the impressions only in the context of the *a priori* forms of the mind, we cannot know how or what the "things-in-themselves" are that give rise to impressions. . . . As long as the things-in-themselves were beyond the capacity of reason, reason remained a mere subjective principle without power over the objective structure of reality.[28]

It is interesting that within the materialism and empiricism of the Greek physicists there are both empiricist and idealist variations. This is important, since materialism is capable of supporting both the mechanical and empiricist traditions of Democritus and the later materialism of Descartes and Hobbes,[29] on the one hand, and also the idealist philosophy of nature of Epicurus, Schelling, and Marx, on the other. There has been increasing evidence that Marx's choice of dissertation topic was heavily influenced by his acceptance of much of Schelling's early philosophy of nature.[30] Sannwald argues that Marx's own philosophy of nature lies closer to Schelling than that of the French materialists, which would explain his very critical attitude toward natural science in the *Paris Manuscripts*.[31] Marx was influenced in this area by the anthropology lectures of H. S. Stevens at the University of Bonn. Drawing on Schelling's *Ideen zu einer Philosophie der Natur* and *Von der Weltseele*, Marx would later critically view the mechanical and mathematical analysis of society through the natural sciences as "explaining the living through a dead process."[32]

Upon reflection of the whole of Marx's writings, the *Dissertation* may thus be read as an archaeological reconstruction of the early Greek critique of natural science in preparing the philosophical foundations for an alternative theory of nature. This philosophy of nature then spills over into Marx's early writings on nature and anthropology, and ultimately affects—as we will see in Chapter Five—his methodology and epistemology in the critique of political economy. The contrast between the positivism of Democritus and the idealist philosophy of nature of Epicurus is the beginning of a long philosophical debate over the nature of science, which ends—according to Marx—in the confrontation between Kant's *Critique of Pure Reason* and Hegel's *Science of Logic*. Unfortunately, after Marx's death this same tradition would then be divided into a materialism grounded in positivism (orthodox Marxism) and a materialism grounded in idealism and critique (critical theory). This has been analyzed by those interested in the issue of the "Two Marxisms."[33] But are there only two possible alternatives and interpretations of Marx?

ATOMIC CONTRADICTIONS, INDIFFERENCE, AND THE CRITIQUE OF NATURAL LAW

The difference between Epicurus's physics and that of Democritus is best illustrated in part 2 of the *Dissertation* by Epicurus's theory of the threefold movement of the atoms: the movement or fall of the atom in a straight line; the deviation (curving away from the necessary motion of the straight line); and the repulsion of atoms from each other. With his theory of atomic swerving (declination) and repulsion, his theory of chance and possibilities, and his meteor theory of the heavens, Epicurus established a break with Democritus's theory of physics and astronomy. The two substantive areas in Greek physics combined with the metatheoretical differences in their approaches to epistemology and science *(Naturwissenschaften* versus *Naturphilosophie)* led Marx to his central theme of the primacy of self-consciousness and the ethical foundations of all science.

According to Epicurus, the atom is the formal principle of determinate being both as the abstract individuality of an imaginative self-consciousness (formal properties) and a self-sufficient body like the heavenly bodies (material properties). The atom as a principle is a pure concept that has not determined itself in the material world, but on which the material world is built. Viewed as a theoretical concept it is the essence of reality, while as a real material particle it is a component building block of all matter. In its abstraction from relative existence, its essence is the pure form of the Concept *(Begriff)* of abstract self-consciousness (a pure Being-for-Self). The material world is built by the process of declination or the swerving of atoms from a straight line and their repulsion and attraction to each other. The cause of this declination lies in the very Concept (logic) of the atoms themselves, and not in any external cause or event.

This one idea of Epicurus, which sets his theory of the atom off from that of Democritus, undermines "the bonds of fate." It builds into his atomism the metaphysical premise of chance and indeterminate possibilities and the ethical promise of freedom and self-consciousness. No longer is the individual bound to the inexorable logic, necessity, and determinism of nature, but is defined from within itself; it gives itself its own laws. The laws of the deviation and repulsion of atoms are defined by the imagination in terms of chance occurrence, abstract possibility, and individual freedom. The concept or principle of the atom is thus a reflection of the human mind and its unbounded creativity. "Repulsion is the first form of self-consciousness, it corresponds therefore to that self-consciousness which conceives itself as immediate being, as abstract individuality."[34] This critique of physical determinism and linear causality in Democritean and Aristotelian physics will establish the foundations of Epicurus's ethical theory and his critique of theology. In the *Notebooks*, Marx quotes from Lucretius's *On the Nature of Things* regarding the ethical meaning for this theory of atomic swerving.

Again, if all movement is always interconnected, the new arising from the old in a determinate order—if the atoms never swerve so as to originate some new movement that will snap the bonds of fate, the everlasting sequence of cause and effect—what is the source of the free will possessed by living things throughout the earth?[35]

The notion of swerving has also been the focus of a major misunderstanding in the history of Western thought, especially in the works of Cicero, Plutarch, and Bayle. This swerving of the atom reflects its own teleology and purpose (Concept) as it swerves away from pain and suffering. It is characteristic of all being, including the gods themselves. Epicurus sees this as a swerving away from "the restrictive mode of being" and represents the Concept in its relativity and its material relationship to others; this knowledge is gained by rational abstraction of individuality from existence.[36] In the process of negating all relations not determined by their own movement, the atoms repulse each other and further determine the conditions of their own existence. Through the declination, collision, and repulsion of atoms, the world of objects is created, along with human self-consciousness. These motions are—for Epicurus—not the result of "blind necessity," but the "realization of the concept of the atom."[37] The essence of the atom is its pure abstract individuality created by declination and repulsion; it becomes an abstract singularity by differentiating itself from the original Greek ideal of linear motion.

For the atom to exist and be real, it must have certain spatial qualities such as size, shape, and weight and thus take on a determinate existence. However, as a determinate being with material existence, the atom must take on qualities or properties that contradict its essence as pure immediacy and abstract individuality (alienation). It is this contradiction between material existence and essence (Concept) that lies at the heart of Epicurus's philosophy and his view of Greek society. Marx saw in Epicurus the first philosopher to incorporate the notion of the contradiction between essence and reality into his thought.

Marx saw these philosophical categories as symbolic of the internal contradictions of Greek society and the breakup of the ideals of the Greek polis. They also represented the further differentiation and repulsion between the ideals of beauty and customs and the reality of the breakdown of the Aristotelian system and the Greek social world.

The contradiction between existence and essence, between matter and form, which is inherent in the concept of the atom, emerges in the individual atom itself once it is endowed with qualities. Through the quality the atom is alienated from its concept, but at the same time is perfected in its construction. It is from repulsion and the ensuing conglomerations of the qualified atoms that the world of appearance now emerges.[38]

Democritus does not deal with the relationship between the materialized atom (properties) and the atom itself, or essence and existence. He does not see the material world developing out of its Concept, but as an expression of the plurality of qualitative relationships that make up an objective world. For him, the atomic structures that compose the real world cannot be known (thing-in-itself) and what can be known is only the empirical reality. Thus, there is no real theory of the atom. Atoms are important to the extent that they are used to explain differences in the phenomenal forms of the experienced world. The atomic structure assumes a hypothetical stance in relation to appearances, since the real is unknowable and the knowable is not real.

Though Epicurus distinguishes between the atom as material substrate or existence (stoicheion) and the atom as a principle, essence, or Concept (arche),[39] the contradiction is never resolved, for the freedom of the atom in its declination and repulsion remains an abstraction from all forms of determination in existence. The Concept as abstract individuality is always at variance with the world of phenomenal appearances, since the atom is a product of the imagination; it is a product of the world of the abstract possibilities of self-consciousness. In its existential form, the specific material properties and movement of the atom are alienated from its own Concept; but through this alienation, the atom is realized. "The world of appearance can only emerge from the atom which is complete and alienated from its concept."[40] Marx uses the categories of Hegel's metaphysics to describe this relationship between the pure concept as essence and the materialized appearances: They are "indifferent" and "contradictory" to each other.

> Thus insofar as the atom is considered as pure concept, its existence is empty space, annihilated nature. Insofar as it proceeds to reality, it sinks down to the material basis which, as the bearer of a world of manifold relations, never exists but in forms which are indifferent (Gleichgültigkeit) and external to it.[41]

In Hegel's *Science of Logic*, the category of "indifference" refers to a deficient mode of being in which the pure concept does not relate or self-consciously understand the process of concrete determination in the physical world. That is, it does not understand how its concept becomes or reflects being. Schelling used the concept of indifference to describe in Kantian fashion the ontological distance between thought and being. Marx uses the category of indifference at least four different ways in his *Dissertation* and *Notebooks*. But there is still an ambivalence here over the relationship between the concept and the external world.[42] This ambivalence appears in his analysis of Epicurus and is tied to the different interpretations that Marx draws from Kant and Hegel, Schelling and Hegel: The nineteenth-century philosophical debates are being fought on the battlefield of Greek exegesis.

At one point, Marx—in Hegelian fashion—indicates that the split is the result of the alienation of self-consciousness. At another point, it appears to be an ontological split, rather than a deficient mode of being or lack of self-consciousness. "Indifference" is used differently (and sometimes indifferently) in his theory of science (methodology), his theory of knowledge (epistemology), and his theory of reality (ontology). At times, Marx states that abstract possibility is indifferent to reality; the concept is indifferent to the material reality; the appearances act indifferently to their essence; and finally, in the "method of the imaginative consciousness," consciousness is indifferent to scientific explanations themselves. Is indifference the result of the teleology of the atom behaving indifferently to its material manifestations (Hegel)? Or is the atom ontologically different and, therefore, indifferent to material manifestation itself (Schelling)? That is, is the mind indifferent to its own manifestations in nature, or is the mind indifferent to nature because—unlike nature—it is self-conscious and free? Finally, is the relationship between consciousness and being determined by ontology or by ethics? Epicurus certainly chooses the latter.

Marx's dissertation is a difficult work to read, because the boundary lines between philosophical traditions are not clearly drawn or articulated. Marx's interpretation contains distinct Kantian moments where he stresses the differences between appearances and essence; the indifference between nature and ethics, pure and practical reason; the abstract possibility of self-consciousness and the real possibility of nature; ethical freedom and the independence of nature; and, finally, nature understood as a series of antinomic relationships between matter and form, concepts and reality, and principles and being. There is also a strong Hegelian moment here, which at times imperceptibly intermingles with the Kantian one. The former is characterized by the dialectic relationship between appearances and essence, the alienation of essence in the appearances, and the priority of self-consciousness and freedom over nature.

Because of the distinctions between matter and form, the atom as abstract individuality "cannot actualize itself as the idealizing and pervading power of this manifold [nature]."[43] The atom is indifferent, therefore, to the substance of the material world. This contradiction is based on a definite ontological separation between concepts and nature, and thereby reflects more of Schelling's insights than any other on this point. However, the notion of indifference is never really clarified, and the ambiguity of its use permits both an Hegelian and a Schelling interpretation. Like Hegel, Marx contends that the existence of material appearances is the result of a necessary alienation of the atom from its own concept; in the process the atom becomes the essential form of nature, but at the same time cannot manifest itself in nature. It exists only in the void. At times the relationship between concepts and reality are indifferent due to lost recognition of the subjectivity underlying appearances, and at other times due to the ontological gap that lies between the two and ensures self-consciousness of its ethical autonomy from natural law. Marx also uses the term in his *Notebooks* to indicate that the consciousness of the physicist is "indifferent" to the explanations of the physical cosmos.[44] Many different explanations are possible and verifiable by experience, and it is this very possibility of different explanations that provides a foundation for the moral autonomy of the individual. Indifference between object and abstract possibility, existence and essence, ends in a contradiction between the atom as an essential principle of physics and the atom as the foundation for matter. There is no connecting link between the two realms of concept and reality in Epicurus's thought, and therefore no resolution of these antinomic distinctions.

Marx's interpretation of Epicurus also reflects a difficulty raised in Kant's epistemology and moral philosophy by the latter's splitting of pure and practical reason in the *Critique of Pure Reason* and the *Critique of Practical Reason*. Kant had hoped to separate the determinism and causal necessity of the physical world from the autonomy and categorical imperative of the moral world. This separation posits the existence of both the transcendental subject and natural science, on the one side, and individual self-consciousness and freedom, on the other. It is clear from Epicurus that the incompatibility of the two realms is a result of the priority of individual moral autonomy over external nature. Human freedom is incompatible with the existence of natural necessity and causal laws. Thus, Epicurus negated the independent existence of these natural laws to preserve the autonomy of the individual, while Kant merely held them distinct.

The variety of possible explanations is limited only by the necessity to consult the senses and appearances. There is no possibility of ever getting to the one correct explanation, to the logic of the nature laws. Marx is reading Epicurus here through Kant's belief that we can never know the thing-in-itself. While Hegel used this to undermine the Kantian notion of the thing-in-itself and to show the development of appearances as the Absolute Spirit manifesting itself in history, Marx reads Epicurus as rejecting any absolute knowledge of nature because of the priority of practical reason. There are always a variety of possible interpretations, but there is never one correct theory. Theories can be falsified by experience, but can never be justified once and for all times. Because of the strong neo-Kantian element in Marx's analysis, there appears to be a connection between Marx's representation of Epicurus's epistemology and scientific method and that of Karl Popper. Both argue that we can never have knowledge of the thing-in-itself; Popper argues that we can never verify or justify a particular theory and that theories can only be falsified or proved incorrect.[45] This is a similar position to that of Epicurus.

After Marx's analysis of the metaphysics of being and the contradictions between essence and appearances, space and time, he develops the implications of this analysis for the Epicurean theory of knowledge. Through an analysis of the concept of time and the changeability of the physical world, Marx concludes that human sensuousness embodies time. "Sensuous perception reflected in itself is thus here the source of time and time itself,"[46] and is measured against changes in the accidental qualities of the external world.[47] Through human sensuousness, the world is mediated by itself as nature hears, smells, and sees itself. This passage from the *Dissertation* is perhaps more famously known in the *Paris Manuscripts* where, after his critique of alienation, Marx calls for the humanization of nature and the naturalization of human sensuousness.[48] The foundations for this evaluation of alienated labor and private property—that is, the critique of political economy in his early writings—lie in Marx's appropriation of the Epicurean theory of knowledge. Marx ends this chapter of the dissertation with recognition of a dual criterion of truth reflecting the dual conception of ontology. Abstract reason is

the "only criterion in the world of atoms," while the senses are the
"only criteria in concrete nature."[49]

While the central focus is on the issue of ethics, there remains an
ambivalence in both Marx's method and his ontology—which will
continue all the way into the *Grundrisse* and *Capital*. In his later
economic theory, the issues of the nature of science and the ontological status of his dialectical categories (do they reflect reality?) remain
crucial. Are the categories of political economy expressions of the
immediate historical reality as they unfold from the logic of capital
(Hegel), or is there a real split between political economy and social
reality—a split that necessitates the intervention of practical action
(praxis) to resolve them (Schelling)? Marx is not very clear on this
point. Does the Concept *(Begriff)* of capital act indifferently to historical reality? That is, are the contradictions and breakdown of capitalism inevitably due to the internal teleology of capital and its iron laws
of historical necessity? Or is there a real ontological split between
theory and reality? Are the categories of political economy and the
contradictions of capital indifferent to the social reality to the extent
that they do not predict the future, but critique the assumptions and
values of its structures and ideology? Finally, does the concept of
indifference push Marx closer to Schelling or to Hegel? Again, there
are no clear answers at this point. But in a sense, the ambiguity is
itself an answer. Marx is battling between two views of method and
science, and there is no winner in the confrontation between the
Hegelian dialectical method and Schelling's philosophy of nature.
This only becomes important in his later writings, when he rejects
Hegel's ontology and replaces it with Schelling's. This acceptance of
the latter awaits introduction of Marx's notion of theory and practice[50]
(see Chapter Seven). However, at this early stage in the development
of his thought, the imprint of both perspectives are written into
Marx's interpretation of Epicurus.

EPICURUS'S ASTRONOMY, SCIENCE, AND ETHICS

Epicurus's really distinctive contribution for Marx, however, lies in
his theory of meteors for it is here that his views of knowledge and
ethics express themselves most clearly.[51] Epicurus makes a break with
the whole of Greek tradition, which had formerly worshiped the
heavens as the eternal sphere of the gods. And it is in the critique of
the heavens and religion that Marx finds the philosophical and ethical

justifications for his later critique of "the plastic gods of the market-place."[52] Epicurus attacks the existence of the divinity of the heavens not because it contradicts sense experience, but because it contradicts the dictates of practical reason (ethics). The purpose of the natural sciences can be nothing other than *ataraxy*, or the peace and happiness of individual self-consciousness. This ethical precept contradicts the generally accepted views of Greek theology and astronomy. The goal of knowledge lies not in ontology, but in ethics—that is, in securing happiness for the individual through a recognition that practical reason has priority over the laws of physics and astronomy. Questions relating to the movement of the sun and the moon, changes in the latter's appearances, and other celestial occurrences can be explained using a multiplicity of theories—all of which may be true. The only criterion of truth in these matters is that they must not be contra-dicted by the sensations.[53] But it is also important to note that Marx emphatically states "there is no interest in investigating the real causes of objects."[54] The only thing important is the peace and happiness of the individual. Science is crucial to the extent that it leaves open the abstract possibilities of nature and furthers the ethical imperative of *ataraxy* by undermining all alternative forms of rationality and natural laws beyond the individual.

Scientific theories are forms of consciousness created to interpret the world in a particular fashion. The relation between ontology and theory—reality and the concept—is problematic and represents more of a Kantian moment in Marx's analysis. That is, theory is an abstract set of principles that does not "mirror" reality (Kantian moment) but is just one possible mode of connection between the mind and external reality (Hegelian moment). The goal of knowledge is neither the accumulation of true facts nor the creation of universally true ideas, but the freedom of self-consciousness from the terror of the heavens. The purpose of knowledge is not to reflect the truth, but to secure human emancipation. This theme of the relation between human emancipation and science is picked up again in his essay "Private Property and Communism" in the *Paris Manuscripts*.[55]

The reason for the study of celestial bodies and their movement is to "tranquilize our minds and remove causes for fear, but also at the same time negate in the heavenly bodies their very unity, the absolute law that is always equal to itself."[56] It represents a critique of all transcendent natural laws, all claims to divinity and false universality. This breakdown of the universal and homogeneous nature of the heavens undermines the conflict between the finite and infinite, human rationality and the divine. The movement of the meteors cannot be limited or explained by a universal law; they move in a variety of unexpected and arbitrary ways (the declination of chance and abstract possibility). This critique of mechanical and causal relationships undermines the essential element in positivist science for Marx. Epicurus was the Greek forerunner to Hume's critique of positivism (the positive side of the Enlightenment), which was later so influential on both Kant and Hegel. The creation of the myths of nature endangers happiness *(ataraxy)*, because it sets above humanity a reality over which it has no control. There is only one universal law, which does not lie outside of human self-consciousness.

> On the contrary, it is an absolute law that nothing that can disturb ataraxy, that can cause danger, can belong to an indestructible and eternal nature. Consciousness must understand that this is an absolute law. Hence Epicurus concludes: *Since eternity of the heavenly bodies would disturb the ataraxy of self-consciousness, it is necessary, a stringent consequence that they are not eternal.*[57]

The theories of Democritus and Aristotle are the result of pure idolatry. Thus, from this perspective, the theories of Democritus and Aristotle—both of whom rely on forms of empiricism and natural science—are inadequate, for they are the result of idle mythmaking and do not reach the level of *Naturphilosophie*. Physics is a subbranch of ethics. Marx does not end his analysis with this recognition, but also tries to explain it as arising out of the internal contradictions of Epicurus's own system and the clash between his theory of atomic physics and his theory of celestial bodies. The celestial bodies are a concrete manifestation of the atoms, as they materialize the abstract individuality of the Concept (atom) into a concrete individuality. The heavens give material substance to the pure formal capacity of the atomic principles and make real the immanent possibilities of the atom. The contradictions in the atom between existence and essence, reality and concept, are transcended in the heavenly bodies. However, this only leads—for Marx—to another, higher level contradiction that encompasses Epicurus's whole system.

The heavenly bodies are viewed as the resolution and transcendence of the contradictions between essence and existence, form and matter, since they are the realization of the atoms on a universal and eternal level. But here is where Epicurus's astronomy comes into conflict with his ethical materialism and his theory of physics. There cannot be these "immortal foundations" to nature, since the existence of an independent nature would undermine his ethical precepts. The existence of an independent, indestructible nature made up of the various forms of motion—when applied in a theory of meteors— produces the belief in an "independent nature" which contradicts the principles of Epicurus's ethics.

Apparently, Marx—following Hegel—would like to have seen an answer to this contradiction that would recognize the dialectical interconnectedness between objectivity and subjectivity. With such a theory, the contradiction between essence and appearance would be overcome: The abstract principle of self-consciousness would proclaim itself as the objectified essence of the celestial world. The concept objectifies and realizes itself in material form, and the independent nature is reintegrated with the subjective. Objectivity has received the abstract form of subjectivity. Epicurus follows a different path. "But now, when matter has reconciled itself with the form and has been rendered self-sufficient, individual self-consciousness emerges from its pupation, proclaims itself the true principle and opposes nature, which has become independent."[58] In the theory of meteors, Epicurus attempts to conceal the antinomies of his physics, since matter is reconciled with its form—external celestial being with self-consciousness—by imposition of the latter over the former. The theory of possibilities of explanation and the ethical priority of *ataraxy* represent a realization of the concrete universal (realization of the individual in the concrete).

Fenves writes that at this point in his analysis Epicurus swerves from his own conclusions, for "the consequences of maintaining the identity of the subject is the annihilation of the object."[59] At one and the same time, the meteors are the solution to the contradictions found within Epicurus's physics and theory of the atom; while, on the other hand, they reestablish a new theology that undermines the ethical priority of individual self-consciousness. According to Marx, this is Epicurus's "most glaring contradiction," which he must have seen because in response he destroys the independent reality of the heavens and restores the primacy of abstract possibility and self-conscious imagination in his theory of meteors. But there are limits to this view of science, as Marx says at the end of chapter 5 of his dissertation:

If abstract-individual self-consciousness is posited as an absolute principle, then, indeed, all true and real science is done away with *(aufgehoben)* inasmuch as individuality does not rule within the nature of things themselves. But then, too, everything collapses that is transcendentally related to human consciousness and therefore belongs to the imagining mind. On the other hand, if that self-consciousness which knows itself only in the form of abstract universal is raised to an absolute principle, then the door is opened wide to superstition and unfree mysticism.[60]

Epicurus resolves the antinomic tensions in nature by destroying its independence and positing the primacy of an abstract individualism. There is no integration, transcendence, or resolution of the contradictions: These are simply theoretically dissolved by the philosopher in the form of scientific abstractions. The reality and importance of the natural world is denied and never integrated into Epicurean science. Marx is aware that the ethical precepts of Epicurus determined the nature of the content of his analysis and forced Epicurus to "swerve" from the conclusions of his own theory of meteors. His materialism imposes a content from without, while the ethical imperatives are viewed as an abstraction from their own content. Here again, the Hegelian critique of Kant's ethics reappears within Marx's dissertation. Individual self-consciousness cannot become real, cannot actualize itself in the real material world, and cannot realize its own ethical imperatives outside of this same world. This is the moral dilemma of Epicurus. "Abstract individuality is freedom from being, not freedom in being. It cannot shine in the light of being."[61] Though an improvement over Democritean positivism, the separation of knowledge from the empirical world cannot result in true science. Abstract self-consciousness transcends the independent reality by destroying it, while Hegel negates the reality of the objective world through recognition that it is a manifestation of the subject (Absolute Consciousness). Epicurus sees that the "abstract possibilities" in nature were determinations of the mind and not a reflection of its "real possibilities." Marx interprets Epicurus as a Kantian who has not yet risen to the level of dialectical science (the negative side of the Enlightenment). Marx thus plays off the two sides of the Enlightenment by viewing Epicurus in terms of both Hume's critique of science and Kant's defense of pure individual self-consciousness.

An ethical implication of all this is that it turns freedom into a "freedom from being" and, in turn, undermines the possibility of a real ethics and science. Marx is critical of the abstractionism of both the Epicurean and the Stoic philosophies, which appear to represent two different aspects of Kant's categorical imperative. Epicurus rep-

resents the philosophy of pure subjectivism divorced from the historical and social reality of moral action, while Stoicism represents the
ethical philosophy of abstract universality. The latter has as its highest
ideal the realization of external abstract virtue and duty, over and
against the individual.[62] In both cases, self-consciousness is separated
from its own material content; or rather, it arises in opposition to the
material world, and not through it. Self-consciousness can affirm
itself only by negating nature. This is certainly an expression of the
strong Hegelian critique of Kant that finds its way into Marx's early
philosophy.

Thus, though the Greek *Weltanschauung* contained many of the
crucial components of a new approach to materialism and science,
they could not realize their own insights because of their underdeveloped notions of science and ethics. In the *Notebooks* Marx plays off a
metaphor of light that he also uses in his dissertation, as he argues
that the "inner light" must come from within the world: That is, the
world itself must become philosophical, while critique must become
immanent. There is to be division between the objective and subjective
components of philosophical critique, between self-consciousness and
the material world, as was experienced with the Greeks. This also
implies a redefinition of the Hegelian concept of the Absolute Idea
and praxis to fit more closely with the ideas developed by Bruno
Bauer and Feuerbach—the concept of human self-consciousness.[63]

> But the *practice* of philosophy is itself *theoretical*. It is the *critique* that
> measures the individual existence by the essence, the particular reality
> by the Idea. But this *immediate realization* of philosophy is in its deepest
> essence afflicted with contradictions, and thus its essence takes form in
> the appearance and imprints its seal upon it.[64]

By assuming a material existence, the pure abstract form of the atoms
takes on the appearance of external, universal, self-sufficient nature
and—in the process—produces a conflict between self-consciousness
and nature that only leads to "anxiety and confusion." The theory of
the atom contradicts the goals of the theory of meteors: The former
was intended to lay the immortal foundations of physics; but when
applied to the heavens, it produces only disturbance and confusion.
Marx argues that Epicurus vehemently opposes any "worship of an
independent nature," which would undermine the freedom and
happiness of self-consciousness.[65]

THE EPICUREAN CRITIQUE OF RELIGION

The method by which the abstract universality of the material world—this "deadly enemy" of abstract individuality—may be overcome is through a science built around the abstract possibilities of nature. Because of the declination of the atoms and their unpredictable and irrational behavior, there is no one explanation that can deal with their origin, movement, and essence. The whole of the phenomenal universe is open to its own abstract and infinite possibilities, to which an equal number of explanations correspond. The eternality and rationality of nature are undermined. With this, the unity and independence thereby produced are negated. The alienated existence of individuality as objectified matter is reflected back into itself as the materialized form of the celestial bodies; and in the process, the objectivity of the universe also is negated. "The Greek philosophers therefore worshipped their own mind in the celestial bodies."[66] However, it was not until Epicurus's critique of religion that this could be seen.

Epicurus connects his theory of possibility from his atomism with his theory of explanatory possibility; he makes this notion a hallmark of physical movement and the scientific method. Democritus saw the method of science as examining the causal relationships between deterministic events through use of the method of real possibility. The latter simply implies that scientific explanations reveal the real and necessary causal conditions, relationships, and interconnections between objects and events. Epicurus—on the other hand—uses the method of abstract possibility. This approach is not limited by physical determinism and the causal connections of the external world. Rather, it is bounded only by self-consciousness and the imagination. The reality or existence of abstract possibility is irrelevant since the goal is not to study the subject matter, but the subject. The goal of theoretical conjectures is happiness; and every theory not contradicted by the sensations is possible, as we have already seen. This theory of the possible and its critique of all external forms of rationality and independence recognize the primacy of self-conscious individuality and moral autonomy. It is this that is more important than the laws of physics, the religious and metaphysical traditions, the eternality of the celestial bodies, and the determinism and rationality of the atomic world.

Sannwald recognizes that Epicurus was creating his theories with two opposing sets of principles: one coming from the ethical individualism of Socrates, and the other from the materialism of Democritus's atomism. "Actually Epicurus wanted to save the freedom of the will, without giving up the materialist basis."[67] The ethical indeterminism is carried over into the indeterminism and arbitrariness of Epicurus's theory of declination. Marx views this conflict between the requirements of physics and the demand for ethical freedom to be the major distinguishing feature of Epicurus's philosophy of nature.

> Marx had brought together the elements of a grounded theory of emancipation with the sensuous reality. The ethical materialism of Epicurus was the pathway. If man has a special nature which can come to itself through the course of history to its real rational form—its true being, that is, to a conscious rational relatedness of individuals to one another (model of meteors), then all forms, in which the individuals can not experience themselves as through their own being, are pre-forms of human development, mystifications over itself, which presents itself to consciousness as real.[68]

Hülsewede clearly recognizes and expands the anthropological assumptions and implications behind this theory of atomic swerving and repulsion. Man is a being in nature who himself is a product of the swerving, repulsion, and attraction of the atoms, but who is also a very special being. He is a being with reason *(Vernunftswesen)*, whose essence is contradicted by his existence. Implicit in Marx's analysis of the physics and ethos of the Greek classical tradition is a social anthropology. There is a highly rationalistic view of human nature implicit in his analysis of the development of physics and the theory of the atom from the crude materialism of Democritus to the concept and principle of the atom as *arche* (Epicurus), along with the corresponding development in the ethics and social ethos of Greek society. From the original emphasis on the nature of substance to the growing self-consciousness and independence of the Greek philosophers, the locus of reflection became centered on moral autonomy and human potentiality. Just as reality is not given in science, the nature of the human being is not given, but develops over the course of time; man is a being who "comes through himself to his real essence, who becomes a being to himself."[69]

Self-consciousness arose historically and philosophically out of philosophical reflections about the natural world to which the individual is bound. For Marx, the actual historical evolution of Greek philosophy represents the transition from a philosophy of nature to a philosophy of man. This reflects the growing individualism and self-consciousness of the Greek philosophers themselves as they reason about changes within themselves, their polis, and their culture. This is certainly a more subtle treatment of the materialism that grounds human nature than is generally applied to Marx in secondary sources.

Epicurus thus leads us to a more sensitive and subtle understanding of the original sources of Marx's notion of materialism. Emancipation and freedom are possible, but only as they emerge from the concrete sensuous world—not when the physical world is rejected.

Throughout the *Dissertation*, there are references to the anthropological implication of Epicurean physics. The individual is viewed as an abstract individuality and self-consciousness. Just as the substance of nature and reality is composed of the free and arbitrary movement of the atoms—through whose repulsion, attraction, and declination the material world is constructed—the individual is also seen as free from all external restrictions and universal laws. This is what is meant by abstract individuality, whether the abstract individuality of man or atom. "Man ceases to be a product of nature only when the other being to which he relates himself is not a different existence but is itself an individual human being, even if it is not yet the mind *(Geist)*."[70]

By grounding physics in the priorities of individual freedom, Epicurus led the critique against religious alienation and mystification, in favor of individual freedom. However, this individuality exists only in the form of an abstract self-consciousness that frees itself from all external limits. At this point, Epicurus falls back behind Aristotle and the latter's notion of man as a political animal. Marx's description of Epicurus's atomic physics reads as if it were taken directly from Hobbes's *Leviathan*. The "war of all against all" portrays the point in both Greek philosophy and Greek life when individualism undermined the social fabric of the substance of Greek life—that is, the integration of individual in society.

> The formation of combinations of atoms, their repulsion and attraction, is a noisy affair. An uproarious contest, a hostile tension, constitutes the workshop and the smithy of the world. The world in the depths of whose heart there is such tumult, is torn within.
>
> Even the sunbeam, falling on shady places, is an image of this eternal war.[71]

The radical individualism of Epicurus was necessary to undermine positivism and religion, but was not adequate to develop a real social anthropology or theory of society based on friendship, citizenship, and public participation. For this, a turn to Feuerbach's notion of species being and Aristotle's view of democracy and citizenship would become necessary.

It would be Marx's immediate task in his early writings to move from one level to the other, to move from abstract self-consciousness and freedom to concrete self-consciousness in the political economy. In order to overcome the contradictions of existence and essence—materialism and ethics—implicit in Epicurean physics, the alienation of the objective and physical world must be overcome through social praxis. The theoretical praxis and ethical critique of the philosopher must be transformed into effective action on the world and a change-over of the institutions of political economy. The *Dissertation* sets the path, the direction, and the priorities for Marx's earliest and later studies on the social relations of production. Just as the *Dissertation* begins with a critique of the foreign externality of nature, *Capital* begins with a critique of the "natural laws" of political economy. It is this relation between self-consciousness and nature in all its material forms—from physics to political economy—that is at the heart and soul of Marx's lifework.

The section on time also has important anthropological implications that help us understand the direction that Marx is taking in his early writings. Epicurus views time as the abstract form of sensation; it is the form in which appearances appear and pass away—that is, the reflection of appearance in itself. Time posits the material world as appearance, rather than essence; but in the process, time does lead back to essence. In a letter written to Herodotus, Epicurus states that time emerges with the distinction between substance and accident; it emerges with sensuous perception and the perception of accidents and change.[72] Thus, sensuous perception is the source of time. Marx seems to be following a straight Kantian view here in describing time as a product of the mind.

As we have seen, Marx argues that Epicurus was the first to recognize the distinction between essence and appearance, and appearance as simply the alienation of essence in the sensuous world. "Human sensuousness is therefore the medium in which the natural processes are reflected as in a focus and ignited into the light of appearance."[73] It is human sensuousness that forms the abstract possibility of appearance and the embodiment of the essence in temporal appearances. As the atom—the essence of nature—is abstract individual self-consciousness, so sensuous nature is materialized empirical individual self-consciousness. As a temporal appearance, the world comes to be through the senses, which form the only criteria of concrete nature. The physical world has its reality through the senses, and the latter are the criteria by which it must be judged.

Conversely, it may be implied that mankind has its reality only through the sensuous world and, therefore, that this world is a human-sensuous world.[74]

> In these thoughts lie already the reversal of the Hegelian system. . . . Rather the consequence for the freedom of the subject is developed from the material substance. From the sensuousness as the concreteness of time man must realize himself as a free rational being *[Vernunftswesen]*, namely as a rational subject in its material nature.[75]

Hülsewede continues that this is the basis for human emancipation in that the individual becomes a rational being only through "the material determined Being" from which humanity determines itself.

GREEK PHYSICS AND PHILOSOPHY IN MARX'S *NOTEBOOKS*

While the *Dissertation* analyzed and compared the differences between the Epicurean and Democritean philosophies of nature and their different approaches to the issues of truth, scientific method, theory and practice, and the antinomies of reality (essence and appearance), as well as the questions of time, necessity, and possibilities in nature, the *Notebooks on Epicurean Philosophy* attended to different issues and offered a wider and more comprehensive view of Greek philosophy. They contained an analysis of the Epicurean and Skeptic views of science; commentaries by Diogenes Laertius, Sextus Empiricus, Plutarch, and Lucretius concerning Epicurus and the latter's relation to other Greek philosophers (Parmenides, Empedocles, Plato, Socrates, and so forth); the relationship between the Greek notion of substance, as developed in Plato's *Republic,* and Christ's emphasis on the principle of subjectivity; the relation between philosophy and religion; and the relationship between late post-Aristotelian philosophy and early Greek philosophy.

The emphasis on two central themes running throughout Marx's *Dissertation*—the priority of self-consciousness, and the critique of religion—develop out of the perspectives and primary interests of the nineteenth-century Left-Hegelians. Marx continues with his critique of religion in the appendix entitled "Critique of Plutarch's Polemic against the Theology of Epicurus" and in the second and third sections of his *Notebooks,* which deal with Plutarch's *That Epicurus Actually Makes a Pleasant Life Possible.* In his response to Plutarch, Marx outlines a philosophical defense of classical German humanism and—specifically—its defense of moral autonomy and individual freedom. These same ideas will be dealt with more systematically and in detail in his *Paris Manuscripts*. Marx's notions of individuality, rationality, and freedom developed from the Greek and German classicists and the later German Idealists. Unlike the perspective of emancipation found in classical liberalism,

> for Marx the emancipation of man meant more than merely a political demand, when also the political freedom would like to stand in the foreground as the next goal in a time, in which the search after a way out of the empty vacuum of abstraction falls together with the general longing after national fulfillment. Freedom is a moment in the comprehensive autonomie of men, the realization of human essence, as Marx later wrote. The humanistic ideal of the German classics with its emphasis on the spiritual universality of men stands in the background, when Marx postulates the emancipation of man, in analogous fashion to the ideal of the wise men in ancient Greece, which was only a partial realization of mankind (complete Stoics, Epicureans, etc.). This goal presupposes that man first remembers the dormant powers in himself and recognizes himself as free from nature. The intention of religion stands against this, which from the frailty of life concludes with the dependence of man on transcendent powers.[76]

Sannwald concludes this idea with a statement from Marx that the critique of religion must be the beginning for all further critique. Though there have been debates over whether Marx was an atheist—debates that still continue today—the *Dissertation* clearly places the critique of religion at the center of his work and the center of his critique of modernity. Though this section in the *Dissertation* is only a three-page fragment, it is clear that Marx directs his attention and criticism to Plutarch's critique of Epicurus's concept of the soul and its dissolution into atoms and the void at death, and against the religious concepts of eternal life and happiness after death. Plutarch holds that this view of the dissolution of the atomic structure of the soul undermines "our hope of immortality." Marx begins the third section of the second book of the *Notebooks* with the statement that "it goes without saying that very little of this treatise by Plutarch is of any use."[77] Containing only "clumsy boastfulness" and "crude interpretations," it fails to capture Epicurus's intentions and misinterprets his philosophical perspectives.

In itself, Plutarch's interpretations and Marx's response would not be terribly important to an analysis of Epicurus's philosophy, except to the most antiquarian historians of philosophy. However, Marx's response to Plutarch throws more light on his own critical perspectives and his very early intellectual development, especially in the area of his critique of religion. Plutarch has not understood Epicurus for he failed to see that Epicurus stands consciously at the end of Greek philosophy as he watches its dissolution. As Marx puts it, "the downfall of ancient philosophy is presented in complete objectiveness by Epicurus."[78] Out of this breakdown and out of the alienation and dissolution of the substance of Greek life and mind into the realm of the spirit comes the rise of critical self-consciousness (pure subjectivity), which in the Greek world culminates in Epicurean philosophy and its view of individual freedom. Beginning with an analysis of the wise men of ancient Greece in the second notebook, Marx shows how this process of dissolution has already taken place theoretically in the consciousness of the Greek philosophers themselves.

In an interesting approach using a sociology of knowledge, Marx shows how the development and dissolution of Greek philosophy was a reflection of the actual development and decay of Greek society. In his own miniphenomenology of the spirit—based on the method of Hegel's major work—Marx recounts the history of Greek philosophy, setting the stage for the place of Greek thought in the German Enlightenment. This was also one of the major themes in Köppen's work *Frederick the Great and His Opponents*. For Marx, it provides the framework within which he understands the development of the cultural and political spirit of Greek society and its own self-conscious reflection on that spirit in its philosophy. Marx traces the transformation of the philosophy of substance and nature to that of self-consciousness and the subject. Similar themes about the relations between substance and subjectivity are found in Nietzsche.

The concept of substance played an important role in Hegel's thought and appears frequently in his *Philosophy of Right, History of Philosophy, Philosophy of Religion,* and *Philosophy of History.* According to Hegel, substance is the Spirit—the principle that expresses itself in various social forms such as in politics, religion, art, social action, and the economy. They are the manifestations of the objectification of the Spirit into the world of social objectivity—the substance of Greek life.[79] A central theme running throughout Hegel's writings is the idea that the truth of objectivity is subjectivity. Out of this substance comes the other component of the Hegelian dialectic: the subject (self-consciousness). With the beginning of philosophy and independent thinking with the advent of the wise men, the process was started by which individuals slowly differentiate themselves from both nature and social life itself. Marx traces the development of the Greek philosophical theories about the universal substance of nature. Beginning with the ontologies of the Ionian philosophers of nature, the Pythagoreans, and the Eleatics, Marx constructs a phenomenology of self-consciousness as he traces the development of substance from nature to the Greek polity.[80] It is this very process of self-reflection and self-differentiation that creates the Greek substance. Philosophy is viewed as something that comes after this historical process, rather than as part of its formation. At each stage of development, there is a further turn from the philosophical search for the eternal and universal in terms of the material substance of nature to more mathematical, intellectual, and—finally—political and cultural categories. The substance becomes the teleology and good of society itself as expressed in the rationality and freedom of its institutions. This is the process of the self-reflective return to self-consciousness and is the basis for all self-reflective critical thought. The very possibility of autonomous thought and moral action lies in the distancing and the eventual returning, in the alienation and the reconciliation of objectivity and subjectivity.

For the Greeks, the social life of the community was the lifeblood of the human being, through which the individual nourished and grew in both wisdom and virtue. Part of the breakdown and dissolution of the Greek world and the Greek philosophical systems (Plato and Aristotle) resulted from the gradual fragmentation and divisions caused when individuals began to differentiate themselves from the substance of this social life and create new forms of human autonomy and freedom. The rise of moral conscience and freedom was seen by both Hegel and Marx as necessary for the development and realization of concrete freedom over abstract formal freedom. Philosophy and the origins of self-consciousness go hand in hand for Marx. Hegel had thought in his *Philosophy of History* that Christianity produced this new form of subjectivity—which must be integrated back into the social community of the state—while the *Phenomenology of Spirit* stressed the importance of the post-Aristotelian Greek and Roman worlds.[81] Marx saw this new turn toward the individual and spirit occurring in Greek philosophy with Epicurus. It was the philosopher in his theoretical praxis who became the "demiurge"—the impetus toward a new relation between substance and spirit, society and individual. The Ionian philosophers were simple vehicles for the vocalization of the Greek social substance—the Greek values and ideals.

With further philosophical inquiry and further differentiation, the philosopher began to emerge distinct from the social substance; the philosopher began to take a critical perspective. With the Sophists and Socrates, and somewhat with Anaxagoras, the subjective element became the basis for further philosophical speculation.

> Now it is ideality itself which, in its immediate form, the *subjective spirit*, becomes the principle of philosophy. In the earlier Greek wise men there was revealed the ideal form of substance, its identity, in distinction to the many-coloured raiment woven from the individualities of various peoples that displayed its manifest reality.[82]

These Ionian philosophers were ideal expressions of the social values of the Greeks; with further development of this ideality and philosophical abstraction, subjectivity becomes the foundation of philosophy. From a simple ideal reflection on the nature of universal substance to the ideality of that same substance, subjectivity as pure self-consciousness confronts the social life as something external and different. We are witnessing—for Marx—the birth pains of true philosophical reason as it develops in dialectical relation with society and nature; it is the actual historical process of alienation and the break between essence and existence that Epicurus's philosophy reflects.

The subject stands both in and outside of the substance, and uses this distance to oppose and compare its ideality to the social reality. It is in this opposition that the dialectic and self-consciousness develop. It is also in this opposition that the individual is able to oppose to the social substance the moral imperative of the subjective spirit. Thus, from this process, morality evolves out of social norms and customs *(Sittlichkeit)*, and self-consciousness out of the social substance.

> First, the fact that this ideality of substance has entered the subjective spirit, has fallen away from itself, is a leap, a falling away from the substantial life determined in the substantial life itself. Hence this determination of the subject is for it an accomplished fact, an alien force, the bearer of which it finds itself to be, the daemon of Socrates.[83]

In this process, "the subject naturally detaches itself from the substantial and the substance loses itself in the subject."[84] The subject is now determined internally by its ability to judge the world standing over and against it and it is through this judging that the self constitutes its own being. This is the same determination-in-itself that we saw in Epicurus's theory of the atom.[85] It represents an epistemological and ethical shift toward self-determination of the individual and the realization of his concept of the "good" through reflective praxis. This is the philosophy of self-consciousness, with Epicurus at one end of the history of philosophy and Hegel at the other.

In reference to this self-determination of wisdom and goodness, Marx—in a manner reminiscent of the early Hegel—criticizes Kant's categorical imperative where the subjectivity is abstracted from the praxis of practical philosophy and the life of the community. The attitude of the philosopher has no place in calculation of the content of practical philosophy as the philosopher applies the transcendent form of the moral imperative—while for the Greeks, it is their very participation in the ethical community (even while standing over and against it, as in the case of Socrates and Epicurus) that characterizes their moral thought. It is from this evolution of Greek philosophy that the critical perspective with its distinction between concept and reality—individual and society—arose. For Marx, Epicurus summarizes this development in his physics and theory of ataraxy and the meteors. All this is missed by Plutarch.

In the third notebook, Marx concentrates on Plutarch's critique of Epicurus. In Marx's analysis and response, he develops a critique of religion that synthesizes the positions of the Epicureans, the Greek materialists, German classicists, and the Left-Hegelians. According to Marx, Plutarch interprets the "fear" of God as experienced by Epicurus to be a psychological reaction of anxiety before a greater and more powerful entity, rather than the result of a philosophical consciousness that seeks self-determination and autonomy. It is not a psychological issue of fear and anxiety, but a philosophical one about individual freedom. As a result of this "sensuous fear," the moral order is maintained and the evil is punished. In addition, the presence of God in human consciousness frees the individual "from sorrow, fear, and anxiety."[86] In fact, according to Epicurus and Marx, the belief in God is only a product of the reduction of man to animal fear.

In the notes on Plutarch in the appendix written after the *Dissertation* at the end of 1841, Marx argues that the ontological proofs for the existence of God are mere "hollow tautologies." Drawing on Holbach's *System of Nature* and the early writings of Schelling in his

"Philosophical Letters on Dogmatism and Criticism," Marx criticizes
the belief in God as a fetter on the free development of the mind,
humanity, and moral integrity of the individual. The existence of an
absolutely free being requires the nonexistence of God. The proofs
begin with the concept of God and can only end where they began,
with the individual recognizing the existence of the concept. "That
which I conceive for myself in a real way *(realiter)*, is a real concept
for me."[87] However, there can be no movement from concept to being,
from thought to reality; the ontological argument cannot be accepted.
The concept of God has a sociological importance in the way it
informs and guides social life, but it is not real. It does possess
existence, but only as a product of the imagination. Kant's critique of
the ontological argument is also questioned, for the existence of both
God and money is only a product of the social conditions within
which these ideas develop. Move from one type of society to another,
and the belief in God and money both change.

For Marx, a belief in 100 talers represents from the individual's
perspective the existence of these talers. The existence of God is a
result of the collective values of the community. God's existence is
determined by human behavior and consciousness, while the concept
itself has no ontological or philosophical basis. There can be no
movement from thought to reality. Even at this early stage in his
intellectual development, Marx is preparing—through examination
of Epicurus—for his critique of the metaphysics of Hegel's whole
philosophical system. Because of his critique of science and religion,
Epicurus is the highest achievement of the Greek Enlightenment, and
at the same time represents the death knell of the Greek polis and
the breakup of the harmony of the Greek community. The goal now
is not to recreate this lost Greek world in a new polis, but to build a
community within the achievements and limits of modernity. To do
this requires a synthesis of the ideals of the Ancients and the social
structures of the Moderns.

Marx is aware of the weaknesses of Epicurus's "natural science of
self-consciousness" and it is in these appendix notes that he clearly
breaks with the notion of "abstract possibility," in favor of the category
of "real possibility."[88] This expansion of the *Dissertation* was directed
against Schelling at the time of his arrival at the University of Berlin.
He had been called there to calm the revolutionary fervor of the neo-
Hegelians.[89] In his discussion of the ontological argument in Hegel
and Kant, Marx analyzes the implications of accepting reality based
simply on the theoretical imagination of philosophical consciousness.

He is beginning to question the power and efficacy of pure speculative reason. A belief in the existence of money or a belief in a certain religious metaphysics will only bring ridicule and laughter in cultural settings where they are not accepted. Thought is limited by reality. According to Baronovitch, this represents the beginning of a break with Bruno Bauer's thesis that social change may be brought about simply by self-consciousness and philosophical criticism. It also represents a reversal of Marx's own position held during the writing of the text of his dissertation. He seems to be moving away from pure reason in the Epicurean and Hegelian traditions and toward critique as a real political activity (praxis) aimed at the material world.[90] Finally, at the end of the appended sections to the *Dissertation,* Marx quotes from the early Schelling—who, as we have seen, is a continuing source of inspiration to him. Here, too, there is a critique of the pure reason that spins laws from itself.[91]

In summary, it has become clear in these writings that many aspects of Marx's later ideas about materialism, science, and ethics are already contained in seminal form in his *Dissertation* and the preparatory *Notebooks.* It has been said that the choosing of a dissertation topic is one of the most important decisions an academician can make, since the rest of academic life is only a further development, explication, and expansion of the original insights. Though Marx apparently travels quite far from his early interests as a Greek scholar, those original insights and visions were with him until his death. He held to a materialism and science that had ties closer to the *Naturphilosophie* of Epicurus and Schelling than to the eighteenth-century Enlightenment materialists and positivists. Epicurus's philosophy reflects a profound interest in an attempt to synthesize science and ethics, materialism and freedom, Democritus and Socrates, materialism and idealism. Through his critique of Democritean science, causal relationships, and the mechanical view of physical relationships, Epicurus established an alternative view of the relationship between man and nature and scientific concepts and the external world. The later writings of Marx express similar views in their critique of fetishism, positivism, and the simple mechanical causality between internal contradictions in the political economy and the various forms of economic and social crises. This view of materialism also contains the concept of alienation as applied to the separation of essence from existence, an emancipation theory implicit in Marx's early critique of religion, and—finally—a social anthropology arguing that human rationality can realize itself only in the sensuous and material world.

"The swerving atom of Epicurus, as the antithesis of Democritean linear motion also represented the negation of material nature by consciousness, the triumph of human thought over blind fate and natural law."[92]

After completing his dissertation and receiving his Ph.D., Marx became involved in the "Cologne Circle" in 1842. Taking over the editing of the *Rheinischer Zeitung* he was embroiled in real political issues, which resulted in publication of his famous early articles on freedom of the press and state censorship and the theft of wood and peasant rights. During this time he met Moses Hess, who introduced him to the theory of socialism (Proudhon, Wilhelm Weitling, Hess himself, and Lorenz von Stein), which further precipitated Marx's break with the ideas of the Berlin Left-Hegelians.[93] By the summer of 1843 Marx had read the *Das Wesen des Christentums* (1841), *Die Vorläufige Thesen zur Reform der Philosophie* (1842), and the *Grunsätze der Philosophie der Zukunft* (1843). Also in 1843 he wrote his *Contribution to the Critique of Hegel's Philosophy of Law*, in which he recognizes the opposition between the ideal and real worlds of the state and rejects the idea that history can be deduced from logic; he also developed an initial definition of a theory of true democracy at this time (see Chapter Four). With this work, Marx was applying his critique of Epicurus in the *Dissertation* to the master himself. Although Marx did become suspicious of the subjective idealism of Epicurus, the centrality of individual freedom and the Greek Enlightenment's critique of mysticism and idolatry were to be part of Marx's social theory throughout his life.

> The radical subjectivism of Epicurus is double-edged. Like Prometheus, Epicurus cuts down from their heaven all gods elevated over and against human consciousness, but with the same stroke he enthrones a dangerously abstract form of self-consciousness as the new idol.[94]

As it turns out, what appears to be an ambivalence in Marx's interpretation of Epicurus is in reality a theoretical balancing act between the *Vernunftsbegriff* of Hegel and the primacy of Kant's autonomous individual. Marx uses Epicurus's ethical theory to transcend Hegel's metaphysics, and uses Hegel's view of historical alienation and intersubjective creativity to compensate for the moral abstractionism of post-Aristotelian Greek philosophy and Kantian practical reason. The subjugation of one moment to the other results in either false individualism or dominating idolatry. The one keeps Marx from developing a metaphysical economic system, and the other keeps him from absolutizing the moral and subjective ideals of the Left-Hegelians and French Socialists. The individual must be understood within the context of historical and real social possibilities.

The stage is now set for a redirection of philosophical critique, a rethinking of the role of theoretical praxis, and a reunderstanding of the social and structural parameters within which the formation of self-consciousness takes place. In 1843–44 Marx also wrote two important essays for the *Deutsch-Französische Jahrbücher: On the Jewish Question* and *Contribution to the Critique of Hegel's Philosophy of Law: An Introduction*. In the former article he makes a further break with Bruno Bauer over the issues of Jewish political liberties, political emancipation, and universal human rights; in the latter Marx incorporates his readings of communist and socialist social theory and develops for the first time his theory of the proletarian revolution. With the critique of the abstract philosophical praxis of Bauer, with the critique of Hegel's Absolute Spirit and his theory of the state, and with the growing importance of Feuerbach and Hess, the meaning and relevance of Marx's understanding of praxis, materialism, and ethics becomes connected with an examination and critique of both political theory and political economy. A dramatic transformation has occurred within the framework of Marx's understanding of Greek philosophy and the moral imperative for realization of human freedom and rational self-consciousness.[95] Ethics must be made concrete to be real. Then in the summer of 1844, Marx wrote his *Economic and Philosophical Manuscripts*.

Chapter Two

Epistemology, Politics, and Social Justice in the Greek Polis: Marx and Aristotle

INTRODUCTION

There has been a good deal written lately concerning the indebtedness of Marx to Aristotle's philosophy, which has certainly broadened our understanding of both intellectual traditions. However, almost nothing has been written on the impact this relationship had on the development of Marx's critique of moral positivism, his notion of theory and practice, and the relation between the concept of praxis as social labor and praxis as revolutionary political activity. This chapter will examine the connection between Greek ethical thought and the social ethics of Karl Marx. A fuller appreciation of the extent of this relationship must wait until the final chapter, when all the pieces from the various chapters are put together to form a comprehensive whole integrating classical ethics and Marx's social theory. The focus of this chapter will be on the relationship between epistemology and praxis. There are two major meanings of the term "praxis" in Marx's writings. The first refers to the category of social labor, which was developed in the earlier works and represents only one aspect of the meaning of the term; the second meaning, which first occurs in *Contribution to the Critique of Hegel's Philosophy of Law*, becomes extremely important in his later works as he begins to interpret praxis as a political category with its roots reaching back to the Greeks.

The term "theory and practice," which is central to Marx's theory of knowledge, can be seen as having more in common with Aristotle's notion of political wisdom *(phronesis)* and political action *(praxis)* than anyone has previously suspected. The conventional wisdom and traditional interpretations in this area have been that Marx's use of the term "praxis" represents a 180-degree turn away from the Aristotelian use. In fact, the concept has been very closely connected with Aristotle's notions of *techne* (productive knowledge) and *poiesis* (fabrication) and is then used by Marx to justify the supposed positivism and science of his later economic writings in the *Grundrisse* and *Capital*. This has been especially true of the modern criticisms of the technical and instrumental character of praxis by Arendt, Lobkowicz, Wellmer, and Habermas.[1] This view of Marx's concept of theory and practice rests on an understanding of praxis as a form of technical knowledge *(Produktionswissen)* used scientifically to explain and predict economic crises and socialist revolution. In this reading, the full impact of Marx's critique of modernity and his reliance on the classical traditions of the Ancients has been lost. This is perhaps another example of the social amnesia of contemporary scholars. This chapter will begin the process of archaeologically recovering the deep formal structures of Marx's social thought. The interpretation of praxis here will turn on an understanding of his ethical theory, his moral epistemology, and their integration in his later political economy.

Some of the different themes in the current literature that detail the relationships between Aristotle and Marx and their common ideas include: (1) their theories of objectification and the relation between Aristotle's four causes and Marx's concept of labor (Gould); (2) the cultural ideals of the Greek polis, praxis, and Marx's notion of species being (Kain, Springborg, and Bernstein); (3) the concept of activity in both the *Metaphysics* and *Nicomachean Ethics* and Marx's species being (Rockmore); (4) Aristotle's ethics of virtue and Marx's social ethics (Brenkert); (5) classical political freedom in the public sphere and Marx's concept of human emancipation (Mewes, Hook, and Arendt); (6) the *zōon politikon* and the species being (Schwartz); (7) Aristotle's natural law and Marx's social being (Mészáros); (8) their theories of nature and materialism (Rouse); (9) the common ground of their philosophical anthropology (Depew); (10) Aristotle's *eudaimonia* (happiness) and Marx's view of self-realization (Gilbert, McBride, Miller, Nussbaum, and Levine); (11) their sociological analyses of class (de Sainte Croix); and (12) their theories of need, use value, and exchange value, and the differences between an economy based on the satisfaction of communal needs *(oikonomia)* and the needs of unlimited self-interest *(chrematistike)* (Springborg and Seidel).[2] It is the complexity of these common and overlapping relationships between the two social philosophers that will help to clarify some of the confusion surrounding Marx's moral and methodological intentions, especially his theories of moral epistemology and social justice. In the process we will see that Marx's critique of modernity is grounded in his understanding of the Ancients.

Behind Marx's critique of political economy, industrial capitalism, and the social relations of power and authority lies a rediscovery and return to the critical elements of the Greek polis and the philosophical tradition of Aristotle. Those elements in Aristotle's thought that had such an important impact on Marx's theories include the former's emphasis on the social and political nature of man, the metaphysical relationship between substance and form—potency and act—and, finally, his distinctions among the different forms of knowledge: theoretical *(episteme)*, practical *(phronesis)*, and productive knowledge *(techne)*. Though some of these ideas have been transformed through contact with Hegel and the Left-Hegelians and by a need to adjust to the historical circumstances of the nineteenth century, there still remains a clear path between Marx's social philosophy and the ethics and metaphysics of Aristotle. Placing Marx within this Greek tradition allows us to see important implications for an interpretation of his ideas of science, moral epistemology, and social justice.

It is in the area of social ethics and Marx's reliance on the natural law tradition that some of the closest links between Aristotle and Marx may be observed. More specifically, the themes surrounding social justice to be discussed in this chapter include the relation between socialist and communist theories of distributive justice; the relation between man's social being and justice; justice and bourgeois ideology; universal knowledge, moral epistemology, and the dilemma of ethical objectivity; and, finally, the relation between Marx's concept of praxis and the Aristotelian notions of practical reason *(phronesis)*, the good life *(eudaimonia)*, and the formal potentiality of human nature. From this list, the reader may well anticipate that the concept of justice for both Aristotle and Marx goes well beyond traditional considerations of the distribution of social wealth. It is this very point that has misled some of the contemporary interpretations of Marx's theory of social ethics. Within this more developed analysis of the Marxian category of justice, we will see a return to the Aristotelian distinctions between science and practical wisdom *(phronesis)*, knowledge and politics.

ARISTOTLE'S THEORY OF JUSTICE: THREE LEVELS

Aristotle's Justice, Level 1: Universal and Particular Justice

Aristotle begins his investigation into the nature of ethics and social justice in his *Nicomachean Ethics* by first raising the question of the ultimate end or final good of human life, or what he calls *eudaimonia* (happiness).[3] This question is literally and figuratively centuries away from the questions of self-interest and pleasure of the seventeenth-century possessive individualism of Hobbes and Locke or the eighteenth-century utilitarianism of Bentham and Mill. Aristotle immediately recognizes the difficulty of such an undertaking, because the form of knowledge most appropriate to the question "Is politics a science?" is very problematic, imprecise, and relies on the contingent world of experience. He approaches the problem cautiously by first asking about the "function of man," in distinction to nature. Just as the musician, carpenter, and sculptor have a function in society—just as nature in general has a function—so too must humanity in general have a function. "What is peculiar to man?"[4] After this is known the philosopher will be in a better position to know the universal purposes of human existence.

> If this is the case, (and we state the function of man to be a certain kind of life, and this to be an activity or actions of the soul implying a rational principle, and the function of a good man to be the good and noble performance of these, and if any action is well performed when it is performed in accordance with the appropriate excellence: if this is the case,) human good turns out to be activity of soul in accordance with virtue, and if there are more than one virtue, in accordance with the best and most complete.[5]

After careful consideration of the concept of the good and after rejecting both pleasure and wealth as the ultimate forms of the good life, Aristotle finally settles on the virtuous life of practical and intellectual activity. This is a life that is self-sufficient—one that is universal and complete, and therefore demands nothing else to augment it. Being final in and of itself, it is not a means to some other end or purpose. Thus, the good life or happiness is identified as one of virtuous, rational activity in the development of the individual soul, which lies as a potentiality within every human individual and may be nurtured through political education *(paideia)*. Books 2 to 4 of the *Nicomachean Ethics* analyze the various types of moral virtues and their corresponding character traits—such as courage, temperance, and virtues concerned with money, honor, anger, and social intercourse. Book 5 is devoted entirely to examination of the last and most important of the moral virtues, which is justice—for it is in a just society that virtuous individuals can exercise virtue not only in themselves, but in relation to other members of the political community. Only in society is self-realization of human potentialities possible, since it is only within the political community that man can truly exercise his moral and intellectual virtues.[6] The individual becomes a true individual—realizing both potential and freedom—in and through society. This is what Aristotle considers to be complete, virtuous activity and the union of individual and community happiness; it is the final goal *(telos)* of man.

Aristotle begins his discussion of justice in book 5 by distinguishing between two main theories: a particular and a universal theory of justice.[7] Particular justice includes distributive *(dianemetikos)*, corrective *(diorthotikos)*, and reciprocal *(antipeponthos)* justice. There has been a good deal of disagreement in the secondary literature about whether reciprocal justice is a form of particular justice or represents a new category entirely.[8] I will argue that it represents both a form of particular justice and its structural preconditions. All three of these forms of justice stress mainly—but not exclusively—the issue of the distribution of the social wealth of society and, thus, economic considerations. On the other hand, Aristotle's more important and complex ideas on a theory of universal justice are summarized in only a few lines. Though he spends a short section defining universal justice directly, his total ethical and political writings are a profound statement regarding his general position. A fully developed theory is not articulated and lies scattered throughout his *Ethics* and *Politics*. However, when it is recognized that his concept of "universal justice" includes his theory of political justice, practical deliberation *(bouleusis)* and political judgment *(phronesis)*, his critique of moral epistemology and universal ethical laws, and his theory of needs and community, the term takes on a wholly new meaning and importance. These are the moments of ethical social life. The emphasis has clearly shifted away from economic considerations to the nature of the polis and political community. Here the concept of justice refers to issues of virtue, moral character, socialization, law, the political constitution, and the self-realization of human potential. This is political justice.

> This is to be found among men who share their life with a view to self-sufficiency, men who are free and either proportionately or arithmetically equal, so that between those who do not fulfil this condition there is no political justice but justice in a special sense and by analogy. For justice exists only between men whose mutual relations are governed by law.[9]

Particular justice analyzes specific instances of the need for justice in certain types of social relationships: initial distribution (sharing) of the wealth of the community, rebalance or redress of individual grievances and wrongs in economic and social relationships, and the establishment of fairness in economic exchange. Distribution, rebalance, and fairness characterize the essential features of particular justice. Universal justice—on the other hand—involves discussion about the nature of society, the nature of justice as a whole, the establishment of the ethical criteria of justice and equality, and the impossibility of establishing natural and universal laws of social justice above the community (the dilemma of ethical objectivity). It is a broader and more far-reaching political category.

Universal Justice

Aristotle starts to develop his theory of universal justice in book 5 by beginning with an analysis of justice as a whole and the common-sense interpretation of justice as being law abiding and fair.[10] For him, the end of law is the realization of the common good measured in terms of some principle, not yet under consideration. Law also functions to produce happiness and harmony within the political community by education and cultivation of virtuous citizens (individuals who are brave, temperate, good natured, and so on). Justice is viewed by Aristotle as the last of the virtues and is the only one of the moral virtues to have a separate chapter devoted to its consideration. It is not simply just another virtue, but also represents the "complete virtue"—for it means that virtue is not only a personal characteristic of the individual, but a characteristic of society as a whole. "Justice in this sense, then, is not part of virtue but virtue entire."[11] It thus deals with the total organization and structure of society and the social relations among its members. All this is done for individual happiness and the good of one's neighbors.

For Aristotle, universal justice represents both a moral state of character development *(paideia)* and the constitutional state of the political character of society *(politeia)*, which creates laws designed to further moral development and just laws for the common good. This is why universal justice is the complete virtue, since the exercise of justice results in the good of the individual and of society, a just individual and a just society. Under universal justice, the law commands us to practice every virtue and forbids us to practice any vice. "And the things that tend to produce virtue, taken as a whole, are those of the acts prescribed by the law, which have been prescribed with a view to the education for the common good."[12] Castoriadis describes it as follows:

> Justice as a whole, total justice—the essential aspect of the law—is thus infinitely more than bidding and forbidding. It is, first and foremost, that which "produces virtue as a whole," and it does this by way of *paideia*, "education," training with a view to the affairs of the community, the whole development of the citizen by which he is transformed from a little animal to a participant of the city. Justice as a whole is the constitution/institution of the community, and it follows from the goal of this institution that the weightiest element of justice should be that which has to do with *paideia*, the formation of the individual with a view to his life in the community, the socialization of the human being.[13]

The goal of justice is not economic equality, but a fully developed, educated, self-conscious citizen. Castoriadis also notices that the notion of total justice is not examined further by Aristotle in the *Ethics*. This along with the almost exclusive emphasis on particular justice in the secondary literature has resulted in a serious oversight in Aristotelian scholarship. All the chapters of the *Ethics*, along with the *Politics*, taken collectively represent Aristotle's investigation into the nature of universal justice. And it is here that the secret of social justice must be sought.

The universal theory of social justice may be viewed as the metatheoretical response to difficulties encountered in establishing a mathematical criterion for the determination of particular justice. At the very start of his *Ethics*, Aristotle recognizes the impossibility of scientifically establishing universal laws of social ethics by joining universal knowledge *(episteme)* and practical wisdom *(phronesis)*. He then turns to a more transcendental approach. (For a further discussion of these issues, see Chapter Six.) In effect, Aristotle raises new questions: What are the transcendental conditions for the possibility of a just society? Under what social conditions are the *polis* and *politeia* possible? These questions also correspond to those relating to the potentiality and final end *(telos)* of human existence, when man is by nature characterized as both a household being *(zoon oikonomikon)* and a political animal *(zōon politikon)*. Findley says that these are characteristics of man viewed as a community being *(zoon koinonikon)*, which presupposes that all associations include a desire for "fairness, mutuality, and common purpose."[14] They are the social and structural preconditions for realization of the *zoon koinonikon*. This idea is further pursued in book 1 of the *Politics,* where man is described as a political animal with speech *(logos)*.

The contemporary Anglo-American tradition when dealing with morality and political theory has focused on theories of justice that emphasize the distribution of the wealth of society, and has lost this broader understanding of the nature of justice and human potential. Much of the discussion over whether Marx has a theory of justice or a moral theory has centered around these very misunderstandings, and therefore represents only a partial treatment of the broader subject found in either Aristotle or Marx. In his *Critique of the Gotha Program,* it is clear that Marx, too, is concerned with these broader types of social and political issues—and not simply with the narrower economic ones. However, the thesis I am developing here is that it is the other theory of justice—universal or total justice—that is the focus of Marx's attention. As one commentator on Aristotle has critically noticed, there are very few analyses of Aristotle's theory of justice as a whole.[15] This has to do with the style, nature, and difficulty of his work, but also with the lack of integration of all its component parts.[16]

Though Aristotle introduces his analysis of universal justice by stating that it involves a moral disposition to act justly, a more accurate and comprehensive picture of the concept would refer to the totality of his ideas concerning political justice—that is, to the nature of the political community *(politike koinonia)*, political constitutions *(politeia)*, political knowledge *(bouleusis* and *phronesis)*, and the nature of political education and socialization *(paideia)* found in the *Nicomachean Ethics,* the *Politics,* and the *Rhetoric.* Aristotle's theory of universal justice is a theory of the nature and constitution of the political community, its legal and economic structures, its patterns of social interaction, and its structures of political deliberation. Because of the problematic nature and status of political knowledge itself, the interaction between the social structures of the community *(koinonia)* and self-consciousness is closely analyzed. But in the end, the real question is: What is happiness and the true goal of human existence? These are also the types of issues and questions that occupy Marx's attention throughout his later works in political economy and that are the foundation stones for his own ethical thinking. The question of distribution of social wealth is not central to Marx's theory of social justice, for the same reasons as it was not central to Aristotle. Justice is essentially related to the nature of social relationships, character development, the formation of self-consciousness, and the possibilities of human potentiality within a free and rational society. The real questions center around the structures of society and political economy and their relation positively and negatively to the potentialities of self-realization of the species being *(Gattungswesen)* or polis being *(zoon politikon)*. For Aristotle, then, the essence of philosophy is to ask: What are the goals of human existence, society, and social justice? What are the ends of individual and social life? What is the nature of the good man and virtuous citizen? It is in this sense that the *Nicomachean Ethics* is a specialized treatment of some of the questions discussed in the *Physics,* with its emphasis on potentialities of the present forms of existence.[17]

Particular Justice

What happiness and the social good mean at this point in the analysis has still not yet been stated. Nor does Aristotle deal with the issue any further, for he immediately changes the subject of discussion to that of particular justice. This only leads to confusion later on in his analysis, but is not unrepresentative of the organization of the material in the *Ethics.* This certainly raises provocative questions as to why he refuses to or cannot deal with some of his own central concerns. Is the problem in the difficulty of the issues he raises or in the manner in which we have received his works? In the secondary literature devoted to an examination of Aristotle's theory of justice, the emphasis is certainly on the study of particular justice, for this contains the bulk of his analysis on the topic. Though not exclusively devoted to economic issues, the emphasis on distribution and fairness of economic exchange are central to this category. In modern thought, the relationship between justice and distribution has made these terms almost synonymous, though they are much more ambiguously and subtly related in Aristotle's thought. The various forms of transgression of society's moral code are called particular forms of moral wickedness; however, when they are done in the interests of pleasure and personal gain, they are called unjust. It is the latter that is considered under particular justice.

While universal justice deals with the law, virtue, and the community, particular justice is concerned with direct and immediate forms of social interaction. *Distributive justice (dianemetikos)* focuses on the distribution of the common possessions of society—social honors, money, and community possessions—to all who have a share in the political constitution based on proportional equality, while *corrective justice (diorthotikos)* is based on an arithmetic proportionality and attempts to straighten out or correct any unjust gain resulting from different forms of social interaction. There are two subdivisions of corrective justice: those based on voluntary transactions *(sunallagmata)*, and those based on involuntary ones. The third kind of particular justice—*reciprocal justice*—deals with the foundations of economic exchange and the basis for equal exchange in the market.[18]

Distributive Justice. Distributive justice or proportional justice is characterized as giving equal amounts of social goods to equals, and unequal amounts to those unequal in merit. However, the difficult question—never answered by Aristotle—relates to the exact meaning and measure *(axia)* of merit. The very criterion and standard of measurement by which equality is defined, analyzed, and measured is made problematic by Aristotle's rejection of the scientific nature of ethics and politics. He states that everyone agrees that distribution should be based "on merit in some sense"—that is, on the amount of contribution to the political community. The difficulty, however, is that the criterion of merit changes according to the nature of the political constitution created in the political community: The measurement of merit in a democracy would be based on the concept of citizenship; in an oligarchy the criteria of evaluation of merit would be standards of wealth or noble birth; while in an aristocracy it would be based on moral excellence *(arete)*. Thus citizenship, wealth, birth, and moral excellence are different criteria *(axia)* by which the standards of equality, inequality, and justice are measured.[19] Aristotle does not immediately resolve the debate over the best standard of measurement or the correspondingly best political constitution in an ideal just society in the *Nicomachean Ethics*, because the discussion of these issues was originally framed within a discussion about the nature of knowledge, truth, and science. The answers cannot be determined philosophically. This may lead one to suspect that Aristotle is an ethical relativist. But this is not the direction he takes. Proportional justice involves four terms: the interrelationship between the two equal persons, and the distribution of the two objects or things. Between individuals, there will be an equal distribution of social goods in the form of geometric proportionality—that is, according to some standard of worth and contribution to society in which equals are rewarded equally and unequals unequally.

Corrective Justice. Corrective or rectificatory justice is based on arithmetical proportion (the total amount rectified based on amount of the offense) and is the legal attempt in civil and criminal law to return to the balance established before the unjust act was committed. It rectifies a social injustice from voluntary transactions *(sunallagmata)* such as sale, purchase, loan for consumption, pledging, loan for use, depositing, and letting. Involuntary transactions include theft, adultery, poisoning, procuring, enticement of slaves, assassination, false witness, assault, imprisonment, murder, robbery with violence, mutilation, abuse, and insult. Neither the moral character of the individuals involved nor their contribution to the general social good—which are the criteria of measurement for distributive justice—is considered part of or relevant to corrective justice. Whether the persons defrauded are good or bad is irrelevant to the legal disposition of this form of justice, as is their social standing. Both parties are considered equal (arithmetic proportion); and justice is thus the equalizing of the inequality created by the offense, by awarding damages to the injured party. Most of the examples used to describe voluntary transactions are economic transactions. Equalization occurs through the use of legal penalties and a corrective balancing of the scales by taking away any unjust economic gains. Corrective justice is thus a mean between the two extremes of unjust loss and gain.

Reciprocal Justice. The third type of justice is reciprocal justice, and it is perhaps the most interesting and unclear of the three types of particular justice. Concerned with the restoration of the self-sufficiency and integrity of the community based on equivalent exchange, mutual sharing, and the absence of selfishness and economic profit, it deals with the social relations of exchange in the market and is viewed by Aristotle as something that holds the polis together.[20] Finley emphasizes that the key word to understanding the nature of reciprocity is *koinonia*, since it is this that holds society together. The notion of *koinonia* has a meaning that is extremely broad and has received different translations. "At the higher levels, 'community' is usually suitable, while at the lower perhaps 'association' provided the elements of fairness, mutuality, and common purpose are kept in mind."[21] Exchange is understood as a community behavior, and not an individual one. It is done for the physical survival of the individual who must earn a livelihood. But it is also the means by which the community is materially formed into an integrated and harmonious whole. This theme of the relationship between political economy and the polis is again discussed in book 1 of the *Politics* in more developed form.

Reciprocal justice is thus part of neither distributive nor corrective justice, and its exact status in Aristotle's theory of justice has been debated.[22] With reciprocal justice, the emphasis is not on virtue or the distribution of social goods, but on the political economy that lies at the foundation of the Greek polis. Though it is not universal justice, it provides the economic foundations without which law, virtue, and community would be impossible. Stated in this fashion, it becomes what today would be considered a metaethical category. Just as the political community is the highest form of association for the Greeks, the marketplace is also the association of exchange that creates the bonds necessary for the state. There is even a religious foundation for these exchanges, exemplified by the "temple of the Graces" established in the public meeting place. Citizens are encouraged to return kindness for kindness and even to initiate a kind act in the future for something done in the past.[23]

The economic foundations of society lie in the proportionate equality that should be present in exchange relations. A real difficulty for Aristotle exists because, while equality of goods is demanded by the proportionate equality of the market, there exists nothing but difference and inequality in exchange relations themselves. How are the products of the farmer and the doctor to be equated for a fair exchange? The history of the interpretations of Aristotle's response has been more tortuous and confused than any other aspect of his thinking on any matter. From the medieval theory of just price, to the classical expression of the labor theory of value, to Marx's theory of value, and to the contemporary neoclassical view of price determination, Aristotle's theory of proportionate equality has been used to justify a wide variety of contradictory interpretations. The economic theory of the day usually prevails and provides the hermeneutical clue for a reading of Aristotle's economic theory.[24] A close exegesis of this theory and its place in the overall context of Aristotle's theory of universal and political justice may provide a more adequate format for its interpretation.

Why are the products of two entirely different economic activities comparable? What is the basis for their commensurability; what are the criteria for the measurement of this commensurability; and what is the purpose of this form of analysis in the first place? What determines the relationship between the number of shoes that must be exchanged for the building of a house? They must be made proportionate. What is reciprocal justice, and what role does it have in the context of Aristotle's theory of universal justice? There has been no agreement on any of these questions, but it is clear that the two key categories that Aristotle himself uses to explain the very possibility of economic exchange are need *(chreia)* and money.[25]

> This is why all goods must have a price set on them; for then there will always be exchange, and if so, association of man with man. Money, then, acting as a measure, makes goods commensurate and equates them; for neither would there have been association if there were not exchange, nor exchange, if there were not equality, nor equality, if there were not commensurability.[26]

Aristotle begins with the assumption that without some mechanism to make the exchange of different products equal, there would be no exchange, and by inference—as we have seen—no political community. Need *(chreia)* appears to be the anthropological and natural foundation for the social division of labor and the exchange process, while money—as the mechanism of exchange—is its legal and conventional measure. "Money has become by convention a sort of representative of demand."[27] Aristotle sees in the etymology of the word for money—*nomisma*—the word for law: *nomos.* It is a social convention created by agreement to express the natural need of humans and an already given exchange relation. Aristotle never really does explain how commodities for exchange are made compatible. In the famous passage from the first volume of *Capital,* Marx states that the answer to Aristotle's dilemma lies in the nature of abstract labor. When commodity production becomes the central economic form of society, when labor is reduced to a commodity, then the essential nature of exchange relations will be revealed. Aristotle lived at the beginning of commodity exchange, and only in its developed form do the secrets become visible.[28]

Immediately after his analysis of the nature of exchange as grounded in need and money, Aristotle examines the nature of exchange and its relation to justice. That is, the social telos of exchange is a form of social justice. Justice is the intermediate or mean between acting unjustly and being unjustly treated. The purpose of exchange as the economic expression of justice, then, is not to acquire wealth at the expense of one's neighbors, but to act in economic matters according to the values of equality and proportion.[29] Marx, too, will consider this very point throughout his writings, and in particular in the section on fetishism in *Capital*. Comparing Aristotle to Marx, it becomes clear that Aristotle does not attempt to base his ethics on an historical critique of economic and social relations of commodity production or the injustice of such an economic system, as is the case with Marx.[30] Rather, Aristotle is concerned with laying the foundations for a theory of ethics and politics in which political economy contains his analysis of human needs, division of labor, and exchange relations.

He concentrates on how they provide the economic foundations for a just society in a fair and proportional exchange system. The goals of Aristotle and Marx are quite different; and therefore, so are their social theories. Though they mean different things by their categories of equality and human labor, the two are by no means incompatible. Aristotle's political economy in the *Nicomachean Ethics* is a very idealized vision of Greek society, as he abstracts from all the forms of commercial capitalism (trading) that exist at the time of his writing. He stresses in this work only the direct exchange among producers themselves.[31] What is important in Aristotle's theory at this point is not the specific substance of his arguments, but the overall logic and structure of these arguments and the inclusive nature of his theory of justice. Of special interest is the relationship between political economy and ethics.

Injustice is an excess and defect, and is viewed as an extreme relation in which there is a disproportionate and unfair exchange between persons. There is also a corresponding social disharmony created by this form of economic injustice in which the exchanging parties have too little or too much. Particular justice (just distribution) has to do with equality and proportion in interactions of various types, with the emphasis on economic transactions; while universal justice (*arete, paideia,* and *politeia*) has to do with the constitution of the polis and the creation of rational, free, and virtuous citizens (*eudaimonia*).

The conception of the State with which complete justice is connected, is that of a moral community of men striving after righteousness, and therefore regulated by a law which expresses their aim. The conception of the State on which particular justice rests is that of an association of equals, which, because its members are equal, is preserved by a principle of equality. Considered in the light of this latter conception, justice means that each individual has his due, and that he is so treated, and so treats others, as to preserve the proper proportion between members of the association.[32]

There is another form of justice mentioned at the end of the section on reciprocal justice: domestic or household justice. This represents a further development of the analysis of political economy begun under the term "particular justice" and becomes the starting point for Aristotle's analysis of his *Politics*.

Aristotle's Justice, Level 2: Economic Exchange, Civic Friendship, and Democracy

The second level of Aristotle's theory of justice concentrates on his economic theory, which has an important place in both the *Nicomachean Ethics* and *Politics*. The categorization of his economics has caused many problems for interpreters, as we have already seen. This is due mainly to the fact that economics is always subservient to the needs of the political community and, in turn, becomes a subdivision of his theory of social justice.[33]

The genius of Aristotle is the manner in which he recognizes the necessary but not sufficient condition that the economy must play in forming the foundations of a self-sufficient community. Anything that tends to undermine the harmonious social and political relations of the polis is criticized by him as destructive of the possibilities of human self-realization. He begins his analysis of the political community in the *Politics* by stating that it is the highest good of man. He continues with his introduction by examining the development of the Greek state, from the earlier social stages of the family and the village to the city-state. Aristotle argues that the state is the natural creation of a large self-sufficient community for the purpose of the "common life." He also contends that the state is the natural end of human existence, since it is its most developed social form. He next affirms these same points again—but at the anthropological level, by arguing that humans are by nature social since they have the characteristic of speech (logos).[34] It is through speech that human beings search for justice and the good life. The etymology of the word logos also refers to questions, arguments, defense of speech, definitions, relationships between terms in propositions, reflections, and solutions.[35]

> For "logos" to the Greeks certainly did not primarily refer to some "cognitive faculty"; it meant rationality as it expresses itself in articulated speech. And this rationality a Greek did not precisely see either in the slave or in the barbarian; rational and articulate speech for the Greek was embodied in politics—arguing and persuading one another and reaching rational decisions based on common agreement.[36]

The development of Greek rationality entailed a political process mediated by the public act of speech. Given this short introduction to establish the naturalness of the political community, Aristotle considers the role of the economy and, especially, the art of the acquisition of wealth (chrematistike), which is his central concern in this book.[37] He gives another short introduction—this time to the economic issues— by analyzing property and slavery, and then proceeds to turn to the heart of his study: the theory of household management (oikonomike) and domestic justice. Aristotle distinguishes between the use value and the exchange value of products, but characterizes the exchange of shoes as a secondary purpose compared with their immediate use. He is interested in developing two major themes in book 1 of the Politics: (1) that economics is important in maintaining the integrity of the polis and the good life; and (2) that the evolution of exchange from barter to commercial trade (kapelike) undermines the priority of the koinonia for mutual sharing, fairness, community, and social justice in the polis.

Karl Polanyi referred to kapelike as "hucksterism written large," while both Finley and Polanyi recognize the importance of the distinction between kapelike—Aristotle's new word for commercial exchange—and emporike, the more traditional word for foreign trade.[38] The earlier stages of economic exchange based on the needs of society and a mutual sharing of the social wealth of the community are lost in a society in which economic profit becomes the primary motivating factor for exchange relations. In effect, Aristotle is very sensitive to the loss of social responsibility for the general welfare resulting from the evolution of a market economy in Greece. Unlike in the Ethics where the emphasis was on the exchange between two producers, in the *Politics* Aristotle examines the impact of commercial capitalism on the polis. Economic theory is an important component in ethics and is always subservient to the ethical and political needs of society. Thus, there is no interest for Aristotle (and later Marx) to discuss the actual mechanism of market exchange and price determination.[39]

In chapter 9 of book 1, Aristotle traces the development of this new phenomenon in Greek social life: (1) from the simple exchange of barter where one good is exchanged for another good, as in C–C; (2) to a more complex form of exchange—characterized by C–M–C— where money acts as the instrument and measure of exchange between two goods; (3) to commercial trade *(kapelike)*, which is characterized by the acquisition of economic profits at the expense of one's neighbor, M–C–M′; (4) to the final form of exchange relations in interest, or M–M′. Aristotle connects his view of the historical evolution of Greek society from the family to the polis—in chapter 2 of book 1—to his theory of the evolution of commodity exchange, in an attempt to show which forms of exchange are natural to the community and which are not. He contends that, with the evolution of the village and the resulting complexity of the social division of labor, exchange was both necessary and natural since some "men had more than enough of some things and less than enough of others."[40] As societies became even more complex and international trade developed along with a money or coin economy, there still remained a degree of naturalness to the exchange relations.[41]

However, with the introduction of commercial trade for profit— that is, commodity exchange—the art of household management turns into an unnatural process characterized by the search for wealth and profits without limit. In fact, the latter becomes the measure of the good life and the criterion by which happiness is calculated. This quest for money without limit is an example of living, but not living well; it is a form of pure existence without moral excellence, for it undermines the very foundations for the possibility of a virtuous and rational life in society.

> But as we have said, this art is twofold, one branch being of the nature of trade while the other belongs to the household art; and the latter branch is necessary and in good esteem, but the branch connected with exchange is justly discredited (for it is not in accordance with nature, but involves men's taking things from one another). As this is so, usury is most reasonably hated, because its gain comes from money itself and from that for the sake of which money was invented [that is, exchange].[42]

At all times in this analysis, it is important to keep in mind that this
economic theory of commodity exchange is only a part of Aristotle's
comprehensive theory of ethics and social justice. A prerequisite for
the virtuous life is property and material pleasure—but in modera-
tion, and secondary to the final end of human existence and the good
life: "human excellence" and "virtue of the citizen."[43] With commodity exchange and commercial profiteering, the goal of human existence turns into the making of money and business success, both of
which are perversions of the potentialities of human existence. Thus,
the economy has a crucial role to play in creation of a just society, for
without it there can be no developed society at all. Exchange is a
prerequisite for the economic survival of complex societies, the integration of their diverse needs, and the maintenance of a fair and just
economic system. Opposed to *kapelike* we have economic reciprocity
(antipeponthos), where need, equality, and mutual sharing maintain a
just economic exchange for the common good. Here exchange is not
viewed as a contest between individuals for private happiness and
profit, but the economic basis for public happiness and social justice.
Reciprocity and mutual sharing *(metadosis)* become the economic
foundations of the polis and the education of the citizen. What is the
nature of the citizen and the political constitution within which the
former becomes rational and free?

   What underlies this reciprocity and justice, as their social form? For
Aristotle, friendship *(philia)* supplies the social framework or social
cement that makes mutual sharing and community possible. Friendship is defined by Aristotle as the "mutual well-wishing out of concern
for another."[44] Mutual recognition, love, trust, and reciprocal wishing
of goodwill toward the goal of the virtuous and good life characterize
this form of social relationship.

> Friendship seems to hold states together, and lawgivers to care more for
> it than for justice; for unanimity seems to be something like friendship,
> and this they aim at most of all, and expel faction as their worst enemy;
> and when men are friends they have no need of justice, while when they
> are just they need friendship as well, and the truest form of justice
> thought to be a friendly quality.[45]

The three types of friendship correspond to the three natures and
reasons for love in social relationships—utility, pleasure, and virtue—
which, in turn, correspond to the three forms of human activity and

purposes of life. Virtue friendship is the best form of friendship because individuals love each other for their individual virtue and good moral character. These friends are courageous, good tempered, generous, honor bound, and just; and these are the qualities that are loved and respected in friendship. Ideally, friendship is also based on equality.[46] Civic friendship occupies such an important position in Aristotle's thinking, since—like justice—it is concerned with the same object or person: the virtuous and rational citizen. Just as there are different forms of justice, so too there are correspondingly different forms of friendship, all of which rest on the existence of the community. There are three forms of the good constitution (monarchy, aristocracy, and polity), and three perversions of these forms of government (tyranny, oligarchy, and false democracy). These good constitutions, in turn, correspond to the types of friendship between a man and his children (merit), a man and his wife (virtue), and that between two brothers (equality). Each constitution therefore involves a different form of friendship, as it does a different form of justice. In the perverted constitutions, there is neither friendship nor justice. While Aristotle examines and compares the interrelationships between the various forms of association, justice, and friendship, he seems to make a stronger case for the importance of the friendship between brothers and comrades.

> The friendships of brothers is like that of comrades; for they are equal and of like age, and such persons are for the most part like in their feelings and their character. Like this too, is the friendship appropriate to timocratic government; for in such a constitution the ideal is for the citizens to be equal and fair; therefore rule is to be taken in turn, and on equal terms; and the friendship appropriate here will correspond.[47]

As the friendship of brother is akin to that of comrades, it is—in turn—akin to that between citizens in a democratic polity. Aristotle picks up this theme of the three forms of constitutions and their three perverted forms in book 3 of the *Politics*.[48] The distinguishing characteristics of the good constitutions is their adherence to the law and the common good, while the defective forms are concerned only with the particular interests of the rulers. Some have argued that Aristotle's ideal political community is an aristocracy based on virtue, while the best *possible* political community is a good democracy based on equality and fairness. They say that Aristotle feels that the latter has the best potential to realize the common good and the good life. Though there seem to be hints to this effect—especially in the

Nicomachean Ethics—I would like to make the case that, when Aristotle does confront directly the issue of the best constitution, it is based on other criteria. It is based on a dilemma of moral epistemology.

In book 3 he ties together a variety of themes from his work with the integration of his theories of friendship and community, the good democracy (constitutional rule by a democratic polity), and assembly deliberation. The purpose of the good governments is to preserve the constitutions—not simply as forms of government, but as forms of social and individual life *(paideia)*, as social forms of education and character development, and as social forms of the ethical ideals of society. That is, the purpose of good government is to preserve the highest character of society.[49]

Aristotle asks this question: What constitutes a political community? Is it geographical contiguity, intermarriage, a set of common laws, trade, or the social division of labor? He argues that, in the end, it is friendship.

> But such organization is produced by the feeling of friendship, for friendship is the motive of social life; therefore, while the object of a state is the good life, these things are means to that end.[50]

This leads to a deeper understanding of the nature of citizenship as civic friendship. Aristotle defines the citizen as he who "participates in the rights of judging and governing," and as the "direct participation in the exercise of sovereignty."[51] Thus, the main political characteristics of the citizen are to hold judicial office and deliberate about the important social issues of the times. Sovereignty—which rests in the citizens—cannot be delegated as in the modern representative government, and must be constantly reproduced by political education and activity. This is a position that both Rousseau and Marx will later pick up.[52]

Aristotle's Justice, Level 3: Practical Wisdom, Deliberation, and Political Judgment

The third level of analysis of Aristotle's theory of justice returns to an earlier problem mentioned at the beginning of his *Ethics:* the imprecise and nonscientific character of political knowledge, which we have already mentioned in the first level of analysis above. To expand on this previous analysis within the context of Aristotle's overall theory of justice is important because it will integrate the different components of his thought—including the epistemological, cultural, social, economic, and political elements. Before they can be integrated into a comprehensive theory, a further discussion on the nature of practical wisdom and political knowledge is required. Books 2 to 5 in the *Ethics* concentrate on the study of "moral virtues," with justice being the centerpiece of the analysis. Book 6 examines "intellectual virtues" and the problematic nature of both practical wisdom *(phronesis)* and political knowledge.

Immediately after dealing with universal, distributive, corrective, and reciprocal justice and the further issues of natural law and conventions, voluntary and involuntary actions, and equity, Aristotle reintroduces from book 1 the complex epistemological question about the nature of moral knowledge and action. Though he started to deal with it at the beginning of his work, it was dropped as a topic for discussion and is only now reintroduced. The question is: Why, and why now? Aristotle reiterates the same theme from book 1 by stating that moral knowledge can never be universal, necessary, or scientific. We can never scientifically determine the appropriate criteria and guidelines for moral and political action because there are, in fact, no universal and precise standards for distinguishing between fair and unfair, just and unjust action. Having considered the nature of political science and the nature of justice and natural law, Aristotle has become skeptical as to whether a universal theory of justice and ethics is even possible. Delba Winthrop writes,

> It may be necessary to conclude that a theory of justice is impossible, because if justice is merely an expedient human creation, then it may have no natural or necessary principles. . . . Aristotle faces with more seriousness than most philosophers and citizens the possibility that there is no natural ground for justice and that if this is known to be so, neither should continue to take justice very seriously.[53]

At the beginning of book 6, Aristotle investigates the five types of knowledge or intellectual virtues: art or technical knowledge *(techne)*, scientific knowledge *(episteme)*, practical wisdom *(phronesis)*, philosophical wisdom *(sophia)*, and intuitive reason *(nous)*.[54] In book 1, Aristotle had mentioned only *techne*, *episteme*, and *phronesis* and had connected these three forms of knowledge with the three prominent forms of social life in the Greek polis: the life of enjoyment by the artisan and laborer *(poiesis)*, the political life of the citizen *(praxis)*, and the contemplative life of the philosopher *(theoria).* These three forms of knowledge are also characterized by the nature of their activity, such as making (productive knowledge), doing (practical knowledge), and thinking (philosophical knowledge).[55] Aristotle's purpose here is to delineate clearly moral knowledge and behavior from all other forms of knowledge and purposes of social activity. By this means, it is also possible to delve more subtly and deeply into the nature of ethical and political activity and to distinguish ethical knowledge and political life from all other forms.

By separating knowledge into five distinct types, Aristotle is arguing that practical knowledge *(phronesis)* cannot—by definition—have the form, characteristics, or goals of the other four types.[56] Their methods, orientations, metatheory, content, logical structure, and use are all different; and a clarification of these differences will lead ultimately to a better understanding of the nature of ethical and political knowledge—that is, the nature of just and unjust activities. Thus, practical wisdom *(phronesis)* cannot have any of the following characteristics: It cannot be scientific, universal, invariable, or necessary; it cannot be demonstrated from first principles, nor have a technical application where the concept (universal) is simply applied in the making of the object (particular)—as in art and work. This is knowledge based on the fragility of accumulated experience and wisdom over time. Martha Nussbaum captures this form of knowledge clearly when she says:

> Practical wisdom, then, uses rules only as summaries and guides, it must itself be flexible, ready for surprise, prepared to see, resourceful at improvisation. This being so, Aristotle stresses that the crucial prerequisite for practical wisdom is a long experience of life that yields an ability to understanding and grasp the salient features, the practical meaning, of the concrete particulars. This sort of insight is altogether different from a deductive scientific knowledge and is, he reminds us again, more akin to sense-perception.[57]

Practical knowledge then is not the knowledge of the mathematician or Greek scientist (contemplation of universal truths), nor is it the knowledge of the craftsman or artisan (domination and control).[58] There has been a debate over the nature of practical knowledge and practical syllogisms in Aristotle.[59] A reading of Aristotle's practical wisdom as a deductive logical syllogism misses the distinctions between *phronesis* and *techne,* and reduces the former to the latter.

> In fact this means that the end toward which our life as a whole tends and the elaboration of it into the moral principles of action, as described

by Aristotle in his *Ethics*, cannot be the object of knowledge that can be taught. . . . Moral knowledge is really a knowledge of a special kind. It embraces in a curious way both means and ends and hence differs from technical knowledge. That is why it is pointless to distinguish here between knowledge and experience, as can be done in the case of a techne. For moral knowledge must be a kind of experience, and in fact we shall see that this is perhaps the fundamental form of experience, compared with which all other experience represents a denaturing.[60]

From the perspectives of modern science and logic, Aristotle's practical knowledge (and by implication, his theory of justice itself) would be viewed as being not only imprecise and not universally applicable, but totally irrational and illegitimate as a form of knowledge. This distinction between *phronesis* and *techne*—between ethics and positivism—is a key to understanding the distance between modernity and the Ancients, and Marx's critique of and distance from the former.

The challenge that Aristotle undertakes is extremely unusual, for his answer to the epistemological problem of the foundation of ethical knowledge *(phronesis)* and political action *(praxis)* lies in the nature of *paideia* and *politeia;* it lies in the nature of Greek social life itself—its political constitution, education, measurement of merit and value, nature of the good life, and (most importantly of all) the community. Moral reflection and practical deliberation *(bouleusis)* are part of the broader process of political deliberation in the Athenian Assembly and Council of 500 *(Boule)*.[61] Level 3 of Aristotle's theory of justice considers the epistemological nature of practical reason, in comparison to the other forms of knowledge and social interaction in the polis. It also rests on the sociological foundations of the other two levels of his theory of justice that have already been considered: economic theory, friendship, and democracy (level 2), on the one hand; and political justice and virtue (level 1), on the other. Therefore, the basis of moral knowledge is justice and a political process based on the self-sufficing and autonomous community.

Ethics is the precondition for justice, and justice the precondition for ethics. Practical judgment and ethical action are based on the previous establishment of a just community (politics), while self-conscious reflection on the nature and principles of ethics and social justice requires reflection on the nature of the economic, social, and political nature of the just community (metatheory). What appears on first consideration to be a simple tautology is Aristotle's answer to the epistemological dilemma that lies behind political science and ethics.

The resolution of the contradiction requires a free and rational community. The political community itself becomes the basis for the resolution of the problems of epistemology and ethics. And reflection on this community is what may be called "metaethics" or "political science."

To return to the specific characteristics of practical wisdom, we may summarize the actual nature of its knowledge, its form of reasoning (syllogism), and its body of proofs *(enthymeme)* as having the following aspects:

> 1) *Persuasion,* which as the aim of the enthymeme differs from *instruction* and *compulsion.* 2) *Opinion,* which provides premises for the enthymeme, does not conform to absolute *truth;* but neither is it absolute *falsehood.* 3) The *probability* characteristic of most enthymematic inferences falls somewhere between *necessity* and mere randomness, or *chance.* 4) And finally, the *enthymeme* itself differs from a strict *demonstration* but without being a sophistical *fallacy.*[62]

Practical wisdom is that form of knowledge by which the moral actor can make virtuous and rational decisions about certain types of ethical and political decisions that have to be made. The citizens must be able to deliberate *(bouleusis)* about what is morally good, and act on that knowledge. Aristotle also stresses that this form of knowledge must reflect upon the attaining of the good life *(eudaimonia).* However, practical wisdom is quite different from all the other forms of knowledge in that it is based on opinions, not certainty and absolute truth; probability, not necessity or chance; deliberation, not philosophical demonstration. Like political science, its conclusions are very rough, imprecise, and in outline form; they are true "only for the most part."[63] These decisions are only made after careful consideration, reflection, and deliberation and are based on general experience and political participation. Moral knowledge can never be taught or learned, as either *episteme* or *techne* can be. "The concept of application is highly problematical"—says Hans Gadamer—since there is no split between the subject and the object or between moral knowledge and the situation in which the moral activity takes place. For him, moral knowledge is not something we have, something we can learn, or something we can forget.[64]

It is rather something that develops with the experience of being actively involved in the world and in moral decision-making—that is, making decisions about the virtuous and just life. It cannot therefore be based on independent and universal categories, since the moral being does not stand over and against the situation as he applies an a priori and invariable set of moral imperatives, as is the case with Platonic and Kantian ethics. Ethics cannot be reduced to a simple mathematical formula or process of calculation. Gadamer calls this a case of "false objectification" and "alienation."[65] What is right and just, what is the correct knowledge and moral attitude for a situation, is determined to a large extent by self-deliberation *(euboulia)* within the social and historical context of the actors. The particulars of a moral situation change, the context changes, and the relationship between the particular situation and the "universal moral rules" is also variable and imprecise. This is not to reduce the issue of moral conduct to a classical variation of modern situation ethics—far from it. Aristotle recognizes that there are, in fact, universals involved in practical knowledge; but they are not the universals of mathematics, physics, or metaphysics. Nor are they the prestructured categories of technical knowledge.

> The man who is without qualification good at deliberating is the man who is capable of aiming in accordance with calculation at the best for man of things attainable by action. Nor is practical wisdom concerned with universals only—it must also recognize the particulars; for it is practical, and practice is concerned with particulars. This is why some who do not know, and especially those who have experience, are more practical than others who know.[66]

For Aristotle the particular method and criterion of truth in the five different forms of knowledge reflect the ontological components of being that they examine. There is thus a close relationship between epistemology and ontology for Aristotle; while in the modern traditions, epistemology (or method) will unconsciously create its own ontology. The other forms of contemplative and technical knowledge have objects and standards of truth that are predetermined (universal); and thus, there is a clear understanding of the objects reflected on, the adequacy of knowledge and its criterion of truth, and the truth of propositions. In practical knowledge, the objects of deliberation are constructed in the practical activity itself, along with the "universal" criterion of truth claims. It is through time, experience, and perception that one acquires practical wisdom.[67] By knowing the laws, traditions, history, moral character, and constitution of one's own society, by engaging in public discourse, by weighing the strengths and weaknesses of various arguments and alternative courses of political action, by public articulation and compromise, and by publicly judging social goals and the means to obtain them, the moral actor and citizen is educated in the process of discursive rationality, public deliberation, and consensus formation. Both the "objects of thinking" and the "correctness of thinking" are formed in the process of *bouleusis* and *boule*.[68]

Gadamer sees Aristotle's analysis of equity *(epirikeia)* as helpful in clarifying the nature of practical knowledge and the application of certain kinds of universal standards to moral decisions.[69] Equity (juridical prudence) is superior to the law in that it adjusts the abstract, formal law to the irregularities and particularities of the concrete circumstances and "matters of practical affairs." Aristotle realizes that the problem does not lie in the abstract universality of the law or in the hands of the lawmakers, but in the difficulty of applying legal universals to particular cases. The danger is that the universal principles may be applied without an understanding or insight into the reality of the particular case under consideration. This would undermine justice, for it would not take into consideration either the fragility of experience or the authoritarianism of the absolute. This same line of argument is later used by Hegel in his criticisms of the terror contained in both the French Revolution and Kantian morality—which is then picked up by Marx in his critique of morality (see Chapter Three). For Aristotle the proper role of the judge is to join the law to the concrete circumstances under adjudication, using his experience and the collective wisdom of the juridical tradition. Through this mediation of the universal and the particular, justice becomes fairness.

After the initial analysis of *phronesis*, Aristotle begins to clarify further the category by pairing it with other cognitive and emotional forms of experience in order to broaden the reader's understanding of the nature and activity of practical knowledge. According to Gadamer, Beiner, and Hardie, practical activity and deliberation also entail the following:

1. political knowledge *(politike)*
2. deliberation *(bouleusis)*
3. understanding *(sunesis)*
4. judgment *(gnome)*
   a. sympathy *(suggnome)*
   b. to judge with
   c. forgiveness

5. ethical virtue *(arete)*
6. moral action *(praxis)*
7. judgment with friendship *(philia)* and harmony *(homonoia)*
8. justice and community
9. rhetoric and public speech
10. mutual deliberation *(boule)* and rational consensus
11. political discourse and democracy[70]

Gadamer—given his primary interest in hermeneutics—is more interested in the relationship between deliberation and understanding, but Beiner is more concerned with the relationships between deliberation, friendship, and citizenship. Reminiscent of Mead's "taking the role of the other," Gadamer stresses that understanding the ethical issues requires that "we place ourselves in the concrete situation in which the other person has to act."[71] Beiner shows the etymological connections between the nature of moral judgment *(gnome)* and understanding *(suggnome)*—the latter term being also translated as sympathetic understanding, judgment with, or forgiveness.[72] All these aspects of interpersonal relations must exist in order for true understanding to occur. Since only friends can have this type of bond based on sympathy and mutual suffering, it is implied in the Greek language itself that for understanding to take place there must be a real community of interests and friendship *(philia)*.

Given Aristotle's initial dissatisfaction with his own theory of justice and the ability to scientifically determine ethics, the complexity of arriving at the real basis for a just distribution, and the problematic goal of reaching a knowledge of the just, it follows that friendship—instead—supplies the needed psychological and epistemological basis on which just actions are grounded.[73] Aristotle's theory of friendship is the metaethical solution to these epistemological problems, since through it a society of justice is developed without having to theoretically predefine the nature of justice itself. Justice follows from friendship naturally, since the essence of friendship is the treatment of individuals fairly, equally, and with mutual respect. Books 1 and 6 raise the dilemma of ethical epistemology, but it is in books 8 and 9 of the *Ethics* and book 3 of the *Politics* that an attempt at resolution is undertaken. Aristotle moves in the direction of solving the epistemological problem through a reliance on friendship within the political community.

ETHICAL OBJECTIVITY AND SOCIAL CONSENSUS

Though Aristotle does not adequately or even directly address the epistemological issue of what has come to be known as the dilemma of ethical objectivity in his ethics, it is never far from his mind.[74] The list covering Aristotle's failure to define once and for all the exact nature of the topic under philosophical discussion in his works is extensive: It might begin with his statements regarding the imprecise and contingent nature of political science; the notion that ethics cannot be scientific; the unwillingness to define universally the nature of justice, the virtuous citizen, and the good society; and the unwillingness or inability to determine the social standards and criterion of measurement for the nature of the best political constitution and the social form of merit and equality appropriate to it (need, citizenship, wealth, or virtue)[75]—and then end with the emphasis in book 6 on the uncertain and contingent nature of political deliberation and judgment for arriving at ethical truths. The various standards for ethical truths and the determination of the good society (teleology) cannot provide the universal and necessary information required by ethics as if it were a science. Universal standards for normative evaluation of the ethical ideals of Greek society were viewed as philosophically suspect, if not epistemologically impossible.

Plato felt the same set of problems, which he solved—according to his satisfaction—in his theory of the Forms. He established a transcendent order of universal truths by which to measure the adequacy of social action in the present. Aristotle, however, was more skeptical in his reaction to the inability to determine scientifically the nature of universal truths. The result has been a hermeneutical ambivalence within Aristotle's theory of social justice. For the most part, interpreters have only dealt with specific passages or sections of the *Ethics,* while failing to integrate them into a comprehensive whole. This chapter has attempted to break down analytically the major components and reintegrate them into an overall theory of social justice. There are three major levels to his theory of social justice: (1) the theory of universal and particular justice; (2) economic theory, civic friendship, and political democracy; and (3) the epistemological dilemma of ethics, ethical objectivity, practical wisdom *(phronesis),* and political judgment.

Aristotle's theory of justice must incorporate these three levels into a comprehensive whole. What results is a very interesting general theory of ethics that includes insight about the epistemological assumptions of the ethical dilemma—in level 3—joined to Aristotle's unwillingness in the *Nicomachean Ethics* to determine universally the best standard of measurement for equality and the best form of political constitution of the state, in level 1. Between levels 1 and 3, there appears to be an unbridgeable gulf, leaving Aristotle in a philosophically very precarious position. He must argue that there can be no universal or scientific truths in either political science or ethics and therefore no universal way of defining "equality," on the one hand, and no objective validity for ethical principles, on the other. He is faced with what appears to be an unsolvable dilemma of ethical reasoning. This could explain some of the confusion, false starts, and unanswered questions in the *Ethics*.

Aristotle does not let the issue hang for long, because in the *Politics* a new and epistemologically important aspect is introduced: the goal of reaching political consensus and social harmony in the community, which takes up economic and political themes from level 2 above and turns them into a way out of the epistemological dilemma of his ethical theory in level 3. With the union of the three distinct levels of Aristotle's theory of justice, epistemology is tied to politics, and ethics to political consensus. This calls into question the idea that Aristotle is in fact developing a theory of social justice—which will cause later hermeneutical problems for his interpreters. He seems to be replacing his initial search for a theory of justice with a theory of metaethics. Philosophy cannot be scientific; it cannot predefine or prejudge the substantive nature of the good life. But it can deal with the structural boundaries within which the issues of the teleology of human nature and the ultimate goal of society are raised. In another context, this has been considered by Habermas to be a movement from epistemology to social theory.

In fact, by setting the equation in this fashion, the problems in the third level are resolved by the second, with friendship and democracy playing the institutional role in mediating between the dilemma of ethical objectivity and the nature of ethics and political judgment. Aristotle was the first philosopher to be cognizant of the inability to determine social and political truths philosophically, and the first to turn toward a theory of political judgment to resolve these epistemological dilemmas. The original position of the dilemma of ethical objectivity turned into a theory of political consensus. Though the cultural and philosophical contexts were different, the problems of ethical objectivity were later picked up by Hume, Kant, Hegel, and

Marx. The solution in Marx's case represented a return to Aristotle (for a further discussion, see Chapter Six). For both men, praxis becomes the solution to epistemology.

In a remarkable anticipation of contemporary debates over the critiques of foundationalism, epistemology, and privileged representations (which question that there can be legitimate bases for the justification of one theory over another), Aristotle recognizes the impossibility of grounding moral arguments and decisions on universal scientific truths.[76] He also undercuts the ontological basis for such an argument by rejecting the preexistence of moral universals. "There is, thus, room for surprise, room for cognitive insecurity and the human vulnerability that the Platonic scientific conception is seeking to avoid."[77] Epistemological objectivity exists only through moral deliberation. The particular and universal components of practical wisdom are changing and situated in both history and artificial convention. Does this reduce his idea of moral judgment to pure relativism, or his idea of the state and social justice to pure conventionalism? He certainly would reject both conclusions quickly. Ethics is constituted in the process of thinking, judging, and acting in the political community. In chapter 7 of book 5 of the *Nicomachean Ethics*, Aristotle defends a position between natural law and conventionalism (mean) concerning the nature of political justice.

As Winthrop has reminded us, Aristotle himself questions the very possibility of developing a theory of justice because: (1) justice is not simply a product of nature *(physis)*, but also partly a social convention (which historically changes); (2) there is no philosophical or scientific basis to determine universally what constitutes equality—the universal principle underlying justice (though he does define justice as treating equals equally and unequals unequally but does not commit himself to a particular definition of equality: equal need, equal contribution, equal wealth, or equal virtue); and (3) there are no universal principles by which to ground his theory of justice. If a "theory of justice is impossible" in his *Ethics*, if philosophy cannot determine the proper criterion for ethical and political measurement *(axia)* and evaluation—that is, the proper definition of equality and merit—then Aristotle does seem to develop a way out of this dilemma in his *Politics*. In this work, he argues that the state and political nature of man are both natural. It is the community itself that provides the universal component in moral arguments and political deliberation. Aristotle seems to be presenting the basics for a consensus theory of truth.[78] Relating to this issue Beiner writes:

> The reason why public judgments are possible at all is that the objects of those judgments are shared by those who judge, or are the focus of their

common concern. For instance, I judge as a member of a community because of a common tradition and shared history, public laws and obligations to which all are subject, common ideals and shared meanings. These "public objects" or public things *(res publica)* allow for judgment of a public character, for these things concern all of us who participate in these traditions, laws, and institutions, and who therefore share in common meanings. Such judgments concern not merely what I want or the way of life I desire, but rather, entail intersubjective deliberation about a common life (how we should be together).[79]

Beiner's position is that there must be a "community of judgment" that underlies any moral and political deliberation and decision, since it is this community that provides the universal standards by which fair and unfair, virtuous and nonvirtuous, and just and unjust actions are evaluated. The application of moral universals in particular decisions—which is deliberation—is made possible by the existence of a just society and a good political constitution.[80] Is this argument circular at this point? Does a moral action require a just society? But what is justice? It is a society that permits individuals to act rationally and virtuously—thus advancing the self-realization of human potential as political animals (their telos). This theme seems to underlie Aristotle's whole work, and it becomes more explicit in book 3 of the *Politics* where he discusses the nature of true democracy and political deliberation.

Aristotle's method of theorizing is based on assumptions—tracing etymologies, common sense, and comparative critiques. There is no developed epistemology regarding the nature of practical knowledge, nor is there an analysis of concept formation in ethics or politics. His emphasis is on comparative study of the various types of truth claims of *episteme, techne,* and *phronesis.* Despite this, an argument can be made that his analysis of democracy in book 3 of the *Politics* represents indirectly an investigation into the epistemological functions of democracy. The political community and shared meanings of the common traditions provide the foundation stones for moral and political judgments. It is ultimately the structure of the Greek constitution that will affect not only the nature of education *(paideia)*, character development *(arete)*, standards of merit, and the nature of justice, but also the form and criterion of truth itself. Praxis becomes the criterion of truth (as it will again in the nineteenth century), but within the context of the political constitution, socialization of human behavior, and relative equality in the economic sphere. It presupposes a metatheory grounding ethics and including political, social, and economic theories. While aristocracy may be an ideal form of government for Aristotle, democracy (constitutional government) is the best actual form since it can combine the best elements of both aristocracy and polity.

> For it is possible that the many, though not individually good men, yet when they come together may be better, not individually but collectively, than those who are so, just as public dinners to which many contribute are better than those supplied at one man's cost; for where there are many, each individual, it may be argued, has some portion of virtue and wisdom, and when they have come together, just as the multitude becomes a single man with many feet and many hands and many senses, so also it becomes one personality as regards the moral and intellectual faculties. This is why the public is a better judge of the works of music and those of the poets.[81]

Whatever the strengths of a society built around an idea of the rule by merit of virtue and the few, collective deliberation and rational discourse in a democratic polity transcend any limitations or weakness of its individual members. For Aristotle, sovereignty rests with the citizens, who have both deliberative and judicial functions; this is a form of direct democracy. Democratic consensus, then, is the real basis for a theory of justice and a just society, since practical wisdom requires a political structure within which public discourse takes place. It is also the place where citizens are educated and become virtuous. Though humans are by nature symbolic and political and though their telos is public participation and deliberation in order to become rational and free, they must be educated to this end. Democracy has an epistemological—as well as economic and political—function, in being the basis for correct reflection. It accomplishes this through the public education of the individual, the building of moral character, and the maintenance of law and justice.[82]

If this be true, then justice is the maintenance of a social and political system within which public discourse enlightens the individual moral being and determines the truth regarding the good life and justice through discursive rationality—public dialogue. It is a system of popular sovereignty built around the assembly, in which every citizen shares in the deliberative and judicial function of the state and in its political power.[83] In book 4 of the *Politics*, Aristotle also recognizes that it is best when there is not too much economic inequality to disrupt the political community. He seems to be making a distinction here between inequality and class, since he calls for a society within which there is some inequality but no real class differences—one based on a middle class. Aristotle recognizes that such a "state aims at being, as much as possible, a society of peers and equals."[84] The political community built around friendship and equity requires the elimination of any extremes of wealth that would disrupt community life and the development of the moral character necessary for popular democracy. A society built around the concern for wealth and class could not possibly have as its goal the concern for others.[85]

DISTRIBUTIVE JUSTICE AND BEYOND

The range and depth of Marx's reliance on Aristotle is extensive—from the basic orientation of his philosophy of man to his overall ontology of being; from his view of materialism and nature to his ideas on human and natural potentialities; from physics to metaphysics; and finally, from his view of social teleology to his theory of social justice. In this section, only the more overt connections between the two men will be analyzed—especially the issues of distributive justice, ethical judgment, and practical action. An adequate understanding of the less obvious and more hidden deep structures that connect their writings will require the further analysis of Marx's theory of democracy, social theory of value, and critiques of liberalism and political economy in Chapters Four and Five. In Chapter Six, historical and sociological substance will be given to the topics of epistemology and politics. Within this general framework—so changed and mediated by his critique of classical political economy—a more comprehensive picture of Marx's general theory of social justice will emerge.

Marx's theory of ethics and social justice will be seen to follow very closely the outline of Aristotle's theory of justice as presented above. Of special interest will be the problem of ethical epistemology, the dilemma of ethical objectivity, the difficulties of precisely and scientifically defining the natures of equality and justice, and the relationship between democratic and public consensus (discursive rationality). The questions, epistemological structures, and ethical dilemmas are from the Ancients, while the general social context of Marx's critique of political economy within which they are framed are from Moderns.

The integration of ethics, political philosophy, and economic theory in Aristotle and Marx is not simply the result of their views concerning the integration of the individual and society, morality and ethics, virtue and a rational society. Rather, it also results from their joint recognition of the problems of determining the ethical objectivity of moral and political truth claims.

Today the divergent philosophical positions regarding social and economic justice—whether utilitarianism, formalism, entitlement theory, or neoliberalism—stress distribution of social wealth in terms of individual pleasure, social contract, market distribution, or fairness, respectively. Since Marx does not emphasize any of these aspects in his theory, he has been understood by many as not possessing any ethical theory at all. In the contemporary mind, justice is distributive justice, while morality is a question of the individual free choice of principles. This is especially true since the "Copernican Revolution" in morality with the Kantian critique of practical reason. This was preceded by developments in Jansenism and Protestantism, and further exacerbated by contemporary analytic philosophy.

However, Marx—for reasons to be analyzed later—believes that the essential questions of ethics and politics lie in an analysis of the nature and structure of the socioeconomic infrastructure and the organization of the productive relations. In *On the Jewish Question* and in the *Critique of the Gotha Program,* he deals with the question of just distribution. However, they still remain for him secondary questions to the primary one of the structure of society; without the latter, the former become impossible. Marx tends to avoid questions of distribution and justice, since they are usually tied to consideration of patterns of commodity consumption and exchange, neither of which are primary areas of real importance as they are expressions of social alienation. Exchange and distribution are secondary issues, since they are decided beforehand by the structures of the mode of production and the prior forms of the class distribution of private property. Therefore, central concern for the former questions have a tendency to generate sociological and moral abstractions divorced from any real historical content of production and class analysis, while at the same time focusing in on secondary social relationships.

Any distribution whatever of the means of consumption is only the consequence of the distribution of the conditions of production themselves. The latter distribution, however, is a feature of the mode of production itself. The capitalist mode of production, for example, rests on the fact that the material conditions of production are in the hands of non-workers in the form of property in capital and land, while the masses are only owners of personal conditions of production, of labor power. If the elements of production are so distributed, then the present-day distribution of the means of consumption results automatically.[86]

Marx reiterates this idea in book 7 and the introduction to the *Grundrisse*, when he states that "the structure of distribution is completely determined by the structure of production." The distribution of goods for private consumption, and the theoretical analyses that flow from it, are not the result of abstract social laws or individual consumption preferences; they result from a prestructured and predefined distribution of the instruments of production and the distribution of individuals within a class division of labor. It is this understanding of the social totality that Marx derives both from Hegel's concept of totality and Aristotle's notion of the organic whole. The understanding of one component necessarily involves the other mediated components. It should be noted that this use of Aristotle—when and where it occurs at the beginning of crucial sections on the structural approach to the whole economic system—is not unintentional. Marx is connecting issues of distributive justice to issues of production.

In the introduction to the *Grundrisse*, Marx—quoting from Aristotle's *Ethics*—uses the Aristotelian concepts of potentiality and actuality in reference to the relationship between production and consumption. "A railroad on which no trains run, hence which is not used up, not consumed, is a railroad in potentiality, and not in reality. Without production, no consumption; but also, without consumption, no production."[87] Marx intends in this section of the essay a twofold objective: (1) to establish a totalistic approach to the categories and structures of political economy; and (2) to establish a methodological framework for the analysis of political economy and capitalism from within the broader framework of Aristotle's *Metaphysics*. This section involves a methodological critique of political economy and its method of interpreting the relationships among production, distribution, exchange, and consumption. Marx was critical of Mill's separation of production and distribution, the abstractions of political economy, and—in some cases—the immediate identification of production and consumption, which ultimately retained the distinction between the two. For Marx, consumption is the finality of production; it creates the object of production, for it gives it a determinate being. The object—unlike a product of nature—comes to be only through consumption. The economic structures mediate and constitute one another in a fashion that will ultimately affect both the methodology of the social sciences and our interpretations of ethics and politics. Marx's ethical epistemology and ethical critique of capitalism are grounded in his anthropology of needs and his views on science, both of which have been affected by his understanding of Aristotle. In the *Critique of the Gotha Program,* Marx begins to examine the issue of "fair distribution" as it changes from bourgeois society to socialism (the first phase of communism) and then to communism itself. He does say that, with the social revolution and the corresponding changes that occur as society moves from capitalism to socialism, there will be a corresponding change in the accepted view of just distribution. As socialism emerges from its capitalist womb, its criteria of equal rights and fair exchange will remain basically bourgeois concepts—but concepts in which "principle and practice are no longer at loggerheads."[88] Though they remain the same principles that legitimated and rationalized capitalist social relations, there will no longer be a dichotomy between ideal expression and real application. That is, the new socialist relations of production will be such as to institutionalize a relationship of equal exchange of labor for equal labor—to each according to his or her contribution. There will no longer be a dichotomy between the form and essence of bourgeois rights and their empirical appearance. In socialism, bourgeois justice will prevail. These were the economic rights articulated by the French Revolution and by the Utopian Socialists of whom Marx was so critical throughout his life. Now these economic rights occupy a stage in the development of his theory of human rights, which will eventually be transcended in the next rung of historical development.

The criteria of labor, value, and exchange are still those of a capitalist society, but no longer structured around the principles of abstract labor, surplus value, and unpaid labor. The most immediate forms of exploitation have been eliminated or at least curtailed by elimination of the class structure. Socialism will replace the structures of political economy and its forms of social organization while temporarily maintaining the latter's ideal political principles, which will regulate social and economic intercourse in its early stages. The sphere of production will be socialist, while that of distribution will remain capitalist. The exchange of equal value prevails as the regulating mechanism in the socialist community. The rights to consumer ownership is determined by individual labor and contribution. Marx does recognize the unequal distribution of abilities, talents, desires, and circumstances that turn equal rights into unequal rights.[89]

> This equal right is an unequal right for unequal labor. It recognizes no class differences, because everyone is only a worker like everyone else; but it tacitly recognizes unequal endowment and thus productive capacity as natural privileges. It is therefore, a right of inequality, in its content, like every right.[90]

With different obligations and social responsibilities, the criterion of equal rights turns into its opposite. This is the stage in which individual contribution legitimates the unequal distribution of social wealth. Even when the form and content of these rights are balanced, they still reveal their underlying antagonisms, since what begins as "equal rights" turns into "unequal right for unequal labour." Marx questions a standard of measurement for a just distribution that is ultimately based on the inequality of physical, mental, or endurance endowments. Is physical endowment an adequate measure for the highest ethical values of society, over which the individual has no say? Some people are born stronger, smarter, and have more stamina than others. Is biology an adequate basis for ethics? The primary ethical principle of socialism remains productive capacity and is still caught in the logic and principles of Enlightenment political economy.[91] Marx clearly sees this as a reduction of individual diversity to a universal standard that narrowly sets the standard of social worth in terms of labor and productive contribution. He is aware that this reduces his rich anthropological understanding of the nature of practical activity to productive activity, and recapitulates in succinct fashion the critique of alienation from his early writings. The result is another form of economic reductionism and social inequality.

To overcome these "bourgeois limitations," Marx calls for rights that recognize individual diversity of personality and the diversity of the species in the exercise of its creative functions. With the coming of communist society, the full transcendence of the principles of bourgeois society—its productive process, its division of labor, its antagonism between mental and physical labor, and its alienation of the social nature of man—and the end of the class system, the principles and structures of communist distributive justice take effect. This final stage leads to a system of equality that can take into account individual and social differences—which, in turn, reinforces the return of the individual to his or her self. "From each according to his ability, to each according to his need." The bourgeois and socialist standard of contribution changes in communism to a standard of measurement based on ability and need. Reminiscent of themes from the *Grundrisse*, this stage is characterized by the fullest "all-around development of the individual,"[92] and not simply by development of the individual's labor power. Self-realization now becomes the ethical principle on which rests the basis for distribution.[93] As the criteria for social justice conforms to the diversity of human needs and personality development, the emphasis on labor and production is lessened.

Castoriadis realizes that Marx is closely following Aristotle at this point in his analysis.[94] At the end of book 8 of the *Nicomachean Ethics*—which deals with friendship—Aristotle raises a question about the appropriate standard of measurement for a fair return to a generous friend on a received gift or benefit. As is his method, he examines the different claims to the proper standard: equivalency based on benefit to the receiver (utilitarian friendship) or benefit to the giver (virtuous friendship), proportionality of virtue, contribution of utility between friends, or simply individual needs. Aristotle sees value in all these criteria and finally decides on a combination of them. To the virtuous individual goes honor, and to the inferior individual goes material gain.

> At all events it seems that each party is justified in his claim, and that each should get more out of the friendship than others—not more of the same thing, however, but the superior more honour and the inferior more gain; for honour is the prize of virtue and of beneficence, while gain is the assistance required of inferiority.[95]

Equivalency, virtue, contribution, and need are the four different claims made on the benefits derived from friendship. Marx raises a similar question with regard to the standards of measurement of a just distribution. He moves from equality of individual rights; to contribution of labor, ability, or effort; and, finally, to human needs. As against contribution, merit, effort, wealth, or status, Marx decides in favor of need. Though Aristotle views the issue of need in this section of the *Ethics* by referring to material assistance, it is Marx who uses the concept to refer to the potentialities of species being.

Depending on one's vantage point, the needs principle may be interpreted as a principle of equality (Geras) or inequality (Heller). To a certain extent, both are correct. The needs principle is a principle of radical egalitarianism, for it establishes the material framework for development of individual abilities and potentialities on an equal footing.[96] However, it can also be interpreted as a principle of inequality because it may result in unequal distribution based on the unequal personal, family, or social situation of the individual. People have unequal needs. Some will have large families, live in isolated areas, have medical problems requiring expensive services, and so forth. "As a result of this deep insight into the problem Marx rejected the value 'equality.' "[97] The two positions are not contradictory if it is recognized that the equality in question is not one of consumption, but of self-development of human potential. Heller has failed to see this and confuses Marx's critique of the universal leveling of property ownership in "crude communism" with the principles of equality of needs and self-realization. The concept of equality appears in both the first and last stages of development toward the communist society. The first stage results in economic reductionism (equality based on the standard of labor and production) and social inequality, while in the second it results in the good society. According to Donald van de Veer, "A dissimilar distribution on the former basis [socialism] makes one man richer than another; a dissimilar distribution on the latter basis [communism] would not since, in more current terminology, it would make the same relative contribution to the well-being of each worker."[98]

Marx's theory of the hierarchy of distribution principles is necessitated because—as Marx says—"right can never be higher than the economic structure and its cultural development conditioned thereby."[99] Ethics abstracted from political economy is an impotent form of social critique and imperative to economic change. The moral imperative for an egalitarian society must first be preceded by the historical and structural prerequisites to this form of social organization. The fully realized concept of distributive justice can only come about when the necessary material, scientific, and structural preconditions for its realization have been given, as was the case with the technological and organizational developments in capitalist society. Viewed in terms of the monumental and voluminous scale of Marx's work, these few comments concerning social justice can only be regarded as cryptic and titillating, to say the least. However, what is interesting here is the continuity with the central concerns of Marx in his earlier writings. Society is not to be structured so as to overwhelm and alienate the individual, but to permit the individual to realize his or her potentialities of rationality, freedom, and individuality. What

Marx has done is to set the methodological framework within which an ethical theory can be developed, but he does not attempt to establish the moral substance himself. These are exactly the same types of issues and formal approaches that occupied Aristotle so profoundly.

In the *Paris Manuscripts*—written about 30 years earlier—Marx dealt with the issue of universal distribution of wealth within a "crude and unreflective communism."[100] For him, this form of distributive justice—which is only a variant of capitalist social relations—would not represent the beginning of a new society, but rather the universalization of the principles of the old. In crude communism, private property had been viewed as fetishized—that is, as simply the objectification of labor as capital without recognition that labor and the social process were its subjective essence. Therefore, the universalism attained by such a system would be "the culmination of such envy and levelling-down on the basis of a preconceived minimum."[101] It would represent—for Marx—universal alienation of the species being, and the loss of a recognition of the contradictions that lie at the heart of modernity.

> But labour, the subjective essence of private property as the exclusion of property, and capital, objective labour as the exclusion of labour, constitute *private property* as the developed relation of the contradiction and thus a dynamic relation which drives toward its resolution.[102]

It is this relationship between subjectivity and objectivity in terms of the essential nature of private property and the alienation of the social being of man that becomes transformed in Marx's later writings into a critique of the objectivity of the categories of political and economic understanding. It is this same idea of objectivity (positivity) becoming fetishized into universal laws of economic development, natural laws, and laws of human nature that forms the basis for his criticism of the economic system. The redistribution of social wealth does not lie at the heart of his ethical theory, since—like Aristotle—Marx's view of social justice is more comprehensive than simply that of distributive justice. In fact, Marx's whole critique of political economy represents a return to the social economy of Aristotle. However—like Hegel—the return is no more than a matter of spiritual and intellectual enlightenment. Marx is more concerned in his later writings with development of the categories of conscious reflection that permit social action and rationality to be developed in the moral individual. This is a critical science, which frees the individual from all forms of religiosity (ideology): religious objectivity in the *Contribution to the Critique of Hegel's Philosophy of Law;* political objectivity in *On the Jewish Question* and the *Paris Manuscripts;* and economic fetishism in the *Grundrisse* and *Capital.*

> The members of the political state are religious because of the dualism between individual life and species-life, between the life of civil society and political life. They are religious in the sense that man treats political life, which is remote from his own individual existence, as if it were his true life; and in the sense that religion is here in spirit of civil society and expresses the separation and withdrawal of man from man. Where the political state has attained to its full development, man leads, not only in thought, in consciousness, but in *reality*, in *life*, a double existence—celestial and terrestrial. He lives in the *political community*, where he regards himself as a *communal being*, and in civil society where he acts simply as a *private person*, treats other men as means, degrades himself to the role of a mere means, and becomes the plaything of alien powers. The political state, in relation to civil society, is just as spiritual as is heaven in relation to earth.[103]

The problems of the organization of society, the issues of the fair distribution policy, the questions of political and economic democracy can be developed only after the metaphysical and religious foundations of the present society are brought to conscious light. This is what Marx means when he uses the phrase "the metaphysics of political economy" in *The Poverty of Philosophy.* All these "creations of fantasy, dreams, the postulates of Christianity, the sovereignty of man," and so forth, must be exposed as concealing unquestioned metaphysical presuppositions and concrete material: social relationships.

Ethical theory concerns itself with the social conditions under which the moral individual chooses and determines the good life, as opposed to the more limiting concerns of economic distribution. It is thus the structural conditions—rather than the individual criteria for choosing a certain fundamental good—that become the basis for his analysis. In Marx's social economics, economic theory is always secondary to his social and political ideals. There still remains this question, however: What possible reasons, within the context of Marx's writings, would he have for choosing as his project this approach to ethics? Within the context of nineteenth-century Germany and its return to the classical traditions, the philosophical movement away from a theory of Kantian morals to that of social ethics places the emphasis of practical philosophy on ethics, politics, and economics. At this point Marx is following Hegel in his return to a social ethics grounded in political economy. The implications of this approach are extensive.

> To appreciate this criticism, it should be noted that the Marxist method of ethical thinking consists primarily in the moral evaluation of social institutions such as private property, social classes, and the division of labor. It examines their consequences for the human individuals living under them and then measures these consequences against the Marxian conception (or ideal) of man.[104]

First, it reformulates the issues of morality—against the arguments of the empiricists, utilitarians, formalists, and rationalists—and places them in a new context that stresses the economic and social preconditions of moral action. Political economy is necessary not only for its effect on the substance of moral decisions, but also since the economic and political institutions structure the very possibilities of moral action (*paideia*). Second, the ideal of the good is now placed beyond individual pleasures of self-interest and beyond the split between the public and the private, the individual and the social, and the political and the civil. By synthesizing moral theory with a philosophical anthropology centered around the social being of the individual, Marx became more sensitive to the questions of both philosophy and sociology, ethics and social theory. He thereby introduced into moral theory a number of issues relating to the "false universality" of modernity, including questions of social rationality, ideology, and false consciousness.

In Marx's works morality becomes part both of critical philosophy and of critical science—that is, part of the reflective analysis of the development of social categories (*Begriff*) and of historical institutions. Morality is transformed from an investigation into the types and criteria for moral choices (happiness, pleasure, equality, market rationality, contribution, or ability) into a reflective critique of the very conditions for moral decisions themselves, without determining fully beforehand the possibilities for future development. The future is open—for Marx—since there are no ideals to be realized, as he says in his work on the Paris Commune. What is to be realized are the potentialities of the species being: its rationality and its freedom. It is no longer a philosophical question of what good is, but a sociological question of the conditions under which good becomes possible. Morality is retransformed into an economic, social, and political issue. Human potential is not limited by a predefined telos or concept in terms of an historically specific category of human nature, natural law, or natural rights, but remains open to further historical and theoretical investigation: "They have no ideals to realize, but to set free the elements of the new society with which old collapsing bourgeois society itself is pregnant."[105] This marks a fundamental break with Cartesian epistemology. It is not a question of imposing concepts and ideals from the outside, but of setting free those ideals and potentialities of the Enlightenment that have been restricted by the social setting in which they developed. Democracy is thus a realization of the universal in the concrete at a particular moment in history (see Chapter Four).

Throughout the writings of Marx, there is little technical and pragmatic recommendation as to the future form the revolution can be expected to take and the nature of the structures of society afterward. In fact, many of the concrete "Marxist" recommendations come from Engels, since only his methodology was capable of generating these types of policy recommendations.[106]

MORAL EPISTEMOLOGY AND THE CRITIQUE OF POSITIVISM

One possible explanation for the paucity of such recommendations in a cookbook approach to social physics and revolution lies in the foundation of Marx's moral epistemology: his ideas on objectivity and on theory and praxis, and his concept of science as critique. For our purposes here, however, let us begin with his critique of the traditional schools of epistemological thought in the *Theses on Feuerbach*. It is in this work that Marx undermines the epistemological legitimations for idealism, materialism, and positivism as possible foundations for a critical social science.[107] These same ideas written in 1845 were to form the heart of the more developed methodological framework in which the *Grundrisse, Capital*, and his historical writings appear. The first thesis contains a critical analysis of the notion of objectivity, which forms the substance of most philosophical investigations into the objects of knowledge—whether they appear as empirically given or as a result of mathematical-deductive studies. Marx sees these approaches as forms of alienated human consciousness (subjectivity).

The concept of objectivity today in the philosophy of science has been reduced to a purely methodological discussion about the correct method of investigation, while traditional philosophy has retained the ambiguity and questioning about the origins of the objects of experience themselves. Though the traditional approach does deal with methodology and objective validity (verification), it also includes issues relating to ontology (the nature of the objective world of experience), epistemology (the creation of the objects of experience in the process of knowing), and anthropology (the relation between both subjectivity, or knower, and objectivity, or objects known).

The sciences that have developed out of empiricism and rationalism are really sciences of a second order: They are ultimately grounded in an unconscious metaphysics. This only raises further questions as to the appropriateness of their epistemological and methodological foundations. The objective world is considered given by these sciences, while in the phenomenological method of both Hegel and Marx the concreteness of both their method and ontology is brought into question and the historical process of these structures of consciousness and social reality are analyzed.[108]

> The facts which our senses present to us are socially preformed in two ways: through the historical character of the object perceived and through the historical character of the perceiving organ. Both are not simply natural: they are shaped by human activity and yet the individual perceives himself as receptive and passive in the act of perception.[109]

Horkheimer has captured Marx's position and his critique of passivity in the process of understanding and in the epistemological assumptions of modern science by showing how the latter fails to consider the practical sensuous activity of the social being, who constitutes and constructs not only the cultural and social-institutional structures (which then further structure human consciousness) but also the very objects of human perception themselves. The world is preconstituted and prestructured by history, which therefore demands a new method or science more appropriate to this dialectical concept of reality and consciousness. This must force us to reconsider the ease with which some theoreticians have categorized Marx as a nineteenth-century positivist social scientist.

The second major point in the *Theses* is that truth is not determined by theory, but entails practical considerations.

> The question whether objective *[gegenständliche]* human truth can be attributed to human thinking is not a question of theory but is a *practical*

question. Man must prove the truth, that is, the reality and power, the this-sidedness *[Diesseitigkeit]* of his thinking in practice. The dispute over the reality or non-reality of thinking which is isolated from practice is a purely *scholastic* question.[110]

Marx is not denying the possibility of objective truth, only that its formulation entails practical questions and that its verification and proof similarly entail praxis; he also contends that the other forms of science (rationalism and empiricism) are modern versions of scholasticism because of their isolation from history and the social reality.

Though the first thesis undermines the positivist tradition of science, it is the second that has really caused the greatest difficulties of interpretation. If one reads the secondary literature closely, it can be seen that praxis is generally defined in terms of theory, and theory in terms of praxis. What these terms really mean, how truth claims may be justified, and how praxis actually relates to theory are all left unanswered in Marxist metaphysics. One assumes the validity of the argument because of the power of the critique of traditional epistemology.

To what understanding of "objective truth" is Marx's statement—that the question of arriving at it is a matter of practice—fully applicable? After a careful consideration one is left with one and only one understanding of objective truth where the question of arriving at it would have really been a matter of practice. To put it bluntly, this is the situation of arriving at objective truth the other way around; the correspondence between thought and reality is still being insisted upon, but the way to achieve it is completely different from that of the classical theory of truth: in the situation we explored in connection with Marx's second thesis it consists in shaping reality according to the concept of it.[111]

As this excerpt reveals, Prokopczyk's analysis of theory and praxis still places the relation between the two within the traditional epistemological schools of thought, which stress a correspondence theory of truth. Avineri, too, is reduced to explaining the relation between the two by defining one in terms of the other within a dialectical relationship that, in effect, dissolves them into a mere tautology.[112] Neither attempts to get behind the ideas to understand the epistemological intention that Marx had when writing the *Theses*. Taken simply within the context of this one work, it is almost impossible to develop adequately an acceptable theory that would develop and explain Marx's dialectical theory of knowledge.

The most common interpretations are that Marx was either referring to a pragmatic or utilitarian determination of truth—that the truth of a theory lies in its ability to influence the masses—or the positivist view that it is through experimentation and scientific verification (practice) that a theory is to be held true (this latter position being also attributed to Engels). However, seen in conjunction with the other theses and his other methodological writings, these interpretations can only be viewed with extreme skepticism. The argument for the dialectical interplay of subjectivity and objectivity, theory and practice—I would argue—must be understood as a synthesis of both the German and Greek philosophical traditions. It represents a synthesis of the classical traditions from both the Ancients and the Moderns—a synthesis of the Hegelian position that truth is the unfolding and self-development of the Concept *(Begriff)* in distinction to the methods of correctness (Locke and Hume) and representation (Kant), and the Aristotelian notion of practical knowledge in distinction to universal science and technical knowledge. The Hegelian concept of truth can be summed up as follows:

> If one tries to express the classical viewpoint by resorting to Hegelian terminology and his way of speaking, then, this classical viewpoint would be summed up as knowledge or, still better, the concept having its objectivity (that is, objective validity, objective truth) in objects. Hegel's own viewpoint, however, expressed in his own words, is just the reverse of the above; he says that "Object *(Gegenstand)* has its objectivity *(Objektivität)* in the concept."[113]

Marx thus utilizes in his later writings the Hegelian method of constructing a "concrete totality" in order to investigate the social reality. Though he borrows heavily from the approach Hegel developed in the *Science of Logic,* Marx clearly recognizes that the historical results of this particular dialectical method are "not in any way a product of the concept which thinks and generates itself outside itself or above observation and conception."[114] Social reality is the product of human creativity (social formations) and forgetfulness (fetishism of transcendent natural and economic laws and rights).

The Hegelian heritage has been studied a great deal. For Hegel, science is the self-expression of the Concept *(Begriff)* as it develops from its immediate form of knowledge to its mediated concrete form in the Absolute Spirit. The objective reality and, therefore, truth is not that of the immediately given empirical world open to modern science, but is something posited in the objectifications of the Spirit in the social values, cultural institutions, and structures of political economy. The representations of perception and the categories of understanding are incorporated within a posited (created) objectivity of the Concept. History, culture, and social institutions are empirical manifestations of the development of pure Mind or Spirit. Claims are made to truth within each historical epoch, but are undermined by the contradictions inherent in all claims based on the historical and the contingent; this is what moves history toward higher stages of development and truth claims. Truth becomes the final recognition of the system and totality of this process and the realization that objectivity (the historical world) is simply a manifestation of subjectivity (the Spirit). Marx takes this idea of truth and develops it within the framework of his analysis of the contradictions of capitalism in his later critique of political economy. He recognizes that to develop the Concept of capital, he must begin with the contradictions contained in its most immediate empirical form as exchange value.

> The exact development of the concept of capital is necessary since it is the fundamental concept of modern economics, just as capital itself, whose abstract, reflected image is its concept, is the foundation of bourgeois society. The sharp formulation of the basic presuppositions of the relation must bring out all the contradictions of bourgeois production, as well as the boundary where it drives beyond itself.[115]

According to Zelený, this concept of capital is "the intellectual translation of the structure of the object itself; the intellectual expression of objectivity existing necessarily."[116] Knowledge is not a simple correlation of social theory to empirical perceptions as is the case with the method of positivism, but is the actual conceptualization of the posited objectivity. Knowledge aims for an understanding of the mediated structures and social relationships of human existence, for it is here that the objects of experience and consciousness itself are forged. This means that the reality we live in is prestructured by the religious, aesthetic, scientific, political, and economic institutions and values of our society. To define truth as simply what is would be to misrepresent it and miss the possibilities inherent in the present as to what could be. It reduces rationality to existence, and knowledge to description and technical control. It also misses the conscious and unconscious structural constraints on human freedom and self-consciousness. Marx's hermeneutics gets to the deep structures reflecting the essence of class relationships behind exchange value and the law of value in volume 1 of *Capital;* and it addresses the economic crises, structural weaknesses, imperialism, and role of the state in volume 3. Marx owes a great debt to the Hegelian idea of the nature of nonpositivistic scientific knowledge; it is from Hegel that Marx develops his notion of theory.

> In the strict Aristotelian sense "a unity of theory and practice" is quite meaningless. Since the two concepts are so defined as to be mutually exclusive, no kind of knowledge can be simultaneously both particular and universal, both applicable and inapplicable. But Hegel twists the traditional meaning of the terms: the eternal, the object of theory, for Aristotle, Nature as a totality of potentials, in Hegel, is shaped by human consciousness. Once the cosmos becomes Weltanschauung, the theoretical becomes a general view of what is practical, or applicable. If the universal and the eternal can be consciously created by thought, then the theoretical can exist only in relation to the practical.[117]

MORAL JUDGMENT AND SOCIAL PRAXIS: MARX'S RETURN TO THE GREEK POLIS

The second moment of the dialectic comes from Greek thought and has not received the attention it deserves, mainly because of the emphasis on the perceived positivism of Marx's economics. In the eleventh thesis on Feuerbach, Marx admonishes the reader to consider that the purpose of science is to change the world by acting on the objectivity of the given structures of both social reality and social consciousness. This constitutes the practical application of the Hegelian/Marxian form of knowledge considered above. The epistemological declaration in the eleventh thesis contains a moral imperative to revolutionize the social relations according to certain normative assumptions about the nature of reality that are contradictory to the principles of the Enlightenment. The use of "practical" here does not have the connotation—within either the epistemology or ethical philosophy of Marx—of having an instrumental or technical character. The latter is the hallmark of modern science and positivism, but is antithetical to the claims of Aristotle, Hegel, and Marx.

Examined from within the total arena of Marx's works on epistemology and methodology, which—one must admit—are few and sketchy, one can tentatively conclude that the Marxian concept of praxis is to be understood as closer to what Aristotle meant by *phronesis* (practical knowledge) than what he meant by *techne* (technical knowledge). This thesis is rejected by most neo-Aristotelian scholars and social philosophers, from Arendt to Habermas. The difficulty in the past has been the inability to distinguish adequately between the various theoretical, epistemological, and methodological meanings and implications of the term "praxis." Thus, while—on one side of the argument—praxis incorporates the meaning of social labor and technical activity and therefore does represent a position antithetical to the Aristotelian categories of practical wisdom *(phronesis)* and political activity *(praxis)*, it nevertheless also incorporates Marx's understanding of self-consciousness, class activity, political knowledge, and critical science, which cannot be reduced to technical knowledge and productive activity. Since there is much more material on the former meaning of the term from his earlier works on labor and alienation, the secondary literature has gravitated toward them to the exclusion of Marx's methodology and epistemology in his later writings, which were surrendered to the positivists. Praxis has been leveled to positivism and technical knowledge. However, once the myth of science is dispelled by a closer reading of Marx's critique of British political economy—along with its substantive tenets, theories, and scientific methodology—the later works cry out for a new interpretation. Into this vacuum of hermeneutics rushes Aristotelian ethical epistemology, which—for the first time—gives us the possibility of a clearer understanding and appreciation of how Marx's notions of the Concept and of objectivity relate to the concrete historical world (praxis). Nevertheless, until the myth of positivism is transcended, the Aristotelian moment of Marx's thinking lies dormant, buried beneath years of fetishized and idolatrous science.

As we have already seen, Aristotle begins his *Nicomachean Ethics* with a teleological explanation of why political science is both necessary and important, but impossible. Though its aim is to examine the nature of the good life and just society, which is a good that both the individual and the state strive for by nature, it cannot be determined scientifically. Once the idea of knowledge, truth, and science become epistemologically problematic, the *Ethics* turns into a work on the nature of knowledge in general. Aristotle thus begins to clarify the nature of practical knowledge *(phronesis)*, as opposed to theoretical wisdom *(episteme)* and technical expertise *(techne)*. According to Lobkowicz, Aristotle's notion of practical knowledge and its applicability in moral action is noninstrumental in character. It is this characterization of practical knowledge that Marx would later take up as part of his concept of theory and praxis—and not the character of knowledge that was developing in the positivism of British political economy or in the "social physics" of French socialism.

Just as there are three dimensions of social being for Aristotle, there are three forms of knowledge appropriate to those dimensions in the polis. They are theoretical, practical, and technical knowledge. It is practical knowledge that Aristotle discusses as the form of knowledge of ethics and politics and that he characterizes as not having the universality and precision of theory; the latter studies the eternal principles—as in mathematics and metaphysics—and does not have the instrumental and calculative characteristics of technical knowledge. It is practical knowledge that investigates the moral good of society and the individual, and is concerned with human freedom and rationality—the telos of man. Its goal is not technically applicable knowledge or knowledge purely for its own sake, but practical truths whose purpose is to guide human action.[118] As opposed to the productive knowledge of the craftsman and artisan, practical knowledge is not a technical art that gives instrumental and concrete guidelines within a means/end schema for accomplishment of a particular task; it is not rational in the Weberian sense of rationalization.

> Our discussion will be adequate if it has as much clearness as the subject-matter admits of, for precision is not to be sought for alike in all discussions, any more than in all the products of the crafts. Now fine and just actions which political science investigates, admit of *much variety and fluctuation of opinion*, so that they may be thought to exist only by *convention* and not by nature. And goods also give rise to a similar *fluctuation* because they bring harm to many people; for before now men have been undone by reason of their wealth and others by reason of their courage. We must be content, then, in speaking of such subjects and with such premises to indicate the truth *roughly* and *in outline*, and in speaking about things which are *only for the most part true* and with premises of the same kind to reach conclusions that are no better.[119]

Hannah Arendt noticed that there was a tendency in Plato to blur the distinction between *episteme* (universal theory) and *poiesis* (productive knowledge) and to substitute fabrication for the practical action of the statesman. The result was that the role of the statesman was changed to that of the craftsman, who now artificially fabricated the laws and constitution with the technical skill of the artisan and the universal certainty and objectivity of the philosopher. Arendt calls this the "instrumentalization of politics."

> The substitution of making for acting and the concomitant degradation of politics into a means to obtain an allegedly "higher" end—in antiquity the protection of the good men from the rule of the bad in general, and the safety of the philosopher in particular, in the Middle Ages the salvation of souls, in the modern age the productivity and progress of society—is as old as the tradition of political philosophy. It is true that only the modern age defined man primarily as homo faber, a toolmaker and the producer of things and therefore could overcome the deep-seated contempt and suspicion in which the tradition had held the whole sphere of fabrication.[120]

It is this confusion in modern thinking with its failure to distinguish between practical and productive knowledge, politics and art, that also lies at the heart of the difficulty of interpreting Marx's theory and practice. Generally, Marx's notion of practical action has been interpreted to mean the productive action of the political craftsman— that is, technical knowledge based on his explanatory and predictive science to be applied at the behest of the working class. But since—as we have seen—Marx did not have the epistemological or methodological foundations that would make such a predictive science possible, he could not have reduced the social and political realm to a purely instrumental and technical world. This would have destroyed the whole Hegelian framework of self-consciousness and the Marxian reliance on class struggle; it would have undermined Marx's views on epistemology and anthropology, and his ultimate social ideals of individual freedom and social democracy. The label "positivism" may be applied to Marx only at the expense of his Greek soul. Even a social philosopher like Avineri has argued that the difference between Aristotle's *theoria* and *praxis* is one in which praxis "contents itself with instrumental, applicable knowledge."[121] By reducing the category of praxis to *techne*, Avineri has misunderstood not only practical knowledge, but also the framework within which Marx himself was working. Avineri does, however, broaden the meaning of the term in his analysis to include aspects of the realization of self-consciousness of the proletariat and the potentialities contained in material conditions of social life. In this process he combines the knowledge of technical social control with the hermeneutical knowledge of an understanding of history in ways that are epistemologically incompatible.

Praxis interpreted as an ethical and political critique *(phronesis)* and as political action *(praxis)* is similar to Aristotle's use of the term; Marx's understanding of the relation between political action and knowledge are similar to Aristotle's critique of ethics and politics as a science; and finally, Marx's epistemological critique of idealism, empiricism, and rationalism, and his rejection of Cartesian metaphysics and modern positivism as a basis for science, force one to look more closely at Aristotle for answers to the difficult questions behind the dialectic of "theory" and "practice." Praxis is noninstrumental, nonpredictive, and nonexplanatory knowledge: It is a form of prudence, guiding one to act in concrete moral and historical situations according to principles that are universal and concrete. Though these principles are not theoretical or scientific, they are generalized principles achieved through moral experience in the search for the good life and happiness *(eudaimonia)* within a society that realizes the telos of man. This telos, however, is open to the possibilities of history.

In his *Theory and Practice* Lobkowicz correctly stresses that the major implication of Aristotle's differentiation of theory and praxis revolves around two points: the potentialities of human rationality, and the freedom of human action. He connects Aristotle's *Ethics* to book 8 of the *Metaphysics* by maintaining that human potentiality and the future courses of moral action are not determined by universal norms, but rather by the key determining factor in Aristotelian ethics: rational choice. It is human decision and choice that determine the actualization and the realization of human potential—not scientific ethics. "It amounts to saying that neither ethics nor political science can decide what ought to be done in each particular instance, and that laws cannot possibly cover everything."[122] This is a form of the concrete universal: Ethics is to guide human action but cannot mechanically rule it, since it is by its nature concerned also with the particular and thus the contingent and the experiential. This is a very subtle distinction brought about by Aristotle's search for both knowledge and freedom (potentiality).

Both thinkers recognize the fragility of human experience and knowledge. It is from within this framework that Marx also deals with the concept of critical science or what may be called here "critical prudence." These distinctions and the primacy of freedom have been part of Marx's vocabulary ever since his dissertation and contact with Epicurean philosophy and the rejection of any idea of a natural, divine order. Beginning with an analysis of the contradictions in commodity production and of the development of the Concept *(Begriff)* of capital from the abstract to the concrete, from the contingent and particular to the universal, Marx's critique of political economy evolves into a critique of the forms of consciousness that legitimate and rationalize modernity. As a reflective and not an explanatory science, it is not concerned with the prediction of future historical events. By tracing the development of the commodity from its internal contradictions of use value and exchange value—material production and value production—to its fullest development in the form of the Concept of capital itself (economic crises), Marx states that these ideas are categories expressing "forms of being"; they are a reflection of logic and history, ideas and ontology.[123]

In this radical calling into question of the epistemological, ethical, and political foundations of capitalism, Marx's main focus is on the discovery that it is man who creates the intellectual and material conditions of his own existence (and alienation). As a critique of the fetishism of the categories of political economy, Marx is creating a new critical science founded on the radicalization of the Kantian method of "critique" in his phenomenological and dialectical method. In fact, science had become one of the major fetishisms and stumbling blocks to understanding the class relations of modern industrial society. Thus, Marx's critique of religion, politics, alienation, and fetishism represents the continuity of his life's work; they are a critique of all forms of consciousness and knowledge that falsify the mediated objectivity of the social relations of production and express the empirical world as a given reality. Marx introduces the critique of the "myth of the given" into the study of history. In both its historical and conceptual moments, alienation results in a failure to recognize and remember the possibilities of human emancipation inherent in human rationality, self-consciousness, and the structures of political economy. Revolutionary social change directed by an emancipated and self-reflective working class would be impossible if science were capable of establishing universal laws and values that would determine or control the outcome of future events. And such a melding of praxis (political action) and *poiesis* (fabrication, work) would not be acceptable, given the wider metatheoretical arguments presented by Marx throughout the development of his writings from the early Feuerbachian to the later Hegelian influences.

In fact, the future—whether in the form of revolutionary projections, planning timetables, forms of social organization, methods of revolutionary overthrow, or maintenance of political power—remains unexamined by Marx, except for limited statements in his more historical writings. There is certainly no metatheoretical foundation (epistemology, ethics, methodology) on which a theory of the future could be developed in Marx's writings. The notions of time and historicity that underlie the Hegelian and Marxian dialectic are not oriented to an open future—as in positivism—but to realization of the potential contained in the past in the form of its logical totality and immanent principle. Like Aristotle, Marx sees ethics and politics not as instrumental sciences *(techne)*, but as concrete universal sciences that determine their own imperatives from within the historical and social context; both Aristotle and Marx reject the ethical scholasticism of their predecessors. The goal of science is not the creation of a philosopher king, technocratic elite, or advanced political party through the instrumentalization of knowledge.

The goal of knowledge is the creation of conditions for the enlightened emancipation of humanity in a free community. Knowledge, truth, and rationality develop within a social matrix and are conditioned by the forms and structures of their institutional setting. Truth involves the dialectical interaction of subjectivity and objectivity to the point where objectivity realizes its Concept (potentials or crisis possibilities) in the subjective revolutionary consciousness of the working class. This class, in turn, realizes the potentials for fundamental structural change inherent in the objective conditions of political economy. Marx's indebtedness to Aristotle and his ethical theory provides us with the beginnings of a theory of social practice oriented to the future as something "not yet," rather than as the unfolding of an immanent principle in the logic of the past (dialectical reason); this must be joined with the theory of praxis that develops out of Marx's critique of ideology and false consciousness.

The relations among critical science, morality, and community describe this Hegelian/Aristotelian synthesis where science—as the critique of political economy—undermines the normative and ethical foundations for capitalist political economy. However, science for both Aristotle and Marx, is itself incapable of establishing the ethical norms for practical judgment and political action directed at the future society. From the Kantian critique to the Hegelian phenomenology to the Marxian critique of political economy, the variations on the common theme of the critical method hold to an idea of the future as tied to the past in the a priori form of either pure reason, the Concept *(Begriff)* of the Absolute Spirit, or the dialectical unfolding

(Begriff) of the logic of commodity production.[124] The German view
of science has been quite different from the Anglo-American tradition; though Marx attempts to demystify the metaphysics of German
Idealism by making the method materialistic and historical, he nevertheless is part of this same tradition and its general critique of
positivism.

The justification for social ethics—the formation of the moral
principles that will construct and guide future social relations—must
come out of practical action within the moral community; it must
spring from the ethical substance of a democratic society freed from
alienated labor and exchange value. Social theory does not produce
the a priori imperatives for social action as it would in the Kantian
framework, which—according to Hegel—could easily lead to immoral
activity because of the abstraction and blindness of the categories of
practical reason. Theory only produces the need for such action by
critically undermining the legitimacy of the truth claims of political
economy, by showing the contradictions between consciousness and
reality—between the Concept and being—and by historically examining the origins and structures of the institutions of social oppression. Science becomes the moral condemnation of the categories of
liberty, freedom, and justice within the capitalist system. Like Aristotle, Marx believes that ethics is a form of political and economic
knowledge. For Aristotle the criterion of truth is that which leads
to the good and to happiness, while for Marx it is that which
leads to liberation and humanization of consciousness. In both cases,
truth is determined not through the classical correspondence of
consciousness and reality, but instead lies in the process of acting
itself.

> Practical knowledge, on the contrary, aims at "practical truth," that is, at
> conclusions whose sole purpose is to guide human actions; it is right or
> wrong according to whether it succeeds or fails in leading man to true
> "happiness."[125]

PRAXIS AND THE FRAGILITY OF THE GOOD LIFE

In the beginning of the introduction to *Grundrisse*, Marx discusses
his critique of traditional political economy and its characterization of
human nature in terms of universal, transhistorical, and individualistic categories. He does this by returning to the Aristotelian concept of
the *zōon politikon*. It represents part of the reconnection of the links

between the early and the later writings of Marx. "The human being is in the most literal sense a political animal, not merely a gregarious animal, but an animal which can individuate itself only in the midst of society."[126] This theme runs throughout Marx's writings and is especially present when he considers the issues of human nature and freedom. The same idea had been expressed in the German Ideology.

> Only in the community [with others] has each individual the means of cultivating his gifts in all directions; only in the community, therefore, is personal freedom possible. . . . . The illusory community, in which individuals have up until now combined, always took on an independent existence in relation to them, and was at the same time, since it was the combination of one class against another, not only a completely illusory community, but a new fetter as well. In the real community the individuals obtain their freedom in and through their association.[127]

Thus the *Grundrisse* begins with a restatement in very succinct form of the position concerning man's species being that is more developed in the *Paris Manuscripts*. Marx is critical of the eighteenth-century "Robinsonades," who defended a natural view of man isolated from society—with the latter viewed as an external necessity only. Marx does not concentrate on this aspect of the problem as he did in his early writings, for his goal is not another philosophical anthropology; rather, it is the connection of the isolated individual and natural rights to the larger methodological problems in political economy of the separation of the various moments of the economic process into distinct stages of production, exchange, distribution, and consumption. His purpose here is to undermine the validity of positivism.

> The aim [of British economics] is, rather, to present production—see e.g. Mill—as distinct from distribution etc., as encased in eternal natural laws independent of history, at which opportunity bourgeois relations are then quietly smuggled in as the inviolable natural laws on which society in the abstract is founded. This is the more or less conscious purpose of the whole proceeding.[128]

For Aristotle, man is by nature a social being since what distinguishes him from other animals is his rationality and speech, both of which involve communication and society. Society is not a utilitarian adjunct of an artificially created presocial being for his protection and property, but the very requirement of rationality and humanness itself. It is the perfection of man's reason and social relations that indicates the good life. Thus, happiness *(eudaimonia)* is achieved by a life that realizes human rationality through the moral development of the individual in both practical and intellectual pursuits. In book 1 and the end of book 10 of his *Nicomachean Ethics,* Aristotle examines the constitutive elements of social rationality and character development. The development of personal dignity and moral integrity through political deliberation and philosophical contemplation realizes the inner potential of man. Though Marx's emphasis is on the social and economic arena, his ultimate goal is similar to that of the classical Greeks with their harmonious and aesthetic balance between the public and private spheres. In the case of Marx, this is to be accomplished through his critique of fetishism and idolatry, the enlightened emancipation from cultural and ideological illusions, the realization of human potential by people themselves becoming the creators of their own social institutions, and the rational deliberation of an expanded public sphere through workers' control—true democracy and human emancipation.

> In the later Marx also, communism was eudaemonistic. Happiness, for Marx, meant the freedom to be a total person, that is, the freedom to indulge all of our productive power and expressive capacities. Culture could not be separated from the realization of human abilities. The fully developed individual was the presupposition of culture.[129]

Marx goes beyond the Aristotelian moment because he must incorporate not only the ideals of the Ancients, but the realities of modernity. There is—however—the same emphasis on the dilemma of knowledge, problems about the nature of science, difficulties about political action, and knowledge of the future; there are the same struggles with the interrelationships between epistemology and politics, moral judgment and political action, and economics and politics—all this under the general rubric of social ethics. With the broadening of Marx's notion of praxis to include the Hegelian, Feuerbachian, and now Aristotelian moments, we can begin to see more extensive ethical and epistemological components to this one idea. Praxis is not simply the conflation of work and interaction—as Habermas and others would have us believe—but includes development of the moral character of man as well as new public institutions of human liberation. Referring to Aristotle, Barker writes,

> Love, affection, friendship, pity are as natural to him as concern with his own good and calculation of what is conducive to his own good. It is

man's natural sociality that is the basis of natural right in the narrow and strict sense of right. Because man is by nature social, the perfection of his nature includes the social virtue par excellence, justice; justice and rights are natural. This natural kinship is deepened and transfigured in the case of man as a consequence of his radical sociality.[130]

This is very similar to Marx's concept of the human being. "Conscious life activity distinguishes man from the life activity of animals. Only for this reason is he a species-being or rather, he is only a self-conscious being, i.e., his own life is an object for him, because he is a species-being. Only for this reason is his activity free."[131] It is only humans who are capable of creating—through labor's objectifica-tion—the universality of the species in their social relationships. This is the reason why the issue of alienation becomes so prominent for Marx: The rationality and realization of human potential depend on the organization and structure of the social relations of production and the creation of a new public sphere. Within capitalism, the individual is alienated from society, which forms the bedrock on which the very possibility of self-consciousness and rationality rest. Without the latter, ethical action and deliberation become impossible, because rationality and morality are not simply the concerns of practical reason but are the fullest expression and realization of the social nature of man. Marx's distinction in volume 3 of *Capital* between the realm of necessity (survival and work) and the realm of freedom is a repetition of an originally Greek view of political life.

> Nevertheless, the Greeks viewed their political life as the realm of freedom, but not solely because they were legally free and equal before the law. More basically, they identified politics and freedom—or politics and the most truly human activity—because in order to take part in the political life just described a man had to be freed from all struggle of survival, that is, released from all or almost all activities concerned with the procurement of the necessities of life. It is against this background that the Greek distinction has to be understood, between "mere life," in the sense of a mere maintaining and preserving of one's physical existence, and a "good life," which achieves man's ultimate destination.[132]

There is thus in both Aristotle and Marx a strong teleological view of man with a corresponding view of ethics and politics, which act as expressions and fulfillments of that telos. Marx's position is different from Aristotle's because of the philosophical developments that had taken place in German Idealism and British political and economic theory, along with actual historical developments with the rise of the industrial system. It is, however, on the teleological view of man as a self-creating entity that Marx is able to base his critique of capitalism as an institutional arrangement that is antisocial and anti-individual. The concept of the social individual, which he gets from reading the *Ethics* and *Politics*, becomes the foundation for a critique of the possessive individualism of the Enlightenment.

For Marx, the future is open within historically defined limits to be determined by human rationality and imagination—the drive to the realization of human potential within a rational society. Unlike in Aristotle, even the form of the teleology is open, for there is no one substantive definition of human nature.

> As we have seen, it is only when the object becomes a human object, or objective humanity, that man does not become lost in it. This is only possible when man himself becomes a social object; when he becomes a social object and society becomes a being for him in this object.[133]

Whether in fact man realizes his potential within his species being or whether he is reduced to a state of barbarism is something that science cannot determine; it is to be determined by the success or failure of the conscious life activity of workers within their social relations. Thus, human beings as social individuals must reappropriate the material basis for the community and their spiritual gifts of *logos* through speech and criticism.

> Communism is the necessary form and the dynamic principle of the immediate future, but communism is not itself the goal of human development—the form of human society.[134]

> But if the designing of the future and the proclamation of ready-made solutions for all time is not our affair, then we realize all the more clearly what we have to accomplish in the present—I am speaking of a *ruthless criticism of everything*, ruthless in two senses: The criticism must not be afraid of its own conclusions, nor of conflict with the powers that be.[135]

The social goal is the humanization of nature and the naturalization of man, the remembrance and recovery of the lost totality and harmony of human existence; it is the return of man to himself, as the Being-in-Itself becomes the Being-in-and-for-Itself. Through an "anamnestic solidarity"[136] with the lost ideals of the Ancients, the power of the ethical spirit of Marx can be revived. But the actual form of this society and the actual content of the good life for both Marx and Aristotle lie in the striving and creativity of man, not in science as *theoria*. The most fruitful of Marx's statements on this matter is found in his examination of the self-governing producer communes established in Paris in 1871.

Horst Mewes has argued that the political democracy of the Paris Commune was itself a revival of the lost Greek ideals of freedom, which transcended the pursuit of individual self-interest through realization of the universal potentials of the species being. According to Mewes, Marx calls for a reawakening of classical political freedoms. One crucial objection to this point might be that Aristotle's notion of praxis was tied to a concept of the public relating to moral and intellectual virtues—furthering the moral character of the individual in the process of public deliberation and speech—while Marx's concept relates to the social sphere of production, consumption, and organization of labor. There are, in fact, major differences between Aristotle and Marx over the question of work that cannot and should not be neglected. The worlds of these two individuals were far apart on some issues. However, within the framework of this important limitation—which has been acknowledged in most secondary interpretations—the formal or metatheoretical aspects of how the two thinkers raised and structured their ideas are very much alike. Their general approaches to ethics, politics, and economics are formally very similar. While manual labor might disqualify someone from being a citizen in Aristotle's polis, for Marx this type of labor is a part (but only a part) of the foundations for objectification, creativity, and freedom. The distinctions are important; but both emphasize the dynamic and creative aspects of human reason, the application of ethical values to political deliberation, and the importance of economics as a foundation stone for ethics.

While Arendt and Wolin have said that Marx reduced and lost the Greek notion of the public in his own notion of society, both Mewes and Schwartz argue that there has been a misunderstanding of Marx's relation to Aristotle and Marx's distinctions in the private/public, social/political dichotomy.[137] Schwartz points out that the notion of social practice refers to political action, formation of the general will (Rousseau), and the process in which the individual is formed through association and interaction with others (Aristotle). The crucial item here is that Marx extended the notion of public by reexamining the idea of property to include both its objective and subjective aspects. Property was not simply a material object, but was also a social relationship requiring maintenance, security, and legitimation: It was thus a class relationship. For Marx, this turned the issue of the use and control over property into an issue for public consideration, and—in the process—turned praxis into an ethical form of social action.[138] Praxis was thus not limited to labor—either manual or intellectual—but became understood as social action, a revolutionary force in which democratic institutions transform class relations and redeem politics as an expression of human creativity and of emancipated social relations.

In Marx's later writings, there is a methodological shift—but not an "epistemological break"—from his earlier philosophical humanism (which he never rejects, as seen in the *Grundrisse*) to an emphasis on dialectical science acting as a critique of political economy. No longer concerned with a philosophical anthropology grounded in the *Gattungswesen* (being and essence) of mankind, Marx shifts his attention to an analysis of the structures of society as a whole that affect this species being, and to the dialectical and logical unraveling of the whole capitalist system in social contradictions and economic crises. However, throughout this redirection of his method, the teleological questions remain alive. They are transformed from those of the telos of the individual to the telos of society. Society—because of its internal dynamics and the contradictions of social production and private accumulation—contains its own formal ends in economic crisis and breakdown. However, as Barker states regarding the Aristotelian position on the dynamic relation between matter and form:

> Generally, it may be answered, Aristotle does assume congruity: the end for the sake of which "movement" arises finds a necessary material suited to itself and to movement towards itself. But it is not always so: a matter may exist which is not congruous with form, and that matter may limit the extent to which movement attains its form. In politics the primary matter may be so rude, that the movement from it never reaches a constitution.[139]

There is in Aristotle this notion that outside forces may affect the working of the formal cause in nature. Certainly the parallels to Marx's method in *Capital* are too strong to be dismissed. Marx treats capital as a Concept or form that has its own internal telos in terms of the concentration and centralization of capital, immiseration of the working class, tendential fall in the rate of profit, underconsumption of capital, overproduction of consumer goods, economic stagnation, and so on. He also delineates "counteracting forces" that can externally deflect the consequences of the logic of capitalist development. Hegel has intervened here between Aristotle and Marx, since Aristotle held that actuality is prior to potency. In the writings of Hegel and Marx, it is formal potentiality that has logical and ontological priority. Both Aristotelian and Hegelian metaphysics—denuded of their ontology—now become important elements in the methodology of critical science. In fact, Marx's terminology in some areas of his writings is directly influenced by Aristotle's notion of the four causes: formal, final, efficient, and material. One example is his description of the labor process.

> But labor is not only consumed, but also at the same time fixed, converted from the form of activity into the form of the object, materialized; as a modification of the object, it modifies its own form and changes from activity to being. The end of the process is the product, in which the raw instrument of labor has likewise transposed itself from a mere possibility into an actuality, by having become a real conductor of labor. . . . All three moments of the process, the material, the instrumental, and labor, coincide in the neutral result—the product.[140]

Marx seems to be interpreting the objectification of labor and the subjectification of the natural world in terms of Aristotle's metaphysical categories of potency and act. It is labor that unlocks and transforms nature from its mere material possibility to its actuality. Unlike Aristotle, Marx considers the teleology of nature to lie in the categories of the laborer and the social relations in which he or she works. This is the potency at the heart of the economic system, which requires the actualization process of human labor and self-consciousness in the form of revolutionary change. And herein we find another unity of the early and later Marx: The inner contradictions of the system require human action to actualize them; the logic of *Capital* can only be fulfilled by the idea of creativity of labor from the *Paris Manuscripts*. Marx also sees the transformative process in terms of Aristotle's four causes, while substituting for the latter's concepts the notions of raw material, instruments of production, formal labor, and final commodity. Throughout his later writings, Marx continues to develop his analysis of commodity in terms of the categories of substance and form, which represent the reincorporation of Aristotle's metaphysics and Hegel's logic into his work. He even continues to use Hegel's terms "Being-in-Itself" and "Being-for-Itself" as a further development of the material found in book 8 of Aristotle's *Metaphysics*.

This chapter has attempted to stress the links between the Aristotelian and Marxian notions of social science and social ethics. Unlike and contrary to Aristotle, Marx includes a wider spectrum of social life. Thus, the notion of praxis includes practical knowledge and political action, but it is also applied to the epistemological constitution of objectivity by the subject in the work process. These other elements of praxis were developed in Marx's confrontations with and interpretation of Hegel's thought. It is this strong, almost blinding Hegelian element in Marx's use of praxis, along with the traditional interpretation of Marx's science as positivistic, that has kept theorists from seeing the more direct relations between Marx and Aristotle. The result of this interrelationship between the German and the Greek worlds is that modern social science has its intellectual and spiritual foundations in the thought of the ancient Greek philosophers. When this is truly and more universally understood the contours and dimensions of social science will have to be rethought and reconstructed, sending nineteenth- and twentieth-century neopositivism to the graveyard of intellectual history.

A more comprehensive picture of Marx's indebtedness to Aristotle will develop when the foregoing analysis of Marx epistemology and politics is combined with his theory of democracy and critique of liberalism (in Chapter Four); his theory of value, and critique of Ricardo and classical political economy (Chapter Five); and his fully developed theory of social justice (Chapter Six).

Part II

The Moderns

Chapter Three

The Nineteenth-Century German Return to Social Ethics and the Ancients: Kant and Hegel

INTRODUCTION

The next area to be examined is the philosophical tradition of German Idealism, with special emphasis on Kant and Hegel and their influence on the ethical philosophy of Marx. Ethics as a subdiscipline within philosophy has been defined by one source as having three main characteristics: "(1) a general pattern or way of life, (2) a set of rules of conduct or moral code, and (3) inquiry about ways of life and rules of conduct."[1] With the approach of modernity, philosophers generally have been concerned with moral philosophy as a means for arriving at universal moral maxims, principles, and imperatives for action. In the contemporary Anglo-American tradition, morality is the branch of philosophy that deals with norms and values of what is right and wrong in relationship to individual decisions and actions. Ethics has become a form of metamorality, in which the foundations and issues of morality are reflected on, logically articulated, clarified, and structurally analyzed; ethics has been reduced to a subbranch of logic and mathematics.

As we have already seen in the previous chapters, the ethical traditions of the Greeks emphasized the relationships between morality and political philosophy, morality and political economy. For them, practical philosophy was composed of ethics, political philosophy, and economic theory; this is social ethics. The contrasts between the

Ancients and Moderns on this issue of the nature of morality must be
clearly understood, since they form the radical juncture and break of
nineteenth-century German social philosophy with the fragmentation
and rationality of modernity. The criticisms of Kant by both Hegel
and Marx are informed by an integration of modern political economy and a return to Aristotle. One characteristic of modern morality
is a loss of the political, social, and economic aspects of moral
judgment and behavior. The social structure becomes immunized
against critical reflection. Moral philosophy has reduced practical
action to issues of the validation of the objectivity and universality of
moral principles and the adequacy of the application of these principles to isolated individual events. This is what can be described as
moral abstractionism and moral *techne*. Ritter says that among the
Ancients the "doctrine of ethics in general" included both a "doctrine
of virtue" (morality) and a "doctrine of law" (legality); but with
modernity, ethics has been reduced to the former—morality—and its
concern with the moral relations between individuals and the inner
freedom and inner self-legislation of moral laws.[2] While Kant is
concerned with inner moral autonomy and personal dignity, Hegel
emphasizes the family, abstract rights, civil society, and the state.
Ritter—referring to Hegel's comments about Greek philosophy in his
Lectures on the History of Philosophy—contends that the Greeks were not
moral but ethical men, concerned with institutional or objective
morality and not subjective or personal morality in the sense of the
modern conscience.[3]

> With Aristotle, ethics is the doctrine of "ethos," taken as the constitution
> of individual life and action in the household and the polis, a constitu-
> tion developed in custom, use, and tradition. . . . "Ethics" is therefore
> the doctrine of what is good and right, which determines the action of
> the individuals as it is rendered universal in ethos and nomos. It is the
> foundation of "politics" insofar as political leadership and constitutional
> and legal statutes have their ground and determination (telos) in the
> praxis "ethically" constituted in the household and the polis.[4]

For Solomon, too, Hegelian ethics deals with all topics within the
broad framework of a search for the good life within community.
This would include political theory, sociology, economics, and history
along with the traditional concerns for morality and theology.[5] In
fact, Solomon splits the whole of ethical thought into two main
philosophical traditions: The Aristotelian, which emphasizes political

virtue and self-realization; and the Kantian, which emphasizes moral duty and individual autonomy. Marx approaches the issues of ethics in a way that joins together both classical ethics and modern morality through the integration of Kant and Aristotle. He places individual autonomy within the broader context of the structural relationships of political economy. This—in turn—has been misinterpreted as a rejection of moral philosophy, as a rejection of the Kantian branch of morality. It is this nineteenth-century German social theory that has tended to confuse contemporary authors and has prompted a number of them to question whether Marx had a moral philosophy at all. Given his understanding of the relationships between essence and appearance, morality—understood as the bourgeois traditions of natural rights theory and utilitarianism—is viewed by Marx as an ideological defense of essential capitalist social relations.

Though his critique of bourgeois morality has been noticed by almost everyone, there exists the danger that bourgeois morality will be taken as the standard for morality itself, as the only form of moral argument possible. When this happens, the debate is over—with Marx having no moral theory to ground his critique of capitalism. However, the key to an understanding of Marx's position in this matter revolves around interpretations of the very nature of morality itself, especially as it develops in the modern German tradition into questions of social ethics and political economy. Here the Moderns return to the Ancients. This transition, which was not unique to Marx, had been made historically and philosophically in the internal development of German moral philosophy from Kant's *Fundamental Principles of the Metaphysics of Morals* (1785) and the *Critique of Practical Reason* (1788) to Hegel's *Phenomenology of Spirit* (1807) and *Philosophy of Right* (1821). As Taylor has noted, the developments within German social theory and the transitions from traditional philosophy to social thought have been very difficult for Anglo-American philosophers to appreciate because of their radically different understanding of the nature, structure, and goals of morality.[6] Both Hegel and Marx—in their different ways—attempt to integrate ethics and political economy. They both have one foot in classical natural law and one foot in modernity. This gives them—probably more than any other modern thinkers—a view of history and human development, an insightful understanding of the past and a vision for the future, that very few others have had. Hegel and Marx lived at a time when the present could still look at its past and future simultaneously, when time itself was an integrated whole. Today, the philosophical and historical past has been forgotten; and with it, the future has been lost.

Knowing of the transition in moral philosophy from an emphasis on *Moralität* to a stress on *Sittlichkeit*, from morality to social ethics, provides us with insight into Marx's own thoughts on ethics and moral philosophy. It helps in explaining why Marx is not so interested in questions regarding the abstract universal norms of right and wrong, good and evil, and freedom and necessity. Rather, he is more concerned with historical and social formations—with their particular institutional and organizational networks for the production, distribution, exchange, and consumption of social wealth. These for Marx are the foundation stones underlying all ethical issues, since they form the basis of his theory of the good life and the good society and also the basis for a realization of the potentials inherent in the human individual's species being. Thus, Marx is interested in analyzing the social and economic world within which moral decisions are made. It is in modern social formations that the very conditions for the possibility of self-realization and actualization, for the internal freedom of virtue and the external freedom of law, and even for social justice, are made possible.

As filtered and mediated through German Idealism, the questions of moral philosophy were becoming less and less concerned with issues of individual reflection, intentionality, choice-making, and free will. Though not denying the importance of these earlier issues, Marx himself then turned to a consideration of the social institutions that distort and repress the free and rational development of the self and to those other institutional structures that would permit a classless nonhierarchical worker-controlled society. The former refers to his critical science, while the latter refers to his utopian vision and revolutionary praxis. Marx's ethics is then intimately bound to both a critical-dialectical science and an anticipatory utopianism; this is ethics bound to the nature of temporality, since different methods apply to the different dimensions of time. The past can be dealt with through the social critique of the dialectical method, while the future is approached through social praxis. Moral philosophy turns into a critique of those social institutions and relationships that hinder and restrict the possibility of truly autonomous moral action and human existence; morality evolves into questions of social ethics and of dialectical contradictions between the social relations of production and the forces of production. Choice, freedom, and rationality must be institutionally structured and protected in order to be real (efficacious). Ethics in the tradition of Hegel and the Greeks now develops into politics and sees the questions of political and economic power, authority and legitimation, as foundations on which the moral community is built. The power of Marx's ethical critique is all the more important when we understand how he integrated Aristotelian ethics and German Idealism.

HEGEL'S CRITIQUE OF KANT: FROM *MORALITÄT* TO *SITTLICHKEIT*

Both Kant and Hegel represent critical turning points in their responses to the traditional theories of man in political science (Hobbes and Locke) and political economy (Smith and Ricardo). It was they who began to interpret the individual in terms of the morally whole and integrated human being. Kant rejected conceiving of the person in terms of legitimacy, political obligations, or social stability and order, or from within the framework of the state of nature. This was a crucial first step in German philosophy, for it was an important critique of the natural rights tradition while still remaining within an individualistic and moral perspective. In so doing, Kant laid the foundation for the all-important distinctions between freedom and liberty, between rational moral decisions and free choices, and between the self-conscious, rational will and the individual with rights and liberties.

From Kant's point of view, the terms "freedom" and "liberty" are antithetical to each other, and an acceptance of the natural rights tradition would undermine the moral autonomy and rationality of the individual. This distinction is not considered important in contemporary political theory, since the two terms are now used interchangeably. However, from the German perspective, it represented a radical break from the natural rights tradition and resulted in two entirely different views of the individual, rationality, and personal freedom. The addition of moral action in the social context, the categorical imperative, and the kingdom of ends gave Kantian moral philosophy its distinctive twist. Most of the secondary literature stresses the categorical imperative, almost entirely to the exclusion of the notion of the kingdom of ends. On the other hand, Lucien Goldmann in his work *Immanuel Kant* has made the latter a central concept in his reading of Kant—as did Marx. The distinction between Kantian philosophy and traditional British moral thought (utilitarian and natural rights theory) can be more easily seen by examining Kant's distinction between duty (obligations to universally binding moral laws) and inclinations (self-interest and pleasure). However, at the heart of Kant's moral philosophy is a radical individualism with an emphasis on rationality and self-determination.

Neither empiricism nor rationalism can supply—according to Kant—the appropriate foundation for moral philosophy. This can be found only in pure reason itself. At the heart of objective moral laws is the notion of the categorical imperative, with its foundation in the logical principle of noncontradiction. The principles on which the moral imperative to universally binding action rest include the following:

1. Act according to the maxim (general rule of action) that every moral action should be universally applicable, become the basis for a natural law, and be bound to the principle of noncontradiction (the principles of universalism, natural law, and noncontradiction, respectively).

2. Treat humanity in the form of every individual as an end-in-itself and never as a means to an end (the principle of human dignity).

3. Act according to the principle that the will of every rational being is a universally legislative will (the principle of moral sovereignty).

4. Act according to the maxim that the principles of practical reason are themselves grounded in the autonomy of the will (the principle of individual autonomy).

5. Act toward every rational being as a sovereign within a social kingdom-of-ends (the principle of the kingdom of ends).

In order to act rationally, an individual must subsume individual judgment and moral action under these five principles, which are applicable in all spheres of morality. Every moral law claiming to have ethical objectivity must conform to these five principles, without which it is invalid. Moral judgment is therefore a self-legislative process, since the determination of moral laws comes from within the individual. Kant's goal is to maintain the freedom, dignity, and moral autonomy of self-consciousness.

Hegel's dialogue with Kant spans the whole of his philosophical writings from his earlier critiques in *The Spirit of Christianity and Its Fate* (1798–1800), *Faith and Knowledge* (1802–3), *On The Scientific Ways of Treating Natural Law* (1802–3), and *System of Ethical Life* (1803–4) through the later *Phenomenology of Spirit* (1807) and *Philosophy of Right* (1821) His critique of Kant's moral philosophy may be broken down into two main areas: (1) a critique of Kant's moral logic and epistemology; and (2) a critique of the loss of social ethics from the Greek tradition. Hegel sees ethics not simply as a concern with individual moral decisions, free will, and individual rational self-consciousness abstracted from history and society. Rather—by returning to the Aristotelian tradition—he shows that ethics deals with the social, cultural, political, and economic framework within which individual self-realization (human potentialities and *eudaimonia*) becomes possible.[7] In fact, there is a real danger in moral philosophy of turning morality into a justification for the immoral by including only abstract formal law—excluding the social component—and making anything possible as a moral law so long as it fulfills formal logical requirements.

Hegel's critique of Kant's moral philosophy (*Moralität*) begins in his early theological writings in Frankfurt with an analysis of the positivity and estrangement of Kant's categorical imperative. Hegel finishes his Kantian critique with his later theory of the state—where he rejects the empty formalism, individualism, and rationality of Kant's moral philosophy, which never developed out of the sphere of the autonomous moral individual into areas of institutional and structural ethics (*Sittlichkeit*).[8] In Hegel's early theological writings, which include *The Positivity of the Christian Religion* and *The Spirit of Christianity and Its Fate*, he undertakes to incorporate Kant's moral philosophy into his own analysis of religion and morality. In the first essay he argues that, in both the Jewish and Christian churches, there is an attempt to undermine the power of human reason in order to determine the objective moral principles that guide human action. Hegel accepts the Kantian definition of objective moral laws as universal and necessary and as expressions of the subjective maxims of the individual. They are also expressions of the individual's respect for duty, and his or her own practical will.

The danger arises in that religion establishes an external set of institutions above the individual—institutions that impose a set of moral beliefs from without, based simply on the authority and power of the church. Closely following Kant, Hegel contends that all moral law must come from within the individual. Morality requires virtue and the respect for duty and human reason. "The right to legislate for one's self, to be responsible to one's self alone for administering one's own law, is one which no man may renounce, for that would be to cease to be a man altogether."[9] Moral laws that are issued from an external authority (positivity) in the form of ecclesiastical statutes undermine the moral freedom and the autonomy of the practical will. And in the process, they bypass human reason and purpose by creating a religious system that "despises man." The church has taken the principles of the subjective will and established them as reified and positive laws of an external authority. This is the social process of religious alienation.

In the essay entitled *The Spirit of Christianity and Its Fate*, Hegel begins his turn away from Kant, for he sees the fragmentation and dualism created by the latter's moral philosophy. The contradictions between inclination and duty, noumenal and phenomenal self, reason and feelings, and the objective and subjective components of moral laws "remain a residuum of indestructible positivity."[10] The difference between the European and Oriental churches—both of which dictate moral positivity—and the moral commands of the Kantian self is that in the former the members are slaves to objective alien laws made by others, while in the latter these same laws are internalized and viewed as the product of subjective reason. Morality—in whatever guise—is a form of domination. Hegel finds the categorical imperative, with its imposition of moral principles based on duty and command and with its fragmentation and estrangement of the self, to be destructive of both individual freedom and rationality.

It is from this perspective that Hegel looks to Jesus and the Sermon on the Mount for a way out of the dilemma of the fragmented moral universe. Jesus transcends morality and the law, positivity and duty, by basing his moral injunctions on love and a virtuous community. Love becomes the highest moral principle. It involves the development of an attitude or inclination to act according to the principles of the law, while taking away its external form of positivity. According to Hegel, love is a synthesis of subject and object, particular and universal, inclination and law. He uses the example of criminal punishment to explain his distinctions between Kantian morality and Christian love. Law is an expression of formal thought and cannot forgo punishment once a law has been transgressed without losing its own character as law. While the punishment results from the logic of the contradiction between the law and the transgression, law is nevertheless then set in opposition to justice—which may not require punishment, but rather mercy. Law involves what is morally universal and necessary; it is pure concept (thought). On the other hand, justice must deal with the contingencies and circumstances surrounding the reasons for certain types of action. This may mean that law and justice will become contradictory to each other and can only be reconciled by love.[11] This is reminiscent of Aristotle's treatment of equity in book 5 of the *Nicomachean Ethics*, but with the addition of Christian morality.

In his work *Natural Law*, Hegel questions Kant's notion of practical reason, for he believes that—ultimately—practical reason renounces law and the social system altogether by turning its pure form into the supreme moral principle. Moral law is then the conformity of human action to its own negative abstract Concept, which alone determines both the form and content of moral judgment.

> But the content of the maxim remains what it is, a specification or singularity, and the universality conferred on it by its reception into the form is thus a merely analytic unity. And when the unity conferred on it is expressed in a sentence purely as it is, that sentence is analytic and tautological. And the production of tautologies is in truth what the sublime lawgiving power of pure practical reason's autonomy in legislating consists of.[12]

Kant had discussed the nature of analytic propositions in his *Critique of Pure Reason*; and to clarify the meaning of these types of statements, he used the example "All bodies are extended,"[13] in which the object of the sentence ("extended") is contained in the subject ("bodies"). Hegel argues that—applied to moral judgments—this type of reasoning has no content since, by definition, the object is already contained in the subject. He continues to criticize Kant for not recognizing the contradiction within his own arguments. Since moral knowledge and truth make universal claims about a particular content or action, Kant has committed a serious logical error by abstracting from all content. He had failed to see that he cannot derive a content from pure reason, because one of the requirements of his own moral philosophy is the abstraction from all content. "Thus it is a self-contradiction to seek in this absolute practical reason a moral legislation which would have a content, since the essence of this reason is to have none."[14] Moral judgments must have a unity of content and form. Hegel questions the exact nature of the content of maxims of the will. Any specific matter or content of a moral maxim may be used to form the content of a moral concept. Any content may be made into the form of a law of practical reason.

Hegel analyzes Kant's moral arguments from the latter's *Critique of*

Practical Reason. There the example is given of a man who steals the possessions of someone who deposited them for security with him, but then died before collecting them again—an example of no-fault theft. Under such conditions that the theft can never be proven, can theft of property become a universal law? Hegel responds by using the moral abstractionism of Kant against him. Within a purely formal argument, there is no contradiction in assuming as an initial premise either the existence of property or its opposite (rejection of property rights and obligations). Looked at from their formal aspects only, either one could become the basis for a moral maxim, but never at the same time. In each case, a substantive moral decision that lies beyond the bounds of the categorical imperative and pure reason itself must be made as to the content of the initial premise. Kant's ethical writings begin at the point where the social content of the moral premise has already been unconsciously decided. Thus, the rejection or acceptance of property rights entails a decision that has been made before pure reason makes its own determination as to the truth of its subjective maxims. There is no logical inconsistency in beginning with either moral premise: the acceptance of private property or of communal property, private property or anarchy, or the reality of the market or the state of nature. According to Hegel, the emptiness and tautology of Kant's practical reason turns into an "absurdity" and a "principle of immorality."[15]

> But by confusing absolute form with conditioned matter, the absolute-ness of the form is imperceptibly smuggled into the unreal and conditioned character of the content; and in this perversion and trickery lies the nerve of pure reason's practical legislation. There is smuggled into the sentence "property is property," not its proper meaning, (i.e., "the identity which the sentence expresses in its form is absolute"), but the meaning: "the matter of the sentence (i.e., property) is absolute." And in this way anything specific can be made into a duty.[16]

Hegel uses another example to show the internal contradictions of Kant's arguments. The moral imperative to help the poor commands an elimination of poverty, just as the imperative to defend one's country demands the elimination of all enemies. However, according to the principle of universalism, a maxim cannot be accepted as universally valid if it destroys its own premise. To actually eliminate poverty or one's enemies means to undermine one's own maxim; and, therefore, it cannot become a principle of moral action. Kant's moral philosophy is built on the formalism of a pure self-consciousness and an empty moral law. He fails to take into consideration the real world, the system of needs in ethical life, and political economy.[17] Certainly, this critique was later to be turned back on Hegel's own concept of the development of the Absolute Spirit in history, by the Left-Hegelians. And on the other hand, Kant's analysis seems to imply an acceptance of natural rights, since—within the bounds established by the principles of universality and noncontradiction—a philosophical moral imperative cannot define its own social and ethical content.

In his *Fundamental Principles of the Metaphysics of Morals*, Kant uses another example of the false borrower in order to further clarify his position. "When I think myself in want of money, I will borrow money and promise to repay it, although I know that I never can do so."[18] He asks how this could possibly become the basis for a universal law and answers his own question in the negative. However, as in his critique of the deposit-stealing example, Hegel responds by saying that this—too—involves an acceptance of substantive moral laws prior to the a priori and transcendental deduction of moral law from pure reason. Whether it is property, contract, binding obligations, or the worth of human life, Hegel's response to the logic of Kant's moral argument is twofold. First, the ethical formalism of practical reason is irrational and contradictory; and second, it assumes the existence of a whole set of prior, unarticulated moral and social values. In later writing the *Philosophy of Right*, Hegel continues this same line of reasoning.

> The absence of property contains in itself just as little contradiction as the non-existence of this or that nation, family, etc., or the death of the whole human race. But if it is already established on other grounds and presupposed that property and human life are to exist and be respected, then indeed it is a contradiction to commit theft or murder; a contradiction must be a contradiction of something, i.e., of some content presupposed from the start as a fixed principle. It is to a principle of that kind alone, therefore, that an action can be related either by correspondence or contradiction.[19]

For Hegel, the law of noncontradiction is inapplicable as the basis for determining moral laws, since there is no contradiction that can arise out of pure subjectivism and formalism. As a method, it is incapable of deciding on the acceptance of property or its rejection, the death of the human race or its collective life. In an interesting juxtapositioning of examples (property, and death of the whole human race), Hegel has joined together the arguments of idealism and empiricism—Kant and Hume. Hume had written that "it is not contrary to reason to prefer the destruction of the whole world to the scratching of my finger."[20] Thus, Hegel is directly equating Kant's rational formalism with Hume's moral positivism. In both cases, Hegel's response is the same: Traditional epistemology is incapable of establishing the validity of morality; it is incapable of defining moral truths through its concepts. Rather, it must rely on implicit concrete and objective assumptions and presuppositions as to the nature of the individual and society—custom, at the expense of reason.[21]

Theft in itself can only become contradictory when property is taken as universally valid within society. There is no contradiction in the statement that "no property is no property." Kant believes that, in the process of willing the moral imperative, the autonomous individual establishes natural law on the basis of his or her own universal rationality. According to Hegel, these arguments presuppose the traditional natural-rights theory and, especially, the rights of private property as the foundation of Kantian morality. Hegel felt that Kant had not developed very far from the natural rights theorists. Dupré has contended that "this [the Kantian categorical imperative] has disastrous effects on moral philosophy, for it allows one to justify any possible behavior in the name of absolute morality."[22] MacIntyre continues this same line of argument when he says,

> The logical emptiness of the test of the categorical imperative is itself of social importance. Because the Kantian notion of duty is so formal that it can be given almost any content, it becomes available to provide a sanction and a motive for the specific duties which any particular social and moral tradition may propose.[23]

Hegel's critique is based on the view that Kant's moral philosophy is too speculative and abstract. The universality of moral claims is validated not because of the categorical nature of morality, but rather because it develops out of the concrete universality of history, culture, and social institutions—out of the ethos of society. The latter entails moral action (*Moralität*), but within a form that includes both objectivity and subjectivity—both the autonomous individual and the laws, customs, and traditions of a society (*Sittlichkeit*). For Hegel, morality develops by necessity into ethics and politics. He sees only pure formalism and subjectivity in Kant, where it is abstract reason that identifies human life, private property, self-development of individual potentials, and the common good as universal principles. The result is that suicide is seen as a contradiction to self-love, and stealing as a contradiction to property rights; and both can then be rejected as immoral. But when the abstract assumptions are contradicted, then moral action becomes impossible.

> On the other hand, since the whole ethical order is per se normative and, therefore, must subsume the real multiplicity of the empirical order under the ideal unity of the spirit, the entire philosophical construction collapses and is replaced by empirical law and custom. Thus, transcendental idealism ultimately turns into some sort of moral empiricism.[24]

It is because of the failure of the synthesis at the moral level of rationalism and empiricism that Kant's moral idealism is transformed into a variation of moral empiricism. With his emphasis on the categorical imperative, the abstract principles of practical reason, and the individual moral actor, the concrete empirical world and the abstract moral world remain unreflectively indistinguishable. There is never a concrete moral universal in Kant's work. As a result, the substance and material of the moral will are unconsciously structured and formed by the principles of practical reason in much the same way that the transcendental consciousness formed and structured the manifold of experience and knowledge itself. However, because moral reason is an abstract formalism, it is ultimately the empirical that structures the manner and content in which the categorical imperative is actually applied; the empirical becomes the true content in Kantian rationalism. This critique has been levied against Kant by a variety of philosophers after Hegel—including Lukács, Marcuse, Colletti, Taylor, Kofler, and Dupré.[25]

> The real trouble with it [Kant's reasoning] is that it misconceives the whole institution of morality. Those who make moral principles a matter of choice in the way explained assimilate the moral life to the life of artistic expression and appreciation; they take it as if it were primarily a private concern. But the truth is rather that morality is first and foremost a social institution, performing a social role, and only secondarily, if at all, a field for individual self-expression.[26]

This helps to explain the emphasis in Kant on an acceptance of life and property as values independent of the law of noncontradiction.

When moral action and principles are conceptualized within an asocial and ahistorical schema, they amount to a justification and acceptance of the status quo because they have been removed from reflective consideration. Kant becomes another moral positivist, because he does not take into consideration the unintended consequences or unintended foundations of the moral dictates of his practical reason. It is at this point that one can read the line, "the real is rational, the rational is real,"[27] as a standard for empiricism. (This is not the meaning that Hegel himself attributes to the statement.) The foundation of morality as a science having the form of an abstract and formal rationality divorced from the social, cultural, and political world is thus interpreted not only as having a normative foundation, but as eventually developing into an empiricist moral argument. Both moral empiricism and idealism end up presupposing and accepting the immediacy and validity of the given social standards in the existing political and economic order as the underlying basis for making moral judgments. In the end, neither empiricism nor idealism have conceptual structures that permit the formation of transcendent or dialectical ideals, which escape the normative structures of the existing social institutions. That is, empiricism and idealism cannot present the system as a whole to the probing eyes of a critical social theorist. The irony of Kantian moral philosophy is that moral judgment cannot be brought to bear on real moral issues.

Finally, the critique of Kant is picked up again in Hegel's *Phenomenology of Spirit*, at first in the sections on Reason entitled "Reason as lawgiver" and "Reason as testing laws" and then in the sections on the Objective Spirit under "Morality." For Hegel, Kant's moral philosophy occupies a privileged place in the development of modernity. Hegel's efforts to trace the development of modern rationality and the Spirit—developed through the realization of self-consciousness and the search for the good life—take him from the realms of hedonism and pleasure, the law of the heart and romanticism, and virtuous activity and pietism to the rationality of Kant's moral philosophy. Hegel sees that the formalism and unconditional nature of the Kantian categorical imperative could not be maintained because—after all—decisions and their effects are under the influence of highly contingent and particular intentions, empirical events, and unintended consequences.[28] As his dialectic moves from Reason to the Objective Spirit, Hegel critiques the moral contradictions underlying the logic of morality and moral action in the real world. He traces the evolution of moral individualism and modernity from the breakup of

Greek culture and society through the ancient Stoics and Skeptics, into the culture of the modern Enlightenment period, and finally culminating in the absolute freedom, anarchy, and terror of the French Revolution.

Just as the community, integration, and social harmony of the Greek polis were destroyed—at first from within and later from without—the attempt to remake the community in modern times is burdened by the ethos of modernity. "Hegel's ideal community is a free state, the state whose citizens willingly accept the common will expressed in the laws, because it is 'spirit of their spirit,' because their own, reasonable, and general will can be found and recognized in its laws."[29] To build a community without the required political, economic, and social infrastructure—to build a community in a market economy characterized by radical individualism and the loss of community—would only (and did) result in the Terror. The *Phenomenology of Spirit* is Hegel's testament to the truth of Aristotle's *Nicomachean Ethics* and *Politics*. Without *politeia, paideia*, the *politike*, and the *oikonomike koinonia*, a free and rational society is impossible; without political philosophy, economic theory, and moral philosophy, ethics is impossible. Kantian thought only reflects and recapitulates the anarchy and terror of modernity—the individual stripped of communal ties and responsibilities and subjected to the alien domination of the imposed authority of modern rationality.[30]

> Hegel believed that the problems of the French Revolution were caused by its attempt to instantiate the principles of natural rights developed by the philosophers of the Enlightenment. The problems with the philosophy of rights were threefold: they rested on (1) a methodologically faulty conception of the self or the subject of rights, (2) a politically faulty conception of the common good, and (3) a morally faulty conception of civic virtue.[31]

The individual as pure abstract self-consciousness living in a social void and a world of absolute freedom (the categorical imperative) will attempt to impose his or her own practical rationality on others. Such an individual will negate the distinctions between self and others, the particular and universal. In distorted fashion, abstract self-consciousness begins to legislate its own moral will upon the world, resulting in a "fanaticism of destruction—the destruction of the whole subsisting social order."[32] In fact, this is the only way that the self knows how to act in the world. The long evolution of modernity has

resulted in a further individualization and abstraction of self-consciousness from the social norms and laws of the integrated and free
Greek social ideal. The skepticism and separation from the social
world of the post-Aristotelian Greeks ends in the moral nihilism and
political fanaticism of the Moderns. For Hegel and later for Marx,
morality divorced from social ethics represents the theoretical expression of this historical transition. Moral philosophy is the philosophy
of the Greek and German Enlightenment and expresses the decay of
man himself.[33] But it is a form of alienation necessary for further
self-development.

The individual is divided against his or her self in that duty and
inclinations, reason and feelings collide—just as society is divided
against itself in that freedom and liberty, moral autonomy and the
inclinations of self-interest clash. This is an historical period characterized by individual political action without a political culture, by
private rights and liberties without public freedoms. Morality is the
last and highest stage in the development of the Objective Spirit and—
according to Walsh—represents "the synthesis of the ethical world of
the Greeks, where spirit is sunk in objectivity, and of the individualistic culture of the post-Hellenic times, where spirit was self-
estranged."[34] But in reality it is a failed synthesis, according to Shklar,
for Kantianism is thus "both a response to and a perpetuation of a
political vacuum" caused by the French Revolution and the rise of
political individualism.[35] By attempting to unite the Greek and modern worlds, it has fallen back behind its own assumptions of moral
positivism and political individualism; and in the process it rationalizes the chief defects of modernity.

Overcoming the alienation of the Enlightenment and the estrangement of the subject from universal cultural values (ethos), Kantian
morality attempts to reunite the particular and the universal, moral
subjectivity and moral objectivity. Kant recognizes the problem and
attempts to solve it with a synthesis of the modern focus on individual
moral choice and the universal laws of the classical tradition. While
Hegel's early writings on religion and natural law are critical of the
Kantian categorical imperative as being too formalistic and morally
oppressive, the analysis and critique of the "moral point of view" in
the *Phenomenology* deals with the incoherence of the logical structure
of morality, and the hypocrisy underlying any form of moral action
in modern culture. With the distinction between moral freedom and
natural necessity that is reflected in Kant's distinctions between practical and pure reason, morality and physics, and duty and nature,
there is—for Hegel—an indifference between the theology and activ-

ities of nature and moral consciousness, an indifference that cannot be resolved within "the moral point of view." Throughout this section, Hegel is aware of the dilemma of ethical objectivity in morality and further recognizes the problem of grounding the validity of moral decisions in the concept of pure moral self-consciousness itself—that is, the postulates of moral reasoning in the "Dialectic" of the *Critique of Practical Reason*. In order for there to be true moral action, there must also be a harmony between moral duty and external nature (happiness), a harmony between morality and sensibility (unity of internal nature), and a unity between the final purpose of self-consciousness and the theology of nature as maintained by God (ontological harmony).[36] These postulates ground the very possibility of morality itself.

> For the Notion gives it this explicit character, viz. that all reality in general has essential being for it only so far as it is in conformity with duty; and this essential being it characterizes as knowledge, i.e. as in immediate unity with the actual self. Hence this unity is itself actual, it is a moral, actual consciousness. This now, *qua* consciousness, pictures its content to itself as an object, viz. as the final purpose of the world, as harmony of morality and all reality. But since it thinks of this unity as *object*, and is not the Notion which has mastery over the object as such, the unity is a negative of self-consciousness for it, or it falls outside of it, as something beyond its actual existence, and yet at the same time is something that *also* has *being*, but a being existing only in thought.[37]

Hegel also questions the very existence of the realm of pure self-consciousness or duty. "There is no moral, perfect actual, self-consciousness."[38] How real or valid are these postulates in the context of our modern culture? The inability to relate correctly the dual aspects of the antinomies ends in the modern tragedy of morality. Hegel contends that the political, cultural, and economic foundations of the ethical life have been undermined, with the result that the very possibility of morality has been negated. The Kantian postulates of the summum bonum (moral duty as happiness), individual moral freedom, immortality, and God are the transcendental conditions on which morality is grounded and made possible. Hegel's concern here is for an analysis of the logical structure of morality and its method of justification; it is a restatement of the dilemma of ethical objectivity in morality. For him, the transcendental postulates that ground moral action are themselves justified only in terms of moral action.[39] Kantian morality is thus founded on not only a logical circularity, but also a contradiction within the *Critique of Practical Reason* between the Analytic (principles and transcendental deduction of morality) and the Dialectic (postulates of morality) of pure reason—which makes its arguments incoherent. It is a contradiction between actuality and pure consciousness (duty). The categorical imperative must assume something about the nature of actual existence, while at the same time claiming for itself a status of pure duty and removal from the actual. To act in the world, consciousness must be made actual; but the nature of the moral point of view requires a pure abstraction for all reality. To act morally, therefore, undermines the very possibility of morality; this is the foundation of the Kantian contradiction, and what Hegel calls "moral displacement."[40]

The postulates of pure reason are therefore embroiled in a series of epistemological contradictions. There is a split or indifference between morality and the object of morality, duty and the real world of moral activity. There is also a question in Hegel's mind as to whether the realization of moral duty was ever really intended, since it would end the moral point of view.[41] There is thus an hypocrisy built into this stage of the Spirit's development in the *Phenomenology*. "The moral point of view is at bottom radically incoherent, and the postulates only distract attention from that fact."[42] Robinson sees the central issue as that of bad faith and hypocrisy. They both accompany morality because "moral experience has transcended ethical life and culture by leaving behind elements which finish by taking their revenge on morality."[43] The very development of modernity as the rise of political, cultural, and moral individualism results in a social vacuum, which has only further intensified the split between culture and morality, morality and nature. This has left us with the crisis of modernity.

The real world is contaminated by contingencies, utilitarian inclinations, external social causes, natural necessities, and unintended consequences—which block the application of any set of independent moral norms of pure reason. At the same time, however, Kant withdraws from objectivity (the world) into abstract freedom and rationality. The choice of moral maxims and laws influenced by these external circumstances, and the necessity to choose and act in the real world, mean that one is no longer acting according to the dictates of pure, a priori rationality.[44] The individual—by being abstracted from the ethical life of the community and the irrationality of the social world—acts in bad faith by refusing to recognize all those circumstances that affect the nature and substance of the moral imperative. Hegel is here expanding his critique of Kant to include the effects of the Kantian antinomies on the indifference, fragmentation, and alienation between humanity and nature. He is thus placing the problem of Kantian moral philosophy in a broader framework of the displacement caused by modern culture, of which Kantian philosophy is an objective manifestation.

Flay writes that, from Hegel's perspective, *Moralität* is the means to overcome the schizophrenia of a culture grounded in the desires of an atomistic utilitarianism (absolute freedom) and the drive toward a universal general will (social totality); as the anarchy and terror of the French Revolution dissolve the moral bonds of society, the social origins of morality are displaced onto the pure individual.[45] But the level of Kantian moral philosophy is fraught with its own contradictions, inconsistencies, and irrationalities; it moves beyond them into the stage of conscience. Here the dichotomies between the external universal and the internal particular, moral duty and utilitarian inclination, and the knowing (theory) and the acting (practice) of the moral point of view are transcended in the immediate presence of conscience itself. Morality was the stage in which moral law moved from the external general will of the state to the individual. While at the phenomenological stage of conscience, moral law is further interiorized in the immediate judgments and actions of the individual. It represents a return to the immediacy of "sense certainty," as the *Phenomenology* comes full circle.[46] However, this stage contains the fulfillment of Kant's kingdom of ends, as the plurality of consciences requires an objective expression of conscientious judgments and duty in the form of language in order for public action to be viewed as stemming from moral obligations. Moral action must be socially recognized as such in order to be valid. This presupposes that a "community of finite individuals, grounded in conscience but nevertheless finite and only attempting to participate in that universal ground, comes into being by mutual recognition of each other's attempts."[47] Though Hegel retreats to the Absolute Spirit and the realms of art, religion, and philosophy to finish the *Phenomenology*, he will later return in the *Philosophy of Right* to his earlier insight that the Absolute Spirit is ultimately realized in the life of the ethical community—the state.[48]

HEGEL AND THE ANCIENTS: THE YEARNING FOR HELLAS

Certainly one of the most important aspects of Hegel's social philosophy is his return to the Aristotelian model of ethics in which ethics, political philosophy, and political economy are united into a comprehensive and integrated whole, as seen in Chapter Two. Hegel was one of the first modern theorists to have read both Aristotle's *Nicomachean Ethics* and *Politics* along with the works of Steuart, Ferguson, Hume, Smith, Say, and Ricardo in modern political economy.[49] In fact, Riedel argues convincingly that the earliest social-ethics work of Hegel to have been preserved—*Das System der Sittlichkeit (System of Ethical Life)*, written in 1802—corresponds at points with Aristotle's *Politics*. One could easily expand this comparison to include the formal structure of both their works in ethics. Hegel responds to the individualism and lack of historical and social elements in Kant's moral philosophy by returning to the classical traditions in general and to the Aristotelian conception of social ethics in particular. As Ritter says, "In his adoption of the standpoint of ethical life, Hegel latches on to the tradition of 'politics' deriving from Aristotle."[50]

Hegel (and later Marx) represents the tail end of a long line of German intellectuals, poets, and philosophers who have tended to look back to the "distant skies of Greece" and the political and aesthetic ideals of Greek society for their inspiration and models of social and ethical life. For Winckelmann, Goethe, Herder, von Humboldt, Hölderlin, and Schiller, the polis represented an ideal by which to measure the inadequacies and strengths of modernity.[51]

> It was precisely in Greek literature and art that the humanist struggle against the degradation of man by the capitalist division of labour found a shining example, for these were the expressions of a society which—for its free citizens, the only ones who count in this matter—still stood this side of such a social structure. Thus it could serve as the ideal and model of a movement which wrote the restoration of the integrity of man on its banner.[52]

Schiller, in particular, had a powerful impact on both Hegel and Marx.[53] He wrote his first work looking back to the Hellenic ideal in his poem "The Gods of Greece," but it was with the publication of *On the Aesthetic Education of Man* in 1795—when Hegel was 25 years old—that his real impact was felt.[54] Schiller saw in the Greek aesthetic a powerful vision of the "ideal Man," which could be used to overcome the fragmentation of modern social life and its philosophical expression in the Kantian antinomies. By returning to Greece, he hoped to transcend all forms of social and cultural fragmentation—"the dismemberment of being and reason"—by integrating the sensibilities and reason, beauty and freedom, labor and enjoyment, and duty and inclinations. "Combining fullness of form with the fullness of content, at once philosophic and creative, at the same time tender and energetic, we see them [the Greeks] uniting the youthfulness of fantasy with the manliness of reason in a splendid humanity."[55] With the rise of modernity "eternally chained to only one single little fragment of the whole, Man himself grew to be only a fragment of the whole." Man had now given way "to an ingenious piece of machinery, in which out of the botching together of a vast number of lifeless parts a collective mechanical life results."[56] Schiller felt that only after the epistemological, moral, and aesthetic dualisms of modernity were overcome would the political and economic divisions also be eliminated.

Many of the same themes running throughout Schiller's works reappear in Hegel's and later in Marx's writings: (1) the idea that everyone carries the moral ideal of humanity within his or her own self; (2) the attempt to transcend social fragmentation through an harmonious reintegration of the individual with society and the individual with self (the aesthetic, rational, and physical sides of humanity); (3) the need for moral autonomy and human dignity; (4) the development of human capabilities and potentialities to their fullest; (5) the defining of personality in terms of freedom and potentiality; (6) the critique of the utilitarian notion of pleasure, and its replacement by the idea that pleasure is the realization of the good life and the expansion of human powers and faculties; (7) overcoming the necessity of nature by realizing that man is the giver of form and law to nature, while at the same time reconciling the dualism between man and nature; (8) the importance of *Bildung* (education, cultivation of the personality and the higher needs of human individuals); and, finally, (9) the human power to change society creatively according to the ideals of reason and the potentialities of humanity.

Hegel—"drunk with Greece as Schiller"[57]—begins his intellectual career and his discussion of ethics by reflecting on the importance of the Hebrew, Greek, and German classical traditions in his *Early Theological Writings*.[58] This is a return to the classical model of both morality and political philosophy, where the two fields were not kept isolated and fragmented from each other. The very analysis of the question of moral rationality evolves into an interest in social ethics and political reasoning. "For Hegel, in contrast, morality can only receive a concrete content in politics, in the design of the society we have to further and sustain."[59] The realization of the human self—

the development of self-consciousness, and the coming to be of the Other—can only be accomplished within the political community (*Gemeinschaft*), as opposed to civil society (*Gesellschaft*). The community is the realization of man's ontological structure, of his being.

> Thus the state which is fully rational will be one which expresses in its institutions and practices the most important ideas and norms which its citizens recognize, and by which they define their identity. And this will be the case because the state expresses the articulation of the Idea, which rational man comes to see as the formula of necessity underlying all things, which is designed to come to self-consciousness in man. So that the rational state will restore Sittlichkeit, the embodiment of the highest norms in an ongoing public life. It will recover what was lost with the Greeks, but on a higher level. For the fully developed state will incorporate the principle of the individual rational will judging universal criteria, the very principle that undermined and eventually destroyed the Greek polis.[60]

The state or ethical community through its laws, mores, customs, and institutions is seen as the essence of man's being. Community is not interpreted as an artificial contract or social construct for the furtherance of individual self-interests, or as an instrument for social order. Rather, it is viewed as a condition for the possibility of human self-realization, self-consciousness, and social freedom. However, this is only part of Hegel's theory of ethical life and must be incorporated into his political economy and theory of civil society.

> Yet Hegel could not agree with the predominant modern view of the state as essentially an artificial product, resulting from a social contract. Though law for him implied a more self-conscious level of understanding than did custom, he was not prepared to grant that law arose solely out of individual intelligence and creative will. The difference between Greek and modern ethical conceptions lay for him in the difference what is created and what is discovered. For the Greek philosophers the principles governing state and society were not created by the individual will but are already existent in the universe. The state involved for Plato the discovery of rational principles, because the principles were implicit in the nature of things. The state was therefore natural as social living was natural; it was only the individual in isolation that was unnatural and illogical. With this fundamental conception Hegel heartily agreed.[61]

In his analysis of natural law, Hegel further attacks the positions of Kant in the *Critique of Practical Reason* and Hobbes in the *Leviathan*. Hegel sees in the development of individualism, the instrumentalism of the ethical and political community, the privatization and atomization of social life, and the positivization of the community. Hegel's goal was to synthesize Christian individualism with the Greek political community—the modern ideals of political freedom within a public context of social eudaimonia. He wished to transcend the one-sided emphasis in Greek and liberal thought on either the community or the individual, and to finally escape from the modern "tragedy in the realm of the ethical."[62] Kant's individualism and abstractionism is, for Hegel, a reflection of the atomism that characterizes Enlightenment philosophy, which further results in the dualism of reason and nature, individual and society, and rationality and instrumentality. The individual becomes alienated from both society and nature; and upon this alienation, modern political science and economics have built their house of cards. Rejecting the moral antinomies of Kantian philosophy, Hegel sees that it is only through language, work, and cultural experience that the subject grows into a self-conscious individual. In *The Positivity of the Christian Religion*, he uses the method of juxtaposing the Greek and Jewish cultural and social experiences in order to dig deeper into the positivity (hierarchy and reification) of the Christian church. The Christian religion undermines moral autonomy and free will; the Greek experience was exactly the opposite.

> As free men the Greeks and Romans obeyed laws laid down by themselves, obeyed men whom they had themselves appointed to office, waged wars on which they had themselves decided, gave their property, exhausted their passions, and sacrificed their lives by thousands for an end which was their own. They neither learned nor taught [a moral system] but evinced by their actions the moral maxims which they could call their very own. In public as in private and domestic life, every individual was a free man, one who lived by his own laws. The idea of his country or of his state was the invisible and higher reality for which he strove, which impelled him to effort; it was the final end of *his* world or in his eyes the final end of *the* world.[63]

Where Christianity has created ecclesiastical rituals, liturgies, and sacraments with its dogmatic moral principles and laws, which only tend to "dumbfound the laws of reason" and deprive human beings of their freedom and autonomy,[64] the classical world of the Greeks offered man a society that was an externalization and actualization of his true self. However, with the wars of imperialism, the acquisition of material wealth, and its resulting economic and social inequality in the polis, the moral integrity and rationality of the Greek system began to change. The concept of citizen in the public sphere was reduced to a few individuals seeking their private gain in the political arena. There were no longer high social ideals that formed the foundation for the community. Sovereignty over the state fell to the aristocracy and a small group of elite technocrats.

The citizens had lost what Hegel—quoting Montesquieu—calls "virtue." This is an internal principle of cultivation of the soul (*Bildung*). Citizens lost the desire to participate and make the laws; they lost the very ideals of state and citizen, the objective and subjective elements of a free society. "The picture of the state as a product of his own energies disappeared from the citizen's soul."[65] In the end—Hegel argues—the state wound up acting to secure the rights to property, while the rights of the citizen were lost. What was really lost was political freedom. "All political freedom vanished also; the citizen's right gave him only a right to the security of that property which now filled his entire world."[66]

The change was so dramatic; the loss of citizenship, community, and political freedom was so traumatic; and the isolation of the individual and the loss of meaning and ultimate purpose was so filled with terror that a world of heavenly immortality had to be created to give purpose and security to finite existence. Christian metaphysics was founded on the destruction of the Greek world, the rise of individualism, and the decay of human rationality.[67] With these political and religious changes came a belief in the corrupt nature of man, with the result that everything good and positive about humanity was externalized into a belief in an all-knowing, powerful, and just God. The political ideals of the classical Greeks were transformed into the mystical doctrines of the church and the metaphysical ideals of the kingdom of heaven, outside the reach of human self-determination. This completed the religious fragmentation of man—the Unhappy Consciousness. "The doctrine of God's objectivity is a counterpart to the conception and slavery of man."[68] Many of the later objections of nineteenth-century German philosophers to religion and metaphysics are already contained in these early writings of Hegel, which were unknown to them.

In Christianity and Judaism, there is a tension between self-consciousness and reason, on the one hand, and moral slavery, on the other—that is, a tension between reason and faith. Religion attempts to give a foundation to moral laws; but in the process, it undermines the very possibility of moral action. It undermines the possibility of rational reflection, decision-making, and individual choice. In Greece—according to Hegel—morality as manifested in the legal system and its laws was an expression of the general will and collective wisdom of its citizens. Inequality of wealth was controlled by restrictions on the ownership of property (as instituted by Solon and Lycurgus). The Greeks recognized that internal class divisions would have undermined the integrity of their political community, with the result that "the freedom of the impoverished might have been jeopardized and they might have fallen into political annihilation."[69] On the other hand—according to Hegel—the Jews were all equal in their subservience to God; they had no rights or freedoms, no political community, no public discourse or social responsibility, and no objective manifestation of a general will.

Though Hegel is aware of the Jewish customs of the Jubilee and Sabbatical years in the Mosaic legal tradition, and of the Jewish notions of stewardship over the land and covenant with God, he saw in these traditions only a base subservience to the external authority and physical force of God and an inability to define and institutionalize rights and freedoms. Because the preconditions (constitutional law and a legislative body) did not exist for a free society, because of the general passivity of Jewish political life (brought about by a desire for the maintenance of physical existence, and no more), and because the Jews tended to flee from reality into the realm of pure ideas (Messianics, Pharisees, and Essenes), they became slaves to an external authority: God. In the end, "the great tragedy of the Jewish people is no Greek tragedy."[70] There was no dualism in the Jewish tradition between subjectivity and objectivity, the divine and the human morality. No conflict between Creon and Antigone, Orestes and Clytaemnestra that had to be transcended.[71] No conflicts that had to be overcome in history. There were immense hardships and sufferings, but no tragic contradictions.

Hegel's treatment of the Jewish tradition is very concise and critical. He believes that the Jewish legal code and the mindless subservience to it have resulted in a moral slavery in which the possibilities for individual development of ethical reason and moral autonomy are made impossible. Judaism is a "life spent in a monkish preoccupation with petty, mechanical, spiritless, and trivial usages."[72] This positive religion creates a cultural milieu in which self-respect and human dignity—the foundation stones of morality—become impossible, since the moral values are imposed by an alien, transcendent, legal system and not by the transcendental powers of reason itself. The passivity, formal legalism, and moral slavery of Judaism have been passed on to Christianity. Religion relies on faith, miracles, and external authority in order to justify its claims to universality and necessity. True morality can only be passed on by the principles of pure reason; and when true morality is institutionalized, there is no fragmentation between individual principles and social norms. Throughout his analysis of Judaism, Hegel presupposes the Kantian assumptions of moral epistemology with their emphasis on creativity and the imaginative synthesis of rationalism and empiricism. With the development of the positivity of religion, the natural right to the development of human faculties (reason and will) have been neglected or unrecognizably distorted.

> The fundamental error at the bottom of a church's entire system is that it ignores the rights pertaining to every faculty of the human mind, in particular to the chief of them, reason. Once the church's system ignores reason, it can be nothing save a system which despises man. The powers of the mind have a domain of their own, and this domain was separated off for science by Kant.[73]

The self-deception, false consciousness, and religious terror that accompany religion are themes similar to those taken up by Marx in his critique of the "opium of the people," as well as his yearning for Hellas.

SOCIAL ETHICS AND POLITICAL ECONOMY IN HEGEL

It is with the work of Hegel in the nineteenth century that the questions of moral philosophy become reintegrated back into the classical natural law tradition and transformed into ethical and social questions. The relationship between individual decision-making, human motives and passions now begins to be viewed within a social, political, and economic context. "What passions and what ends the individual has and can have are a matter of the kind of social structure in which the individual finds himself."[74] With Hegel and—in turn—with Marx, there is a shift in the manner in which moral questions are handled. With the critique of positivity, empiricism, and individualism in Hegel, questions of morality become questions about the development of self-consciousness within the community, about the relationships between community and civil society, and about the differences between morality and social ethics, individual freedom and social freedom. The parameters within which moral philosophy had previously developed—whether in terms of the moral rationalism of Hobbes and Locke, the moral positivism of Hume, or the transcendental subjectivity of pure reason in Kant—now shift to questions of virtue, freedom, morality, and justice with a new sociological premise: Man is a social being, and no issue relating to morality can be divorced from the historical and social institutions that structure and define its conceptual frameworks and moral principles.

Previously, man was seen to be free in a state of nature, in a social contract, or as an autonomous moral being. But with the raising of the issue of the relation between morality and society—namely, ethics and sociology (political economy)—the meaning of morality and freedom also began to change. Questions began to develop as to how social institutions could structure, limit, or enhance the realization of moral autonomy and how the potentialities for moral enlightenment and social action could be inhibited by social restraints and false consciousness (Stoicism, Skepticism, Unhappy Consciousness, moral individualism, and so on) and by social structures (slavery, serfdom, alienated culture, the political anarchy of the French Revolution and Terror, and so on).[75]

The first systematic treatment of political economy is found in Hegel's early work of the Jena period called the *System of Ethical Life*. Here he views the ethical life (*Sittlichkeit*) as an organic social system in which the universal—as the objective cultural and ethical values of society—is indifferent to or integrated into the moral life of the subject. Thus, morality and ethics are reunited again in Hegel's work, as in the classical tradition of the Greeks. Previously opposed categories such as the universal and the particular, and morality and natural law, become identical or are characterized by what he calls "absolute indifference."[76] The ethical universal no longer appears—as in the Kantian tradition—to be something objective and alien; it no longer appears as a sign of domination of the law over the individual. The ethical life of the moral community represents the possibilities of the virtuous life of the individual.[77] This synthesis brought about by education (*Bildung*) results in a realization of the essence of man, beauty, and freedom. Note that, through this very dense and abstract text, Hegel's discussion of the nature of ethical life clearly reflects a return to the Greek tradition with its emphasis on virtue, education (*paideia*), the ethical community (*politeia*), and the harmony of the universal and the particular. Where there is an interesting break with the Greek tradition is in Hegel's treatment of the movement of ethical life. Here the transcendence of all individual differences is understood as analogous to the production process, in which the final product shatters the particularity of its different pieces. This is a very nonclassical model on which Hegel bases his understanding of modern culture and the social totality.

Hegel recognizes that there are social forms that mediate between the individual and universal ethical life. These are the social classes: the military aristocracy, the bourgeoisie, and the peasantry. Here—too—description of their roles in society, their functions, their relations to the other classes, and their various virtues seem to take much from Aristotle's *Nicomachean Ethics*. This is also true of Hegel's interpretation of equality as equality within a class but inequality and utility between classes. Hegel's analysis of justice is distinctly reminiscent of Aristotle's treatment of reciprocity, critique of the Pythagorean view of justice, and—finally—the view that value and price of a commodity are determined by universal need as measured by money. The analysis is too sketchy to contain many implications for a coherent social theory, but it is clear that Hegel has returned to Aristotle to get some very important social categories, which he then joins to his readings in modern political economy.

In this first systematic modern treatment and integration of ethics and economic theory, Hegel introduces the notion of the "system of needs." This term refers to the integrated nature of modern society, as it is based on the socially interdependent creation and satisfaction of human needs in the marketplace. No one is independent; there are no Robinson Crusoe–type persons, since everyone is dependent on everyone else for their physical existence. The value of what is produced, in turn, is determined by the workings of the market—"an alien power" (*eine wenig erkennbare, unsichtbare, unberechenbare Macht*) over which any single individual has no control.[78] The value of production and needs are determined by the unconscious and indifferent workings of the economic system—what Hegel, following the Scottish Enlightenment economists Adam Ferguson and Adam Smith, calls in his later works "civil society." Hegel's treatment of the market is taken from classical political economy, as he relies heavily on the laws of supply and demand to distribute both the economic surplus and the technical skills of the population. In a pathbreaking work on Hegel's economics, Lukács—quoting from Rosenkranz—states that Hegel's view of civil society, need, labor, the division of labor, poverty, taxation, and the state are taken from James Steuart's *Inquiry into the Principles of Political Economy* (1767), which Hegel first read in early 1797 at Frankfurt while writing a draft of *The Spirit of Christianity and Its Fate*. In fact, Hegel wrote a lengthy commentary on this work in the spring of that year—a commentary that has not survived.[79] It is during the Jena period (and—Lukács believes—even earlier in Frankfurt) that Hegel in his *Fragment of a System* (1800)—having already read Smith—appropriates the idea and importance of work as the central form of human activity, mediating between subjectivity and objectivity. Work as a form of "purposive destruction" destroys the reified positivity of the ethical life of modernity and the deadening fragmentation and mechanization of the class-structured workplace. It is also at this time that, through newspapers and journals, Hegel is kept abreast of the latest developments surrounding the Poor Laws, factory legislation, and parliamentary debates taking place in Britain around the turn of the century.

Hegel sees the market as a natural mechanism satisfying human needs; it is a social mechanism whose nature is balanced in equilibrium between the totality of needs and the ability of the economy to realize it. Questions about the ability to satisfy the needs of society with sufficient production and the choice of certain types of needs are both settled within the market mechanism. He refers to the market disturbances ("empirical oscillations") of the natural equilibrium of the economy as "external conditions" and "empirical accidents."[80] However, the examples that he gives to explain these disturbances undermine his characterization of them as external to the system of needs itself. Poor harvests may be due to external climatic, geographical, or even astronomical conditions; but lower prices and lost markets resulting from the competition of a neighboring community reflect internal disturbances to the natural equilibrium.

For Hegel it is the role of the modern state to intervene and reestablish the lost universality and harmony of the system of needs. The government must consider the implications and effects of the "abstraction of equilibrium"—the finite indifference or unconscious workings of the market—since it can result in prices being too high (thereby making it more difficult for people to enjoy life) or too low (making it difficult for a segment of the population to earn a living). Hegel is extremely perceptive of the interaction and interdependence of the economy and the polity. He even recognizes the dangerous aspects of the development within modern society toward economic inequality and a new class system. Though Hegel believes that inequality and social class are necessary features of the modern economy, he also recognizes the new form of master-slave relationship. This is no longer a particular relationship between two individuals, but a universal relationship in which the individual is slave to the class structure and market mechanism itself. Hegel calls it an "absolute particularization and dependence on something abstract, an *ens rationis.*"[81] He describes the business class as having a "bestial contempt for higher things."

> The mass of wealth, the pure universal, the absence of wisdom, is the heart of the matter [*das An-sich*]. The absolute bond of the people, namely ethical principle, has vanished, and the people is dissolved. The government has to work as hard as possible against this inequality and the destruction of the private and the public life wrought by it. It can do this directly in an external way by making high gain more difficult, and if it sacrifices one part of this class to mechanical and factory labor and abandons it to barbarism, it must keep the whole [people] without question in the life possible for it.[82]

These class relationships undermine the integrity and organic solidarity of the social whole (totality), as well as its universality (law). Hegel does not call for dissolution of the class system, but for dissolution of its excessive abuses—in particular, the disproportionate distribution of social wealth and its accompanying system of social domination. The business class—the power broker—is asked to permit greater participation in the ethical life of the community. And while his descriptions of the unconscious workings of the market remind one of Smith's notion of the "invisible hand," it is this reliance on the constitution, on the limiting of inequality, and on the organic nature of society that reminds the reader of Hegel's return to Aristotle and the Greek *politeia*. For both Aristotle and Hegel, the nature of the constitution is much broader than simply an outline of the form of government. Rather, what is at stake is the nature and telos of society, based on universality (law) and citizenship. As if to emphasize these points, Hegel finishes this section with an analysis of justice in both civil and criminal cases, the creation of universal mores in education (*Bildung*), and the direct copying of Aristotle's distinctions between good (democracy, aristocracy, and monarchy) and bad (ochlocracy, oligarchy, and despotism) governments.[83]

Besides the system of needs, there are two other components to the organization of society: the system of justice, and the system of discipline. These three aspects of civil society will be further developed in Hegel's later work, the *Philosophy of Right*. What is of interest in the early formulation of these social structures is that the system of justice (criminal and civil justice) and the system of discipline—which includes education and training as well as discipline and the police— are both viewed as necessary to correct the "tragedy of the ethical life" and the breakdown of the substance of the organic whole. The market dislocations, the class divisions, the division of labor in the factories, the mechanization of human life, the increasing disparity between wealth and poverty, increasing forms of social domination, the blind and unconscious direction of society, and—finally—the personal and social estrangement characteristic of modernity must be held in check and transcended. This is the role of criminal and civil law, the education system, and—if necessary—the police. If the process of fragmentation and estrangement is characteristic of modernity, then so is the dilemma of ethical life. Are these other social institutions adequate to the job of a reintegration and harmonization of the various social components and classes in society? Has Hegel gone too far beyond the classical model by attempting to integrate the classical ideals and rationality of the polis with the irrationality and conflicts of the market mechanism (political economy)? Hegel appears to have used a mechanical response to the problems created by the contradictions between the ethical life of Plato and Aristotle and the economic imperatives of Steuart and Smith. However, he has redirected the critique of modernity away from aesthetics and toward political theory and political economy.

These ideas on political economy are further developed in his Jena economic lectures of 1804–5 entitled *Realphilosophie*, in the sections on the philosophy of nature and the spirit. These lectures, which would not have been available to Marx, contain some of Hegel's most critical statements regarding the development of the capitalist system. The mechanization and specialization of labor in the workplace has proceeded to the point "that because of the abstraction of labour, [the worker] becomes more mechanical, more deadened and more mindless. . . . The strength of the self consists of its rich comprehensiveness; this is lost."[84] Throughout these lectures, Hegel condemns the stupefying conditions and effects of mechanization, the loss of a diverse personality, the misery of the class system, and the irrationality of the market. It is a system that Hegel characterizes as "a life of the dead with its own momentum (*ein sich in sich bewegendes Leben des Toten*)."[85]

All these ideas will find their way into his later masterpiece, the

Philosophy of Right. The tragedy of modern ethical life becomes expressed in the Rousseauean language of the dualism between the bourgeois and the citizen, civil society and the state. The radical critiques of modernity from his earlier economic lectures become lost in the overall goal of transcending all divisions and conflicts in society: Aesthetics regains its supremacy over politics just at the point when politics assumes center stage in his writings. In this way, the state takes on a key role in his thinking. This later writing is also an expression of the change from Hegel's early outspoken criticisms of the structures of political economy and the mechanization and fragmentation of work (the *System of Ethical Life* and the *Jenaer Realphilosophie*) to his later accommodations with modernity. Hobbes's political theory with its hypothesis of the state of nature and the *bellum omnium contra omnes* and Smith's notions of the division of labor in the workplace, self-interest, market rationality, and the invisible hand of the market are still the central structural features of Hegel's theory of civil society. His general attitude to them has softened substantially, along with his coming to terms with modernity. He argues that, by "developing itself independently to totality, the principle of particularity passes over into universality, and only there does it attain its truth."[86] What appeared under a very critical light in his early works is now subdued in his later writings. The particularity of civil society with its emphasis on self-interest and the satisfaction of individual needs, caprices, and subjective desires; the market competition that is likened to a civil war of all against all; and the mechanization of the organization of production, all become only moments toward an integrated and harmonious society—toward the ethical universal. Rather than stressing the negative aspects of these changes in political economy, Hegel stresses the hidden structural universality they entail, or at least could entail.

> At the same time, this abstraction of one man's skill and means of production from another's completes and makes necessary everywhere the dependence of men on one another and their reciprocal relation of the satisfaction of their other needs. Further, the abstraction of one man's production from another's makes work more and more mechanical, until finally man is able to step aside and install machines in his place.[87]

Hegel views the development of modernity as a dialectical evolution in which "subjective self-seeking turns into the mediation of the particular through the universal."[88] These transformations result in a society characterized by greater social integration and economic inter-relationships rooted in the division of labor, the development of the structural foundations for a community of ethical life, and a greater ability to satisfy general social and individual material needs. The negative aspects of modernity are transcended by the very movement of the Concept (*Begriff*) of modernity itself. The Concept of the state produces its own structural determinations (property, family and civil society) from within itself, as the potentiality of its own Idea. Many of the most disturbing problems are solved within civil society by its own internal development, through the creation of greater social interde-pendency and a developed industrial sphere. Lingering elements of particularity, which might disturb the harmonious functioning of the community, are resolved by the activity of the modern state. The state protects the property as well as the personal and formal liberties of the law and also establishes a legal and court system to maintain order within the system of needs. Hegel is aware of the social psychology of poverty and economic inequality, the creation of a "rabble of pau-pers," the loss of self-respect in a class society, and the broader implications of the loss of political freedoms. However, one real problem here is that Hegel defines self-respect, morality, and individ-ual freedom from within the context of civil society. The standards of social measurement have changed from the ideals of the Greek polis to that of civil society. Hegel has moved from Aristotle to Smith.

The negative structural implications of inequality and poverty are that they violate the principles of a market economy and classical political economy. Hegel's whole philosophy of the state is so inter-connected with classical political economy that he cannot get out of the contradictions established by the market. He says that "excessive poverty" and a "penurious rabble" are part of the very structure and nature of modernity, because society is simply not wealthy enough to solve its own problems. There are two major options: In the first, the wealthy class has the fiscal option of either providing a set of welfare programs from their own pockets to relieve the suffering of the disenfranchised, or else using public services for this purpose. A second option would be to provide work for the unemployed. Both options undermine the logic of capitalist social relations. The first is impossible because self-respect can only come through individual work, and the second is impossible because the major macroeconomic crisis of capitalism has been caused by overproduction and underconsumption of commodities. The state cannot give people work, for that would only exacerbate the economic crisis by producing more in a society already facing overproduction; it cannot give public charity, for this would undermine the whole principle of civil society. Hegel merely states without commentary that in England and Scotland the poor have been left to their fate (economic necessity) as beggars. It is this class contradiction that drives society beyond its own limits (*Grenze*) or barriers (*Schranke*)[89] to an expansion abroad into new undeveloped markets. The economy already has countervailing tendencies that resolve the initial contradictions of the class society. Hegel never recognizes that this involves its own new contradictions and is simply another moment in the dialectic development of the Idea. It will take Marx to develop these points and to show the connections between the internal contradictions of capitalism and the role of the state in maintaining the stability of the social system.

The state is the concrete definition, articulation, and realization of ethics in private and public social institutions; it is the manifestation of the Objective Spirit and the rational embodiment of individual freedoms—"the rational life of self-conscious freedom, the system of the ethical world."[90] The traditional view of the state as the social mechanism designed to protect life, property, and liberties is too narrow for Hegel. Rather, he sees it as the actualization of pure rationality and mind in the ethical ideal of the modern community.[91] The family, economy, and state are structural components of the logic and development of the Idea from its moments as individuality and particularity to universality. All internal divisions within civil society are transcended in the actualization of rationality in the state. "The fundamental characteristic of the State as a political entity is the substantial unity, i.e., the ideality, of its moments."[92] The sovereignty of the state is expressed in the monarchy, which—together with the corporations (interest group organizations)—integrates all the diverse and divisive elements in society into an harmonious whole whose chief goal is the general good.

> What the service of the state really requires is that men shall forgo the selfish and capricious satisfaction of their subjective ends; by this very sacrifice, they acquire the right to find their satisfaction in, but only in, the dutiful discharge of their public functions. In this fact, so far as public business is concerned, there lies the link between universal and particular interests which constitutes both the concept of the state and its inner stability.[93]

Hegel fails to consider the social implications of his appropriation of classical political economy. He fails to take a critical stance to this tradition in his later writings. In turn, his ideals of the Greek ethical life and the communal nature of man are lost in his mechanical and speculative treatment of the nature of the modern state and its role in overcoming internal social and economic contradictions (politics as logic). Marx responds directly to the political theory of Hegel in his *Contribution to the Critique of Hegel's Philosophy of Law*. An analysis of some of these critiques will be contained in Chapter Four. It should also be mentioned here that some of Marx's criticisms of liberalism, with its narrow emphasis on egoism and self-interest, come from Hegel's critiques in the *Phenomenology of Spirit* as well as later works on the abstract individualism of political economy, Kantian morality, and the French Revolution.[94]

KANTIAN AND HEGELIAN ETHICS AND MARX'S POLITICAL ECONOMY

Marx saw the development of moral philosophy in terms similar to Hegel. At the center of his social theory is the concept of man as a species being (*Gattungswesen*), which means that the individual is both a social being and a being within a commonwealth. It is this idea that permeates all of Marx's thought, from the *Paris Manuscripts* of 1844 to *Capital* of 1867. As Avineri states,

> Modern civil society, based on individualism, violates, according to Marx, man as a social being. Individualism in this sense implies a model of man as an entity whose social relations are only means to his own private ends; it regards individual existence as man's supreme purpose, and juxtaposes society to the individual as something external and formal. Such a society cannot, by its very nature, develop a socialized model of man.[95]

It is this notion of man as a social being that lies at the foundation of Marx's social ethics; and this concept mediates every aspect of his philosophy, sociology, and economics. Thus, beginning with his work *On the Jewish Question*, Marx's social ethics can be viewed as a critique of bourgeois individualism and justice, as a critique of the division of labor and alienating social relations of production (the *Paris Manuscripts*), as a critique of moral philosophy divorced from political economy (*The Poverty of Philosophy*), and as a critique of the fetishism of social relations and the idolatry and ideology of capitalist concepts (*Grundrisse* and *Capital*). In all cases, the critique is being leveled by Marx at the theory and reality of capitalism as fundamentally destroying the possibilities of the commonwealth (the materialized ethical substance) or the ethical community (the classless society). In capitalist society, the individual is forced by the necessity for physical survival and economic success to make decisions that undermine the species content of his being and—ultimately—his own individuality and freedom. While this social content was presupposed by Kant, it becomes problematic for Marx. Under these conditions, Kantian philosophy is impossible because moral philosophy must be supplemented by sociology. The two became inseparable.

Marx stresses the fact that personal decisions are dictated and determined by the logic of the market, and species' choices are eliminated from consciousness and the public sphere. Aristotle had recognized that a change in the political constitution of society results in new standards of justice. Democracies, aristocracies, and oligarchies produce different types of individuals with different social ideals, political institutions, and ethical standards. The dialectical interplay between the individual and society is also accepted by Marx. An example of this would be Marx's underlying ethical values, which affect his understanding of the nature of man and the structures of social institutions. It is through the social organization of work and the democratic organization of the economy and polity that the individual defines and creates his or her self in society. These are the universals that create the species being in concrete institutions and further determine the historical nature of the human being. They provide the structural framework of the political economy and supply the very possibilities for self-realization.

Marx took over the radicalization of the Kantian community of ends and Hegel's notion of the concrete universal of the social ethic in abstract right, morality, and ethics (the family, civil society, and the state). Through the process of the Feuerbachian transformative method and critique, he began to analyze the process of social production and the class society.[96] Understanding the Marxian concept of ethics entails also understanding the revolution that occurred in moral philosophy and critical social science in the nineteenth century, along with a rethinking of the world in light of the German turn to Greek social and ethical thought. Hegel transformed Kantian morality into a question of the state and politics, while Marx transformed it into a question of power, class, and economics. From being simply a critique of political economy, it became a theory of social praxis and workers' revolution. Marx's goal is to denounce the moral content and bad faith of the ideologies of natural law theorists, utilitarians, and political economists—which, he believed, were the intellectual barriers to a self-conscious community built around the moral criteria of human dignity and individual freedom.[97] Marx turned away from modern moral philosophy with its roots and assumptions grounded in self-interest, private property, and capital accumulation. Therefore, we can see that his moral philosophy was inextricably bound to his ideas of sociology and economics, in ways similar to Aristotle and Hegel.

The objectification and alienation of work in the process of production, in the objects created by the process, in the self, and in the community destroy the life activity of man, his relation to nature, his species being, and his relation to other individuals in society. If society and politics are—as Hegel believes—the real content and foundation for the concrete universality of the moral will and obligation, then— for Marx—the concrete content of Kantian morality can only be this alienation "from his own body, external nature, his mental life, and his human life."[98] The key to the transcendental subjectivity of morality lies in political economy; the key to self-consciousness, freedom, moral autonomy, and the kingdom of ends lies in the structures that bind us to everyday life.

According to Marx, it is within the context of social relations of production that man manifests himself as a species being. Rather than being simply a means to further life, productive activity is an essential expression of the human being. Man's contact with others and his theoretical appropriation of his inorganic self in nature is accomplished in the very act of creating—through objectification— the institutional arrangements and structures that identify and give meaning to human life. Marx's concept of work is here joined to the classical Greek and German notions of *paideia* and *Bildung*, and represents a very radical treatment of those ideas. The constitution of society cultivates the social nature of man. Marx is following Hegel's integration of classical ethics and political economy within a method that emphasizes the importance of physical and cultural labor in a material world of social and natural relationships. These institutions are created within the dual moments of objectivity and subjectivity— that is, within alienated private property and the subjective division of labor. As a result, the possibilities of self-consciousness and a reintegration of the individual into the moral whole of the community are lost. Life itself becomes simply a means to the furtherance of capital appropriation.

> The practical construction of an *objective world*, the *manipulation* of inorganic nature, is the confirmation of man as a conscious species-being, i.e., a being who treats the species as his own being or himself as a species-being. . . . The object of labor is, therefore the objectification of man's species life; for he no longer reproduces himself merely intellectually, as in consciousness, but actively and in a real sense, and as he sees his own reflection in a world he has constructed.[99]

Private property—like the gods—appears as the objective manifestation and derived result of alienated class relationships in bourgeois society. The social products and socially constructed wealth of society are divided on the basis of power and authority relationships, directly connected to the ownership and control of the means of production. Marx has transformed the subject-substance theme from Spinoza and Hegel into an analysis of the social relations that underlie the division of labor and property ownership in modern industrial society. These social relationships appear in classical political economy only in their outward forms as contracts, capital, property, and the universal laws of the marketplace. Marx believes that a critical social science must uncover the deep structures and unconscious social layers that are the real determining factors in understanding modernity.

This dualism between the sociological (class and social relations) and the economic (technological and economic rationality of the marketplace, including its utilitarian ideology) factors of production forms the basis of Marx's critique of both false consciousness and alienation, on the one hand, and positivism and science, on the other. Self-consciousness is constituted when the working class sees itself as Subject—as the truth of the objective economic laws—since behind the technical and instrumental rationality of the economic system lie class oppression, exploitation, and social alienation. Behind the appearances stands the social reality of authority relations based on property, power, and class. The goal of analysis pushes us toward creation, within a new economic and political community, of a common being of man, humanity who will understand these relationships—understand their historical evolution, their internal mechanisms and laws (the logic of capital), and the possibilities they present for social change.

Marx's ethics is grounded in the call for a human society. "Thus society is the accomplished union of man with nature, the veritable resurrection of nature, the realized naturalism of man and the realized humanism of nature."[100] It is a self-conscious society of ends—in which the criteria for rationality do not lie in instrumental elements and utilitarian presuppositions, but rather in the free, democratic, and articulated expressions of the moral community. No longer to be based on arbitrary needs, the false universalism of the liberal democratic state, or the anarchy of private production, the new society will be a true democracy that synthesizes the universal commonwealth and the particular species being. This requires not only the technological achievements of industrialism and a new form of rationality by which society will create and control its own history, but also a coming together of modernity and the classical traditions— which calls for rational self-reflection and a spiritual recapitulation of the cultural foundations of modernity. For Marx it is very clear that this necessitates a return to the Ancients. When all is accomplished, the Kantian questions of modern morality with their emphasis on individual decisions will again become important. But this time it will be integrated into a social context that encourages and nurtures the development of personal autonomy and a self-legislative moral being.

Alienation in the early works of Marx was explained as the situation where subjective class relationships are perceived in terms of objective property relationships. In the later works, the concept of fetishism refers to the particular circumstances of economic laws holding the position formerly held by religion and the church before the Enlightenment. Universal, unalterable, immutable, and totally rational are some of the characteristics attributed to the new economic system. But it is ultimately a system that devalues society and social relationships into their abstract universal forms of price and marketability; this is the false universality of exchange value. This perspective of Marx certainly relies on the criticism of economic exchange found in the moral philosophy of Kant, and the latter's recognition of the importance for moral action of an autonomous and free individual. In his work *From Substance to Subject: Studies in Hegel,* Rotenstreich asserts that Marx's notion of the fetishism of commodities comes from Kant's analysis of the "realm of ends."[101] He quotes from Kant's *Foundations of the Metaphysics of Morals:*

In the realm of ends, everything has either a price or a dignity. Whatever has a price can be replaced by something else as its equivalent; on the

other hand, whatever is above all price, and therefore admits of no
equivalent, has dignity. That which is related to general human inclinations and needs has a market price. . . . But that which constitutes the
condition under which alone something can be an end in itself does not
have mere relative worth, i.e., a price, but an intrinsic worth, i.e., dignity.

Now morality is the condition under which alone a rational being can
be an end in itself, because only through it is it possible to be a legislative
member in the realm of ends.[102]

If this is Marx's understanding of the relation between morality
(dignity) and price (fetishism), then the idea of developing a moral
philosophy with its universal and abstract maxims of moral behavior
would be contradictory to Marx's understanding of philosophy. Moral
philosophy becomes impossible when the social content of the philosophy would be moral fetishism. Here again, Kantian morality—which
we have seen start with a critique of empiricism, but end in an
affirmation of empiricism—now begins with moral autonomy and
human dignity, but in the end undermines both, along with the very
possibility of morality itself. It is at this point that *Capital*, which
begins with the contradiction between use value and exchange value—
or the social production of products for individual use and the private
appropriation of commodities for the production of individual profits—may be viewed as the completion of Marx's ethical theory. From
his critique of religion, the state, natural law theory, and utilitarian
moral philosophy, to this critique of the class structure and economic
rationality of the marketplace, Marx is criticizing various forms of
"metaphysical subtleties and theological niceties"—that is, the various
aspects of theological manifestation, whether in the form of an
ontological concept or an economic and political concept (and their
structural and historical correlatives).

In the earlier manuscripts Marx discussed the process of objectification in terms of the objects of labor themselves, but in *Capital* he is
interested in the social totality of the economic laws of capital development and accumulation. In both places the critique focuses on the
alienation of human consciousness and human community, which
makes self-consciousness and freedom impossible. If laws of economic
and social development have godlike qualities and are viewed as the
realization of rationality, then the possibility of moral action and
human freedom is lost. But Marx kept that one truth of Hegel close
to his heart: The Subject is the truth of Objectivity. What appear to
be objective laws of economics—grounded in the universal psychology

of the state of nature or utilitarian behavioral presuppositions—are in reality only the theoretical and institutional expressions of a particular, phenomenal form of social-class relationships (subjectivity). This is the heart of historical materialism, especially as it relates to moral issues.[103] When the particular is mistaken for the universal, idolatry occurs; when the particular is mistakenly made into a universal theory, then metaphysics occurs; and finally, when people act on these mistaken universals, oppression occurs. Only after one has attained this insight are the real social conditions for the possibility of moral action possible.

> The fetishistic illusions enveloping all phenomena in capitalist society succeed in concealing reality, but more is concealed than the historical, i.e., transitory, ephemeral nature of phenomena. This concealment is made possible by the fact that in capitalist society, man's environment, and especially the categories of economics, appear to him immediately and necessarily in forms of objectivity which conceal the fact that they are the categories of the relations of men with each other. Instead they appear as things and the relation of things with each other. Therefore, when the dialectical method destroys the fiction of the immortality of the categories it also destroys their reified character and clears the way to knowledge of reality.[104]

And with this knowledge of reality comes the possibility of creating a society based on the fulfillment of real human needs, self-consciousness, and freedom. The reintegration of society presupposes the reintegration of culture—modernity incorporating the Ancients.

FROM THE HEGELIAN SYSTEM OF NEEDS TO THE MARXIAN THEORY OF NEEDS

While Hegel accepted classical political economy without resolving its internal contradictions, he also did not investigate the nature of the needs created by the system of needs in civil society. For Aristotle, Hegel, and Marx, needs are the social glue holding society together. This is a feature also characteristic of classical political economy, but it is only Marx who investigates the relationships between the type of needs created and the imperatives of the social system. His theory of human needs, which he begins to develop in the *Paris Manuscripts*, centers around the issues of human nature and species being and continues throughout his works, even to the *Grundrisse* and *Capital* with their discussions of self-realization and social needs. The place that Marx's theory of needs occupies in his theory of social justice will be dealt with in Chapter Five. Agnes Heller has argued that Marx's theory of needs is the foundation stone for his theory of labor power and surplus value.[105] The concept of needs was assumed in classical political economy as only applying to expressions of capitalist wants within a market economy. Marx's theory, which is a response to both the utilitarian view of the shopkeeper and to Hegel's uncritical acceptance of the capitalist system of needs in civil society, refers to both the material and spiritual nature of needs created within society.

Marx rejected the idea that need is purely an economic category, whose content can only be defined by the marketplace. Not only can needs be determined outside of capitalism, they can be seen as a response to the logic of capital itself. A theory of needs provides Marx with some of the normative foundation and assumptions for his critique of capitalism throughout his early and later writings. Needs have become the biological, psychological, and social expression of alienated and fetishized social relationships. Those that cannot be articulated or have difficulty being actualized in capitalist society provide a theoretical framework for the critique of political economy itself. Marx has rejected the metaphysical foundations of the need for life, liberty, and property (needs that are articulated in a market economy) and seeks instead the social expression of other types—for example, the need for community, common good, the environment, culture, education, the public sphere, work, and the social nature of man. "The wealthy man is at the same time one who *needs* a complex of human manifestations of life, and whose own self-realization exists as an inner necessity, a need."[106] The man with the greatest wealth is he who has friends. The return to Aristotle is apparent.

These social needs cannot be expressed as reflections of individual self-interest in the competitive private sphere; they have great difficulty being articulated in a society in which needs are reduced to market categories and market logic; and finally, they are not reflections of utilitarian patterns of private consumption or the satisfaction of personal material pleasures. Marx borrows heavily for his theory of needs from Kantian notions of human dignity and the kingdom of ends, the Feuerbachian concept of species being, the Aristotelian idea of self-realization within the political community, and the Hegelian return to Hellas. Marx's whole theory rests on the idea that physical needs are only a small part of the question, with the fullest development of human potential in the "realm of freedom" being the most important aspect. From the discussion of self-realization of the species being to that of self-realization within the realm of freedom—from his earliest to his later works—it is this Greek notion of needs, supplemented by the classical German tradition, that is the key to understanding of Marx's theory of needs.

In his analysis of alienated labor, Marx assumes that work is a need of the species being. The individual is fulfilling a need for self-development and self-actualization in producing himself or herself as a person and as a communal being. Externalization and objectification are moments in a nonalienated situation by which individual and social creativity is manifested. This creativity involves the production of both material and cultural wealth, of both economic and social institutions. Developing the social and anthropological implications of Kant's epistemology (the constitution theory of truth) and Hegel's phenomenology (phenomenological reconstruction of history in self-consciousness), Marx evolves a theory of needs from his understanding of the species nature of man. Where Kant dealt with pure reason creating the world of experience through a synthesis of the manifold of representations (material cause) and the categories of understanding (formal cause), and where Hegel talked about labor—albeit spiritual labor—as creating the cultural forms that are manifestations of the Absolute Spirit's quest for self-identity and self-consciousness, Marx deals with the self-conscious, free creativity of the individual in both manual and intellectual labor.

For Kant, creativity is an epistemological creation of the world of perception; for Hegel, it is the Spirit's unfolding of itself in social history; and for Marx, it is the creation of the institutions and social relationships of political economy. This conscious-life activity becomes forced and alien labor in modernity. "It is not the satisfaction of a need, but only the *means* for the satisfaction of other needs."[107] The need for productive expression of the species being in the private and the public spheres—and in economic, political, social, and cultural areas—is an expression of life itself and thus of the true needs of the individual. It reproduces both the individual and the species as self-conscious and free, according to the laws of aesthetic and political integration and harmony. With the modern social organization of production characterized by division of labor and power, private property, and the class structure, "productive life"—along with self-development, community, and social interaction—are made impossible. The species' need for community, social interaction and recognition, economic and cultural creativity, and control over private and public decision-making becomes part of Marx's theory of needs. This is a critique of the system of needs found in classical political economy. It espouses a need for expression of the universality within the species.

Needs in capitalist society—however—are reduced to expressions of the particular rationality of the market, and to private property. Here the simple act of "possessing or having" is the only manner in which the individual appropriates social reality in an egoistic fashion. At the level of the sensibilities and consciousness, this further intensifies the abstract individualism found in the political sphere. "Private property has made us so stupid and partial that an object is only *ours* when we have it, when it exists for us as capital or when it is directly eaten, drunk, worn, inhabited, etc., in short utilized in some way."[108] Productive life is turned into a means for the further accumulation and ownership of property, rather than the self-expression of human potential. The needs of modernity are those of Smith and Ricardo, and not those of Aristotle and Epicurus. The overcoming of the dualisms and contradictions of modernity are necessary for Marx not because of some universal and deterministic understanding of history, but because of the moral necessity for the existence and realization of other types of social needs than merely economic accumulation. The necessity for communism lies in the moral necessity for development of the spiritual and higher needs of the individual, which are not capable of realization (or even articulation) in a capitalist society.

Modern needs are artificial and alien qualities resulting in self-stupefaction, and are established in individuals to bind them to the social system. Needs become another mechanism for social domination and control, rather than an expression of individual freedom. "The need for money is, therefore, the real need created by the modern economic system, and the only need which it creates."[109] Under the guise of friendship, these needs produce universal exploitation—according to Marx—for they disguise the real basis for social interaction, create "unhealthy appetites," and in the end result in the "bestial savagery" of the worker.[110]

> First, by reducing the needs of the worker to the miserable necessities required for the maintenance of his physical existence, and by reducing his activity to the most abstract mechanical movements, the economist asserts that man has no needs, for activity and enjoyment beyond that; and yet he declares that this kind of life is a *human* way of life.[111]

By reducing needs to simply economic needs, the utilitarianism of the political economists has abstracted from the true nature of human social activity. When society is built around communist principles, "their association itself creates a new need for society—and what appeared to be a means has become an end."[112] For Mészáros, this is the only criterion of moral assessment that should ever be applied to society.[113] As both Rousseau and Kant stressed, human dignity requires that individuals control their moral lives and that there be no division between individuals and their society—universal and particular. Though the specifics of their ideas were different, both Rousseau and Kant argued that, only when the moral law of the general will or pure reason is not imposed but expresses the individual will, only then can individual freedom be preserved. When following universal moral laws, individuals are in effect following the dictates of their autonomous free will. However, in a society characterized by the economy's invasion of sensibilities, perceptions, tastes, needs, and morality, the very acts of eating, drinking, discussion, exercising aesthetic interests, and so on are no longer the social bases for public communication, but simply means for making money and accumulating wealth. The realization of man's potentials—as Marx states—is reduced "to the realization of his own disorderly life, his whims and his capricious, bizarre ideas."[114]

While the theory of needs in his early writings centers around his view of human nature, social psychology, and human sensibilities, Marx's later writings stress the structure and logic of capital and their effect on self-realization of the individual.[115] In the *Grundrisse* and *Capital* the theory of needs is tied to the broader historical and institutional framework of the Concept (*Begriff*) of capital. The whole of economics is understood as the "sacrifice of the human end-in-itself to an entirely external end."[116] With transcendence of the internal contradictions of society and alienated labor, the general elimination of labor and labor time as standards for creating wealth, the elimination of measuring social need and utility by exchange value, and—finally—the implementation of human emancipation, a situation is then created that results in

> the free development of individualities, and hence not the reduction of necessary labour time so as to posit surplus labour, but rather, the general reduction of the necessary labour of society to a minimum, which then corresponds to the artistic, scientific, etc. development of the individual in the time set free, and with the means created, for all of them.[117]

When the necessary labor time is measured by the needs of social individuals—by their species needs for self-realization—true wealth will be created, with the result of an increase in leisure time. For Marx the real wealth of society lies in its members and not in its profits. "For real wealth is the developed productive power of all individuals,"[118] which has been made impossible given the nature of capitalist economy. The full development of productive powers in capitalism means success in the market, for capitalism reduces all higher strivings into means for capital accumulation. Those human potentialities that are not economically productive cannot survive. The theory of needs supplies the normative foundations for his theory of man in Marx's early works, while in his later ones it provides the basis for his structural and historical critique of political economy. For Nussbaum his theory has direct ties to Aristotle's theories of happiness, human functioning, and human capability. Two major points Marx borrows from Aristotle are:

> that truly human living requires performing all one's natural activities in a way infused by rational choice and rationality; and that the capability to function in this human way is not automatically open to all humans, but must be created for them (brought forward from rudimentary capabilities) by material and social conditions.[119]

Chapter Four

The Ancients, Democracy, and Marx's Critique of Classical Liberalism

INTRODUCTION

This chapter will examine Marx's critique of liberalism as it develops throughout his early and later writings, along with his vision from the heights of the Ancients—which gives the critique its distinctiveness. With the critique of liberalism and the development of his theory of economic democracy, another important piece in the puzzle of Marx's ethics falls into place. Along with the theory of needs and species being, his theory of social democracy provides a substantive framework for further analysis of Marx's theory of social justice. Liberalism is here understood not simply as a political phenomenon represented by Locke and Mill, but as the integrative spirit of nineteenth-century British society. It is the social whole comprising the major institutional and cultural aspects of modernity: epistemology and science, ethics and politics, psychology and human nature, and the state and economics. To fail to appreciate how these parts are so tightly integrated is to fail to understand the truly radical nature of Marx's critique of liberalism and modernity. Focusing on this material is also another means by which we may look more closely at the integration of his early and later writings—an area that has been dealt with already by others, as well.[1] Marx's critique of liberalism may be broken down into the following areas:

Critique of the Epistemological Foundations of Classical Liberalism[2]

1. critique of liberal epistemology and science
2. liberal theory of consciousness

3. philosophical dichotomies or Kantian antinomies
4. moral epistemology
5. fetishism as an epistemological and methodological category

Critique of the Political Philosophy of Classical Liberalism

1. critique of liberal psychology and view of human nature
2. liberal philosophy of rights and morality: natural rights theory
3. political liberalism
4. philosophical anthropology of liberalism
5. liberal notions of freedom, individualism, and property
6. liberal theory of the state
7. utilitarianism: its view of happiness and the principle of the greatest good for the greatest number

Critique of the Economic Theory of Classical Liberalism

1. critique of alienation
2. reification of social relations of production
3. commodification of labor
4. liberal theory of needs: utilitarianism and classical political economy
5. theory of economic contradictions
6. labor theory of value
7. economic crisis theory: disproportionality, overproduction, and underconsumption

This chapter will combine a variety of different works to form a sense of the comprehensiveness and totality of Marx's critique of liberalism. Generally, secondary interpretations have stressed the chronological or developmental stages of his thought, with special emphasis on the various differences between distinguishable methodological, epistemological, and sociological periods in his life. The traditional bifurcation of Marx's writings into separate stages, time periods, or epistemological shifts undermines the depth and scope of his general analysis. The emphasis here, however, will not be on his methodology, but on his overall critique of modernity. The broad strokes of the picture will stress the integration of his philosophical, sociological, political, and economic critiques of the capitalist social system, as his thinking ranges from the critiques of epistemology to modern consciousness; from modern science to the technological alienation of nature; from individual liberties to the irrationalities of the market; from economic exploitation in the workplace to the loss of self-consciousness; and from economic crises and distorted societal development to the distorted development of the human personality.

Marx's social theory does not represent a condemnation or rejection of only one aspect of the social system, but a rejection of all its social and cultural forms of oppression and inequality—from the economic and political institutions to the formation of modern consciousness itself. There are places in Marx's writings, however, where specific features of liberalism are positively evaluated as stages toward the future emancipation of humanity: the scientific and technological achievements of modernity, the establishment of political institutions on the basis of political rights and civil liberties, and the philosophical insights of some of modernity's brightest minds. Marx's analysis represents both a critique and negation of liberalism as well as a radicalization of the emancipatory potential within it. The newly emancipated society will come from within liberal society itself. The critical moments of liberalism are then united to the ancient traditions.

Though suspicious of much of classical political economy, utilitarianism, and political philosophy, Marx's radicalized humanism and liberalism was based on his interpretations of Rousseau, Kant, Hegel, J. S. Mill, and Ricardo.[3] This way of approaching Marx will be beneficial to the extent that Marx's critique of liberalism can then be understood from two vantage points: the comprehensive critique of liberal political economy, and the acceptance of certain liberal values and rights—such as the protection of personal freedom and individual rights. But this acceptance is only fully appreciated when the full weight of all the elements in his analysis are integrated. When they are not, they make little sense; and the usual result is that Marx is interpreted as being against individual freedom in particular and ethics in general.

Marx's response to the problems of modernity should not in any way affect our understanding of his political respect for individuality and rights, which are part of his notion of human emancipation. His investigation of social psychology and his critique of the ideology and false consciousness of natural rights should not be confused with his own political philosophy and understanding of the political freedoms in a rational society. The critique of morality and natural rights is a general critique of seventeenth- and eighteenth-century individualism and its various expressions in social psychology, epistemology, and political theory, all of which are ahistorical and asocial. They have been so closely joined together in the consciousness of liberalism that a critique of one is viewed as a critique of the other: A critique of liberal morality is viewed as an attack on all morality, just as a critique of modern science is interpreted as a rejection of science itself. Modern social theorists certainly have been guilty of mistaking the particular for the universal. This is a contemporary form of idolatry.

Marx critiqued the philosophical, epistemological, and structural foundations of liberalism in order to free its key insights of individual freedom within the public sphere from the restrictions of its limited philosophical and economic base. The contradictions of modernity— as seen in the contradictions between civil society and the state, the bourgeois and the citizen, and the rights of man and the rights of the citizen—were first analyzed in a different form with Marx's early juxtaposition of the individualism of Epicurus and the social nature of man from Aristotle. The limits to Greek self-consciousness and the application of its social ideals to modernity lie in its distance from the contradictions of modern society and the social, political, and economic means for transcending these contradictions. Thus Marx's epistemology and ethics, freed from the limitations of classical political economy and placed within the broader context of the social relationships of liberalism, open up an enormous wealth of questions and issues not conceived by traditional or contemporary liberalism. The emphasis here will be on an analysis of the various aspects of political liberalism. The philosophical foundations of liberal epistemology and science has been dealt with earlier, while the critique of economic liberalism will be examined in the next chapter.

LIBERAL PSYCHOLOGY, THE WORKPLACE, AND DISTORTED SELF-DEVELOPMENT

For Marx, workers realize themselves in the process of production; they develop their innate and individual capabilities and talents in the act of producing the material goods of society. But besides this subjective creativity, they also create social objectivity: the objects of perception, cultural life, and social institutions, along with the necessary material goods that are the products of their activity (praxis). In fact, this activity is the defining characteristic of the human being for Marx. In this creative activity, the individual forms the subjective and objective conditions of human existence. It is this aspect of the concept of praxis—which Marx derived from Hegel—that is central to an understanding of Marx's concepts of objectification and alienation. The products that make up the objects of the social world with all its institutions, values, and customs are the result of the objectification of labor itself. In a social setting in which the worker is free from all artificial and historical forms of oppression, the worker creates a world in which the products become the very manifestation of his or her self-conscious being. It is this form of creativity (objectification) that distinguishes human work from that of animals. Man produces for reasons of physical survival and for the realization of his universal nature as a species being. The community is the manifest expression of this universal nature, and it is through the community that objectification and freedom become possible. Freedom is the fullest expression of the particular and universal nature of man in the process of production. It is here that the individual expresses his or her specific needs and, in return, acquires the goods that themselves are the material preconditions for creation and maintenance of the community. Only in the latter does man have the opportunity to become truly human. Marx treats the issues of political economy as a form of social economics in the same manner as Aristotle; neither one is a political economist in the classical nineteenth-century sense of the term.

By abstracting from the social relationships expressed in the theoretical and material realm, classical liberalism also abstracted from the issues of power relations and their effect on the formation of consciousness itself. Consciousness is viewed as a given, prestructured, and preformed reality—existing already made and ready to act.[4] Liberal psychology with its inadequate understanding of consciousness is itself an ideology and form of false consciousness.

> No psychology for which this book . . . remains closed, can become a *real* science with a genuine content. What is to be thought of a science which stays aloof from this enormous field of human labour, wealth of human activity means nothing to it except perhaps what can be expressed in the single phrase—"need," "common need"?[5]

The question of the transformation of the concept of consciousness from the psychological to the political area is not considered. Does the formation of consciousness constitute an important political question? Do the manner and form of its creation, and the social institutions within which it is created, also constitute political questions? If its formation is not made problematic in the conceptual abstractions of liberal psychology and political philosophy, then freedom can be seen as simply freedom from external coercion.[6] The monad has an independent atomic structure that admits of no external influence and, therefore, no external coercion. But this seventeenth-century psychology is totally inadequate to the development of sociology and history, which are crucial ingredients in the *Geisteswissenschaften* of nineteenth-century German social thought. Once socialization is recognized as an important consideration, then the formation of consciousness becomes a crucial issue in political philosophy. The traditional liberal split between negative and positive freedoms—between freedom from external physical coercion and freedoms that make possible certain types of activity—can no longer be maintained.

Once it is accepted that individual consciousness is formed through language, norms, and social structures, then the traditional split is dissolved, for there is no longer any negative and positive freedom and no longer any split between the individual and the social. "Freedom from" must now entail a "freedom toward," since different social structures will lead to different forms of consciousness and different opportunities to express and realize one's sense of self and individuality.[7] Negative freedom is possible only when the individual is so divorced from the social structures that any intrusion of the latter is viewed as a political infringement on the rights of individuality; Marx has rejected both the epistemological and psychological foundations of this view of liberalism.

The effects on society built around private property run so deep that even the senses are affected as we have already seen at the end of Chapter Three when discussing Marx's theory of needs. Marx calls the senses of seeing, hearing, smelling, desiring, thinking, and so forth "the organs of individuality," since it is through them that we experience our initial contact with the world and distinguish ourselves from it. By means of them, the objective world is appropriated—and with it, human reality and consciousness. This objectivity has already been constituted as the false objectivity of alienated labor. The act of appropriating this external world is itself part of the alienated process. Productive social relations of modernity reach deep down into the perception and consciousness of the individual to structure our relations with the world. Freud's theory of the unconscious and the social repression of the id are extremely important contributions to social theory. However, his ideas about the repression of sexual drives should be augmented by the primacy of the social repression brought about by the logic of capital. In both cases, the impact is made on the formation of modern consciousness. For Marx, then, the crucial point is that the objects of a human being's creation should "confirm and realize his individuality" with the goal of creating human senses that correspond to "all the wealth of human and natural being."[8] The objects would then become part of the creation and manifestation of the essence of man: the hopes, values, customs, and social norms by which his life is constructed and his particular individuality realized. When the social institutions disrupt this process of the objectification of the self in work, then the power relations, logic, and structural imperatives of capitalism are further integrated into the psychology and consciousness of the individual.

THE CRITIQUE OF LIBERAL MORALITY AND NATURAL RIGHTS THEORY

Marx did not develop a theory of morals, and his statements regarding morality are—as Steven Lukes has pointed out—anything but consistent and clear. The classical liberal values of liberty, equality, fraternity, and justice are—for Marx—expressions of modern mythology, which only confuse and misrepresent the real issues at stake. These values create the image of utopian ideals to be realized, while they abstract from the real issues of the end of human nature, the realization of the individual in a human society, and the class system itself. Lukes offers a number of reasons why Marx is so critical of the theory of natural rights in the liberal tradition. Rights theory (theory of *Recht*) is inherently ideological, for it conceals the exact nature of class society and class conflict.[9] In this sense it is similar to the nature and social role of religion. Both create false illusions about equality in very unequal societies; fraternity in societies governed by the commodification of labor, alienation, and fetishized social relations; liberty when there are continuous organizational and market forces manipulating the consciousness and supposed rational decisions of individuals; and social justice in class societies, which are incapable of equality, fraternity, and liberty.

Lukes says that, to get at the heart of the nature of rights theory, one should raise this question: "To what problems are these rights a response?"[10] What one uncovers is a view of the individual and society that is antagonistic and "potentially catastrophic." These social conflicts require authoritative rules and standards that are capable of regulating social intercourse. By rationally distributing the rights and obligations of the individual, the theory creates a situation where restrictions on freedoms and activity are justified. Thus the psychological (natural inclinations, self-interests, and egoism), sociological (social conflict and social antagonisms), and economic assumptions (material scarcity and competition) are all ideological presuppositions of a class society, which become ingrained in the theory of natural rights. They are not the theoretical expressions of objective and natural principles of right and wrong, independent of any particular social interest; nor are they carriers of universal moral ideas. Rather they ideologically distort the true nature of the social relations of production, tend to stabilize the disequilibrium created by the unstable class conflict in modern society, and retard the process of critical self-reflection capable of recognizing and changing these relationships.

> For Marx, on the contrary, both the rights and the principles governing the relations of civil society, and the state itself, were rooted in and means of stabilizing the production relations and thus the class relations of a given social order.[11]

The psychological, sociological, and economic assumptions (the metaphysics of natural rights) that underlie natural rights theory are manifestations of a certain type of society whose institutional and social structures should be historically changed through revolution. As a footnote to this, Engels's critique of Dühring in his 1878 work is considered by many to be the foundation of the orthodox Marxist-Leninist view of morality. That is, all morality is class morality, and there are no universal value systems because there are no universal social relations. There is only class conflict and discord. This initial position of Engels is developed further in the later debates between Mehring and Tönnies over the *German Society for Ethical Culture*; in Kautsky's critiques of Cohen, Vorländer, and Bernstein over the importance of introducing the neo-Kantian ethical concerns into a materialistic analysis of economic and political institutions; and in the later discussions by Adler and Vorländer.

Marx's understanding of morals is complex because morality itself is a complex social form. It contains contradictory elements such as moral ideals and pictures of utopian society based on unrealized moral principles, on the one hand, and social ideals that conceal the underlying social antagonisms and contradictions of class society and hinder self-consciousness and the possibility of their negation and transcendence, on the other. Marx asks,

> But how can I be virtuous if I am not alive and how can I have a good conscience if I am not aware of anything? The nature of alienation implies that each sphere applies a different and contradictory norm, that morality does not apply the same norm as political economy, etc. because each of them is a particular alienation of man: each is concentrated upon a specific area of alienated activity and is itself alienated from the other.[12]

Marx raises the question as to whether the relationship between morals and political economy is accidental and therefore unscientific, or whether it is "essential." He does not really answer this question because, for him, morals is itself caught up in the alienation of the capitalist social system. In the end, Marx states that "political economy expresses, in its own fashion, the moral laws."[13] By establishing the laws of the economy, the political economy of Ricardo in turn establishes moral laws. The reason for this apparent contradiction and ambiguity between both lies in the nature of the economic laws of capital and the moral principles themselves. The latter are reflections—ideological manifestations—of the ideals and theoretical principles by which the system works. This was Hegel's original critique of the moral positivism inherent in liberal morality. Though conscience and bourgeois moral virtue could be used as the basis for a social critique and could thus bring political economy and morality into opposition, there is also the point that underlying the moral principles are the psychological, sociological, and economic assumptions of a particular historical social system. All of which Marx rejects. Though morals could be used as the basis for a partial critique of the system, their principles are ultimately tied to and reflect that society. They only appear to contradict each other: In reality, they represent only different forms of the same social reality. The strength of a critical social theory rests in its ability to distinguish between essence and appearance, ideals and ideology, cries of the people and moral opium.

The morality of political economy may be expressed as work, savings, and the denial of material pleasures—what is later to be called "the Protestant work ethic." But despite this seeming harmony of purpose, there is a clash between morality and needs. Parading as the "truly moral science," its main thesis is "the renunciation of life and of human needs."[14] Physical survival, the sensibility of man, and the development of self-consciousness all cease to be human needs. Every need is used as the fulcrum by which to further integrate the individual into the system, to reduce moral relationships to commodity relationships. Needs become no longer the directing force of subjectivity toward its creation in objectivity; needs are no longer the expression of individuality and creativity toward the natural and social world; and needs are no longer tied to human creativity and freedom, but become a calculated mechanism for the artificial and manipulative creation of wants.

> Just as every imperfection of man is a bond with heaven, so every want is an opportunity for approaching one's neighbor, in simulated friendship and saying, "Dear friend, I will give you what you need, but you must know the *conditio sine qua non*. You know what ink you must use in signing yourself over to me. I shall swindle you while providing you enjoyment."[15]

This creation of appetites does not expand the free choices available to the individual, but creates artificial needs and dependencies by which sensuousness and consciousness are further tied to the logic of capital. The depiction of possessive individualism and personal liberty and the critique of political intrusion into individual decisions are not recognized in classical liberal thought as serious threats to individuality or freedom. The market is viewed as impartial and objective and an exchange between equals who have full information and are conscious of all the possible choices and ramifications of their decisions. The moral ideals of thrift and savings are viewed by Marx as an extension of alienated consciousness. "The less you *are*, the less you express yourself, the more you *have*, the greater is your *alienated* life and the greater is the saving of your alienated being."[16]

Another way of expressing this idea within the context of exchange itself is that the opening up of new possibilities—new forms of consumption and self-expression—result not in the extension of individual freedoms, but rather in their further limitation. Though Marx in his theory of needs emphasized the effects on consciousness of this form of alienation of self, there is another way of looking at the issue. The freedoms, forms of self-expression, choices, and individuality that are available in a market economy are the result of the creation of false needs and a real limitation and reduction of choices to marketable commodities and consumer goods. Choices are limited and not extended by the expansion of a consumer culture, because they are the only choices that can be made within the context of the logic of the market and capital.[17] That is, it results in the "universal exploitation of human communal life." Implicit in Marx's analysis is the idea that, by measuring needs in terms of money and profit, one loses the ability to conceive of needs in the context of self-realization within the community. The market reduces all needs to those that can be satisfied by private consumption and defines out of existence (social unconscious) all alternative forms of real freedom in productive activity (praxis). In the third volume of *Capital* Marx writes:

> Freedom in this field can only consist in socialized man, the associated producers, rationally regulating their interchange with Nature, bringing it under their common control, instead of being ruled by it as by the blind forces of Nature; and achieving this with the least expenditure of energy and under conditions most favorable to, and worthy of, their human nature. But it nonetheless still remains a realm of necessity. Beyond it begins that development of human energy which is an end in itself, the true realm of freedom, which, however, can blossom forth only with this realm of necessity as its basis. The shortening of the working-day is its basic prerequisite.[18]

As Kamenka has stated, the goals of Marx are self-realization and human dignity within humanity.[19] In capitalism, one can easily "acquire art, learning, historical treasures, political power."[20] One can appropriate anything that can be purchased by money. Everything is reduced to the needs of the system and the continuance of its logic. But what cannot be chosen under this system is the productive creativity of the individual within a community of his or her own creation—a community based on love and friendship, whose priority is the realization of human potential. These are universals not capable of being articulated by the rationality of the market. So what appear to be extensions of liberties and individual freedoms end as gross limitations on the range and types of choices available. One cannot choose to live in a free nonalienated society, in a real community built around the self-expression of the universal nature of man as species being. On the contrary—Marx says—the modern worker finds fulfillment of self and realization of needs in the self-stupefaction of the English gin-shops. "Their luxury reveals the real relation of industrial luxury and wealth to man."[21]

THE CRITIQUE OF POLITICAL LIBERALISM

Marx's critique of political liberalism is very complicated and does not represent a simple rejection of its political values and traditions.

In fact, he quite clearly states that the political freedoms gained by liberalism—though they are not the highest forms of human emancipation possible—do represent significant progressive steps in the development of mankind. "Political emancipation certainly represents a great progress. It is not the final form of human emancipation, but it is the final form of human emancipation within the framework of the prevailing social order."[22] He is well aware of the importance for human emancipation of the political revolution against feudalism culminating in the French Revolution. This revolution was against the political forces of feudalism and was also a revolution of civil society. In feudal society, the social system was based on integration of the economic and the political—where property, family, and occupation were all intimately bound up with the elements of political life itself. The revolution of liberalism overturned this structure of the manorial land system; government and the creation of laws became affairs of the people, and the decisions of the state a matter of general concern.[23] However, in abolishing the political nature of the economy, liberalism resulted in a splitting of the political from the economic, with the creation of distinct public and private spheres of social life.

It is also fairly clear that Marx's distinction between "rights of the citizen" and "rights of man" are to be seen within this context of the dichotomy between the political (idealism of the state) and the economic (materialism of civil society). The general and universal human rights—as articulated in the famous document of the French Revolution, the "Declaration of the Rights of Man and Citizen" of 1793—are broken down by Marx into the rights of the citizen and the rights of man. The former are political rights that refer to the citizen's "*participation* in the *community* life, in the *political* life of the community, the life of the state."[24] These are the rights of political liberty and civil rights. They are necessary but not sufficient conditions for emancipation and real freedom for—as Marx says—"the state may be a *free state* without man himself being a *free man*."[25] Marx did not detail the specific articles in this revolutionary document that would correspond to the rights of the citizen, since his interest in writing the essay was to respond to Bruno Bauer's essay on the issue of Jewish political rights and to critique the rights of the economic man as they developed in the documents and constitutions of the French Revolution. In spite of this failure, it could be argued that the rights not directly attacked—and that do refer to political and civil liberties—would be defended by Marx. In fact, most are defended in his later work on the Paris Commune.

Specifically, Marx mentions the rights of man in civil society from the 1793 French Declaration articles 2, 6, 7, 8, and 16 (although he also quotes from the state constitutions of Pennsylvania and New Hampshire). These are the rights of the economic man—man as the free consumer of commodities, the product of alienated labor, and the beneficiary of private property and economic exploitation.[26] It should be noted that Marx does not mention articles 1, 3, 4, 5, 9, 10, 11, 12, 13, 14, 15, 17, and following.[27] The five articles listed as the rights of man and directly criticized by Marx deal with personal liberty, equality, and property rights (article 2), individual liberty to act in ways that are not injurious to others (article 6), the right to religious freedom (article 7), security and protection of personal liberty and property (article 8), and free disposal of private property (article 16). The rights not mentioned but that are presumably rights of the citizen—and positive moments of the political emancipation of the French Revolution—include: the political rights to general welfare (article 1), the equality of all men by nature and before the law (article 3), law as the free expression of the general will (article 4), and public office open to citizens and free elections (article 5). These are the rights to free speech, public assembly, and the right to freely participate in the political process. The articles listing civil rights include: rights against arbitrary arrests or force (articles 10 and 11), the legal presumption of innocence (article 13), fair trial (article 14), proportional and fair penalties to violators of the laws (article 15), and so on. These are the rights accorded by the rule of law in society; they protect the individual from arbitrary and illegal forms of coercion.

When attempting to unravel the complex interplay of issues in Marx's writings, it is not difficult to appreciate the variety of interpretations regarding whether Marx has a theory of rights or not. There are three important questions involved here. Does Marx discuss the nature of rights? Does he have a theory of rights? And does he reject all bourgeois rights? The answers to these questions are yes, possibly, and definitely no, respectively. To indicate the extent of confusion on these matters, Joseph Femia has provided us with a good example.

It is worth noting the content of the rights dismissed by Marx. In the 1791 Declaration, Articles 10 and 11 defend the "unrestrained communication of thoughts and opinion" and guarantee that "every citizen may speak, write, and publish freely"; while Article 8 states that "no right ought to be punished, but in virtue of a law promulgated before the offense and legally applied." Marx never abandoned his dim and depressing view of human rights; and in a much later work, *The Critique of the Gotha Programme* he referred contemptuously to "rights" and other bourgeois moral ideas as "obsolete verbal rubbish" and "ideological nonsense," intellectual schemes for facilitating economic competition and guaranteeing security of property.[28]

There is much debate over whether Marx has a moral theory and theory of rights, but there is no debate whatsoever that he used the concept of "rights" throughout his writings. Femia has mistakenly identified Marx's critique of the underlying anthropological assumptions of the natural rights tradition with its presumptions of egoism, liberty, false consciousness, and loss of community. Marx comes out of the ethical tradition of Spinoza, Rousseau, Kant, and Hegel with its radically different view of human nature and freedom.[29] Femia combines different critiques from different works—disregarding their various intentions—and focuses them into one general condemnation of Marx's rejection of rights and morality. Thus, Femia combines Marx's critique of egoism and the limits of political emancipation from *On the Jewish Question* with his critique of abstract morality from the *Critique of the Gotha Program*. The purposes for which these essays were written and the forms of their critiques of the natural rights tradition are different; they cannot be combined without explanation and clarification. Femia then proceeds to join together his claim that Marx reduces individual freedom to collective cooperation—thereby losing all individual freedom—and his belief that Marx rejects all "permanent principles" by which to judge society (sociology of knowledge). Just throwing these hermeneutically different approaches together does not make a coherent statement regarding Marx's position. To criticize the liberty accorded by the French Revolution does not mean to criticize all forms of individual freedom; and to criticize bourgeois morality and rights, in turn, does not imply a generic critique of all morality and rights. We have already discussed the reasons behind the Hegelian and Marxian criticisms of Kantian morality and individualism.

It should be noted that Marx is very specific in choosing which articles he wishes to attack. Even when criticizing article 7 he is very careful to criticize only the section that refers to freedom of religious worship, while not mentioning (or criticizing) the other parts: The article says that "the right of manifesting ideas and opinions, either through the press or in any other manner, the right of peaceful assembly, *and the free exercise of worship* may not be forbidden."[30]

Peaceful assembly, free press, and free rational discourse were part of Marx's view of a free society—from his earliest writings on freedom of the press, his defense of the rights of the peasants, his articulate defense of liberal democracy in his critique of Hegel's *Philosophy of Right*, and his praise for political emancipation in the defense of Jewish civil rights, to his later criticisms of all forms of conspiratorial societies, and his defense of the economic democracy of the Paris Commune of 1871. Marx's view of individual freedom and rights is much broader than that of eighteenth- and twentieth-century social theorists.

> Although the liberal state guarantees religious freedom, free labour, freedom to own property, and political emancipation to the working class it is not enough. Marx's concept of freedom is absolute: man ought to be freed from all kinds of alienation, oppression, exploitation, estrangement and domination. What is more, he should be freed also from his illusions about his position in the civil society (i.e., from ideology).[31]

Marx fears that, in a society founded on two contradictory premises and systems of rights—the practical rights of the community and political participation, on one hand; and the economic rights of property, egoistic liberty, and maintenance of the class system (security), on the other—the latter will always prevail and be destructive of the former. The two systems of rights are in contradiction with each other and reflect the contradictions between man as a species being and citizen, and man as a bourgeois and part of civil society; they reflect the contradictions between Rousseau and Locke, Aristotle and Ricardo. One view of rights leads to the inclusion of people in the decisions that affect their daily lives, the development of their personalities and their own subjectivity, and the social constitution of themselves through the creation of their own laws and the furtherance of their own moral and political education in the public sphere.

On the other hand, with the natural rights of the private sphere, the citizens are stripped of any rights to participation, equality, and moral self-development—for these are reserved for the privileged few owners of private property and become impossible, given the imperatives of civil society. Thus, there seems to be a major conflict within the social system between competing rights. One system of rights undermines the other and leads "every man to see in other men, not the realization, but rather the limitation of his own liberty."[32] It is the conflict between a theory of rights founded on the notion of the species being and another founded on the egoistic man. For Marx the latter undermines and destroys the community, participation, and the freedom necessary for true human emancipation, while it offers personal liberties, participation in the market, and a community of free choice (consumer community). The conflict between the idealism of the state and the materialism of the economy cannot be resolved within the capitalist social system, just as the contradictions within natural rights theory cannot be resolved from within the theory itself.

Marx's critique of these rights of man reflects a view similar to his analysis of capitalist productive relations. They isolate the individual from the community and reduce the latter to a mere means for furthering the rights of economic accumulation and competition. "Political life declares itself to be only a means whose end is the life of civil society."[33] The major assumption of the rights-of-man perspective is that the competitive, aggressive, and egoistic individual represents the authentic nature of man, since the purpose of every political agreement is the preservation of these rights of possessive individualism.

> None of the supposed rights of man, therefore, go beyond the egoistic man, man as he is, as a member of civil society; that is, an individual separated from the community, withdrawn into himself, wholly preoccupied with his private interest and acting in accordance with his private caprice. Man is far from being considered, in the rights of man, as a species-being; on the contrary, species-life—society—appears as a system which is external to the individual and as a limitation of his original independence. The only bond between men is natural necessity, need and private interest, the preservation of their property and their egoistic persons.[34]

Holding strongly to the traditions of practical philosophy from Aristotle to Hegel, Marx sees that political life is sacrificed to the ends of the economic. There is also the real danger in this situation that, with its distorted social priorities, the political rights in a liberal society could easily be suspended or eliminated when they threaten the primary rights of personal accumulation.[35]

Because the political revolution of liberalism only freed civil society from various forms of political control, it resulted in a limited form of liberation and a correspondingly limited form of individual freedom and self-consciousness. In order that they might participate in the political process, citizens were liberated from requirements of private property, religion, social rank, education, and occupation. But this liberation from the need to comply with formal requirements to express political freedoms was not the end of the problem, since these requirements were never really transcended or totally abolished. Being curtailed in the public sphere, they were given free reign in the private sphere. So the freedom from private property in the public sphere conflicts with the freedom to own private property in the private, and ultimately affects the original intentions of those introducing political emancipation. For these to exist simultaneously in theory and in practice, a fiction must be maintained that separates the private from the public, the economy from the state.

The universality of interests and common good of the state is only an "unreal universality." These two theories of rights based on two different social spheres cannot by synthesized—for they involve contradictory views of human nature, the social good, and the nature of democracy itself. The ability to keep these two theoretical and practical moments together is a real religious juggling act of liberalism and constitutes the heart of its metaphysics of politics. Human emancipation requires the progressive elements of liberalism, but only as a stage toward its realization; human emancipation will, in turn, liberate the true emancipatory potential of liberalism and the general political rights of the citizen. Only then are true freedom and authentic rights possible. Marx's discussion of political and human emancipation at the end of *On the Jewish Question* is very inadequate, for it does not deal with the structural nature of the modern economy. This will be one of his future theoretical projects.

POLITICAL PARTICIPATION, REALIZATION OF SPECIES BEING, AND THE GREEK POLIS

Though all aspects of liberal society—including its social, cultural, political, and economic systems—come under very close scrutiny and criticism in Marx, there are areas that contain possibilities for further development in another social setting. Marx nowhere rejects the liberal values of equality, individual freedom, and political and civil rights. There are elements in liberalism—with its democratic ideals and its natural rights theory—that Marx wishes to preserve in a transformed way, as we have seen.

At the time of his writing about Hegel's philosophy of the state in his *Contribution to the Critique of Hegel's Philosophy of Law*, Marx accepts the general orientation of the Hegelian analysis. That is, he views the state as "the spirit which knows and wills itself" and as the final form of the objective spirit.[36] The essence of the individual is the state as the social mode of being. Marx's view of rationality and the essence of man are the same as in Hegel's philosophy. The real distinction between them lies in Marx's refusal to accept Hegel's notion that the state is a result of the logical deduction of the Concept, the self-determination of the Idea itself. In his critique of Hegel's theory of constitutions, Marx argues that democracy represents the true "self-determination of the people." Marx uses Feuerbach's transformative method and critique of religion, and states that—as in religion—the state and its constitution are the products of the people, and not the other way around. The basic uniqueness of democracy, for Marx, is that it is the only political form that corresponds to and reflects man's essence as a species or universal being. All other forms of political constitutions fail to express the universality and rationality of the human individuality. Rather, they appeal to man as a *gesetzliches Dasein*. Democracy is a realization of the universal—the concrete universal. It is the only form of rational social existence, because it is created by the people and reflects their needs and interests—rather than being imposed on them from above—thereby, reflecting particular social interests.[37] As Dick Howard has stressed, the initial understanding of the Marxian idea of the disappearance of the state is contained in these early writings. In a sense, democracy represents the abolition of the state as an independent political realm—a realm independent of the people.[38]

The modern state is a false universal—an abstract, pure form—since the real content of the state lies in civil society. It is this one clear insight that will be the foundation for Marx's later critique of liberalism, natural rights theory, and morality itself. The heart and soul of the political realm lie in the economic sphere, and it is in this private sphere that answers to the questions posed in the public sphere must be sought. He also recognizes the close relationship between political liberalism and the rise of liberal capitalism. Without the creation of an independent private sphere, the constitution of the public sphere remains an impossibility, as it did during the Middle Ages. "It is obvious that a political constitution as such is formed only where the private spheres have achieved independent existence."[39] Only with modern industrial society—with its distinction between the state and civil society—is political democracy a possibility. With liberalism, according to Howard, "the principle of individualism is consecrated, splitting man's particular existence from his universal existence, and making any reconciliation of the two impossible."[40] This remains even today the heart of the dilemma of political liberalism—the split between the two spheres of society: one that demands self-interest, competition and individualism; and the other that stresses the political community, general welfare, and universalism. For Marx the two spheres of modernity are incompatible: They express incompatible imperatives, forms of rationality, and views of the individual. However, at this early stage in his intellectual career, he still believes in a reconciliation based on a rejection of estates liberalism and social antagonisms. Essential to the political process and the formation of true individuality as species being is the direct participation in the political process. Actualizing one's existence— realizing one's potential as a universal and rational being—lies in creation of the laws that govern society.

> To take part in the legislature is therefore to take part in the political state, is to demonstrate and put into effect one's *being* as a *member of the political state*, as a *member of the state* . . . Hence, that civil society should penetrate the *legislative* power *in the mass*, if possible *in its entirety* . . . The striving of *civil society* to turn itself into *political* society, or to turn *political* society into *actual* society, appears as the striving for as *general* as possible a participation in the *legislative power*.[41]

Marx calls for the universalization of voting rights as a means for the achievement of real democracy—as the unification of universal and particular, and the realization of the essence of man. Political freedoms and participation realize the true individuality, which is species being. At this time in his life, Marx believed that the power of reason and the universalization of the right to vote would overcome the distinctions between public and private, particular and universal. With his later letters to the founders of the *Deutsch-Franzözische Jahrbücher* and *On the Jewish Question*, Marx came to realize that this, too, is only another form of mystification—for the truth of civil society is not in the political, but in the economic realm. The content of political liberties will always be the egoism and competition of the market. This marked an important turning point in Marx's analysis, for now he began to direct his attention to the study of civil society and political economy. He was moving in the direction of an examination of the material and social conditions of human life and to a fuller development of his own dialectical and critical method.

It is crucial here to note that this rather clear movement and direction in Marx's thought was set up by the insights of each previous stage in his analysis. However, his early emphasis on democracy, humanism, and individual freedoms and rights were never rejected in his later works. In fact, they formed the essential moral basis for his later critiques of the political economy of capitalism. What makes his position difficult to follow throughout its very complex winding course during his lifetime is his attitude to the development of a pure theory of morality and rights, on the one hand, and the later theory of economic democracy, on the other. The traditional categories of political liberalism were left behind as the central area of analysis because these forms of social expression were not the main determinations within the productive social relations and alone could easily be manipulated and turned into forms of false consciousness and ideology. Political rights, democracy, and liberalism were still tied to the logic of capital, and to break this relationship between civil society and the political sphere would necessitate a rethinking of the political ideals of liberalism.

From the practical side, a change—even a reformulation—of the political ideals themselves, which would require a transformation of the political consciousness of liberalism, necessitated some change in the social relations of the economy. The latter structured and "determined" the framework and parameters within which the political and social spheres developed. For someone who called for social revolution to continue developing treatises on morality, natural rights, political ideals, and so forth would be to undermine the whole project of social change. One could even call this an error of misplaced concreteness. It was not that these ideals were no longer important or that Marx no longer accepted their relevancy or validity; the issue was that the turn to political economy was necessitated by his realization that freedom was to be realized not in the abstract idealism of the state, but in the concrete material spheres of the economic world. Germany had been free in its ideas and slaves in its reality for too long for Marx to make this mistake again.

> Freedom, the feeling of one's dignity, will have to be awakened again in these men. Only this feeling, which disappeared from the world with the Greeks and with Christianity vanished into the blue mist of heaven, can again transform society into a community of men to achieve their highest purposes, a democratic state.[42]

For Marx, the realization of human possibilities as a universal being demands a more radical critique and a more structural transformation of society. The universalization of voting rights would not be a sufficient condition for the free society; this would necessitate a radical political economy and social revolution. The change in Marx's orientation was dictated by the imperatives of critique and revolution, and not by a rejection of the underlying belief in humanism and democracy. Certainly this is proven by the later writings of the *Grundrisse, Capital,* and the *Critique of the Gotha Program.* From his earliest writings, Marx distinguishes between moral autonomy and heteronomy. Only in the former are ethical laws self-determined by the individual. Marx's critique of censorship of the press by the Prussian government is one of his earliest essays and reveals the heart of his major concern: the moral autonomy and freedom of the individual. Justice cannot be an adequate basis for the analysis and normative critique of society for a variety of reasons: its subservience to the ideology of liberalism, the notion that society determines the context of ideas and consciousness, and Marx's own rejection of utopian ideals. The ideals of liberalism may be a basis for inspiration and hope, for immanent critique, and even for a "cry of the oppressed," but they cannot support an analysis of the structural conditions for change or an analysis of future possibilities. Nor does justice alone supply the institutional support necessary to carry the weight of a new system. This is a repetition of his earlier argument against the domination of abstractions found in the Left-Hegelian criticisms of religion and Kant.

MARX'S EARLY THEORY OF DEMOCRACY: LIBERAL DEMOCRACY AND THE CRITIQUE OF HEGEL'S THEORY OF THE STATE

At this stage in the early development of his thinking—writing at Kreuznach in the spring and summer of 1843—Marx is still very much a child of the liberal tradition. It is out of this liberalism that his critique of Hegel develops. He begins his analysis of the latter's *Philosophy of Right* by quoting the section that declares the state to be both the external necessity and the immanent end of the family and civil society. For Hegel, concrete freedom lies in a synthesis and identity of the general interests of the state and the particular interests of the individual in civil society and the family—that is, in overcoming the fragmentation of modern social life. Marx understands that this unity derives from the fact that the duties and rights of the state are in reality rights to property.[43] The essence of the political is the economic. Marx begins to stress the methodological weaknesses of speculative philosophy and the reversal of the relationship between the private and the public spheres. For him, Hegel's philosophy is a reflection of an "alien spirit," since the actual relationships are subjugated by development of the Idea of the state. The private spheres of the economy and the family are viewed as moments and expressions of the ideality of the state—the state as mind. "The actual idea, mind, divides itself into the two ideal spheres of its concept, family and civil society."[44] These separate spheres are produced by the world spirit as it externalizes itself in social institutions: The family and civil society are products of logic.

The state is the fullest expression of the objectification and rational form of the ethical spirit and the institutional basis for the realization of self-consciousness; freedom is the essence of the state. In this reversal of the relationship between the state and the economy, there lies a confusion over the nature of concrete freedom. The definitions of the state are "logical-metaphysical definitions," which lead to an understanding of freedom with the same mythical characteristics. The state is understood not according to its own nature, but according to the internal logic of the Concept (Mind) itself. The notion of the state, the state's relation to civil society and the family, the internal constitution of the state, and its activities and functions are expressed as logical relationships developed from the Concept.[45] The metaphysical unfolding of self-consciousness into the objective world of historical and social institutions is the framework for Hegel's analysis. He fails to consider the actually existing relationships between these social institutions. Logic has replaced history as the framework for understanding social relationships. This has dramatic effects for Hegel's view of human freedom and individual self-consciousness. Thus, the real subject of Hegel's analysis is the logical (and thus ontological) unfolding of the Concept of the state. It is the mystification and distortion of the actual relationships existing between the state and the other social institutions. The former is only the existential and phenomenal form in which the real subject matter of the analysis—the mind—is examined.

This logic is further strained when "personality" and "subjectivity" are expressed only in terms of the personification of sovereignty in the form of the monarch. They are characteristics of the essence of the state manifested in a singular person. Though Hegel is conscious of the split between the person as an abstract entity within society and the person, whose concept is actualized in the state, Marx maintains that this is a further extension of the initial metaphysical understanding of the state. Instead of seeing the "person" as a real being who actualizes his or her self through "species-forms"—that is, the social institutions—Hegel sees the person as the actualization of the Concept, as an expression of the development of the Absolute Spirit. Political philosophy is inseparable from both logic and metaphysics. "Rationality consists not in the reason of actual persons achieving actuality but in the elements of the abstract concept doing so."[46]

By interpreting the state as an abstraction and development of rationality, Hegel confuses the real relations, institutional forms, and historical content of the state with philosophy. While he speaks of the sovereignty of the state as expressed in the monarch, Marx immediately puts his emphasis on the side of the sovereignty of the people. In a monarchy, the people are governed by a political constitution whose mode of being is determined by the particular (monarch), and not the universal (people). In a democracy, the political constitution "appears only as one determination, that is, the self-determination of the people."[47]

> Democracy is the solved *riddle* of all constitutions. Here, not merely *implicitly* and in essence but *existing* in reality, the constitution is constantly brought back to its actual basis, the *actual human being*, the *actual people*, and established as the people's *own* work. The constitution appears as what it is, a free product of man.[48]

This is why Marx writes that democracy is the unrecognized truth of the monarchy. The political constitution represents the union of essence and existence: the institutionalization of the self-conscious creativity and species being of man. All other forms of political constitutions are phenomena that, like religion, hide the alienation of man's social being. It is man who creates all forms of the social and cultural institutions—religion, and the state—in the process of objectification. Only democracy is the self-conscious form in which human creativity as the ground of historical institutions is recognized. "Just as it is not religion which creates man but man who creates religion, so it is not the constitution which creates the people but the people which creates the constitution."[49] The state is the product of man's creativity, rather than the other way around. The reality of this in a monarchy is not made self-conscious, but is hidden from public view. In the process of creating a democracy, the activity itself is a manifestation of the species being of man, and the product becomes the content of the people itself. Since it is the people who make the constitution, the political constitution of a monarchy would not have a self-conscious and rational content.

This is why democracy is the truth of the monarchy. Marx realizes that the true content of the political constitution—even a monarchy—is an historical product of human praxis. Though a monarchy represses this, proceeds to universalize itself in a transcendent and divine form, and then rationalizes itself in an otherworldly metaphysics removed from the historical, Marx claims that this denies the real content of that form of political institution: human creativity.[50] At this point in his analysis, it is clear that the Marx is reading Hegel through the eyes of Rousseau. The general will is formed and is the forming principle; it becomes both the form and the content of true political activity.

At this early stage in the development of his thought, the relationship between the state and religion is succinctly but clearly stated. Both the state and religion are seen as alien expressions of human activity, since both are forms of external necessity outside of man that rule his life—even though they are, all the same, products of human activity. "To democracy all other forms of state stand as its Old Testament."[51] Marx is self-consciously relating the Old Testament critique of idolatry (fetishism) to his study of the modern state. The state is not a particular political institution that binds us, and for which we exist; the end of human existence is not to serve the purposes of the state. The state is a human production of objectification and praxis, and, therefore, represents the true form of all human creativity.

To mistake the products of political activity and turn them into pure political constitutions abstracted from this self-conscious understanding leads to a situation where the products of human activity rule us. It is this concern for the general issues of domination and control and this critique of all forms of metaphysical laws—whatever their phenomenological appearances (religion, state, economics, and so forth)—that lie at the heart of Marx's work ever since his dissertation on post-Aristotelian Greek philosophy. It is in this sense that democracy is the truth of all the various forms of the state. Democracy is being used here as a symbol for the direct expression of self-creativity—as synomous with the being of man. However, in the modern state, there is no longer this recognition of the self-conscious universal reason that underlies political activity. Instead,

independent private property, i.e., abstract private property, and the corresponding *private person* are the supreme construction of the political
state. Political "independence" is construed as "independent private
property" and the "person of this independent private property."[52]

All forms of political constitutions are defective to the extent that,
though they are all the result of human creativity, they are not all
self-consciously aware of this. They are not aware that they are
expressions of the human essence. This latter requires the self-
conscious understanding of the relationship between subjectivity and
objectivity. Marx is so explicit on this point that he calls all constitutions that are not expressions of the will of the people "practical
illusions." The people must understand that the political institutions
are the product of their own universal rationality and species-being.
"Socialized man" is the essence of all political constitutions. "In
democracy the constitution, the law, the state itself, insofar as it is a
political constitution, is only the self-determination of the people, and
a particular content of the people."[53] This philosophical understanding is institutionalized and made real through universal suffrage.

In both monarchical and republican states, the particular—as the
monarch or private property—rules over the universal—reason and
the people—through the "mediation" of the bureaucracy and civil
servants. However, in modern society the essence of the political
constitution is private property. On the other hand, true democracy
is the fulfillment of all other forms of political organization because,
in it, the law has been created "for man"—rather than the individual
having been made for the law. Here again, Marx recognizes and
distinguishes between the producer and the product: The former
creates the latter and must never be mistaken for it; the latter must
never rule the former. Law is a manifestation of human freedom and
creativity in democracy, while in other forms of political constitution
the individual is simply an abstract person having rights and is
subservient to the law. In modernity, the emphasis is on rights, but
not on real power to make decisions and affect change. Marx makes
the distinction between human manifestations and legal manifestations to express this political difference. While the principle of abstractionism occupies a central place in this early work as a critique of
the "abstraction of the state," it will continue to be a key category in
his later writings with his theory of abstract labor. Marx recognizes
that Hegel wishes to view the state as the rational expression of the
self-conscious will. However, Marx is keenly aware of the discrepancy

in Hegel's view of the modern state between the in-itself and the for-itself—that is, substance and the Concept, subjective and objective freedom, formal and substantive democracy. "The separation of the *in itself* and the *for itself*, of substance and subject, is abstract mysticism."[54]

"Only democracy, therefore, is the true unity of the general and the particular."[55] Only in democracy are the laws, constitution, and political infrastructure the result of self-conscious human creativity through universal suffrage.[56] The state does not stand outside the people as a false generality "that dominates and determines everything particular."[57] As Marx mentions, French liberalism holds that true democracy entails the annihilation of the state. Marx is not requiring the disappearance of the political realm as a precondition for freedom, but only the disappearance of political domination—the suppression of the general by the particular. In a democracy, the content and form—as universal expressions of the general will—are united, so that the difference between the particular constitution and the general populace is negated.

The monarchy and the republic are both characterized by Marx in very pluralistic language—stressing that the state is only one institution among a variety of others (contract, property, marriage, civil society). The particularity of the state is matched by the particularity of the various other social institutions in civil society. In reality, the state acts as the rational ordering principle for the logic of the pluralist society: the rationalization of a market economy. "The constitution is what rules, without really ruling—i.e., without materially permeating the content of the remaining, non-political spheres."[58] The state cannot assume a dominant position in relation to these other institutions. The state is only one form of social existence, whose content is the product of these other social forms. Its determinate being is the result of an alien social content. Note that the critique of the discrepancies between the content and form of Hegel's theory of the state is very similar to Hegel's own critique of Kantian moral philosophy. In both cases, it is the unrecognized social reality that gives content to the abstractions of legal and moral philosophy.

Democracy, on the other hand, is defined as the constitutional support for popular sovereignty. Marx—like Thomas Jefferson—recognizes that the people have the right to give themselves a new constitution when they are aware that the existing one does not correspond to their will.[59] Universal suffrage is viewed as the mechanism for the expression of the peoples' general will. From this perspective, Marx's view of democracy and the state is in the tradition of Rousseau and Hegel, rather than Locke and Montesquieu—for the latter saw voting as an expression of individualism, and rights in the context of the separation of political powers. For Marx, "*participation in the legislature* is an *innate* human right," and not a right of nature (birth).[60]

> In a really rational state one might reply: "*All should* not *individually* participate in deliberating and deciding on the general affairs of the state," for the "individuals" participate in deliberating and deciding on the *general affairs* as "all," i.e., within the society and as members of society. Not all individually, but the individuals as all.[61]

The question of whether the democracy of possessive individualism and the British government should be representative or direct is irrelevant, since in both cases democracy occurs within the abstractionism of the present political state and the dichotomy between civil society and the state. This represents a continuation of the fragmentation of social life between the citizen and the bourgeois, at another level of abstraction. Here Marx is taking up a series of familiar themes from Rousseau: (1) the importance of direct democracy as opposed to representative government; (2) defining democracy by distinguishing between public participation in terms of the general good or "individuals as all" (Rousseau's General Will) and the particular interests of the ego or "all as individuals" (the will of all);[62] and (3) defining freedom as a social rather than individual category. Marx believes that individuals must participate directly in the "general affairs of the state," which would include discussion about both public and private issues. This participation is an expression of the social being of man at the self-conscious level: The state is not something that one takes part in (occasionally), but is something that is a part of one's social being through deliberation. This is certainly a view of the political that represents a return to the Aristotelian definition of deliberation and democracy. Marx will move even closer to Aristotle's position when—as we have seen in Chapter Two—he begins to see the relationships between epistemology and politics and develops his mature understanding of democracy through an analysis of the Paris Commune of 1871. This in itself would be an important contribution to social theory; but, when joined to his critique of epistemology and positivism, it also further strengthens his ties to Greek materialism.

To recapture the intent of democracy and save liberalism from the abstractionism and formalism of the modern state, Marx recommends that both the political constitution and the civil society be dissolved and replaced by a new political system.

> Civil society has *really* raised itself to abstraction from itself, to *political being* as its true, general, essential mode of being only in *elections unlimited* both in respect of the franchise and the right to be elected. But the completion of this abstraction is at the same time the transcendence of the abstraction. In actually positing its *political existence* as its *true* existence, civil society has simultaneously posited its civil existence, in distinction from its political existence, as *inessential*; and the fall of one side of the decision carries with it the fall of the other side, its opposite. *Electoral reforms* within the *abstract political state* is therefore the demand for its *dissolution*, but also for the *dissolution of civil society*.[63]

The political state of Hegel is an abstract formalism that hides its real content: civil society. " 'Real private property' is then not only the 'pillar of the constitution' but the 'constitution itself.' "[64] Though Marx does not clarify or expand on this theme, he does indicate that the split between the public and the private, politics and the economy, will be transcended and that the self-determination of the people will involve a direct voice in the constitution of all affairs of the state, including those in the economic sphere. It will thus involve removing private property as the essence of the modern state.[65] Marx argues that the particularity and self-interest of civil society, which is the heart of Hegel's constitutional monarchy, will be transcended by the incorporation of all social elements into the new political sphere by means of universal suffrage. This would eliminate the abstract nature of the state, its split and isolation (independence) from civil society, and the disenfranchisement of the majority of people. It is a call for true democracy within a radicalized form of liberalism. This is a picture of Marx as an idealistic, humanistic, and liberal political philosopher.

How this would really change what Marx sees as the real problem is unclear, but the solution certainly appears from within the framework of the European liberal tradition itself. At the end of Chapter One it was mentioned that Marx develops and changes his ideas very quickly during this period, with the publication in the *Deutsch-Französische Jahrbücher* of *On the Jewish Question* (1843) and *Contribution to the Critique of Hegel's Philosophy of Law: An Introduction* (1843–44). With the former piece, he goes beyond his flirtation with liberalism toward a new philosophy of socialism and human emancipation; in the introductory piece to Hegel's political philosophy, Marx begins to develop his ideas of critique and social praxis, the turn to political economy, class struggle, proletarian revolution, and radical social change to accomplish his ideals of a true democracy.

Against this view of the ideals of democracy stands a recognition that the reality of the social situation does not, in fact, correspond to this hope. It is Hegel who lays the foundation for the view of the modern state—with his recognition that there is a fundamental split between the state and civil society—while it is Marx who recognizes the historical and institutional contradictions between the two, and the necessity for the democratic sovereignty of the people.

> He supposed the *separation* of civil society and the political state (a modern condition), and expounded it as a *necessary element of the idea*, as absolute rational truth. He has presented the political state in its *modern* form—in the form of the *separation* of the various powers. He has given the bureaucracy to the actual, *active* state for its body, and set the bureaucracy as mind endowed with knowledge above the materialism of civil society. He has counterposed the intrinsically and actually general aspect of the state to the particular interest and need of civil society. In short, he presents everywhere the *conflict* between civil society and the state.[66]

Hegel argues that it is the state bureaucracy that mediates between the state and civil society, while the estates—acting as representatives of civil society—further mediate between the two social spheres. In this synthesis lies the reconciliation between the particular and general interests. Civil society is "the battlefield of the individual private interest."[67]—the *bellum omnium contra omnes* from Hobbes's *Leviathan*. The secret of the state, however, is that "the political constitution at its highest point is therefore the constitution of private property."[68] The main purpose of the state—according to Marx—is the maintenance and continuation of private property. Hence the state is not an expression of the mind, but is the social institution whose function is to preserve the power of private property and the abstract nature of the individualism associated with political rights. While Hegel would like to understand private property as the social form within which separate wills recognize themselves and each other in a common will (social contract), Marx sees it as the misapplication of the principles of civil law to the constitutional realm (recreation of the state). While Hegel sees the realm of abstract rights—that is, property rights—as a foundation for later developments in the family, the state, and social intercourse based on interdependent self-recognition, Marx sees private property as a form of religious barbarism and brutality.

> Hegel described civil law as the *right of abstract personality* or *abstract right.* And, in truth, it must be expounded as the *abstraction* of right and thus as the *illusory right of abstract personality,* just as the morality expounded by Hegel is the *illusory being of abstract subjectivity.* Hegel expounds civil law and morality as such abstractions.[69]

Morality is closely connected in the eyes of Marx to this exposition of Hegel's view of law and the state. It is the morality of the modern state in that the former expresses not the life of the ethical community and the highest expression of self-determination, but rather the complete moral abstraction of the individual from the social totality. That is, morality becomes an expression of the social relations within the modern state characterized by contradictions between civil society and the state, private interests and general interests. The theoretical expression of these social contradictions appear in the form of the abstract person and natural rights of the individual; these, in turn, are merely expressions of the rights of property and class, however. The concepts of the abstract personality and abstract subjectivity form the foundation for a morality based on a specific historical form of social relations of property ownership, and thereby guarantee both philosophically and institutionally the social relations of civil society. The state comes to guarantee the rights, obligations, and structural network necessary for continuation of the political existence of the market economy. It has no independent reasons for existence other than the needs of other institutions, since its primary purpose is to guarantee the constitutional and civil rights of private property and profit. At this point in his argument, Marx makes an interesting statement regarding the nature of morality.

> Civil society is actual political society. In this case, it is nonsense to raise a demand which has arisen only from the *notion of the political state* as a phenomenon separated from civil society, which has arisen only from the *theological* notion of the political state.[70]

The content of the political state lies not in its own Concept, but in the substance of civil society and property relations. It is thus foolish to create moral theories about the nature of the just society based on a failure to appreciate this historical fact. Morality and political philosophy—raised on this separation—are products of a religious consciousness that produces theological categories of moral behavior. Though the specific content or social goals of these theories may have some worth—for example, theories about self-realization, self-determination, and democratic social justice—they can only become further manifestations of this moral abstractionism. They only obscure the real underlying structural problems and solutions. Marx is here criticizing the morality of liberalism, in both its Hegelian and Kantian forms since it is based on theological principles, and not on an understanding of the actual historical relations of property. This is similar to the arguments leveled against the Utopian Socialists, who have also failed to understand the structural relations underlying economic activity. Left to themselves, moral principles do not even have the positive side effect of moving toward these utopian visions of better future societies, since the conscious content of moral theories is ultimately overwhelmed by its unconscious political and economic imperatives of the marketplace. The quest for justice, freedom, self-determination, individualism, and democracy founder on the underlying normative assumptions and political ideology of possessive individualism, estates democracy (class democracy), and liberty to own property.[71]

MARX'S LATER THEORY OF DEMOCRACY: ECONOMIC DEMOCRACY AND THE PARIS COMMUNE

We have seen that Marx's views on natural rights theory and morality are generally complex, ambiguous, and dialectical. Rights theory is ideological since it conceals the real power relations of society and distorts the possibilities inherent in the actual. However, it still contains emancipatory elements that may transcend its ideological role. In *The Eighteenth Brumaire of Louis Bonaparte* Marx writes that, in periods of intense class conflict and social discord, the traditional liberal values of freedom of the press and protection of personal liberty and the whole structure of the parliamentary system with its petitions, critique of authoritarianism, open discussion, and majority decisions become serious hindrances to the further maintenance of class stability.[72] Then, in times of crisis, the traditional values of liberalism are called socialistic. Marx does not reject this insight, since

the bourgeoisie had a true insight into the fact that all the weapons which it had forged against feudalism turned their points against itself, that all the means of educations which it had produced rebelled against its own civilization, that all the gods which it created had fallen away from it. It understood that all the so-called bourgeois liberties and organs of progress attacked and menaced its *class rule* and its social foundations and its political summit simultaneously, and had therefore become *"socialistic."*[73]

According to Marx, this is the "secret of socialism": that the democratic institutions of liberal capitalism turn against its original founders and become a hindrance to their continued class rule. In order to maintain its economic and social class rule, liberalism's own political institutions and parliamentary system must eventually be dismantled. Marx continues by saying that "in order to save its purse it must forfeit the crown."[74] In other places he states that the world is rational, but exists irrationally. The truth will not appear external to the historical moment, either in the form of another liberal ideal or an independent set of moral principles. Rather, truth and rationality are—for Marx—immanent to the historical moment, while revolutionary parxis is simply the exploited class applying and realizing that repressed rationality. Thus, Marx's critique of liberalism is not total or unconditional. Liberalism is not absolutely negated in socialism, but is to be transcended—transformed into a higher level of rationality and freedom. This work written in his later period reflects the same interest in public participation and freedom of personal expression that characterized his early writings.

In the third section of the *Civil War in France*, the actual institution of true democratic political rule is described in the form of the Paris Commune. On coming to power in March 1871, the Paris Commune proceeded to dismantle the old governmental structures of repression: the governmental bureaucracy, the army and police, the clergy, and the judiciary. Though first all formed as a response to the ineffectualness and oppression of the residual feudal institutions of the French monarchy, these institutions had then been used for the maintenance of bourgeois power over the working class in France. With the dismantling of the secret police and the other arms of political coercion, along with the ideological arm of the state in the name of the church, the new Commune created its own institutions of government based on workers' control and popular sovereignty. It was—as Marx says—"the self-government of the producers."[75] State power and the rule of capital over labor were dissolved, as the real power came under control of the majority of its citizens. Universal free education and universal suffrage were instituted in order to free the development of the consciousness of the population from "class prejudice" and false consciousness. These had been created and maintained by ideological control over the formation of consciousness in the hands of the state and the church. The standing army was disbanded, and a citizen's army of the national guard created. The division of labor in the old government was replaced with a commune that combined the powers of the legislative and executive branches; members of the Commune were to be elected by universal vote, and the majority of its members were to be of the working class. Its members would be paid at the prevailing workers' wages, thereby taking government positions away from those who would seek economic enrichment. To further protect the community and place democratic controls over the political process, the right of immediate recall became part of the new political form.

> While the merely repressive organs of the old government power were to be amputated, its legitimate functions were to be wrested from an authority usurping pre-eminence over society itself and restored to the responsible agents of society. Instead of deciding once in three or six years which member of the ruling class was to misrepresent the people in Parliament, universal suffrage was to serve the people, constituted in communes, as individual suffrage serves every other employer in the search for the workmen and managers in his business.[76]

At the end of his introduction to this work, Engels says that the Paris Commune represented the true picture of the "dictatorship of the proletariat."[77] What is really important about this concept is that, though it represents a "withering away of the state," there is no implication in Marx that this means there is a corresponding dissolution of the public sphere. With the disappearance of the bureaucratic state, there comes a spiritual rebirth of public participation and democracy.[78] The key political transformation is the destruction of all centralized power uncontrolled by democratic institutions and values. Certainly, the picture Marx paints of the political and economic organization of the Commune is quite different from the institutions that have characterized the development of any later forms of communism or liberalism in the twentieth century. Voting was no longer to be a plebiscitary acquiescence to those chosen by the ruling class— what is today referred to by political scientists as the circulation of elites and pluralism (the theory of democratic elitism).[79] Democracy was something through which the workers were to organize their political opinions, decide the issues discussed, and have general control over the direction that their society and government were to take.

> Capitalism's alien political structure retained none of the positive features of the Greek *polis*. But the workers' Paris Commune could recall, embody and transform the potential for political community prefigured in Greek politics.[80]

Democracy was no longer viewed as a passive political system in which participation was limited to simple voting, while the important issues that affected the majority were to be determined by a small economic and political minority that would need the police and military to maintain its class hegemony. Just as an employer has a free hand in decisions that affect his or her employees, so too would the members of the Commune have a similar power over the decisions that affected their daily lives. Thus, Marx uses an example from the private sphere to clarify the nature of democracy; the traditional distinctions between public and private, democracy and the economy, would wither away in an economic democracy. Marx's view of the Commune certainly prefigures the rise of a new public sphere to fill the void left after the political marketplace had been dissolved. In fact, as we have seen, the public sphere was to be extended in the opposite direction, to cover decisions made in the private sphere. Once political power had been established in the democracy of the Commune through universal suffrage, the next step was the economic emancipation of labor. "The political rule of the producer cannot coexist with the perpetuation of his social slavery."[81]

The social slavery of class rule and wage labor was to be dissolved. Labor was to be transformed so that it would no longer have its old "class attributes." Marx was describing the actual institutionalization of human emancipation—originally dealt with in his early works. Private property as the control over social capital and—especially— over labor was to be abolished. This expropriation of the expropriators was to "make individual property a truth by transforming the means of production, land, and capital into the instruments of free and associated labor."[82] With the abolition of private property, economic democracy and worker control were to be accomplished. Also with the end of class rule and private ownership, the wealth of society was to be returned to the people, thereby increasing—not decreasing—their individual or "personal" property.

As cooperatives were to determine the running of the factories, a national organization of cooperatives was to coordinate national production through social and economic planning. The anarchy of the market, the fetishism of the commodities, unemployment, and the economic contradictions and periodic crises—which are not part of natural law, but the logic of capital—were to be overcome. Rational and democratic decision-making was to be the foundation of the economy—and not the anarchy of production through which class rule is hidden from public discourse and deliberation. Unlike the liberal theories of democracy, there were no set objectives to be realized other than the praxis of democracy and the recontrol of human existence in terms of rational self-conscious decisions. The Commune had, in fact, unlocked the secrets of liberalism and radicalized liberal democracy. Thus there appears to be a break between Marx's early ethical writings on democracy and liberalism and his more historical analyses grounded in a mature view of socialism. The values of Hegel's self-consciousness and Rousseau's direct democracy are just below the surface of Marx's analysis.

Workshops and factories closed by manufacturers were to be placed under the direct control of the workers' cooperatives. Traditional measures of increasing surplus labor by intensifying work or increasing the workday were to be outlawed. In the end, this new experiment in working-class government was guided by a single ethical principle: "the government of the people by the people."[83] Marx had followed and written about the U.S. Civil War, and was well aware of the historical context and social implications of these words from Lincoln's Gettysburg Address.

However, the greatest ideals of bourgeois liberalism were to become reality only within the short-lived working-class cooperatives of the new Commune. Through the machination of the Prussian government, the violent repression of the French government of Theirs at Versailles, and the mistakes of the Commune, the end came on May 28 as the last defenders of the Paris Commune were either killed or captured on the hills of Belleville.

What are the ethical implications for Marx of his later historical writings on rationalization and democracy? As we have seen, he believes that rights are an expression of the underlying bourgeois social relations and structures. This, however, does not mean that moral values are wrong in and of themselves. The emphasis in Marx's writings has been on materialism and the laws of social evolution. To develop a theory of morals without first developing a social theory would undermine the prospects of clearly articulating the normative foundations of present and future societies. Ethics, thus, becomes extremely important as the basis for a normative critique of capitalism in the form of the early immanent critique using Feuerbach's method or the later critiques based on a theory of needs and social democracy. Critical science rests on an ethical foundation; but without history and sociology, a true ethics is impossible. A purely ethical theory would not get to the real reasons and potentialities behind the social appearances: It could neither historically explain the causes for social oppression, examine the institutional structures of continued exploitation and alienation, nor offer real possibilities for social change. Without a political economy, ethics becomes another form of mystified consciousness and abstract universality. One of Marx's real difficulties is that the power of the natural rights tradition is so strong that to attack it directly is perceived as a direct attack on all basic rights and freedoms of the individual. We have seen that this is incorrect and that Marx wants to see rights as both formal and substantive species rights.

The critique of private property, private appropriations, competition, alienated labor, crude communism, and the ownership of "having" presupposes the idea that man is an autonomous being who creates himself in his objectifications in nature (Marx's early writings) and in his democratic participation (Marx's later writings). The individual is truly human when the satisfaction of his or her needs results also in the satisfaction of the needs of others.[84] To support the natural rights of equality, liberty, and fraternity would be to support the social foundations on which these rights rest. That is, to articulate an ethical theory would be to support a social system built on egoistic needs, competition, and self-interest. These are the very principles that Marx rejects in his early writings. Because ethical theory cannot be divorced from political economy, Marx never developed such a theory. But such a theory is implicit in his political economy. To develop a true ethics requires that equality, liberty, and fraternity rest on the economic and political structures of the Commune. He was critical of the ideological implications of bourgeois rights and its distortions of the truth of capitalist social relations, but ultimately his critique rests on the fact that natural rights are built around the egoistic individual, and not the species being. They reflect a distorted development of the individual, and not the development of true individual potentials. Despite this, however, a great many theorists have recognized that underlying Marx's own theory are ethical propositions and principles about the nature of man, social relations, the proper political economy, and the ultimate goal of communism.

These imperatives rest on a long tradition in Western philosophy from the classics of Ancient Greece to nineteenth-century German Idealism and British liberalism. Marx mediates between Athens, Tübingen, Berlin, and Glasgow. Thus the natural rights tradition presupposes an historically specific social system; to accept the former is unconsciously to accept the latter. To develop an alternative critical ethical theory would be an exercise in the clarification of one's own ideals and the traditions on which they rest. However, it would not be critical in the sense of going to the roots of the social problems. These are uncovered through the use of political economy. One can see the ambivalence clearly here. On the one hand, ethical thought—because it is tied to defense of a particular social formation (capitalism)—is ideological; while, on the other, a critique of political economy rests on moral values and normative assumptions. This is why, although Marx did not develop an ethical theory of individual rights, there is no reason internal to his writings that ethics cannot be part of the Marxist social theory, since the ethical theory was always there—but just never philosophically articulated. The ideals of the French Revolution still remained the foundation for the later development of socialism.

> The principles, indeed, of social and political regeneration have been found fifty years ago. Universal suffrage, direct election, paid representation—these are the essential conditions of political sovereignty. Equality, liberty, and fraternity—these are the principles which ought to rule in all social institutions.[85]

But these ideals of a revolutionary modernity are joined with the ideals of Aristotle's democratic polity.

> One factor of liberty is to rule and to be ruled in turn. For the popular concept of justice is to have equality according to number, not worth, and if this is the concept of justice prevailing, the multitude must of necessity be sovereign and the decisions of the majority must be final and must constitute justice, for they say that each of the citizens ought to have an equal share.[86]

Part III

The Synthesis of Ancient and Modern in Marx

Chapter Five

Metaethics and the Critique of Classical Political Economy: Marx and Ricardo

INTRODUCTION

In the first two parts of this book, the issues surrounding the normative and ethical assumptions of Marx's works were discussed in detail. Of particular interest was how the classical ethics of the Greeks and Germans affected his philosophical anthropology and his initial critiques of political economy. We also saw that the traditional positivistic interpretations of Marx's understanding of science in his later critique of political economy have been mistaken. The epistemological, methodological, temporal, and ontological (materialism) dimensions of his dialectical science draw heavily on eighteenth- and nineteenth-century German philosophy as well as Aristotelian and Epicurean materialism. The Hegel-Schelling-Feuerbachian nexus provides an entirely different insight into the implications of his critiques of empiricism and rationalism. Since the first chapter of this book, we have been reading in the direction of developing Marx's theory of ethics and social justice.

We have already considered four crucial aspects of such a theory: (1) the analysis of the integration of classical ethics in Marx's social theory and political economy; (2) the epistemological critique of positivism, science, and foundationalism; (3) Marx's theory of needs and the self-realization of species being; and (4) the relations between the epistemological dilemma and Marx's theory of democracy (epistemology and politics). The fifth aspect will entail an analysis of his historical and structural critiques of the classical versions of the labor theory of value. This will provide a social and historical content to his ethical theory. With the addition of this part of the puzzle, we will have provided the five major preconditions to Marx's theory of ethics and social justice: classical social ethics, epistemology, anthropology/ psychology, democracy, and political economy. Though some have argued that Marx's view of science does not permit ethical evaluations (the Tucker–Wood thesis), the real debate is over the exact nature of these normative and ethical assumptions—not whether they exist or not.[1]

In his critique of political economy, Marx discovers the ethical substance for his theory of justice. Behind the appearances of the classical labor theory of value, behind the appearances of the cyclical business crises, and behind social inequality and conflict lies his theory of the social relations of production and exploitation, his theory of the lost possibilities of self- and species-realization—the lost possibilities of rational self-consciousness in a kingdom of ends—and, finally, his theory of the social and economic irrationalities of an inefficient and crisis-ridden system (social contradictions). When placed within the broader context of his appropriation of the ethical and epistemological critiques of German Idealism and through it the classical traditions of the Ancients, Marx's revisions of the labor theory of value take on much greater meaning for an understanding of his overall social theory. To emphasize the point of his revisions of the classical theories of labor and value, labor and property, and value and price—and his radical break with these traditions—the term "labor theory of value" will be replaced by the term "theory of value."

The purpose here is simply to deontologize the concept of labor as the mystical substance of either the natural right to property (Smith) or the determining factor in the price of commodities (Ricardo). Marx's theory of value has nothing to do with these classical approaches to labor, as is implied in the subtitle to many of his later works: "Critique of Political Economy." Rather, his interests were in the structural, organizational, and historical evolution of a social system that had resulted in the transformation of labor into exchange value. To jump ahead: Marx in *Capital* was not supplying a direct moral theory on which to build his critique of capital, but—rather— was developing a metaethics by reworking the traditional labor theories of value from Locke, to Smith and Ricardo into a sociological and historical theory of value. Also, for Marx, the real transformation problem was that from labor to exchange value, and not that from exchange value to price.

By criticizing the metaphysics of political economy—its underlying epistemology, method, and theory—Marx lays the foundation for his metaethical critique of capitalism. It is this difference between ethics and metaethics that is so important in understanding Marx's real contribution to social theory and social critique in his later economic writings. The distinction between them corresponds to the difference of emphasis between his anthropology and political economy, between his philosophical and his historical/structural works. In his later writings, Marx does not attempt to lay out—as he did in his early material—the specific moral and ethical values on which the social individual would act. Rather, he wishes to present a critique of the social structures of political economy within which these values could or could not be created. In fact, there is a dialectic between the two as the values inherent in the social institutions affect both the formation of self-consciousness and the values reflected in ethics. In this context, we can see how the traditional ethical theories and values are integrated and transcended in Marx's political economy. The classical traditions materialize within the framework of Marx's understanding and alteration of classical political economy and its view of the law of value. It is here, then, that Marx's interpretation of the crucial first two books of Ricardo's *Principles of Political Economy and Taxation*[2] become joined to the books 5 and 6 of Aristotle's *Nicomachean Ethics*; this will also be an important theme in our next chapter. By beginning with values similar to Aristotle's theory of justice and equality, and joining them to his critique of Ricardo's theory of value, price determination, and the tendential fall in the rate of profit, Marx establishes the substantive and historical foundations for his critique of liberalism; that is, his general theory of social ethics. The formal and methodological foundations—as we have seen—lie in his integration of the dialectical and materialist "critique" of both German Idealism and ancient philosophy.

MARX'S THEORY OF VALUE AND THE CRITIQUE OF RICARDO'S POLITICAL ECONOMY

For Ricardo, labor is simply the quantitative measurement of the value of a commodity and its comparative exchange worth.[3] Marx develops Samuel Bailey's critique of Ricardo's concept of value as determined by labor, from Bailey's *Critical Dissertation on the Nature,*

Measures, and Causes of Value. Marx seems to be beginning where he left off in the *Paris Manuscripts*, with an analysis of work. The difference, however, is 20 years of intellectual effort and growth; it also represents a shift from philosophical questions to ones concerned with the structures of capitalist production. Ricardo separated form from content by recognizing the crucial importance of labor in the formation of the value of exchange commodities. Marx spends most of his time in his later writings investigating the structures of this social formation and the nature of work it produces. Besides the structural and historical studies, he will attempt to undermine normatively the traditional ethical and economic justifications of a social system based on individual liberties and productive efficiency.

The theory of value is the crucial category in Marx's later writings—and possibly the most difficult, if not the most misunderstood even by his supporters. There has been a great deal written on this subject; and one would think that if the issue had not yet been resolved to the satisfaction of everyone, then at least the major issues would have already been expressed and explored. I must argue—though—that, when Marx's theory of value is understood in the overall context of his critical epistemology, his dialectical method, and the ethical foundations of his writings, then the nature of his law of value becomes clearer. We begin to see it as an expression of his metaethics. Together with his theory of a rise in the organic composition of capital and a tendential fall in the rate of profit, the theory of value represents Marx's project to secure the foundations for his general critique of capitalism. It is neither a purely rationalistic analysis (deductive categories), an empiricist analysis (inductive categories), nor even merely an historical analysis. All of these are joined to form a metaethical critique of modern capitalist society.

As articulated in his *Theories of Surplus Value*, Marx's critique of Ricardo's political economy represents the theoretical link between the historical analysis of the structural prerequisites and development of capitalism in the *Grundrisse* and the dialectical presentation of capitalism's internal contradictions in *Capital*. The key point raised again and again throughout the second volume of the *Theories of Surplus Value* is the fact that Ricardo failed to investigate "the peculiar characteristics of labour that creates exchange-value."[4] Nor does he understand the meaning of money as something beyond a mere medium of exchange. Ricardo's service to political economy is that he has examined the underlying physiology of the bourgeois economy, "its internal organic coherence and life process"; explained its appearance using the scientific method; and exposed the essential class contradictions in capitalism.[5] This last point will be especially important for the later development of the Ricardian socialist tradition.[6] But there are real deficiencies in both Ricardo's method and his structural analysis of the underlying foundations of capitalism. According to Marx, the important elements of Ricardo's theory are contained in the first six chapters of his *Principles of Political Economy*, while—in fact—his real contributions to political economy are contained in the first two chapters: the first on value, and the second on rent.[7] The most important theoretical insight of Ricardo is that he reduces the science of political economy—and, therefore, the explanation of bourgeois society—to one overarching economic law: the labor theory of value.

Despite this real theoretical advance over Smith and the classical tradition of political economy, Ricardo himself is not able to unravel the theoretical confusions behind his own labor theory of value. They are created by his inability to articulate any real analytical and structural differences within his value theory (such as the differences among abstract labor, exchange value, and surplus value), within its theory of capital (the differences between constant capital and variable capital), and in the relationships between the two—the organic composition of capital, the rate of surplus value, the rate of profit— and the resulting economic tensions and crises caused by these interrelationships. Marx levels a litany of criticisms against Ricardo's political economy.[8] He argues that: (1) Ricardo failed to see a variety of crucial distinctions, such as between a theory of profits and a theory of surplus value; (2) Ricardo did not recognize the various forms of surplus value (profit, rent, and interest); (3) he also confused relationships such as those between constant capital and fixed capital, value and profits; (4) he confused surplus value and profit, cost and value, natural price and the value of commodities; (5) he failed to distinguish between constant and variable capital and labor and labor power; (6) he failed to perceive the various components in the organic composition of capital and their implications for an analysis of the differences between the rate of surplus value and the rate of profit; (7) Ricardo's theory also lacked an adequate definition of capital, which is limited by him to variable capital (wages); and (8) in the end he also accepted the economic and structural implications of the "metaphysical equilibrium" of Say's law and the resulting belief in the inherent stability of the economic system.[9] According to this last-mentioned theory of equilibrium between production and consumption—supply and demand—there is no inherent tendency to either overproduction or economic crises.

This is an interesting array of theoretical confusions, from Marx's perspective. But is the issue simply that Ricardo did not have a theory similar to that of Marx? Throughout the second volume of *Theories of Surplus Value* there is one overriding theme that encapsulates Marx's fundamental theoretical disagreement with Ricardo's political economy. Though Ricardo failed to articulate analytical differences between the various categories of political economy within his labor theory of value, his real error was that he did not develop the historical and structural foundations of the modern concept of work in this theory. That is, his theory of exchange value did not entail a theory of abstract labor. He did not really understand the social nature and historical form of work in capitalist society. This is so simple a point, yet so profound in its implications. It resulted in merely a quantitative understanding of the value and price of a commodity based on the amount of labor contained in the finished product (positivism); Ricardo's approach to labor was ontological and metaphysical—not historical.

The quantification of value and price is not a real concern of Marx's, though much of the contemporary debate about the labor theory of value centers around this very issue. In fact, much of the debate over Marx is really a disguised debate over contemporary issues, while simply using Marx's name; this has certainly happened with Aristotle's theory of needs, as we have seen. Marx was not interested in pursuing the issue of the utility (use value) of the commodity or that of its quantitative constitution: the amount of labor time contained in it. He was interested in examining its historical and organizational foundations—that is, the historical and structural conditions for the possibility of an economic system based on money exchange, abstract labor, and profit.[10] These relationships are what characterize modernity and have made the capitalist economic system unique in history. What makes such a society possible? What is the social basis for money circulation, exchange value, and commodity production? What are the power relations that underlie the social basis itself? The question is not how much labor is contained in a particular commodity—which would give it its price—but what social form of labor makes a market economy and price (money) possible. In order for there to be an exchange between corn and wool on the market, there must have been a major social revolution that preceded it at the point of production and distribution. This is Marx's central concern, and this is the purpose of his theory of value—not to determine the price of a commodity, but the reasons behind commodity production itself.[11]

> Ricardo starts out from the determination of the relative values (or exchangeable values) of commodities by the *"quantity of labour."* This is the basis of Bailey's criticism and, at the same time, of Ricardo's *shortcomings*. The character of this "labour" is not further examined. If two commodities are equivalents—or bear a *definite proportion* to each other or, which is the same thing, if their *magnitude differs* according to the *quantity of "labour"* which they contain—then it is obvious that regarded as exchange-values, their *substance* must be the same. Their substance is labour. This is why they are "values." Their magnitude varies, according to whether they contain more or less of this substance. But *Ricardo does not examine* the form—the peculiar characteristic of labour that creates exchange-value or manifests itself in exchange-value—the *nature* of this labour.[12]

The philosophical discussion surrounding the category of substance—which has filtered down from the Greeks to the Moderns through Spinoza and Hegel and into Marx's economic theory— indicates that behind the discussion of quantity, value, labor, wages, market prices, and so forth lies one subject: the social form of production. The substance of value is "social labor."[13] This entails both a micro- and macro-examination of the particularities of the nature of work. The former analyzes the immediate social and power structures in the workplace and in the social relations of domination at the point of production. This was certainly the emphasis of Marx in his early writings. The later writings focus on the macrosocial relations, the "laws" of the development of capitalism, and the broader questions of domination within the structure of the economy as a whole—that is, his theory of exploitation and profits. The integration of both macro and micro categories is certainly one reason why Rubel included the *Paris Manuscripts* as part of his published edition of *Capital*.[14] Ricardo's inability to distinguish between various crucial economic categories ultimately reflects his inability to see that the categories of classical political economy are categories of historical and social power relations.

In chapter 25 of his book on Ricardo's theory of surplus value, Marx notes in a very short section that between 1797 and 1815 the price of corn and nominal wages rose in England, while the daily number of hours worked by the workers increased (absolute surplus value). The intensification of economic exploitation in the workplace—facilitated by social control over private property, and social organization of the production process—was a direct response by the capitalists to the falling rate of profit at the time. The interesting aspect of this short analysis is that Marx's critique of Ricardo in the next paragraph gives us an important methodological insight into the total analysis.

> Ricardo did not consider this at all since he investigated neither the origin of surplus-value nor the absolute surplus-value and therefore regarded the working day as a given magnitude. For this case, therefore, *his law*—that surplus-value and wages (he erroneously says profit and wages) in terms of exchange-value can rise or fall only in *inverse* proportion—*is incorrect.*[15]

The investigation of the historical origins and foundations of exchange value and abstract labor lies in analysis of the commodity, the social forms of production, and the foundations of the structures of political economy. It is not simply work that creates value—and exchange value, in particular—but an historically specific social form of work found only in capitalist societies. Marx's analysis of these historical foundations and structures in the *Grundrisse* is framed within a transcendental approach; his goal is to understand the transcendental conditions (historical foundations) for the origins and development of capitalist social relations. Both history and sociology are excluded from political economy, and Marx's *Theories of Surplus Value* critiques this crucial weakness of the classical tradition. Therefore, his purpose is to reintegrate history (*Grundrisse*) and the structures of domination (*Capital*) back into a critique of political economy, so as to develop a theory of social economy along the lines of Aristotle.

Exchange value, surplus value, and abstract labor are not simply economic categories expressing aspects of or factors of production; they are not residual metaphysical categories, left over from nineteenth-century political economy and social theory; nor are they ontological categories reflecting a labor theory of value and its view of universal human nature, such as developed by Locke and Smith;[16] and, finally, they are not abstract analytical attempts at explaining market costs and prices.[17] The secret to understanding these categories is the secret to understanding the metaphysics and fetishism of classical political economy. This is the theme of the added section at the end of chapter 1 in the first volume of *Capital*: the fetishism of the commodity.[18] These categories are the theoretical expression of particular historicosocial relationships and the underlying structures of domination in nineteenth-century political economy. They are also categories of human self-alienation.[19]

THE THEORY OF VALUE: CRITICAL SOCIAL THEORY OR ECONOMIC PRICE THEORY?

Marx argues in the chapter on capital in the *Grundrisse* that in the character of money and exchange relations is found "all the inherent contradictions of bourgeois society,"[20] including those found in more developed production relations. They appear, however, in an immediate form that hide these same contradictions. In his analysis of the simple form of exchange and the exchange of equivalents in the market, Marx recognizes that bourgeois democracy and economics distort the essential social relationships by appealing to the central concepts of equality and freedom as the foundation for the exchange relations.[21] In its pure form, the interchangeability of exchange value is an expression of the social function of market circulation, in which the exchange process is abstracted from all other characteristics. The subjects in this market transference are formally equal, and the commodities being exchanged are equivalent.

The two major characteristics of this social relationship are: (1) the abstraction from all other determinations and aspects of the individual outside the equality of the immediate exchange; and (2) the use of each individual by the other as a pure means in this process. For Marx, the whole process of exchange is necessitated by natural differences in needs and productive capabilities. These natural differences create the social framework for reciprocal exchange based on an equality of commodities and subjects. "Each serves the other in order to serve himself; each makes use of the other, reciprocally, as his means."[22] This exchange realizes nothing of a higher social nature, as it represents only "the generality of self-seeking interests."[23] The realization of the being-for-self is accomplished only by becoming a being-for-another and by reducing every other person in the market exchange to a means.[24]

This abstraction from individual characteristics, from the worth of individuals—while stressing their equal treatment as common possessors of exchange value, and the reciprocal utilitarian approach to market exchange itself—characterizes, for Marx, the anthropological and social assumptions of economic equality and freedom. As Marx very succinctly puts it, "the exchange of exchange values is the productive, real basis of all equality and freedom."[25] The necessity to participate in this process of exchange is the apparent result of each person's own needs and nature ("totality of needs and drives"), and not the result of some alien force determining each one's activity. The development of classes and a gross inequality of wealth distribution then becomes a product of the people's own free will. The purpose of an historical and critical science is to show how these exchange relations—from which all contradictions are seemingly removed—have a deeper dimension than their surface phenomena or appearances studied by modern science. As one moves from simple exchange relations to a complex capitalist society, the contradictions inherent in the social relations and in their ideal expressions (freedom and equality) become visible.

> It is forgotten, on the one side, that the *presupposition* of exchange value, as the objective basis of the whole system of production, already in itself implies compulsion over the individual, since his immediate product is not a product for him, but only *becomes* such in the social process, and since it *must* take on this general but nevertheless external form; and the individual has an existence only as a producer of exchange value, hence that the whole negation of his natural existence is already implied; that he is therefore entirely determined by society.[26]

These are social and historical relations that undermine the equality and freedom of individuals and reduce them to being mere suppliers of exchange value. Marx is also quite explicit that these earlier and more simple forms of reciprocal exchange and commodity production contain in themselves the deepest contradictions, which only become visible in the more fully developed stages of the social relations of capitalism. This is also the reason why Marx is then so critical of the French Socialists, who wished to keep an idealized or purified form of commodity exchange while yet rejecting exploitative social relations.[27] They believed that, freed from the limitations and perversions of money and capital, a social system grounded in the ideals of equality and freedom could be realized. For them, property relations were a question of the fair distribution of social wealth, rather than class structures of domination and unequal power relations in production. They did not understand the relationship between economics and political ideology—nor the fact that the "exchange of exchange values" is the real foundation for the political ideals of equality and freedom. For Marx, an ethical theory must also be connected with historical materialism.

At this point in his analysis, Marx is developing the structural implications of his earlier criticisms of bourgeois social ideals from *On the Jewish Question*. Here—as elsewhere—the substance of the critique of capitalism remains the same. What has been altered is the method (critical science) and the focus of attention (structures of production process). The money system as the realization of exchange value is also the realization of equality and freedom. This apparent conflict between the economic and political dimensions is understood by Marx, as he states that the realization of equality and freedom "prove to be inequality and unfreedom."[28] His critique of the economics of the nineteenth century—which is still applicable to today's economic theory—is that the complex economic and social relationships of capital and wage labor are ignored in preference to "simple determinants" and "infantile abstractions." The historical and political analysis of capitalist society is reduced to the mechanism of a simple exchange of commodities. Everything is reduced to simplistic models of exchange relations based on formal abstraction from the nature of needs, the commodities produced, and the complex social relations inherent in modern capitalist society; it is capitalism without the Industrial Revolution. This results partly from the attempt to reduce the social variables to manageable conditions in order to make scientific predictions and to depoliticize the social relations of production. Economic abstractionism fails to consider the following: (1) the nature of work; (2) the structure of work organizations; (3) the power and authority relations of the workplace; (4) the class structure of society; (5) the role of the state in maintaining a system of exchange value and production based on profits and wage labor; and (6) the importance of land appropriation, exploitation, wars, and imperialism for overcoming its internal contradictions (counteracting influences).

Some economists have argued that there is a contradiction between volume 1 and volume 3 of *Capital* (the transformation problem). They say that Marx started to develop a theory of relative prices of production in a manner similar to Ricardo. Thus, his labor theory of value is in reality a theory of price determination, where value is determined by labor time.[29] This theory states that commodities tend to be exchanged at prices that correspond to their value. By the third volume, Marx began to see that prices could not be equated with the value of the commodity and that, in fact, there are permanent divergences between them. The result is a logical inconsistency between the two volumes of *Capital*. This argument does not take into consideration, however, the sequence in which the volumes were created in Marx's mind nor his overall intentions in his later writings. Karl Korsch writes that to perceive Marx as attempting "to calculate the price of a particular commodity with mathematical exactitude" is "a catastrophical misunderstanding of the economic theory of Marx."[30] Marx was simply not interested in developing a labor theory of value in this direction, for the same reasons that Aristotle in the *Politics* never developed a theory of prices based on his theory of needs.

> Nowhere in the *Politics* does Aristotle ever consider the rules or mechanics of commercial exchange. On the contrary, his insistence on the unnaturalness of commercial gain rules out the possibility of such a discussion, and also helps explain the heavily restricted analysis in the *Ethics*.[31]

This issue and the further debates converge at this one crucial point. Did Marx intend to develop a theory of relative prices in his analysis of capital? The first logical question to follow from this would be: Why would he be interested in doing so? Certainly, the full extent of his sociological and ethical critique was directed against this form of social system, which dehumanized and degraded the individual so that even the ideals of bourgeois society would be incapable of being realized. No: To seek an understanding of Marx in this neo-Ricardian fashion is to take up a question that simply did not and could not interest Marx. Alfred Medio has written that, in both an 1862 letter to Engels and in the *Theories of Surplus Value*, Marx was cognizant of the disparities between prices and value. Quoting Marx, Medio wrote, "Ricardo's identification of the value of commodities with their *cost price* is fundamentally false and traditionally accepted from A. Smith."[32]

This rejection of the direct relationship between the price and value of particular commodities is also present in the *Grundrisse*. "Price is not equal to value . . . because labour time as the measure of value exists only as an ideal, it cannot serve as the matter of price-comparisons."[33] And ultimately, for Marx, value is a qualitative social relation not reducible to quantitative comparisons. In fact, commodities have value only because of the social relations, and not because of labor per se. The value relations are expressed in a variety of phenomenal forms, such as the wage contract, money, costs of commodities, exchange value, and so on; but these forms should not be mistaken for the reality of value itself.

In the third volume of *Capital*, Marx's interest in the issues of production price and profits does not represent a reversion to the classical theory of value of Smith and Ricardo, and therefore to the relative determination of the prices of exchange. Rather, the purpose of introducing the question of prices and profits is to show the interconnection between the capitalist social relations (law of value) and the later developing economic crises of overproduction and the tendential fall in the rate of profit. Profits are related to exchange value and surplus value and ultimately to economic crises—not to the determination of consumer interests and costs, supply and demand. To see price determination—rather than the historical analysis of social relations—as the central issue is to miss both the sociological critique in his law of value and the very pointed analysis of his fetishism critique.[34]

The critique of fetishism contains key elements of Marx's early concept of alienation, but it is now built into the methodological foundations for his study of the social relations within the production process.[35] This critique should represent a clarification of the direction and purpose of Marx's theory of value. Its goal is to examine the commodification of money, work, personality, and (most importantly of all) the labor process—the structure of work under capitalism and the creation of abstract labor. The aim of social critique is not to deal with social relations as things (*Wertfetishismus*), not to examine the economy as the arrangement of the technical factors of production (*objektive Wertlehre* or *Rechnungslehre*), not to examine the interaction of universal psychological principles within social contract relations (*subjektive Wertlehre*),[36] nor to examine the laws for the distribution of the social wealth of society. Thus, this certainly means that Marx would reject any attempt to calculate the relative price of commodities on the basis of socially necessary labor time.

The metatheoretical implications of this section in chapter 1 of volume 1 are enormous, for they entail a break with the natural science method of the classical tradition. The direction of Marx's analysis was to undermine the whole reified approach of political economy (fetishism), in order to develop social categories—to undermine the *Begriffszauberei* and discover the secret of value. Only in this manner would the historical and logical contradictions between the social relations of production and the productive forces be unearthed. Also, this would have been the only method by which to criticize the psychological and political universalism in classical political economy. Franz Petry argued that what really separated Marx and Ricardo was much more than German Idealism: It was the fact that Ricardo was an economist using a method that mirrored the natural sciences— while Marx, "despite his naturalistic make-up, mirrored an unmistakable change in the methodological interpretation of the social life."[37] This methodological transformation was the direct result of his incorporation of the "method of critique" from the classical German philosophical tradition. But it also included the critique of all forms of false universals first developed by the Ancient traditions.

Marx is interested in an examination of the development of this type of society characterized by a specific social form of workplace organization, production relationships, social organizations, class structure, and private property and—in turn—their historical foundations in the development of agrarian capitalism, the enclosures, banking developments, the evolution of the modern state, its military protection of nascent international and domestic markets, and so on. "The specific character of work comes from its social form," which has been confused traditionally with the utility of the commodity (use value), with its relationship to human physiology, and with its immediate legal rights [Rechtsverhältnisse].[38] Not only is work the result of social relations, but so too is money, surplus value, and private profit. "The supposed 'objects' of economic knowledge are themselves only the objectively [dingliche] clothed expressions for the existing determined relationships, which men enter into in the social production of their lives."[39] Ricardo has failed to see that the categories of political economy are historical and social categories.

The distinction between the first and third volumes of *Capital* lies not in the reevaluation of a subjective theory of value, but in the correspondence between the sociological relations within the law of value and the logical/historical economic crises that develop from them. Marx's theory of value is an objective law of the social institutions of capitalism and their inherent contradictory claims, drives, and effects. It is not the same theory of value as that of classical political economy, for his goal is to critique the system—not justify it.[40] The critique of fetishism also results in a critique of the separation of sociological from economic categories—the reduction of the former to the latter, and of the latter to simple quantitative relationships between things (naturliche Sachenzusammenhang).[41]

Though this can be interpreted as referring to a seminal theory of social psychology, it would probably be more accurately viewed as a rejection of the reification of social relationships in all its theoretical forms: *Naturgesetze, Naturwissenschaften,* and *Naturrecht.* "The concept of value receives through Marx's point of view, in so far as [*insoweit*] he stands in the service of the analysis of social relationships, a totally other meaning."[42] More specifically, it is a critique of all forms of false universals in the humanities and social sciences, and therefore represents a further development of his earlier ideas relating to political theory in *Contribution to the Critique of Hegel's Philosophy of Law* and *On the Jewish Question* and to his critique of classical political economy. The range of Marx's critique of false universals is extensive, whether it be the reification of personal relationships (social psychology); the critique of utilitarianism and the enjoyment of use value (political theory); the critique of the subjective theory of value, its idea of the quantitative exchange of things (*ein einfaches ökonomisches Rechenexempel*),[43] and its corresponding price determinations (classical political economy); the critique of the exchange process as a form of biological and psychological satisfaction; or the critique of the circulation process as the simple exchange of things and a production process where social relationships are turned into "factors of production"—or whether it be the whole methodological approach in these areas, which takes the form of natural science.

> The size of the produced worth by the workers in the products of their labor beyond the compensation of wages or the amount of the "surplus labor" toward the production of "surplus value," and the relation of this "surplus labor" to the necessary labor (that is, the current "rate of surplus-value" or "rate of exploitation" for a determined time and a determined country) is thus in the capitalist manner of production not the result of economic calculation. It is the result of a social class battle.[44]

The concept of capital is the result of a synthesis of volume one and its analysis of the essential unity of production (law of value) with volume three and its study of accumulation (economic crises of overproduction and tendential fall in rate of profit). The underlying logical/historical foundations for economic stagnation and crises rests in the creation of value in commodity production. The production of value is the barrier beyond which capital cannot proceed; it also sets class limits to the accumulation of capital, by limiting the manner in which exchange value and surplus value may be extracted in the production process. The barriers are not natural, but are the result of the social organization of production—the very thing Ricardo failed to consider.

VALUE THEORY AS AN HISTORICAL THEORY OF THE SOCIAL ORGANIZATION OF PRODUCTION

For Petry, the central focus of the value concept (*Wertbegriff*) is "the analysis of the social structure of the capitalist economy."[45] It represents an analysis of the laws of marketplace, the fragmentation and specialization in the division of labor, the competition in the market, the mechanization of labor within the factory system, the homogenization and deskilling of labor, and the alienation of labor. This is the structural substance of the objective law of value, and not value as interpreted as the interaction between psychological subjects (utilitarianism) within the sphere of consumption and circulation. These are the objective and structural characteristics of abstract labor; as the category becomes more concrete in the logical development of the Concept (*Begriff*) of capital, Marx also makes it concrete by giving it historical and social determinations.

Petry views the differences between the antinomies of *Wertgesetz* and *Wertbetrachtung*, *Verteilungsproblem* and *Preisproblem*, and objective *Wertlehre* and subjective *Wertlehre* as a reflection of the fetishized approach to the analysis of capitalism used by the classical political economists.[46] The analysis of the *Wertbegriff* and the *Wertlehre* both imply a sociological and historical analysis of work relations and a fundamentally ethical orientation to these structures. Though Petry sees the problem of the different approaches to the law of value and argues articulately that the heart of Marx's analysis lies in the social organization of work, he also contends that the value concept of Marx has no normative worth of its own since it is simply a "theoretical principle of the value relationship."[47] Whether Marx's theory of labor involves a theory of exploitation is another issue heatedly debated.[48] Geoffrey Pilling—though he does not dismiss the importance of Marx's theory of exploitation—indicates that it is secondary to the latter's theory of contradiction. Pilling argues that Marx was primarily interested in developing a theory of the internal physiology of the social system, with its contradiction between the social organization of production (volume 1) and the accumulation process (volume 3). This was originally expressed as contradictions between exchange value and use value.[49] The weakness of this approach is that it abstracts Marx's theory of value from his historical critique in both the *Grundrisse* and *Capital*. It also abstracts his critique of political economy from the ethical foundations of his thought in the Ancients.

While Ricardo stayed at the level of price appearances, competition, and the natural distribution of profits to the different classes,

Marx dug deeper, for he understood that behind the price movement
stood the completed distribution not as the distribution of finished
consumer supplies within the isolated classes of the people, but as the
distribution in human work of the liquidated products, of the total value
and through it as the social relations of producing men.[50]

For Marx, the labor theory of value developed first by the classical
bourgeois theorists becomes the framework within which he analyses
the historical and social forms of material production. The social
relations of production form the heart of Marx's analysis in his later
economic writings—not the technological categories of economic
analysis.[51] Rather than being concerned with questions of price determinations, the relationship between value and price, and worker's
wages and profits—all within a theory of prices—Marx utilizes his
theory of value for an analysis of the qualitative determination of the
social relationships specific to capitalist society in England during the
nineteenth century. Thus, the theory of value does not provide a
basis for the quantitative calculation of the price of commodities, but
is rather a key to determining the qualitative relationships of capitalism that lead to worker exploitation and to economic crises.[52] The
contemporary attempt by the neo-Ricardians of the Cambridge
School to eliminate Marx's theory of value and its supposed metaphysical remnants in order to combine Marx's sociological class analysis within a neoclassical theory of price is a further example of the
misunderstanding of the radically qualitative and sociological nature
of his theory.[53] It is also an underestimation of how radical his critique
of political economy really is.

The law of value is intended by Marx to give us insight into the
social organization and structure of the production process—the
exploitive nature of the creation of surplus value, capitalist profits,
and wage labor in general. It is not intended—as we shall see—as a
mechanism for the determination of quantitative relationships between things (commodities) in the market (the critique of commodity
fetishism). The emphasis for Marx is clearly on the production
process and, more specifically, on the social forms of interaction—not
on the exchange and distribution process. Certainly the failure to
distinguish between exchange value as part of production and exchange value as part of distribution (price) has accounted for much
of the confusion over his reluctance to develop a theory of justice
based on fair distribution of the social goods of society. This also
accounts for a good deal of the misunderstanding in regard to the
nature of his theory of value, his crisis theory, and his metaethics.

Another way of stating the same idea is that Marx's understanding of the theory of value, and thus his historical and materialist analysis of political economy, involves a recognition that in a society characterized by the workings of a labor theory of value, it is not possible to realize the ethical norms of the community and equality developed out of the Greek, Hebrew, and German traditions. These are metatheoretical concepts (institutional and structural prerequisites)—for without community and equality, the free self-conscious development of the individual becomes impossible. Metaethics contains the structural preconditions for the realization of ethics. The necessity for these two social and structural preconditions for self-consciousness and individual freedom (human emancipation) is a theme that was explicitly developed in the *Paris Manuscripts* and is only just below the surface in his later writings.[54]

ABSTRACT LABOR, EXCHANGE VALUE, AND THE STRUCTURES OF POLITICAL ECONOMY

Let us now investigate the historical nature of commodity production and exchange relations. The value of a particular commodity is determined by the socially necessary labor time required for its production. The discussion about the nature of value has centered around the meaning, relevance, and application of the concept "labor." It is not a social fact that any particular object may be exchanged at any particular time and place. For an exchange to occur, a social metamorphosis must first precede it. The unprecedented, dramatic, and revolutionary nature of this social transformation was only first recognized by Marx and was then immediately suppressed with the rise of neoclassical economics. To change a product into a commodity—to change a use value into an exchange value; to transform something that has subjective worth into a commodity with a price—requires a major transformation of the whole social system. This is why Marx states in the beginning of *Capital* that he is not interested in a discussion of use value, which is a physiological and biological category that transcends the particularity of history and social systems. The emphasis of his research is on the specific historical nature and characteristics of exchange value.

In his analysis of commodity exchange, Marx returns to Aristotle's *Nicomachean Ethics* and the Greek attempt to deal with the issue of the commensurability and exchange of products. Aristotle recognizes the need to find the "common substance"—the basis for equality—that underlies the exchange process and makes it all possible. Marx argues that Aristotle was incapable of developing his theory of exchange any further because Greek society was built on the prerequisites of inequality and slavery, recognizing only the differences between human beings. What was needed was the development of modern society and its political notion of the equality of all humanity—which is later expressed by Marx in economic categories as "abstract labor." "Aristotle therefore, himself, tells us, what barred the way to his further analysis; it was the absence of any concept of value."[55] Marx states that the common substance Aristotle sought is labor. Castoriadis has picked up this discussion between Marx and Aristotle in order to further analyze the first chapter of *Capital* in more detail. Castoriadis believes that the whole analysis of the commodity is a logical tautology based on the metaphysical foundations of the concept of substance.[56] In fact—he continues—the notion of simple labor is the common substance and, thus, the essential category in Marx's labor theory of value. Besides confusing the relationship between appearances and essence—substance and subjectivity—in Marx's method, it is Castoriadis who has turned Marx's notion of labor into an ahistorical and metaphysical category. A further reading into the chapters on money and capital should have indicated to him the direction that Marx was taking.

For a commodity to be equated with all other commodities in terms of its objectified labor, to be comparable in terms of the amount of labor value contained in it, and to be the necessary basis for market exchange, distribution, and consumption requires more than simply labor time. In every society, the production of the goods necessary to satisfy human needs is always the result of the application of human labor on nature. Labor in itself is not the major distinguishing characteristic of commodity production.

> The existence of value in its purity and generality presupposes a mode of production in which the individual product has ceased to exist for the producer in general and even more for the individual worker, and where nothing exists unless it is realized through circulation. For the person who creates an infinitesimal part of a yard of cotton, the fact that this is a value, exchange value, is not a formal matter. If he had not created an exchange value, money, he would have created nothing at all. This determination of value, then, presupposes a given historic stage of the mode of social production and is itself something given with that mode, hence a historic relation.[57]

Value determination and the creation of exchange value are thus not simply the result of the application of labor in the production process (labor theory of value), but—rather—the transformation of the commodity into a quantitative relation in which all other commodities are theoretically equivalent to it. This, in turn, presupposes a transformation in the nature and rhythm of work, its technical and social organization, and the class structure within which it develops. The relation or measurement of all commodities in terms of what is produced—and later, the quantitative relation of all commodities in terms of a third commodity, such as gold and silver—exists at the level of symbolic thought. This third commodity is not a particular commodity and represents labor time as such—that is, it is a social symbol of exchange values.[58] This characterization represents a conceptual abstraction from all the natural properties and use values of the commodities, and considers them only in terms of their commensurability or relation to other commodities. Commodities by themselves are not naturally exchangeable against every other commodity. This only occurs when a commodity becomes an exchange value. The basis for the commensurability of commodities is then the labor time necessary for its production, and it is on this basis that the exchange between one product and another takes place as an numerical expression. One pound of bread will be exchanged for ten nails.

The commensurability of all commodities in terms of money takes place not because of the objectification of labor time in the commodities themselves, but because of a historically specific, qualitatively different kind of labor that is produced in capitalism. This is the heart of Marx's theory of abstract labor.[59] He is very well aware of the historical changes that must occur in the structural patterns of labor before it becomes possible to think simply about the commensurability (exchange value) of commodities. His goal is to produce a theory of value that stresses the historical specificity of this production process, and the qualitatively different form of labor created in it. His theory of abstract labor and value has changed from an ontological and anthropological form into historical and sociological categories; labor and value are expressions now for historically specific forms of social and work relationships characteristic of capitalist societies. This point cannot be overemphasized, along with the idea that "the commodities to be exchanged are transformed in the head into common relations of magnitude, into exchange-value and are thus reciprocally compared."[60] Labor in general is not capable of this. It is the social relations among people—materialized in the production process—

that later takes on an independent existence as prices and profits.[61]
The historical nature of the category of value may be seen in Marx's
discussion of the nature of labor and exchange value in *A Contribution
to the Critique of Political Economy.*

> As useful activity directed to the appropriation of natural factors in one
> form or another, labour is a natural condition of human existence, a
> condition of material interchange between man and nature, quite inde-
> pendent of the form of society. On the other hand, the labour which
> posits exchange values is a specific social form of labour. For example,
> tailoring if one considers its physical aspect as a distinct productive
> activity produces a coat, but not the exchange-value of the coat. The
> exchange-value is produced by it not as tailoring as such but as abstract
> universal labour, and this belongs to a social framework not devised by
> the tailor.[62]

THE STRUCTURAL PREREQUISITES OF CAPITAL: MARX'S "COPERNICAN REVOLUTION"

In its natural properties as a product having a certain use value for
its producer, the commodity is not exchangeable or even measurable
against other commodities. This is something that occurs when commodities are abstracted from their material content and natural
properties, and become exchange values. When commodities are
transformed into these abstract symbols, they become comparable to
other commodities, and thereby measurable in terms of a universal
equivalent. Note that the symbolic meaning attaching itself to the
commodity as exchange value is not an inherent property of the
commodity—is not a component of its natural properties—but,
rather, is the result of a mental process whereby the commodity
becomes an exchange value for the individual and, in turn, becomes
exchangeable with other commodities. This mental process itself
requires a structural transformation in the nature of work, production, and distribution.

In the first notebook of the *Grundrisse* Marx seems to indicate that
it is a mental process whereby individuals simply express the "worth"
of a commodity in the form of a symbol. He uses the example of
certain natives in West Africa who transform commodities into "bars."
Each commodity is worth so many bars in the mind of the owner;
commodities are compared to each other in terms of these bars, and

exchanged accordingly. As Marx says, these bars have "a merely imaginative existence," but they permit exchange to take place. Commodities become transformed quantitatively into an expression of exchange value: That is, they have a quantitative measure in relation to another commodity containing use value or another commodity acting as a universal equivalent (money). They must also be transformed qualitatively.

> In becoming an exchange value, a product (or activity) is not only transformed into a definite quantitative relation, a relative number . . . but it must also at the same time be transformed qualitatively, be transformed into another element, so that both commodities become magnitudes of the same kind of the same unit, i.e., commensurable. The commodity first has to be transformed into labor time, into something qualitatively different from itself.[63]

As the materialization of labor time, these commodities are the product of an historically specific kind of labor that results from a particular set of historically formed social and economic institutions. Though Marx starts with a recognition that exchange takes places as a mental abstraction from the material particulars of the commodities and requires a symbolic mediation during exchange process, it is the historical foundation of this process that interests him. In fact, the implicit question that follows him throughout the *Grundrisse* is: What are the conditions for the possibility of exchange value (measurability and commensurability)? In the third notebook, he pushes the question further by asking: What are the conditions for the possibility of surplus and capitalist profit? The historical conditions on which rest the transformation of all products and activities into exchange value require the establishment of a national and international market economy, wage labor, and private property.[64] In the first two notebooks, Marx examines the nature of exchange value as a social abstraction, and the social formation necessary for its existence. The emphasis here is on the process of exchange and circulation in a money economy.

> Exchange, when mediated by exchange value and money, presupposes the all-round dependence of the producers on one another, together with the total isolation of their private interests from one another, as well as a division of social labor whose unity and mutual complementarity exist in the form of a natural relation, as it were, external to the individuals and independent of them. The pressure of general demand

and supply on one another mediates the connection of mutually indifferent persons.[65]

Early in the first notebook, Marx briefly outlines the historical and social forms of production of exchange value.[66] The first major characteristic of commodity production is "the dissolution of all fixed personal (historic) relations of dependence in production."[67] This would require the dissolution of the small independent farmer, the cottage industry, the local community and all self-help groups (social welfare systems), along with any political and economic power that might transcend or negatively influence the operations of the market mechanism. This also entails undermining the extended family structure, which results in creation of the nuclear family. It involves the dissolution of all social and economic relations that protect the individual from or restrict the individual from entry into market relations—such as the Elizabethan Poor Laws.[68]

All external economic forms that interfere with the working of the market must be eliminated, and a new network of social relations created in which all producers in general depend on all others. Reciprocal dependence is instituted and maintained through the creation of a system of needs, regulated by a series of different commodity exchanges. At the point of production, this dependence is further intensified by a new division of labor in which all production activities are interrelated and integrated (abstract labor) by the managerial center of capital. As consumption and production are structured around the market in general and the production of exchange value in particular, the forms of social dependency that now develop are objective and formal—totally unlike that of the personal and family dependency of the eighteenth-century cottage industry. The new structural changes produce a new type of social relationship, and this whole structure is what produces exchange value; this latter presupposes alienated labor and private property as structural prerequisites.

The reducation of individuals to Hume's "bundle of sense impressions," and the collision of individual atoms in Newtonian physics, require the destruction of Aristotelian *physis* and the creation of a new science. For a money economy to fully develop, these other social forms must disappear and be replaced by the anonymity of a market economy ruled by the mediation and exchange of money. In this system, even the production process is determined by the requirement to purchase labor as just another particular commodity.[69] Production in a communal setting, on the other hand, with a different set of social arrangements produces "a specific share of the communal production,"[70] but does not produce exchange value.

In the second notebook, Marx begins to specify the nature of work and the distinction between the use value and the exchange value of work itself. The exchange value is determined by the labor necessary to regenerate "the general substance" of the worker's labor powers and the further capacity to work. At this point, Marx is still interested in the exchange value of labor from the perspective of circulation only. In the third notebook, his interests move from an analysis of the exchange value of labor to an analysis of wage labor at the point of production, for purposes of explaining the creation of surplus and profits. The major characteristic of free labor is that it does not produce exchange value in itself, but is seen as only pure use value for the capitalist. The second notebook ends with an important point regarding one condition for labor exchange of the worker: "His *valuelessness* and *devaluation* is the presupposition for capital and the precondition of *free* labor in general."[71]

The third notebook begins with an analysis of the relationship between capital and labor. Though the language is at times densely philosophical and theoretically abstract, Marx attempts to outline the anthropological and sociological aspects of the nature of work in capitalist society. The opposition of labor and capitalist, the indifference of the worker and capitalist to the content of labor, and the mutual indifference and lack of specificity between labor and capital are the main characteristics of this economic and social arrangement.

> This economic relation—the character which capitalist and worker have as the extremes of a single relation of production—therefore develops more purely and adequately in proportion as labour loses all the characteristics of art; as its particular skill becomes something more and more abstract and irrelevant, and as it becomes more and more a *purely abstract activity*, a purely mechanical activity, hence indifferent to its particular form; a mere *formal* activity or, what is the same, a merely material activity, activity pure and simple, regardless of its form. Here it can be seen once again that the particular specificity of the relation of production, of the category—here, capital and labour—becomes real only with the development of a particular *material mode of production* and of a particular stage in the development of the industrial *productive forces.*[72]

What Marx is describing in this abstraction from all particularities of work is the structure of a political economy that has created alienated labor. Abstracted from the ends of work as self-realization and from the goals of the community, work is structured around a formless and purposeless—mechanical—activity, whose purpose lies in the hands of the capitalist and no longer with the worker. Alienation here is perceived not as a philosophical or anthropological state, but as the necessary development of a particular material mode of production and productive forces. This is the structural mechanism of political economy behind the process of alienation. This is the further working out of the arguments of the early writings, where Marx states that private property is not the cause of alienation, but its result; the cause lies in the division of labor—that is, the social organization of the capitalist mode of production. His intention is not simply to lay the foundation for an anthropological or moral critique of capitalism, but rather—through the theory of value united to his economic crises theory—to lay the foundation for a metaethic. Both are necessary for a complete ethics.

The third notebook deals with labor's relation to capital in the production process. Labor at this point is the mere possibility of a value-positing activity, since it is the pure subjective existence of labor without any form of objectivity. The phrase "without objectivity" refers to the fact that labor—as a pure abstract activity indifferent to its form, as an activity divorced from the technical means of production (private ownership), and therefore as a pure possibility without any capital of its own—possesses in itself no means for the realization of its own activity. This is just a more philosophically abstract way of describing the implications of the dispossession of private property in a class society. This is the modern form of labor stripped of the structural means for its own self-realization. Marx has moved from the arena of exchange and money to that of capital and production. As he expresses it here, the relation between labor and capital has all the appearances of the contradiction between subject and object, subjective labor and objective labor, activity and passivity.

Capital is a social activity and relationship determined by a particular mode of productive relations. It is not a thing (fetishism), but a social relationship. The elimination of capitalists does not really change the system, since commodity production and capital may be institutionalized and realized by someone else. Labor is exchanged for the exchange value of money, which is then turned into payment for basic necessities. What is purely a means for existence and exists only as exchange value for the worker is transformed by the capitalist into capital—that is, into something that continues to reproduce more and more surplus value. It is not that labor has changed from one thing into another, but rather that it has changed its social form. The social relations of production are controlled by the capitalists through the legal ownership of private property. Because of this control over objectified labor, and now subjective labor—dead labor, and living labor—they have control over the whole process of production, and thereby over the creativity and productivity of labor. This means that a class has control over ontology itself: It controls how the individual and society are defined and structured. It controls the underlying values, ideals, and social goals—which constitute the essence of reality for the species being. And in this process of control, it undermines the ethics valued from the Greek philosophers to the German Idealists, and makes human rationality and freedom impossible.

Labor—as we have seen—has only an unreliable potential, and the real productive capability of labor lies outside itself; productivity of labor can only be realized in the exchange between labor and capital and the consumption of labor by capital. The conclusion is explicitly made by Marx that the productive potential and its realization can only take place through the alienation of labor. Marx's economic theory is here recapitulating his earlier insights from the *Paris Manuscripts*. "Thus all the progress of civilization . . . enriches not the worker but rather capital."[73] Alienation is the structural precondition for the further development of wealth from money to capital. Other economists such as Ricardo and Sismondi have presented the case that only labor is productive, that capital is only the ideal form of value, and that capital is accumulated labor. Marx argues that the manner in which labor and capital confront each other should be enough to arouse some suspicions regarding a purely economic interpretation of this relationship.

THE THEORY OF SURPLUS VALUE AND THE *VERWERTUNGSPROZESS*

The other side of this simple production process is the activity of realization (*Verwertungsprozess*) whereby labor and capital not only unite in the productive process to make a commodity, but unite actually to increase value and not merely to reproduce it. This is the mechanism for the creation of surplus value. Central to the concept of abstract labor is the historical process of dissolution, whereby workers are separated from the objective conditions of production. By this means, the free laborer is created. For Marx—then—this separation of the workers from the instruments of production, and thereby from any form of autonomous economic activity, was considered to represent freedom. This process was preconditioned by the transformation of money into capital or the development of merchant wealth into surplus production. The fact that all the crucial elements of production—the raw material, the instruments of labor, and labor itself—can be purchased or (which is the same thing) turned into exchange value requires the prior historical transformation of society and the alienation of labor.

> A presupposition of wage labour, and one of the historic preconditions for capital, is free labour and the exchange of this free labour for money in order to reproduce and the realize money, to consume the use value of labour not for individual consumption, but as use value for money. Another presupposition is the separation of free labour from the objective conditions of its realization—from the means of labour and material for labour. Thus, above all, release of the worker from the soil as his natural workshop—hence dissolution of small, free landed property as well as of communal landownership resting on the oriental commune.[74]

Within the context of the debates in classical political economy over the nature and cause of wealth, it is Marx who sees it less as a technical creation of labor and technology than as the result of specific historical circumstances. The latter required social relationships with which all autonomous social foundations of production be illuminated: the dissolution of landed property relations, the dissolution of the guild system, and the dissolution of client relations. All forms of social relations external to the market must be dissolved so that production of use value and direct consumption can be replaced by production of exchange value. "Capital does not create the objective conditions of labour."[75] The existence of monetary wealth and the dissolution of old property relations do not necessarily lead to a capitalist social formation. There is no historical necessity as societies change from one social form into another. This new form occurred only with the expropriation of land and the creation of free workers, who were freed from community responsibilities and duties at the same time they were freed from their property. They then became part of the mass labor market. The state was also necessary in this process as it created the stable social order in which this historical development could proceed unimpeded, by means of passing and implementing the Acts of Parliament and the Poor Laws. First through its police power and its control over force, the state was able to use the gallows and public whippings as mechanisms for social control and peace. The state placed an important priority in these early times on dissolution of the old property relations and modes of production. "The *governments*, e.g., of Henry VII, VIII, etc., appear as conditions of the historic dissolution process and as makers of the conditions for the existence of capital."[76] Capital was influential in increasing the tempo of this process of dissolution; but it did not create it, nor did it create the objective condition on which this new mode of production developed.

> For the domination of exchange value itself, and of exchange-value-producing production, *presupposes* alien labour capacity itself as an exchange value—i.e. the separation of living labour capacity from its objective conditions; a relation to them—or to its own objectivity—as alien property; a relation to them, in a work, as *capital*.[77]

The fifth notebook is primarily an analysis of the historical conditions for the dissolution of feudal property relations and the creation of the labor market and the free worker—that is, the objective and subjective conditions of capital. In the sixth notebook Marx starts to analyze the nature of surplus value and profits within the production process, and explains how surplus value arises neither out of capital (wealth), the instruments of production (which merely transfer their value but do not add to it), nor the act of exchange. The secret lies in the mode of production itself and its newly formed social relations. The dissolution of old property relations and the formation of the free worker were preconditions for capital accumulation. The extraction of surplus and, thus, wealth from the production is a reflection of the class structure and its relations of domination and control. If capital is to realize itself, it must not only preserve itself, but increase over time.

Marx argues that profit within the whole system cannot be created through commercial interaction. Though a particular merchant may buy cheap and sell at much higher prices—and thus obtain a greater profit—this does not explain the nature of profits as a whole. It does not explain the production process—how a product is made—nor does it explain the value of the various component parts that go into making the final product. What role does the value of the instruments of labor and labor itself play, insofar as they are consumed in the production process? Where does capital and surplus value come from? "The only thing which can make him into a capitalist is not exchange, but rather a process through which he obtains *objectified labor time*, i.e., *value*, without exchange."[78] Surplus value is thus obtained when—over and above the exchange of equivalents—something extra is added in the production process. Marx poses the answer in the third notebook. "By giving in exchange only the labour objectified in the worker"[79]—by paying only for the productive powers of the worker, and not for the total amount of the results of the worker's production—the capitalist thereby reaps a surplus. The capitalist purchases the use value of labor and receives in exchange the full harvest of what the worker is capable of producing. Therefore, surplus value is not a product of labor, but a product of the structures of domination found in modern political economy.

To pay for the necessary use value of the worker may require only one-fourth of a day's labor, while the other three-fourths is a surplus or—as Marx says in *Capital*—unpaid labor. The worker labors for the sustenance of his or her body for only a small part of the day, while working free for the capitalist for the rest of the day. It is this distinction between necessary labor (wages and sustenance) and surplus labor (profits) that is the basis for the creation of surplus value. What interests Marx in this development is the disenfranchisement of the worker; this is expressed in his constant reference to the foundations of surplus creation as "the separation of labour from its objective elements of existence."[80] The existence of the capitalist and wage labor rests on this process of dissolution.

> We see therefore that the capitalist, by means of the exchange process with the worker—by indeed paying the worker an equivalent for the costs of production contained in his labour capacity, i.e., giving him the means of maintaining his labour capacity, but appropriating living labour for himself—obtains two things free of charge, first the surplus labour which increases the value of his capital; but at the same time, the previous labour materialized in the component parts of capital and thus preserves the previously existing value of capital.[81]

At this point in his analysis, Marx recognizes that the various components of the process—the machinery, the raw material, and the labor—are joined for only one purpose: the production of surplus value and the free extraction of living labor from the exchange process. The components of the production process have no other goal than this; and when the creation of surplus value becomes difficult or impossible, production ceases. Here is the real link between volume 1 and volume 3 of *Capital*, and the answer to the vexing transformation problem.[82] It is not for the common good of the members of a community, not for realization of use value, nor for the satisfaction of basic human needs that production continues. But when production does cease, so too does any possibility for supplying the basic necessities for human life and social equilibrium.

THE CLASSICAL EQUILIBRIUM MODEL OF SUPPLY AND DEMAND AND ECONOMIC CRISES

Though Marx does not go deeply into an analysis of the issues surrounding modern economic crises and overproduction in the *Grundrisse*, he does reject the simple equation of supply and demand held by Say, James, Ricardo, and J. S. Mill as well as the equilibrium model on which it is based.[83] The debate revolves around the issue of whether capitalist production contains (posits) its own realization within itself. These economists "conceived production as directly identical with the self-realization of capital—and hence were heedless of the barriers to consumption or the existing barriers of circulation itself."[84] Though Sismondi does recognize the existence of barriers to self-realization of capital, they are portrayed as external barriers created by customs and trade. For Marx, the barriers and limits of capital lie in capital as the production of exchange value for exchange on the market. Production is not maintained for the purpose of human consumption or for the creation of use value. Rather, it is for the creation of surplus value and capitalist profits. The difference between these two purposes of production is the difference between two entirely different social systems, with differing social goals and relations of production. By not seeing the distinction between use value and exchange value at this point, the classical political economist misses the crucial limitations to the self-realization of capital in both the nature of the work force and the underlying purposes of production (surplus value). The demands of the social system based on use value (mass of needs) and exchange value (surplus value) produce different types of structural demands and stresses on the economic system.

"Supply itself is demand for a certain product of a certain value."[85] This subtle play on the concept of value indicates the social divisions in society, which create so many different problems. Commodities have a value as a price on the market, they have a use value to satisfy a social need, and they also have an exchange value that presupposes the totality of social relations in capitalist production. These distinctions between use value and exchange value, between social needs and the needs of capital, between needs in general and needs capable of being fulfilled (money), are the deep causes on which rest the crises of the economic system. Marx contends that the economy is not a closed system regulated by the costs of production and the market (Ricardo), but is ultimately regulated by the laws of production and the law of value—that is, by the historical foundations of a social system that creates capital and wage labor. Capital is not simply wealth for production, nor is wage labor simply work. Capital and wage labor describe a social arrangement with specific relations of domination, work structures, and political and economic institutions, including their corresponding cultural values and ideals. These relationships, their class contradictions, and the economic contradictions between supply and demand—production and consumption—are the reasons for the crisis of overproduction and underconsumption.

At this point, Marx does not get into the details of his analysis. Both aspects of the economy—production and consumption—have different structural imperatives, which contradict one another; it is as if two railroad engines were hooked up back to back, pulling in opposite directions. On the one hand, production strives to overcome the internal and technological limits established in the production of surplus value by reduction of necessary labor to a minimum, by improvement in the productive forces (science and technology), and by intensification of the labor process (exploitation). However, this process is further restrained from realizing the creation of surplus and profits (*Verwertungsprozess*) because there are structural limits placed on the ability of workers to consume by these very same imperatives of production, as established by the social relations or class system of capital. The first requirement of capital is to keep necessary labor time (wages and consumption) to a minimum. Thus, the drive for surplus and the lowering of labor costs and wages contradicts the realization requirements for higher levels of mass consumption to complete the production–consumption cycle of surplus value. The crisis of overproduction is regarded by Marx as "the fundamental contradiction of developed capital."[86]

The contradictions of capital reverse the priority of production from the production of goods to the maintenance of established social relations. For Marx, this distorted priority of capitalism undermines its own productive capacity. These structural limits, in turn, produce economic crises, but "coincide with the nature of capital, with the essential character of its very concept."[87] This is why these limits are not simply structural barriers resulting in economic and social crises, but are expressions of the Concept (*Begriff*) and logic of capital itself. They can never be transcended and never fully counterbalanced. Marx summarizes these limits as follows:

> (1) *necessary labour* as limit on the exchange value of living labour capacity; (2) *surplus value* as the limit on surplus labour time; and, in regard to relative surplus time, as barrier to the development of the forces of production; (3) *transformation into money*, exchange value as such, as the limit of production; (4) the *restriction of the production of use values by exchange value.*[88]

These limits are structural and logical limits to the potential extraction of surplus value, to the realization of capital in consumption, and to the production process as a whole. The minimum requirements for reproduction of the work force (wages for survival) place limits on the exchange value of living labor capacity: Wages cannot be reduced beyond a certain limit necessary for basic physical survival. This, in turn, limits the amount of surplus value and surplus labor time that are necessary for the creation of profits. The requirement (limit) of capital to realize itself in consumption—since it does not produce for immediate consumption in the first place (exchange value)—places an extra burden on the production process. The requirement to transform commodities into money thus limits the amount that can, in effect, be produced by capital.

Finally, the restrictions on the production of use value by the prior requirements of exchange value, and the restrictions on the social satisfaction of human needs by the prior requirement for realization of private profits, result logically and structurally in an economic system that moves in the direction of constant overproduction. The entire credit system created in England was an attempt to overcome these restrictions to production, but the transcendence of the crisis is only temporary—until the next higher level of economic crisis is reached. The process starts again, but at a higher and more technically advanced level of production and contradiction. Marx has shown that a social system based on private property, capital, and wage labor creates its own internal barriers to the realization of accumulation and equilibrium.

Profit is the ultimate barrier of production in a society in which production and consumption are distinct economic spheres; overproduction is connected with the requirement to minimize necessary labor. Marx draws heavily on the classical tradition—and Malthus, in particular—in order to show that "the demand of the labourer himself can never be an adequate demand."[89] It is at this point in the fourth notebook of *Gundrisse* that Marx comes to the critical and ethical heart of his analysis.

> To begin with: capital forces the workers beyond necessary labour to surplus labour. Only in this way does it realize itself, and create surplus value. But on the other hand, it posits necessary labour only *to the extent and in so far as* it is surplus labour and the latter is *realizable as surplus value*. It posits surplus labour, then, as the condition of the necessary, and surplus value as the limit of objectified labour, of value as such. As soon as it cannot posit value, it does not posit necessary labour; and given its foundation, it cannot be otherwise. It therefore restricts labour and the creation of value—by an artificial check.[90]

Not only are there limits and checks on the production process caused by the social relationships between production and consumption and between capital and wage labor in capitalist society, but the production process is itself only an epiphenomenon (technological reflex) of the social relations of production. The basic requirements for human survival, the requirements of production in general, and the production of use values are accomplished only to the extent that profit is realized, the class system with its repression of workers is maintained, and the law of value remains as the essence of the production process. Only to that extent does production proceed and—in the process— undermine the priority and importance of basic human values. The same drive of the system to increase surplus and profits through an increase of the productive forces also limits these same productive forces. As the system becomes more and more technologically advanced, the class structure further limits its possibilities for satisfying human needs, both physical and spiritual. All this occurs because capital is separate from wage labor, and the wage laborer severed from the objective conditions of his or her existence.

In the third section of the seventh notebook, Marx develops the beginnings of his theory of the tendency of the rate of profit to fall. There seems to be no direct connection made by Marx between the theory of overproduction in the fourth notebook and that of the tendential fall in the rate of profit in the seventh notebook. Both are viewed as distinct aspects of the underlying contradictions of capitalist production. In *Capital*, the former will be more integrated into the latter, and the theory of the tendency of the rate of profit to fall will have a more central place in his general economic theory.

For our purposes here, both overproduction and the tendential fall in the rate of profit represent economic and social effects of the contradictions of capital and the workings of the law of value in the economy. In the last two notebooks of the *Gundrisse*, Marx evaluates the repercussions of this system on individual freedom and self-recognition and shows how the capitalist social formation is antithetical to both. For him, the equating of individual freedom and economic competition in the market produces nothing but its own opposite.

> This kind of individual freedom is therefore at the same time the most complete suspension of all individual freedom, and the most complete subjugation of individuality under social conditions, which assume the form of objective powers, even of overpowering objects—of things independent of the relations among individuals themselves. . . . The statement that, within free competition, the individuals, in following purely their private interests, realize the communal or rather the *general* interest means nothing other than that they collide with one another under conditions of capitalist production, and hence that the impact between them is itself nothing more than the recreation of the conditions under which this interaction takes place.[91]

These illusions about the free individual and free competition form the normative and ethical foundations of bourgeois social science and social philosophy. It is clear that, beneath Marx's analysis of the structures of modernity, the ethical prescriptions of the early manuscripts are still present. However, the emphasis is now on metaethics. That is, it is on the social and structural forms that inhibit and distort the goal of self-realization—the social forms that distort the ideals developed in the *Paris Manuscripts*. One could argue even further that the historical institutions of political economy are what really give his ethical ideas their force. Ethics by itself is pure ideology; but uniting ethical considerations to his "critical science" and the law of value forces the reader to interpret both ethics and science in a new way—one that synthesizes ethics and materialism. This is a theme we have seen already in Marx's *Dissertation*. The ethical component of his analysis becomes even more pronounced in *Capital*. The result of his historical and social investigations in the *Grundrisse* is a complete ethical condemnation of the whole economic and social system developed under capitalism. It is a system that undermines the ethical aspirations that have been a part of Marx's social theory from the start and that represent his synthesis of the classical theories.

Marx sees that, from the perspective of its technological rationality, the system is spurred on by its own internal logic and historical development, which push society in a direction where the straight application of labor time is replaced by development of the full forces of modern science and technology. Wealth comes to be viewed less as control over alien labor time than as control over the "agencies" activated by the revolutionizing of the productive forces. As we have moved from simple exchange to simple production to capitalist production and wage labor, Marx now sees on the horizon a new social system in which the industrial and technological advances of modernity become the real basis for human freedom. But these possibilities are prevented, as science and technology are still under the control of the social necessities of capital. The reduction of necessary labor time to a minimum, the free development of individual capabilities ("individualities"), and the development of artistic and scientific accomplishments become cornerstones of the possibilities inherent in the old system. But liberalism is incapable of fostering the moral autonomy, human dignity, and political community necessary for these new forms of freedom and social development.

> In the *Grundrisse*, Marx continued to talk in terms of the "universal development of the individual." He tried to demonstrate how full development was impossible inside capitalist society because of the barriers to full production, the inherent contradictions of the private enterprise system. In order for the individual to achieve his full development, it was first necessary for the "full development of the forces of production" to become the "conditions of production." . . . With expanded productivity, human beings would have greater opportunity to actualize and express their inherent capacities.[92]

Marx points out further that the modernization of industry attempts to make the creation of social wealth independent of the laws of value, while—at the same time—these forces of industry are limited by the structural imperatives of capital. This is an example of the contradiction between the productive forces pushing one way and the social relations of production pushing the other. This very contradiction is the "material condition to blow this foundation sky-high."[93] The transformation of social wealth into capital is the final barrier to the development of capitalism and its political ideals of equality and freedom. Wealth is transformed into capital, work into wage labor, and disposable time into surplus value. This is the system founded on alienation, poverty, and economic exploitation.

> Since the theory of labor value provides the key to the problem, unsolved by classical political economy, it reveals the true nature of its justifications. The actual substance of the abstract freedom of civil society is now recognizable as class antagonism, the exploitation of wage labor by capital, the substantive bondage of the proletariat.[94]

HISTORY, SOCIAL STRUCTURES, AND ETHICS IN *CAPITAL:* THE SOCIAL THEORY OF PRODUCTION

The theory of value is the heart of Marx's analysis in *Capital*. The first three chapters of volume 1 on commodities, exchange, and money represent a summary of his work *A Contribution to the Critique of Political Economy*, published in 1859, while the historical aspects of his theory of value involve a development of his historical analyses contained in the *Grundrisse*. There does exist a transformation problem; but it is a theory of the transformation of work into a commodity, the transformation of the production of material goods into commodity production, the transformation of social relationships into fetishized relationships between objects, and transformation of production for the satisfaction of human needs into the satisfaction of profit accumulation. This is the real transformation problem that Marx dealt with in his *theory of value*. Also, the theory is historically grounded in the *theory of abstract value* (division of labor, fetishism, private property, and the market). While it is a theory by which the exchange of commodities is understood as exchange value (distribution), its main focus is on explaining class structure and exploitation of the working class in the production process (*the theory of surplus value*) and the economic crises of this social system in the overproduction of capital and the tendential fall in the rate of profit (*the theory of profits*). Thus, the theory of value is inextricably connected with Marx's analysis of production and distribution: the theory of surplus value and the theory of profits. These two aspects of commodity production are then viewed by Marx as being historically based in a certain type of socioeconomic system characteristic of capitalist societies: *the theory of abstract labor*.

Since the relative form of value of a commodity—the linen, for example—expresses the value of that commodity, as being something wholly different from its substance and properties, as being, for example coat-like, we see that this expression itself indicates that some social relation lies at the bottom of it.[95]

Marx's real contribution to economic theory is his theory of value, which is the historical theory of value is a structural component of his broader ethical theory. In this category he deals with all aspects of the processes of capital accumulation and the creation of value (exchangeable congealed labor). Thus this ethical theory is also a social theory of production—or theory of the social organization of production which may be summarized as follows:

The Exchange Process: This process provides the legal and moral justification for the whole social system because of the apparent equality and freedom expressive of the market exchange process.

The Reduction Process: This entails the social organization of production around abstract labor, the division of labor (isolation of stages in the production process and the forced independence from each other), the technicalization of manufacturing, the separation of labor power from the means of labor, the separation of labor from labor power, constant from variable capital, and abstract labor from concrete labor, and the concentration of ownership in the hands of a few. This is the theory of abstract labor.[96]

Historical Foundations of Capitalism: Here Marx examines the historical conditions for the possibility of commodity production in primitive accumulation, the enclosures, state intervention to protect the "theft" of property, and the colonization of the Third World for access to cheap resources and labor. The theory of value is an historical theory of the reorganization of society and the production process for the purpose of creating private economic surplus. Exchange value can be the central social form only in a capitalist society, because it is a product of abstract labor. Closely connected with this theory of abstract labor is Marx's theory of the modern state and the latter's part in laying the foundations for the process of accumulation and reproduction of capital. The state "is itself an economic power."[97]

Production of Surplus Value: This is accomplished through the intensification of the process of production and the creation of surplus labor and surplus value by means of private control over the social organization of production, the division of manual and intellectual labor, introduction of science and technology in the workplace, intensification of the work load (theory of relative surplus value), and lengthening of the workday itself (theory of absolute surplus value). This part of his theory also contains Marx's theory of exploitation.

Profit Realization and Economic Crises: Here Marx examines the various theories of crisis such as disproportionality, overproduction, underconsumption, and the tendential fall in the rate of profit theories. The bottom line in this analysis is that the economic system during its normal functioning is incapable of maintaining an adequate rate of profit and tends toward economic stagnation. Commodity production—in the third volume of *Capital*—involves both an ethical and an efficiency problem. The capitalist production process is structurally deficient, systemically crisis ridden, and grossly inefficient and unproductive measured by its own material potential. The system neither provides the material goods necessary for a human existence, nor fosters development of a moral personality. The system is unjust in its exchange and distribution of the social wealth of society, unjust and exploitative in its social organization of production (social distribution of capital), unjust in the historical manner in which capital accumulation has occurred (primitive accumulation), and unjust in the manner in which it undermines the potential for human emancipation (*On the Jewish Question*), man's species being (the *Paris Manuscripts*), human potential for self-realization (*Grundrisse*), and true human freedom (*Capital*). Thus, capital synthesizes in its theory of exploitation and economic crises both ethics and political economy. The two are never really separated in Marx's mind, nor in the minds of Aristotle and Hegel. The theory of value is an ethical theory. Marx's *Grundrisse* and *Capital* are works in the field of social ethics.

Throughout this analysis, Marx is making an unmistakably clear ethical statement about the production process in capitalism. To deny the centrality of the theory of exploitation and its expression in economic and political institutions and the social relations of production would be to miss the key element in his analysis. In the same tradition as the Ancients, Marx's ethical theory is a theory of society united to an analysis of modernity and the critique of classical political economy. The separation of ethics and politics, ethics and political economy, and ethics and science is a characteristic of modernity and a failed understanding of both morality and epistemology. By returning to Aristotle and Epicurus, Marx reintegrates at the theoretical level the positive moments in the classical and modern traditions. It is a theoretical reintegration of modernity and the Ancients, which anticipates and precedes the reintegration of the species being into a truly human and democratic society.

Chapter Six

Marx's Theory of Ethics and Social Justice: Toward a Materialist Consensus Theory of Truth

INTRODUCTION

This final chapter will bring together the various elements of Marx's ethics and theory of social justice found in the previous chapters, with special emphasis on the relationship between epistemology and politics in his later economic and historical writings. A further clarification of the meaning of the concept of praxis in his "theory and practice" and its importance for laying the foundations for his ethics is also examined. It is well known that Marx actually published only volume 1 of *Capital* during his lifetime and never completed the extensive project, which was outlined in the *Grundrisse*. Since volumes 2 and 3 were arranged and published by Engels, any statements regarding Marx's overall method can be only limited. Within this limitation—and before a comprehensive understanding of his later economic writings can be developed—Marx's actual method (or methods) used in *Capital* must first be unraveled from their complex interconnections with each other, and then analytically ordered so that a clearer appreciation of his intentions may come through. Only when this is done can we get a more adequate understanding of Marx's method, its implications, and the possible further developments of his thought.

The real problem of articulating Marx's method in *Capital* is that the work is a composite of many different approaches, all intermin-

247

gled with each other—with no clear statement by Marx of their exact relationships to each other. Therefore, though an ordering of the methods presents only the normal difficulties of exegetical analysis, the relationships between them and the overall intentions and direction of their author remain an exercise in speculative social theory. In *Capital* there are seven distinct methods used in his critique of political economy; all have their own distinct methods, orientations, intellectual traditions, and epistemological and ethical assumptions. However, they also appear to converge at a common point and on a common theme, which makes a synthesis possible and necessary. This common theme is not simply the critique of classical political economy, but the synthesis of classical ethics and political economy into a comprehensive critique of capitalism. Implicit throughout is Marx's theory of ethics and social justice.

The issue of the relationship between Marx's ethics and political economy has been debated since the late nineteenth century. The famous Marburg School of neo-Kantian philosophy—which included such illustrious thinkers as Cohen, Staudinger, Stammler, and Vorländer—believed that at the heart of Marxism is the categorical imperative and the moral drive toward a human society where all individuals are to be treated as ends-in-themselves.[1] The Marburg School maintained that the moral development and education of an individual could take place only within a human community (*menschliche Gemeinschaft*).[2]

In more recent U.S. literature on the subject—especially among those who defend the Tucker–Wood thesis—it is argued that Marx rejected ethics and social justice as being forms of bourgeois ideology; this position also contends that Marx is a positivist attempting to establish the scientific foundations of his economic theory. The thesis also holds that Marx's critique of capitalism is not based on a recognition of its inherent injustice or immorality.[3] It was Robert Tucker who first articulated this position when he stated:

> The fundamental passion of the founders of Marxism was not a passion for justice. Their condemnation of capitalism was not predicated upon a protest against injustice, and they did not envisage the future communist society as a kingdom of justice. In general, they were opposed to the notion that socialism or communism turns principally on the matter of distribution.[4]

The two schools of thought have much in common, even though their conclusions differ greatly. Both argued that ethics is not systemic or integral to Marx's own social theory—with Tucker and Wood rejecting any link whatsoever, while the neo-Kantians attempted to integrate Marxian political economy with the Kantian theory of practical reason and the categorical imperative. Both positions are incorrect. Though Marx never developed an explicit theory of ethics and social justice, it is clearly there to be uncovered. In the previous five chapters, the pieces to his overall theory have been laid out. Now is the time to pull them together into a comprehensive whole.

This chapter will restate briefly an analysis of the understanding of morality and ethics in the classics of German Idealism and the Ancients, and then proceed to discuss the issue of the ethical foundations of Marx's thought. The various elements of his ethical theory have been developed in the following: Marx's critique of individualism and utilitarianism (*On the Jewish Question*), his critique of private property (the *Paris Manuscripts*), the analysis of alienation and exploitation (the *Paris Manuscripts, Grundrisse,* and *Capital*), the relation between his philosophical anthropology (man's social being) and his social ethics (the *Paris Manuscripts*), the examination of the *Grundrisse* and *Capital* as ethical texts, and the development of a materialist consensus theory of truth (*Theses on Feuerbach* and *Civil War in France*).

ETHICS, POLITICAL ECONOMY, AND MARX'S THEORY OF SOCIAL JUSTICE: THE DEBATE

Recently there has been a great deal of controversy over the issue of Marx and social justice. Whether Marx does have such a theory or not has become a central question. So far, much of the debate has centered on a generally very narrow exegesis and definition of justice.[5] It has been this definition that has decided the issue, a priori. Therefore, we should recapitulate the explanation of the classical ancient traditions and how their understanding of the relationships between political economy and social justice affect Marx's own position. When this is done, we will see a much closer parallel between Marx and the writings of Aristotle on ethical and political ideas. However, the contemporary controversy should be mentioned first, and a nice summary of the opposing viewpoints has been provided by Norman Geras.[6]

Marx Against a Theory of Social Justice

1. There is a fair exchange between labor and capital for the worker's labor power and any surplus is "a piece of good luck for the buyer."

2. Ideas about justice are "obsolete verbal rubbage" and "ideological nonsense about rights and other trash so common among the democrats and French Socialists."

3. In historical materialism, morality and justice are phenomenal forms of the superstructure determined by the economic base. These standards are always relative and correspond to the social and economic circumstances of the times. The standards appropriate for judging the economic relations of capitalism are only the standards of capitalism itself.

4. Morality and the concepts of justice are ideological categories and only reflect the underlying economic substructure.

5. Marx is concerned with the social relations of production, and not the sphere of distribution—and thus, not with distributive justice. As Marx says, "To clamour for equal or even equitable redistribution on the basis of the wage system is the same as to clamour for freedom on the basis of the slavery system."

6. Interest in a change in distribution and exchange is a concern for "moral enlightenment and legal reform," and not a revolutionary transformation of the material base of society.

7. The principles of justice are juridical and require the whole state apparatus for its organization and implementation. Since Marx calls for the withering away of the state, he could not be concerned with this form of justice.

8. The principle of need and the principle of distribution in Marx's postcapitalist society point "beyond justice." Justice is no longer necessary because the new society is also "beyond economic scarcity," and the former is always a function of the distribution of scarce social resources. Also, in communist societies, universal values will no longer be needed because new societies are capable of treating people in their individuality. The conditions that create the need for justice will have disappeared. The "circumstances of justice"—that is, the circumstances that in a capitalist society require the intervention of justice—will no longer be present.

9. Marx's theory is based on the ideals of freedom, self-realization, and the community. These are different values than the desire for justice; some say they are even nonmoral values.

Marx in Favor of a Theory of Social Justice

1. Once beyond the sphere of exchange and into that of production, the social relations between worker and capitalist become class based and exploitative—thus requiring social justice.

2. Marx does not discuss justice per se; there is no developed theory of justice, but he does use moral terms such as "robbery," "theft," "exploitation," and so forth, to describe the capitalist appropriation of surplus value.

3. From the use of categories of moral condemnation we can see an implicit theory of social justice based on transcendent, universal moral standards of social judgment and critique.

4. Some have mistaken Marx's moral realism and critique of the ideology of morality and natural rights as a form of moral relativism. He recognizes—however—that, for moral principles to be realized, one must turn to an examination of the actual structures of society, since it is the latter that ground and sustain the moral principles of justice. With a change in these structures, there will be a corresponding conceptual change in the nature of justice. Rights cannot be "higher than the economic structure." To show that morals and rights are grounded in the structures of political economy does not mean that Marx's own standards of evaluation are so grounded.

5. Though the emphasis is on an examination of the social relations of production, Marx is still concerned with distribution in general, which is the result of the prior distribution of the means of production—that is, class structure.

6. When moral argumentation is made in conjunction with a sociological analysis, there is nothing reformist involved. Ethics is a legitimate form of social critique when not separated from political economy.

7. Marx's critique of justice and its close connection to the coercive mechanism of the state apparatus can be transcended when the principles of justice are based on nonjuridical, universal, and ethical standards.

8. The principle of needs is an ethical standard of social justice and can form the basis for a theory of rights—a right to the material goods of society in order to achieve the fullest expression of the individual and self-determination. This is the right of "equality of self-realization." It is part of the individual's hierarchy of rights based on contribution, effort, and needs.

9. The distinction between moral relativism of his sociology of morals and moral universalism of self-actualization and freedom is unjustified in Marx. The application of a critique of ideology would be applicable to all values—whether moral or nonmoral.

Geras has nicely and succinctly outlined some of the main features of the debate and summarized an extensive list of authors writing in this field. What can be clearly discerned—especially in reviewing those who would argue that Marx does not have a theory of ethics—is that their concept of ethics is very narrowly defined to correspond to its modern form, rather than its nineteenth-century German usage. Even Geras is locked into the debate as it is presently defined, in his efforts to offer a different view of the material. However, a broader interpretation that incorporates Marx's critique of modernity and political economy requires that he be understood in light of his connections with the ethical traditions of the classical Ancients and the nineteenth-century German Idealists. This also entails that the liberal concept of science as positivism be transcended. Only this will provide a better standpoint from which to deal with these questions. With a redefinition of ethics and the relations between ethics and political economy, we can recognize that the nine points for and against a theory of social justice are not so contradictory as they may appear at first glance. The reason is that they entail entirely different understandings of the nature of ethics. They address different logical and even ontological levels of argument, and do not immediately correspond to each other: One level is the critique of ideology and bourgeois morality, and the other is a developed ethical and social theory. Though the category of "ethics" appears in both, it refers to different entities.

The key idea in this analysis of ethics must be to show how its component elements are integrated into a living ethical whole that makes sense of Marx's own writings and the traditions on which they are based. Drawing from issues discussed in previous chapters of this work, the following elements should be included as constituents of Marx's theory of social ethics:

1. Theory of Freedom—ethics as individual and social freedom from alien external laws (Chapter 1: Marx and Epicurus)

2. Theory of Self-Realization—ethical values of self-realization and the realization of species being (Chapters 2 and 3: Marx, Aristotle, and German Idealism)

3. Theory of Fetishism—defense of individual freedom against the mechanism of modern production, alienated labor, the laws of the market, poverty, and class (Marx and the prophets)

4. Theory of Human Emancipation—inadequacy of bourgeois values of equality and freedom. Marx calls for a drive beyond Bentham and Mill to human emancipation. (Chapter 4: Marx, liberalism, and democracy)

5. Theory of Democracy—Marx's theory of popular economic democracy and workers' self-determination (Chapter 4: Marx, liberalism, and democracy)

6. Theory of Needs—based on Marx's view of species being, human creativity, and praxis, and his aesthetic view of human nature (Chapter 3: Marx and German Idealism)

7. Theory of Distributive Justice—distributive justice of social wealth in production and consumption (Chapter 2: Marx and Aristotle)

8. Theory of Rights—based on the distinction between the rights of economic acquisitive man in civil society and the rights of the political citizen in the public sphere; (*Critique of the Gotha Program* and *On Jewish Question*) (Chapter 4: Marx, liberalism, and democracy)

9. Theory of Economic Exploitation—synthesis of Marx's theory of value (history of capital), economic crisis theory (structure of capital), theory of social contradictions (logic of capital), and irrationality of social system (rationality and capitalism) in his critique of political economy. The critique of exploitation more specifically stresses the rate of the extraction of surplus value and the dehumanization of labor with the mechanization and intensification of labor in the workplace. Marx's views on the economic irrationality of the whole social system are founded on his critique of classical political economy and its acceptance of an equilibrium theory of the economy, the balance between production and consumption, and the rejection of the possibilities of overproduction and economic crises. In the ethical components of his crisis theory, Marx maintains that the social system does not provide material foundations for the realm of freedom or possibilities for individual self-realization. Contradiction between the forces of production and the social relations of production is the basis for his analysis of the logic of capital and his ethical critique of capitalism. The social system is—by its underlying dynamic inefficient, crisis ridden, exploitative, and dehumanizing; it undermines the potentialities of human existence. (Chapter 5: Marx and Ricardo)

10. Theory of the Public—Marx's materialist and democratic consensus theory of truth, which belongs to the area of metaethics and involves the relationship between epistemology and politics. Primacy of the community and public sphere requires true equality and freedom. (Chapter 2: Marx and Aristotle)

A simple listing of various ethical components does not constitute a developed and integrated theory. The components must be synthesized into a comprehensive theory of society. Nor do the normative assumptions that underlie Marx's thought provide us with an insight into an historically particular view of the emancipated society. It is extremely rare for Marx to make specific concrete references to the emancipated future. One could argue that interpreters have had this same difficulty with Aristotle's *Nicomachean Ethics*. Rather than providing us with specific recommendations for the just society, what both social theorists provide us with is a metaethical theory or a social theory of justice. With modernity has come philosophical theories of justice based on an abstract individualism and the market economy. A return to the Ancients provides us with a different social theory of justice: the rejection of scientific and universalistic ethics and the development of a theory of society within which the ethical values emerge through public discourse and consensus. Marx gives us a broad outline of the general structural features—usually negatively defined through his critique of capitalism—within which values arise and are validated, rather than direct statements relating to a mirror image of the emancipated society itself. That is, he provides us with the broadest structural parameters of political economy through his critique of the nineteenth-century classical tradition. This, along with the substantive ethics in his specifically philosophical writings of the early period, provides us with the normative assumptions necessary to construct a theory of social justice that draws heavily on the Greek experience. Marx's critique of political economy, the ethical assumptions of his analysis, his theory of needs, and—finally—his theory of democracy provide the foundations for this social theory of justice.

ETHICS AND METHOD: THE LEVELS OF ETHICAL CRITIQUE IN *CAPITAL*

We are now in a position to begin filling in the outline of Marx's ethics and theory of social justice. What first must be done is to mention the distinctions between the various components of any ethical theory: (1) ethical epistemology; (2) the methodology of ethical critique; (3) the particular ethical norms and standards of judgment themselves; (4) metaethics or critique of the structures of political economy; and (5) metaethics as the structural basis for social praxis and revolutionary change. The attempt here is to give a comprehensive and integrated outline of the nature of social ethics and its various levels, from its concept and theory formation (1) to its application in social change (5). It is a holistic approach in the same manner as Aristotle and Hegel, and therefore represents a critique of the modern view of morality; it is based on the traditional distinction between—and later integration of—*Moralität* and *Sittlichkeit*. Though it recognizes differences between self-realization, freedom, equality, and material security, it does not mistake analytical for ontological categories, nor artificially distinguish between moral and nonmoral ones.[7] And finally, it reintegrates moral values, political philosophy, and economic theory into a comprehensive theory of social ethics. Not one of these categories is raised to primary status at the expense of the others, though the central idea is always the freedom toward self-realization (species being) within the community. Based on the model of classical ethics, these elements must be viewed within an overall integrated theory of justice, as the categories themselves are dialectically interrelated. Morality is not an isolated (and alienated) form of philosophical reflection, but becomes part of a more expanded theory of modernity.

Though the first and second components above have been more adequately dealt with elsewhere,[8] it would be beneficial to present the different methods used in *Capital* and their relationship to ethics. The next section of this chapter will then examine the connections between ethics and economics; and in the section following that, I will summarize the whole of the relationships between ethics and metaethics and the integration of modernity and the Ancients. The final two sections develop the implications of Marx's social ethics for a materialist consensus theory of truth. A simple analysis of the different methodological levels of "critique" will provide us with a firmer foundation on which to base Marx's ethics, his critique of political economy, and his social theory. That is, distilling the pure substantive values from the first three levels of critique in *Capital* and integrating them with the ethics of his earlier writings will leave us with the building blocks for a complete theory of social ethics. The other four levels of critique are part of his formal metaethics and thus constitute his theory of social justice.

The seven distinct but interrelated methods of critique in *Capital* include: (1) the normative critique, (2) the immanent critique, (3) the critique of fetishism, (4) the critique of political economy, (5) the dialectical critique, (6) the historical critique, and (7) critique as crisis theory.[9] The first three methods make up his ethics (substantive values and morality); and the last four, his metaethics (historical and structural critique of political economy). The method of normative critique, which was first developed in the *Paris Manuscripts*, is built around the ethical ideal of the species being and the self-realization of the individual in the social and political community; it has a long intellectual tradition from Aristotle to Rousseau, J. S. Mill, and Marx. The immanent critique also comes from the early writings beginning with the *Contribution to the Critique of Hegel's Philosophy of Law*, proceeds by accepting provisionally the leading progressive normative claims of bourgeois economists and political theorists, and then compares them to the actual historical institutions within which they are said to be realized. This method undermines the validity of ideas by revealing their contradictions to reality and to themselves.

The third method is the critique of fetishism, which is a metatheoretical critique of the categories of classical political economy. These categories have turned social relationships between individuals into relationships between reified institutions that appear to have an independent life and reality of their own beyond human control. Marx criticizes the false objectivity of bourgeois social science. The critique of fetishism is the methodological and epistemological application in a critical science of the early Marx's critiques of false universality, alienation, and the natural rights tradition in *On the Jewish Question* and the critique of Hegel's notions of rights, freedom, and the state in Marx's *Contribution to the Critique of Hegel's Philosophy of Law*. The critique of political economy shows the internal inconsistencies and contradictory logic resulting from the claims to legitimation made by the classical tradition; it also contrasts the latter's value system to both Marx's substantive ethics and actual historical developments.

The fifth method—the dialectical critique—develops when Marx applies Hegel's logic (*Science of Logic*) to social reality in order to show how the structures and direction of capitalist society are built on contradictory social imperatives. These appear in the form of contradictions between the productive forces and the social relations of production, between the satisfaction of human needs and the realization of profit, between the production of material goods and the production of surplus value, and between the production of social wealth and the production of capital. The sixth method of critique analyzes the historical and social foundations of the capitalist system as it evolves out of its premodern social forms. Marx examines the various changes brought about by a society based on the institutions of exchange value, abstract labor, surplus value, and capitalist social relations of production. Finally, the seventh method of critique utilizing crisis theory—which includes the analysis of the overproduction of consumer and capital goods, the disequilibrium between production and consumption, and the tendential fall in the rate of profit—is an examination of the foundations of modern economic crises peculiar to the capitalist social system.

Relating these methods and developing some arrangement of them into a more comprehensive understanding of their meaning within an overall social theory must be approached with a great deal of hermeneutical skepticism. To make sense of Marx's work, however, we must take the plunge. At first, we notice that the normative, immanent, and fetishism critiques are clearly based on ethical assumptions about the nature of man and society; while the critical method of the dialectical critique, historical critique of the law of value, and crisis theory deal more—though not exclusively—with the institutional structures of society, with an emphasis on their historical makeup or logic of development. Then, this analysis also seems to unify the different methodologies utilized by Marx throughout his writings. Applying this breakdown of his critical methods, we begin to see more clearly the unity between the earlier and later works, and how particular pieces of the grand puzzle fit neatly with each other.

The older debates over the relationship between the early and the later—the philosophical and the scientific—Marx are simply unfounded, given the methodological makeup of *Capital*. *Capital* becomes a beautiful (though jumbled) montage of critiques regarding distorted and alienated subjectivity, class conflict, economic exploitation, fetishized social relationships, delegitimation of the natural rights tradition, and the irrationality of distorted social and economic development. Throughout the analysis, however, the crucial moral components of the normative, immanent, and fetishism critiques are present—mentioned, but never really studied. The clear emphasis is on the historical and logical structure of capital as it tends toward economic crisis. Nevertheless, a substantive moral critique still lies at the heart of the first three forms of critical method. One could certainly argue—as some have—that Marx's critical methods represent the final victory of positivist science over the philosophical and Hegelian remnants of political economy. As we have seen, however, even the last four methods represent critiques of the positivist tradition and have a different epistemological and methodological understanding of the nature of science than positivism does.

The first three critiques appear too often in both the *Grundrisse* and *Capital* to be simply forgettable remnants of the philosophical past of his early writings. And the critique of fetishism has such a prominent place in *Capital* that the only reasonable interpretation is to see the first three critiques as providing the cornerstones of Marx's thought and full critique. This is further justified by his later analysis of the Paris Commune in *The Civic War in France*. What conclusions can we draw from this? The major one is that underlying Marx's first three methods of critique—which contain ethical values in his theories of the communal nature of man, his notion of self-realization, and his ideas on freedom, equality, and social justice—is the belief that alienated labor (the anthropological critique), bourgeois natural rights (the immanent critique), and economic crises (the political economy critique) distort and undermine the species being's quest for self-realization within the public sphere. They undermine the ability of individuals to realize their potentialities and capabilities within a democratic consensus (social praxis). We thus see—if this is a reasonably correct interpretation, if not somewhat speculative—that at the heart of Marx's critical science lie both ethics and metaethics (justice). That is, Marx's condemnation of capitalist social arrangements rests on an ethical critique based on his ideals of self-realization and his theory of needs, but within an historical framework for an understanding of the modern structures of capitalist political economy.

His ideals of democracy, equality, and freedom from his early and later writings establish a second metaethical basis for the critique of society, based on whether the society permits and supports the public institutions—in both the political and the economic spheres—that would promote democratic consensus and self-realization. There is thus an individual and a social component—an individual ethics and an institutional metaethics—at the foundation of Marx's critique of political economy. Marx has integrated his philosophical and institutional analyses; they are no longer in conflict. Ethics without the metaethics of political economy is blind, but metaethics without ethics is meaningless. History and political economy without an understanding of their own normative frameworks, the values of the society under investigation, or the ethical ideals of an emancipated society result in a rationalized positivism. Ethics without social science ends in pure metaphysics. Though the emphasis is clearly on the last three methods in Marx's later writings, it still can and should be maintained that the intellectual heart lies in his original moral values. This also means that the vision of the Greek polis and the ideals of beauty and reconciliation that marked the neohumanism of the nineteenth-century German academy and Marx's early works are also the cornerstones of his later political economy.

The Foundations of Ethical Critique in *Capital*

1. The *normative critique* is based on species being and self-realization; the critique of alienated labor and distorted subjectivity are grounded in the tradition from Aristotle through Spinoza and Hegel.

2. The *immanent critique* concerns the contradictions between concept and reality within classical political economy; it is a critique of individualism and private rights as undermining community and the common good through the fostering of self-interest and destructive egoism. This was the method of Hegel and Feuerbach.

3. The *critique of fetishism* attacks the alien objectivity contained in the positive science of political economy, which establishes an objective social world independent of human intervention and values. This is the critique of religion transferred directly into economics and contains both a critique of the methodology of classical political economy (fetishism and metaphysics of economic categories) and a social psychology of fetishized social relationships. This critique developed from the critiques of mythology and natural law by Epicurus and the critiques of idolatry and false gods by the Hebrew prophets.

The Foundations of Structural and Historical Critique in *Capital*

4. The *critique of political economy* represents a structural analysis of capitalist social relations at the point of production—analysis differing greatly from that of the classical political economy of Smith and Ricardo. The epistemological, methodological, and historical foundations of Marx's analysis turn away from this classical tradition, even though confusingly similar categories are borrowed from it—including the notions of the labor theory of value, the tendential fall in the rate of profit, surplus value, counteracting social forces, and so forth. The subtitle of both the *Grundrisse* and *Capital* point in this direction of a rejection of the roots of classical political economy.

5. The *dialectical critique* recognizes the contradictory elements and the irrationality of the capitalist social system based on the contradiction between the productive forces (economic technology) and the social relations of production (class structure). This is a critique of the logic of capital.

6. The *historical critique* is based on the historical law of value and abstract labor. Methodologically this is a transcendental critique, resting on the actual historical and social conditions for the development of capitalism. Used in conjunction with immanent critique, it

reveals the underlying social reality and deep structures of exploitation and human deprivation on which rest the *appearances* of the bourgeois values of equality, individualism, and freedom. It unites the later concepts of abstract labor in the *Grundrisse* with the earlier notion of alienation from the *Paris Manuscripts*. Specific sections of *Capital* analyze primitive accumulation, division of labor, mechanization, and the technological intensification of labor.

7. *Critique as crisis theory* involves two main variations: (1) a crisis theory resting on the overproduction of consumer goods because of the inability of capital to realize itself in the market, due to the low wages of the workers; and (2) a crisis theory based on the contradictions of the social system and the logical development of the law of value in an overproduction of capital and a tendential fall in the rate of profit. The former is emphasized in the *Grundrisse*, while the latter is central to *Capital*. The inefficiency and irrationality of the social system based on exchange value and abstract labor leads to a distinction being made between the realm of necessity and the realm of freedom.

For too many interpreters, the fifth and the seventh critiques form the foundation of the positivist critique of capitalism and the explanatory predictions within a philosophy of history. With the apparent failure of these predictions, it has been relatively easy to dismiss the Marxian paradigm, even while accepting some of the earlier—more philosophical—aspects. But as more recent scholarship on the subject has revealed, neither the dialectical critique nor critique as crisis theory rests on a positivist model of science that abstracts from ethics and normative elements. Also, the critique of political economy using the law of value and the theory of exchange value and abstract labor has at times been defined as a theory of price determinations. However, this too places Marx within the positivist tradition and abstracts from all normative elements as being metaphysical. It has been my intention in this book to show that the last four forms of critique rest on the first three types. Marx's political economy is based on a repudiation of capitalism for destroying just those possibilities of freedom and self-expression that it claims to actualize. Ethics has primacy even in his economic theory. The spirit of Epicurus is never far from his later works.

The variety of critiques seem necessary in order that the full range of human activity be encompassed. That is, there is a critique of the historical foundations of capitalism, a critique of the logic of its own internal dynamic, and a critique of the rationality that underlies a system incapable of realizing its own publicly stated aims. There is a critique of the value system that legitimates the political and economic structures of capitalism (natural rights and the market exchange), and of the form of science that leaves these institutions and social relationships unquestioned (positivism). Finally, there is the normative critique itself, drawn from his early and later writings in which Marx explicitly mentions the value system that directs his research and critiques. This value system—as we have seen—develops out of Marx's understanding of the classical ethics of Greece and Germany.

There are a variety of different methods or levels of analysis because of the necessity in *Capital* to capture the totality of social relationships. To fetishize these relationships and their corresponding critical methods is to objectify society into a reified corpse that only positivism could animate. Under the structuralist critique, we see the logical and historical components to Marx's developed crisis theory. The normative and immanent critiques juxtapose the differing ethical values of bourgeois and Marxian social theory. The fetishism critique mediates between both the ethical and structural critiques in that it lays the epistemological foundation for the critique of political economy and evaluates a social system in which personal relations are viewed as relationships between things.

Fetishism is both a critique of alienation in social relationships and the basis for a method of historical investigation that uncovers the deep social relations at the base of a mechanical world. This critique prepares the methodological way for a recognition that in capitalism all social relationships become exchange relationships in which class power and domination are subsumed under reified categories of the laws of supply and demand, production and consumption, profits and prices.

ETHICS AND THE CONTRADICTIONS OF CAPITALISM

Materialism is neither a form of rationalism nor positivism, but relates to Marx's humanistic critique of the abstractionism in idealism and the ideology of the immediacy (facts) in empiricism. The contradiction between the productive forces and the social forms of economic organization is a contradiction that is grounded in the economic priorities and social constraints on the application of modern technology in the production process. This is caused ultimately by the initial contradiction between production for immediate use (use value) and production for exchange on the market (exchange value).[10] This means that the development of modern technology and the satisfaction of human needs is restricted and retarded by the socially prior requirements of a class society in which production leads to the realization of surplus value and private profits.

After Marx had gone through an analysis of the types of economic crises in volumes 2 and 3 of *Capital*—disproportionality, overproduction, underconsumption, tendential fall in the rate of profit, and class conflict—an underlying problem remained: the social requirements of the logic of capital. That is, the necessity in a capitalist society to reproduce surplus value remained at the heart of the economic system and was the underlying cause of the various phenomenal forms of crises. Here again, we have an integration of volumes 1 and 3 of *Capital*—a synthesis of the law of value and economic crises.[11] This synthesis, as we have seen, was not built on the foundations of a labor theory of value as in the manner of Locke, Smith, and Ricardo, but on the foundations of the social and historical structures of modernity.

The analysis of the economic and social forms of crises throughout *Capital* is, in fact, a result of the contradiction in society between the machinery and technology of work and the social organization of work patterns (abstract labor). As long as capitalism is grounded in private property, exchange value, surplus value, and private accumulation, the social arrangements around production appear as a technical force of production itself—a way of conforming labor to the necessities of private production. Economic crises result not because of the inability of the economy and society to supply the basic material goods necessary for its survival or continued production, but because the society is incapable of making a sufficient rate of profit for the capitalists. The problem is not that there is no demand, but that there is no effective demand; there are needs to be met, but few individuals who can pay for the market commodities. The methods of social organization of work are inadequate to the production of surplus value. Thus, the overproduction of capital and underconsumption of commodities and the growing disproportionality between production and consumption are aspects of one central theme: the contradiction between the economy and its social relations. These social relations are phenomenal appearances reflecting the underlying economic problem (essence) that the realization of surplus value is not sufficient to keep the economy going.

Though these laws themselves have been viewed incorrectly as natural laws or positivistic laws predicting the "breakdown" of the economic system, they in fact represent a fundamental ethical critique of capitalism. Just as the theories of rights, distributive justice, and economic exploitation are ethical critiques of capitalist legal, political, and economic relations, so too the theories of economic crises provide a macroeconomic and structural critique of the failure of species self-realization and freedom. Because of the nature of the distinction between contradiction (logic and essence) and crisis (historical appearance) in the economy, problems are endemic to the social system. Looking from the perspective of the productive forces, the social forms of work organization and the macrodivision of property and resources are forms of social organization that restrict the ability of society to produce material goods. Capitalist society's production ability is thus extremely inefficient and results in cyclical downturns that manifest themselves in periodic and systemic economic crises, unemployment, physical suffering, exploitation, intensification of alienated labor, and loss of opportunities for the development of public self-consciousness and democracy. The state is reduced to being the administrative and technological arm of a crisis-ridden economy, which results in lost possibilities for freedom. Marx's economic theory is an ethical theory. Its subject is not another political economy, but the social economy; and, as a "critique of political economy," it is part of a broader theory of social ethics in the manner of Aristotle's ethics and politics. This synthesis of science and ethics recapitulates in a different theoretical form the synthesis of Epicurean science and ethics for the purpose of the "happiness (*ataraxy*) of self consciousness." Historical critique based on a dialectical science is grounded ultimately in social ethics.

Society is incapable of providing the material goods necessary for the "realm of freedom" and the leisure to objectify and express one's multifarious forms of talents and abilities. Its economic wealth is incapable of matching its real wealth of human needs.

> In fact, however, when the limited bourgeois form is stripped away, what is wealth other than the universality of individual needs, capacities, pleasures, productive forces etc., created through universal exchange? The full development of human mastery over the forces of nature, those of so-called nature as well as of humanity's own nature? The absolute working-out of creative potentialities, with no presupposition other than the previous historic development, which makes this totality of development, i.e. the development of all human powers as such the end in itself,

not as measured on a *predetermined* yardstick? Where he does not reproduce himself in one specificity, but produces his totality? Strives not to remain something he has become but is in the absolute movement of becoming?[12]

Freed from the drudgery and necessity of supplying the basics for physical survival, humanity would be free to realize its potentials in the form of social and individual creativity in an emancipated democratic society. The emphasis in the new society would be on political judgment, discourse, and aesthetic creativity; it would be on the creative control over all aspects of human life. No longer to be ruled by transcendent physical, religious, ontological, or economic laws, men and women would be free to create their own forms of social arrangements, along with their own histories. Viewed from the perspective of capitalist social relations, the economic technology (of which the social organization of production and the social method of production in the workplace are part) dehumanizes and alienates workers. It undermines their ability to realize their nature as species beings and their need for community participation and self-realization through creative production; it divides them into competing groups, separates their mental and physical powers, alienates their labor, distorts their personality development, and reduces reason to the technological production of surplus value (*techne*, rationalization, and value realization).

The social contradictions between modern science and technology and the social forms of economic organization result in an inefficient and irrational society with its economic crises, poverty, human misery, unemployment, overproduction, and underconsumption, which in turn results in further worker alienation and social estrangement. The key point here is that the causes are human and not natural. Productive forces and the social relations of production are analytically—but not institutionally—distinct elements of the basic contradictions of capitalist societies. As we have already seen, ethics is not limited by Marx to a theory of social justice based simply on economic distribution of material goods, but necessitates consideration of the distribution and organization of the sphere of production as well as the totality of all human social relationships. Social justice deals with the totality of human relationships in a given society and how these same relationships hinder or aid in the development of rationality, self-consciousness, and freedom. This is certainly the meaning of universal justice for both Marx and Aristotle.

Aristotle certainly knew this, despite his attempts to support aristocracy, for he cited an economic relationship in which the equality of exchange and the equality of persons, via the equality of needs, became the crucial relationship for society. He tried to develop an "economics" which would be conducive to justice, a friendship, and a community which could be sustained and humane. His requirements for such a community amounted to a de facto definition of a just economic relationship, and their contravention by capitalist society should be indicative of the unjust status and eventual self-destruction of that society. Aristotle's stipulations for a sustainable community and Marx's for the same, accord to a remarkable degree.[13]

Marx's economic theory is primarily a theory about justice and the community, because the real minimal intent of a true economic system—viewed from its economic base—is to supply the material conditions for survival and satisfaction of physical needs. These are necessary for the further development of the human individual's spiritual and intellectual needs. From the perspective of the social relations of production, the goal is the development of species being and the satisfaction of the human needs for social interaction, creativity, community, and friendship (*philia*). "Marx had in the back of his mind the primary constituent concepts of justice and community (*koinonia*), as the defining considerations of economics."[14]

Capitalism is therefore condemned, because it is economically irrational and inefficient at the point of production and undermines the community basis for a free democratic society (metaethics). Marx's economic writings are much more extensive than Aristotle's, for they are built on the problematic of modernity: With modern society, the economy becomes the key social mechanism through which the individual is defined (as "the economic man"); and the structures of political economy are much more complex than they were in the fourth century B.C. In spite of these differences and the theoretical distance that lies between the two men, Aristotle's theory of exchange, money-making (*chrematistike*), and commercial trading (*kapelike*) fulfilled the same function and purpose as Marx's analysis of economic contradictions and crises. In both cases, the social economy is viewed as something necessary for human survival and a prerequisite for self-realization within the community. While bourgeois equality and freedom from the French Revolution are reduced to ideological expressions of exchange relations, the Ancients offer an alternative for they went beyond this limited perspective. With them, equality and freedom were the basis for the community, for exchange, and for the political constitution—not the basis for private consumption.

> Equality and freedom are thus not only respected in exchange based on exchange values but, also, the exchange of exchange values is the productive real basis of all *equality* and *freedom*. As pure ideas they are merely the idealized expressions of this basis; as developed in juridical, political, social relations, they are merely this basis to a higher power. And so it has been in history. Equality and freedom as developed to this extent are exactly the opposite of the freedom and equality in the world of antiquity, where developed exchange values was not their basis, but where, rather, the development of that basis destroyed them. Equality and freedom presuppose relations of production as yet unrealized in the ancient world or in the Middle Ages.[15]

MARX BETWEEN TWO WORLDS: CLASSICAL ETHICS AND THE CRITIQUE OF MODERNITY

We are now in a position to summarize the whole of Marx's theory of ethics and social justice, which incorporates his epistemology, ethics, metaethics, political economy, social theory, and theory of democracy. Though Marx draws on a wide range of classical authors ranging from the Hebrew prophets to Diogenes Laertius and Lucretius, the towering figure in his ethics is certainly Aristotle. The following list summarizes the relationship between Marx and Aristotle, and thereby the unconscious ethical structure of Marx's works. Though the correspondence is not always exact on particular points, the overall structure of their arguments is surprisingly close.

Theory of Social Ethics and Justice
Marx	Aristotle

I. Ethical Epistemology:
1. critique of epistemology, science, and foundationalism from Hume to Hegel

    1. critique of ethics as science (*theoria*) and universal knowledge (*episteme*)

2. dilemma of ethical validity and objectivity: the philosophical problems of verification of ethical truth claims
3. Hume's critique of induction and deduction and the philosophical justification of science
4. Hegel's phenomenological reconstruction of the formation of modern consciousness and science as his response to the critique of epistemology and foundationalism
5. Marx's use of "theory and practice" to solve the dilemma of objective validity of science and the inability to ground universal moral norms
6. no ideals to realize except immanent principles of bourgeois society; future open to democratic deliberation and practical activity
7. critique of pure theory and positivism: future not to be decided or determined by abstract theory, but by the experience of the working class within the objective structures of political economy
8. epistemology, politics, and consensus theory of truth: social interaction and democratic consensus as the foundation of Marx's ethical and social ideals

2. dilemma of ethical objectivity and validity
3. ethics based on the fragility and contingency of experience
4. ethics as political judgment and deliberation
5. epistemologically unable to define the universal standards of measurement (*axia*) for equality and the just constitution
6. no universals in ethics and politics
7. theory of justice based on ethical universals deemed impossible
8. ethical epistemology and politics: political consensus and moral norms

II. Methodology of the Ethical Critique of Political Economy:
1. normative critique of bourgeois anthropology, natural

1. empiricism and *sensus communis*

rights, and parliamentary democracy
2. immanent critique of bourgeois morality and justice
3. critique of fetishism: positivism and science
4. critique of political economy: classical economic theory
5. dialectical critique: the logic of capital
6. historical critique: the law of value
7. critique of crisis theory: economic irrationality, inefficiency, and stagnation

2. etymological origins of ethical categories
3. essence (rationality) in existence
4. *epagoge*—induction
5. *nous*—grasp of first principles (*arche*)
6. dialectical discussion about conflicting first principles
7. deliberation and practical rationality

III. Substantive Ethics: Social Anthropology:

1. the primacy of freedom, self-determination, and the critique of natural laws (Epicurus)
2. goal of human life as self-realization and happiness (Aristotle)
3. critique of idolatry, class inequality, and poverty as undermining man's communal being (Hebrew prophets)
4. emphasis on the moral worth and human dignity of the individual in a kingdom of ends (Kant)
5. human behavior as free, rational, and creative in work (Hegel)
6. essence of human nature as species being (Feuerbach)

1. man as a moral and political animal
2. expression of man's being through virtuous and political activity of citizen (*praxis*)
3. role of citizen to be involved in the judicial and deliberative functions of the polis
4. end of human existence defined as self-realization and the good life (*eudaimonia*)

IV. Formal Metaethics: Critique of Political Economy:

1. critique of political economy: alienation and exploitation
2. historical and structural critiques of capitalism
3. social economy and economic crisis theory: from disproportionality to the tendential fall in the rate of profit
4. historical materialism
5. sociology of knowledge and critique of ideology: theory of socialization and the formation of distorted consciousness

1. critique of false constitutions: dictatorships, oligarchies, and false democracies
2. economic theory and critique of commercial profit (*chrematistike*)
3. theory of democracy and political deliberation
4. theory of political constitutions (*politeia*) and socialization (*paideia*)

V. Formal Metaethics: Structures of Social Praxis and Theory of Justice:

1. theory of social revolution
2. theory of democracy and workers' control
3. theory of needs of species being (social eudaimonism)
4. theory of equality and social justice
5. theory of political emancipation, distributive justice, and human rights
6. theory of freedom and human emancipation

1. theory of social justice: general, distributive, corrective, and reciprocal justice
2. theory of social economy, exchange, and economic equality
3. theory of happiness (*eudaimonia*)
4. life of *phronesis* and *episteme*, *praxis* and *theoria*

Marx's theory of ethics and social justice entails the integration of all five of the above levels of ethical thinking. Level I sets the stage with an analysis of his epistemology and the central concerns of the dilemma of objective validity and ethical objectivity that runs throughout eighteenth- and nineteenth-century German philosophy. Marx attempts to answer this question: How are theory and morality justified? Level I may be broken down further into epistemology and metaphysics, epistemology and method, and method and political economy.[16] Level II examines the variety of Marx's methods used in the *Grundrisse* and *Capital*. The seven aspects of critical method—the variety of methods and their procedures for ethical justification (philosophical anthropology, historical materialism, critique of political economy, and crisis theory)—provide the methodological diversity of Marx's later economic writings. Marx's immanent critique of natural rights, liberal psychology and human nature, and utilitarian and Kantian moral philosophy—along with the fetishism critique—provide an internal normative basis for his critique of modernity, while the law of value provides an institutional and structural analysis of the economic irrationality, inefficiency, and disequilibrium of modern political economy. The social and political philosophy of the French and German Enlightenment provide the external perspective for a normative critique on the basis of belief in the moral dignity and autonomy of individual self-determination, the primacy of self-consciousness, rationality, and freedom in human development, and the final goal of self-realization as a social being in level III.

Levels IV and V supply the metaethical foundations for Marx's theory of social justice. Metaethics is the part of social ethics that contains political economy and social theory. Here the structural conditions of modernity are analyzed. These structural elements are important in an ethical theory because they provide the social preconditions under which the general will, free communication, and deliberative rationality can develop unhindered by class divisions, inequality, economic crises, and alienated labor. They are the social requirements or conditions necessary for the possibility of moral autonomy and self-determination. It is here that the historical and dialectical studies of capital provide the critique of all social forms that distort human freedom and self-consciousness. Metaethics was a method used both by Aristotle and later by Rousseau in their defenses of the integrity and freedom of the moral being.[17].

As the above list indicates, for every level of social ethics in Marx there is a corresponding one in Aristotle. Levels IV and V also provide us with the foundations for a materialist consensus theory of truth and an ethic of public discourse (*Diskursethik*).[18] This book began with an examination of Marx's work on Epicurean ethics and philosophy of nature. His dissertation on Greek philosophy expresses the guiding principle of freedom as the essence of Marx's writings and his understanding of the nature of species being itself.

However, what is more important to Marx is that Epicurus subordinates his natural philosophy to a moral conception of man. He points out that the real goal of the Epicurean natural philosophy is not the establishment of scientific knowledge but "the *ataraxia* of self-consciousness." Anything which could disturb the autonomous, self-contained development of the human spirit towards this ideal must be rejected, including both physical laws and the so-called divine heavenly bodies. In fact man's autonomy is conceived in such a radical fashion that there can be "nothing good which lies outside of him; the only good which he has in relation to the world is the negative movement, to be free from it."[19]

The critique of religion and natural laws—the critique of heaven and earth—become the hallmark of Marx's early and later works. Whether it is a belief in an independent being in religion, an independent and universal view of human nature in liberal psychology, or adherence to the independent natural laws of the capitalist economy, Marx criticizes all forms of idolatry and fetishism in which the individual as a social being becomes lost in a metaphysical system over which it has no control. It is a world become meaningless, for man has failed to realize that what appears as natural and objective laws are only objectifications of the conscious and unconscious being of man. Marx's goal is to reestablish the moral priority of the individual and to regain control over these unconscious laws, whether they be the laws of the "transcendental unity of apperception," "the cunning of reason," or "the invisible hand."[20] It is in the area of economics that the central locus of Marx's thinking coalesces on these ethical issues of human dignity and self-determination.

Bourgeois economic theory sees the relations of bourgeois production as natural relations, that is to say, it holds "that these are the relations in which wealth is creative and productive force developed in conformity with the laws of nature. These relations therefore are themselves natural laws independent of the influence of time. They are eternal laws which must always govern society. Thus there has been history, but there is no longer any." For Marx, however, capitalism was only an historical form of social production.[21]

The critique of political economy was necessary in order to undermine the political legitimacy of the social structures of modernity that distort human development, undermine communal social relations, and repress individual striving toward self-determination and self-legislation. His understanding of Greek philosophy left an indelible impression on him of the importance of an egalitarian community to social justice. Aristotle criticized gross inequality, class, and poverty as detrimental to human freedom and social life. Marx combines his analysis of Ricardo and the critique of modern political economy with the general form of Aristotle's search for justice in the *Nicomachean Ethics* and *Politics* and the soul of Epicurus's desire for freedom, self-determination, and critique of the natural laws. Though these components are manifestations of the substantive side of Marx's ethics, they also form the metaethical basis for his critique. The classical ethics of the Ancients as well as the classical ethics of German Idealism were used to provide Marx with the normative foundations for his critique of modernity.

ETHICAL VALIDITY AND DEMOCRATIC CONSENSUS: FROM GREEK POLIS TO MODERN COMMUNE

The decidedly U.S. and Canadian debates in the last few years over morality, justice, and Marxism have set in motion an intense discussion of these issues. With the large mass of published material out there to be analyzed, it appears that there is no possible resolution to the debates. They are just another in a series of deep philosophical arguments that have no conclusion. This is quite possibly so. It may be especially the case with the interpretations of particular sections of Marx's writings. However, certain aspects can be resolved. First, the question of whether Marx uses morality in his critique of capitalism has—I believe—been clearly and positively answered by a review of the secondary literature and by a rereading of Marx. Second—as Geras has said—the real issue is not whether moral values are used, but the kinds of moral values used and where their emphases lie. Lukes and Brenkert have argued that the central moral category in Marx's social thought is freedom, while others have stated that it is justice.[22] Third, it is clear that Marx was not a moral philosopher and did not leave us with an explicit philosophical treatise on ethics. Fourth, what appears to be a contradiction between those who view Marx from the perspective of a sociology of morals and critique of ideology, and those who view him as having a theory of justice, turns out—on further investigation—to be not a contradiction at all: The two positions are not incompatible. And fifth, the real and most difficult issue is the one about Marx and a theory of justice.

It really is a matter of focus and emphasis—whether the analysis is on the appearances of bourgeois moral values and their critique, on a critique of political economy from a moral perspective, or on the social values and ideals of an emancipated society. Marx's attitude changes depending on the direction and emphasis of his analysis. It also changes depending on how broadly the categories of morality and justice are defined in the secondary literature. The narrower definitions of these subject matters are not necessarily wrong. When they exclude relevant material in Marx's writings, they not only limit the range of debate to their preconceived definitions of morality and justice, but distort Marx's own writings. The view that Marx does use moral and juridical categories is superior to the arguments laid out in the Tucker–Wood thesis, because the former is truer to the variety of material in Marx's own writings and is more inclusive.

The final question to be resolved, then, is the real problem of whether Marx has a theory of social justice. Here too the issue will be resolved by dealing with the narrow and expansive definitions of the term. Those who argue that Marx does use the categories of moral philosophy and has an implied theory of morality, but who disagree as to whether he has a theory of justice or not, rely on different definitions of justice. Scholars like Brenkert and Lukes—by emphasizing the importance of freedom and human emancipation—say that Marx does not deem justice or a theory of rights as part of his moral theory; they accept the argument that law and rights are the ideological expressions of capital. Now we have reached the real heart of the issue. Do the social categories of freedom and emancipation exclude or include the notion of justice? Or put another way: Does the idea of justice—as we have been developing in our analysis of the natural law tradition to the present—include freedom and emancipation, along with the categories of the good life, community, species being, and social democracy? I believe that the answer is a most definite "yes". To the extent that the secondary literature focuses on distributive justice and Marx's critique of the "rights of man," not only his ties to the Ancients are missed, but so too is his own general theory of justice. He does deal with distributive justice, which is most explicitly detailed in his famous dictum: "From each according to their ability, to each according to their needs." But as we have already seen, this is a too narrow interpretation of justice and must be supplemented with a more general theory of social justice that would include the other ethical categories. "Both Gould and Marković have suggested equality of freedom or self-determination as the most adequate jurisprudential translation of Marx's understanding of just social relations."[23]

Justice is not simply a question of the rights of man in civil society, individualism, law, and the state; nor is it simply a question of the distribution of the social wealth of society based on some standard of measurement such as work, effort, ability, status, or need. We cannot permit liberalism to define the conceptual structure of socialism. Rather, justice and ethics—more broadly defined—deal with the issue of the final goals of society and the individual: the nature of the good life, realization of the common welfare and happiness (*eudaimonia*). They also involve the full realization of human potential (telos) through the education and development of the individual personality in and through society (*paideia* through *politeia*). Though Marx's concept of man as praxis and activity includes the concept of work— a perspective the Greeks would have rejected—it also includes much more that they would have accepted. Work is only one of the defining characteristics of the essence of man as free, self-conscious, productive activity. The overall structure of Aristotle's argument about ethics, justice, and the polity was incorporated into Marx's social theory; it supplies Marx with the deepest structures of his thought. When the importance of the Ancients is understood and accepted, then much of the debate over morality and justice in Marx simply disappears.

> While Marx differed with Aristotle on many specific issues (the alleged incapacity for happiness among slaves, barbarians, or women, the primacy of contemplative activity), he also emphasized objective features of individual lives which would profoundly influence happiness (display of social connectedness in genuine forms of friendship and political community, freedom from exploitation, freedom from physical handicap, possession of the opportunity to realize one's capacities, perhaps realization of some of one's higher capacities), yet still allowed a distinctive modern wide leeway for individual choice of specific activities to be undertaken. . . . In some fundamental respects, therefore, Marx could have regarded his argument as a correction and refinement of Aristotle's eudaimonism, not a replacement of it.[24]

In the classical ethics of Aristotle, virtuous activity, practical wisdom, ethical judgment, the good life, friendship, happiness, education and socialization, and the political constitution of the state were all considered part of the question surrounding his theory of justice. In fact, discussion of the nature of justice was not separated from moral theory, political philosophy, or economic theory.[25] All were aspects of the general discussion about the nature of man and the good society—questions about the meaning and purpose of human existence. All these categories are so tightly interwoven that it is impossible to discuss one aspect of ethics without discussing them all. Joining them together resulted in further questions relating to the being of man, the nature of society, human needs and commercial profits, equality of economic exchange, the development of moral character, self-realization of the political animal, the fair distribution of the wealth of society, equity in civil and criminal law, the nature of the citizen, equality and the free society, the strengths and weaknesses of democracy and aristocracy, and the epistemological relations between ethics and science. These questions of Aristotle in his *Nicomachean Ethics* and *Politics* are the same types used by Marx when considering the issues of man's species being; the nature of capitalism and communism; political emancipation; the emancipation of human consciousness, sensibility, needs, and self-realization; fair distribution of the social wealth based on contribution, ability, or need; the nature of equality in crude communism, utopian socialism, and an emancipated society; the development of democracy from the rational kernel of liberalism to the popular democracy of workers' control; and finally, the epistemological dilemma of ethical objectivity in ethics inherited from Hume, Kant, and Hegel.

While ethics deals with the development of the moral and political character of the individual in the good society, the Aristotelian concept of justice also refers to what today would be called metaethics or social theory. Metaethics refers to the social and institutional setting within which virtuous activity, ethical deliberation, and political judgment occur—that is, to the social structures within which self-realization is made possible. Therefore, it entails a discussion of the legal, political, economic, and educational spheres in society that "determine" (*bestimmen*) and influence the success or failure of the telos of man—that aid or hinder the fullest development of human potential as a *zōon politikon*. If one makes this analytic distinction between ethics and metaethics, then Marx is certainly dealing with both. He emphasizes in his writings the metaethical side and does, in fact, have a fully developed theory of metaethics with his historical materialism, critique of political economy, theory of democracy, and social theory in general. Metaethics examines the social and structural preconditions for virtuous and practical activity. For Marx, it represents the examination of the political, cultural, and economic institutions that are the preconditions for moral and species development: self-determination and freedom. He also borrows heavily from Spinoza, Rousseau, Kant, and Hegel's moral philosophies, which introduced the important categories and isolated the rational kernel of bourgeois thought in the form of individual moral freedom and dignity; the formal, legal freedoms of subjectivity; the kingdom of ends; the political freedoms of the French Revolution and the modern state; the public rights of the citizens; universal suffrage; and the freedoms of assembly, public deliberation, and the press. Like Hegel before him—who integrated Kant and Aristotle—Marx integrates modernity and the Ancients, *Moralität* and *Sittlichkeit*, individual freedom and species development.[26]

The substantive ethical standards used by Marx to critique capitalist social relations are grounded in his philosophical anthropology—his views on work, praxis, species being, and human creativity ("the unfulfilled promise of substantive or concretized freedom" in bourgeois society);[27] his theory of distributive justice; and his ideals of individuality and freedom. This is where the real difficulty of understanding Marx's theory of social justice develops. Reducing ethics to the moral philosophy of Kant would be a failure to recognize Marx's theory of ethics and social justice. On the one hand, there are the overt normative elements in his ethical critique of capitalism; on the other hand, there is the metaethics of his political economy and social theory. Thus, his early philosophical period corresponds to a theory of substantive ethics, while his later economic theory corresponds to a theory of metaethics. The former provides the normative and moral substance for his critique of capitalism, while the latter provides an analysis of the structural basis for ethics and self-realization in the institutions of modernity. Metaethics is a social theory that critically examines the political and economic institutions of industrial capitalism in order to show how the system is incapable of realizing the ethical ideals of the classical ancient and modern traditions (transcendent critique) and, at the same time, incapable of realizing its own ideals of bourgeois society (immanent critique).

What clearly is missing is a structural analysis of the ethical ideals of the emancipated society. Marx is very pointed on this issue as he states:

> In that case we do not confront the world in a doctrinaire way with a new principle: Here is the truth, kneel down before it! We develop new principles for the world out of the world's own principles. We do not say to the world: Cease your struggles, they are foolish; we will give you the true slogan of struggle.[28]

> Communism is for us not a *state of affairs* which is to be established, an *ideal* to which reality [will] have to adjust itself.[29]

Relating to the issues of the objectivity and validation of ethical values, Femia argues that Marx's scientific method undermines two essential ingredients for democratic decision-making: epistemological uncertainty, and epistemological equality. If there is no uncertainty about the nature of knowledge and truth and no free and open discourse, then social evolution will be determined by a social physics directed by scientific experts and technocratic elites. Epistemology and politics would be reduced to a social technology. O'Neill has responded by saying that Marx's science is a proletarian science, which—though having the predictive ability of positivism—does not have the ability to control historical events. Both authors are working within a framework that accepts the traditional view of modern science—one claiming Marx's science is antithetical to democracy, and the other that it is not. It is this very dichotomy between critical knowledge and democracy that is transcended by Marx, who rejects the categories and method of positivism.[30]

The "critical method" of Marx is epistemologically incapable of incorporating a concept of the future as a "not yet" into its methodology of the critique of political economy. Its view of the future is that of the dialectical unfolding of that which has already been *in potentia*; this represents a rejection of the positivist view of the sociology of explanation, and rejection of a predictable future.[31] The goal here is the historical and dialectical understanding of the nature of capitalism—and not a form of social engineering to direct change in the future. Thus, the institutional and temporal dimensions of the future are missing and the ethical norms in Marx's works do not provide the missing pieces to his overall theory. They do not give us the substantive and concrete information about the nature of the institutions of the free society; nor do they offer us much of a guide in determining the institutional specifics or operational definitions for his theory of needs, his notion of species being, or his theory of democracy.

What do the categories of Marx's social theory mean when applied to the concrete historical world of political economy? How is work to be divided and structured in a complex industrial society? What is normal and abnormal division of labor? What are acceptable levels of alienation? What are the institutional networks for the macro- and micro-structures of economic democracy? What is a fair and equal distribution of social wealth toward the satisfaction of human needs in a free society? What is the structure of exchange without exchange value and surplus value? What are the ultimate ends for the individual and society, and what constitutes human happiness? And what are the meanings of these ethical standards when applied to the real world? Though Marx is less restrained than Aristotle in defining the criteria for ethical judgment or the standards for the measurement of equality and justice, there is no discussion of what these standards would mean in the real world—as opposed to the world of philosophical speculation. Nor is there any analysis of how they are to be applied. Finally, there is no discussion about how these standards themselves are to be justified.

> The question naturally arises as to how Marx thought the principles exemplified in certain practices might be justified. What test must be satisfied or what requirement met? We have very little to go on at this point. Marx appears to think that some normative principles are *rational*, but he does not specify what canons of reason are involved in the vindication of a moral principle.[32]

Here again the overlap between Aristotle and Marx is enlightening, if not surprising. While Aristotle begins his *Nicomachean Ethics* with the statement that ethics and political science cannot be scientific and universal, Marx comes to the same conclusion through the tortuous and circuitous route of Hume's skeptical critique of science and its philosophical justification in deductive and inductive logic; Kant's critical method, his constitution theory of truth, and his synthesis of rationalism and empiricism in the critique of pure reason; and Hegel's phenomenological critique of epistemology and foundationalism. Marx's theory of "theory and praxis" is his response to the modern dilemma of epistemology and failure of the search for certainty—the dilemma of objective validity and critique of science begun by Hume and expanded in the writings of German Idealism.[33]

This notion of theory and practice gives us a perspective from which to criticize the traditional epistemologies of empiricism and rationalism. Knowledge is not arrived at through the deductive unfolding of categories from first principles; nor is it arrived at by reflection on the immediacy of the given objectivity. There is a dialectic between the knower and the object known, in which process both are formed and transformed. This form of knowledge is therefore not reducible to a correspondence theory of truth, which assumes the independence of both subjectivity and objectivity, or to absorption of the latter in the former with the unfolding of Hegel's Absolute Spirit.[34]

There is a good deal written on this subject analyzing the sociology of knowledge, the constitution theory of truth, the critique of idealism and positivism, and the relation between theory and social activity, essence and reality, and science and objectivity.[35] Praxis is also examined as constituting the basis of knowledge, the objects of knowledge, the criterion of knowledge, and the verification of knowledge. Others argue that praxis creates reality, but is not the criterion of the truth of that reality.[36] Kolakowski writes that

> man's practical activity has been elevated to the rank of an epistemological category, so that its functions are not limited to verification of . . . correspondence . . . but are broadened to encompass the defining of the very concept of truth, falseness, and nonsense. . . . The truth of a judgment is defined as a practical function of the usefulness of its acceptance or rejection.[37]

These ideas have been very helpful in the development of the secondary literature dealing with Marx's materialism, method, and epistemology. However, we must return to the question raised above. In spite of all these important contributions, the real questions—to which these others are simply prolegomena—have not been answered: How are the principles of moral action justified? How are these principles to be implemented? What will the future look like? And what institutional arrangements will express these principles?[38] Though we have some initial thinking in this area, responding simply that practical activity as an epistemological category defines the nature of truth or is involved in determining truth does not answer these more probing questions. It only creates another metaphysical realm of truth claims. There is no developed theory of truth, no standard of measurement of truth claims, no criterion of analysis, and no basis on which to make a universal judgment about the truth and falsity of truth statements. The category of praxis has been helpful in raising a variety of new questions about the nature of knowledge and criticizing the traditional approaches, but has not been able to move beyond them and deal with the most important types of issues. Sánchez Vázquez realizes that one of the most important questions when dealing with the epistemological aspects of praxis is that of validation.

> But how can I affirm that practice proves the truth or falsehood of a theory? Although Marx never offered a solution to this question, an answer can be found in his concept of praxis as a real, material activity adopted to certain ends. . . . In the end it is practice that submits our

theoretical conclusions about things to the test; if we base our hope for
the achievement of certain ends on a given judgment about reality, and
those ends are not achieved, it follows that our judgment was false. At
the same time we must be wary of interpreting this relation between
truth and success, or falsehood and disaster, in a pragmatic way, as if
truth or falseness were determined by success or failure. If a theory can
be applied, it is because it is true; the reverse, however, is not necessarily
true. Success does not constitute truth; it simply reveals the fact that
thought can adequately reproduce reality.[39]

Though this position extends the argument further by criticizing the
idealist, empiricist, and pragmatic views of truth, it does not really
help us too much. It does not give us any clearer insight into the
nature of the criterion of truth other than as a variation of pragmatism.

Though Marx introduces a new historical and materialist method
grounded in his theory of political economy, he recognizes and
responds to the same epistemological problems as the eighteenth-
century philosophers. Though the traditions of the Moderns and
Ancients are different, the results are very similar. Both Marx and
Aristotle reject the universal foundations for ethical and political
judgments in theory or pure knowledge; and both turn to a materialist consensus theory of truth grounded in a theory of deliberation,
political judgment, practical action, and democratic consensus.
Though Marx does not use this terminology, the meaning is still
present. Both social theorists respond to the problems of epistemology by turning to praxis as political activity. Praxis as politics is an
idea that is part of Marx's early philosophical and later historical
writings.

> The only general condition of rationality cannot inhere in the qualities
> of the measures taken but in their democratic formulation . . . for there
> can be no other criterion of correctness. . . . Marx's reluctance to give
> descriptions of communist life is a most correct attitude to take comple-
> mentary to grasping that the achievement of rationality is not a question
> of goals but of truly democratic means. An equally correct attitude is
> represented by the line of Marx's analysis of capitalism, where funda-
> mentally economic restrictions on the mass democracy of social self-
> consciousness are criticized, leaving the future open in the light of the
> removal of these restrictions.[40]

From another perspective, Herbert Marcuse stresses Hegel's advance
over empiricism with his idea that reason and the development of

human potential are the criteria by which the world should be judged.[41] Marx takes this one step further by implying that a rationality of political discourse is not only an active rationality, but the real criterion of knowledge and truth. Democracy itself becomes the criterion for the validity of truth claims, since every other epistemological argument implies some form of unjustifiable foundationalism and metaphysics. Through political judgments and deliberation, through the formation of a social consensus in the public realm (commune), through the development of human reason and interpersonal interaction in an emancipated society, those issues of the fundamental norms that guide human life will evolve out of democracy—and not out of pure theory.

> Politics does not rest on justice and freedom; it is what makes them possible. The object of democracy is not to apply independently grounded abstractions to concrete situations but rather to extrapolate working abstractions from concrete situations. In a word, politics is not the application of Truth to the problem of human relations but the application of human relations to the problem of truth. Justice then appears as an approximation of principle in a world where absolute principles are irrelevant.[42]

Though Barber is referring to pragmatism's critique of "Cartesian epistemology" and "the politics of certainty," this statement nicely reflects the foundations for both the Greek and German perspectives.[43] As in the case of Hegel's Owl of Minerva, theory comes only after the fact; it never predicts the future, but gives meaning and coherence to the present.[44] The development of the future is guided by a theory that is not universal and scientific, but that springs naturally from social reality itself. This explains much of Marx's critique of bourgeois ethics, which is imposed on reality from without; it is, therefore, always unnatural and ideological. Truth and moral values are constituted in the very process of the constitution of reality, sensuousness, consciousness, personality, and the species being. As Aristotle has misgivings about defining the nature of equality and justice, Marx has similar misgivings about defining the nature of the future society and its institutions and social ideals. When he does discuss moral norms, it is in the context of metaethics—that is, in the context of establishing the sociological preconditions for the epistemology of social praxis. Metaethics analyzes the structural preconditions under which deliberative reason, public discourse, and establishment of the sovereign will finally could take place unhindered by class domination and exploitation, inequality, and alienated labor.[45] Democracy for both social theorists provides the epistemological clue to overcoming the crisis of epistemology and science, the dilemma of ethical objectivity, and the "fallacy of independent ground."[46]

For both Aristotle and Marx, the epistemological dilemma about the nature of knowledge and truth becomes translated into issues of social praxis. The search for ethical and political standards becomes grounded in the political process itself, rather than in pure theory. The epistemological foundations for this has been established by Aristotle's distinctions between *praxis* and *episteme*—between practical wisdom and universal scientific knowledge—by his special emphasis on the imprecise nature of both ethics and politics, and by the inability to theoretically establish standards for the meaning and measurement of justice, equality, sovereignty, the correct political constitution, and the best mechanism for political decision-making (*Nicomachean Ethics* sections 1094b12–28, 1098a24–28, 1104a4–8, 1131a25–29, 1134b28–30, 1135a3–4, 1137b30–32, 1140a31–1140b4, 1140b8–13, 1142a23–28, and 1142b8–13; *Politics* sections 1281a8–13, 1282b22–24, 1283b8–10, 1283b26–28, and 1286a26–27). It is important to note that Aristotle continues to have doubts about whether the good, the rich, the noble, or the middle class should rule—even after he has discussed the nature of the democratic polity as the best solution in book 3 of the *Politics*.

> But on the other hand in matters which it is impossible for the law either to decide at all or to decide well, ought the one best man to govern or all the citizens? As it is, the citizens assembled hear lawsuits and deliberate and give judgements, but these judgements are all on particular cases. Now no doubt any one of them individually is inferior compared with the best man, but a state consists of a number of individuals, and just as a banquet to which many contribute dishes is finer than a single plain dinner, for this reason in many cases a crowd judges better than any single person. Also the multitude is more incorruptible—just as the larger stream of water is purer, so the mass of citizens is less corruptible than the few.[47]

Whenever Aristotle deals with the democratic polity in book 3, it is always in the context of the resolution of the epistemological problem of being unable to universally establish the principles for ethics and politics. A popular democracy of citizens is finally decided on as the best political constitution, mainly because of its ability to generate superior political judgments in these matters. Again, the criterion by which one constitution is conceived as superior to another is decided on the basis of its resolution of the epistemological dilemma.

Marx also faces the same problems relating to the establishment of his fundamental ethical and political principles. With his constitution theory of truth; his critique of rationalism and empiricism; his critique of epistemology, and the philosophical ability to ground and justify social norms and theories; with the methodological importance of his theories of objectivity, false universality, ideology, and fetishism; with the development of his notion of theory and practice and the practical activity of man in the social sphere for purposes of self-realization; with the special nature of his dialectical method as the critique of political economy; and the development of his views on emancipated society and economic democracy, Marx too turns in the direction of "political praxis" to establish the validity of his ethical ideals. As we have seen in Chapter Two, Marx in the "Theses on Feuerbach" clearly states that theory cannot decide the truth claims of its own ideas. They can be validated only in practice; any other method would be guilty of scholasticism.[48]

The role of theory is one of relentless criticism of everything accepted on the basis of nothing other than its immediacy: It simply is. All forms of individual alienation—from religion and politics to economics—must be brought before the judge of human reason to be unmasked as illusions and distortions. Self-conscious and deliberative reason must regain its authority in order for the individual to regain moral integrity and self-determination. But Marx is aware that this theory is not that of the isolated philosopher criticizing the developments of modernity, since theory must become the practical need of the proletariat. Theory must be made a real force in people's lives; it must change their consciousness, and must enlighten for the purposes of real social transformation. Theory can never be separated from the practical activity of the self-conscious working class.[49]

> The weapons of criticism cannot, of course, replace criticism by weapons. Material force must be overthrown by material force. But theory also becomes a material force once it has gripped the masses. Theory is capable of gripping the masses as soon as it demonstrates *ad hominem*, and it demonstrates *ad hominem* as soon as it becomes radical.[50]

Marx recognizes in a fashion similar to Aristotle that discursive rationality and the deliberative function are social in character and cannot be separated from one another. Reflection and self-consciousness arise in public activity when the people try to free themselves from all forms of social bondage. Theory is thus a public activity (political and economic), which must be institutionalized to give it "material force"; and it is the working class that will provide the theory, with its subject and driving force. But what will the institutional structure of this materialized theory look like? It is here that the Paris Commune provides us with some important sociological and epistemological insights, since it was here that theory became real. Though Marx says that the Commune had no ideals of its own to realize, he also does not develop—beyond very abstract and general statements—his theory of needs, distributive justice, or the good society; nor does he deal with the period of transition, the operational or technical implications of his ethics, or the institutional setting within which social praxis would take place in the emancipated society. Marx's analysis of the structures of social praxis is very underdeveloped when compared with his analysis of classical political economy and German Idealism. In spite of this, it is clear that the form of knowledge of Marx's social praxis and political activity is *phronesis* (political wisdom). The use of the term "praxis" in his analysis of the Paris Commune represents a return to his earliest use of the term "political activity" in his critique of Hegel's *Philosophy of Right.*

Theory is a practical activity undertaken in the quest for unionization, more worker rights and benefits, republican democracy, and—finally—socialist revolution.[51] The Commune was characterized by universal suffrage, direct recall, popular sovereignty, worker cooperatives, egalitarianism, and the dismantling of the institutions of social repression (church, bureaucracy, and the army). Marx stresses the "self-government of the producers"—"a government of the people by the people" created for the purposes of eliminating all forms of class slavery.[52] It is also important for him that this political constitution has gone beyond political emancipation to human emancipation. The Commune was a working—not representative—government, with both the executive and legislative branches in the hands of the people. The citizens had the power to deliberate, and to publicly decide and act on their decisions. Implicit in this is that the people must be free from all forms of self-alienation, economic exploitation, class fragmentation, and distorted consciousness. These are the materialist and democratic foundations for his consensus theory of truth.

This is why Marx views it as important that the internal repression and distorted consciousness of false ideology—resulting from the "parson power" of the church—be destroyed. In his early writings, Marx said that criticism begins with the criticism of heaven and moves to the criticism of earth. Here he is saying that the formation of self-consciousness and the critique of ideology are necessary in order that the people become citizens and participate in self-legislating their own values, principles, and social arrangements. "The whole of the educational institutions were opened to the people gratuitously, and at the same time cleared of all interference of church and state."[53] Popular sovereignty demands an egalitarian society in which the citizens can deliberate, judge, and acquire political wisdom. This is the major reason why Marx is so opposed to the "alchemists of revolution" and their conspiratorial forms of social change: They eliminate popular support and undermine democratic ideals.[54] The people learn through experience and the cultivation of a critical self-consciousness by participating in the creation of their own future.[55] There are no goals to be realized, because of the radicalness of Marx's views on the self-realization of human potential undistorted by prior definitions of the ultimate goals in life, his views on popular sovereignty and self-legislation by the democratic community, and his views on human reason and self-consciousness as a social process (*praxis*) and not a theoretical one (*theoria*).

Some have mistakenly interpreted the notion of the "withering away of the state" to mean that Marx favored the dissolution of the political sphere along with all forms of political rights. We have seen that—though critical of the rights of possessive individualism—Marx wanted to protect basic "human rights" and the "rights of the citizen." These are the very rights incorporated in the Commune, and it is through political participation that the species being is self-consciously and rationally created.

> The transformation, through the division of labour, of personal powers (relations) into material powers, cannot be dispelled by dismissing the general idea of it from one's mind, but can only be abolished by the individuals again subjecting these material powers to themselves and abolishing the division of labour. This is not possible without the community.[56]

Marx is drawing on a rich intellectual tradition from Aristotle to Kant and Hegel. "Marx fused an ancient vision of the political life of free men with the experience of modern working-class political action."[57]

Here—with the emphasis on citizenship, the poor, the critique of property and classes—Marx is drawing heavily on Rousseau and his theory of the General Will, popular sovereignty, and the critique of representative government.[58] Rousseau's critique of inequality and property and his call for an egalitarian democracy supplies the structural link connecting Aristotle's notion of citizen and *phronesis* with Kant's idea of the dilemma of objective validity and the self-legislation of practical reason. Praxis had been turned into labor by an alienating and depoliticizing political economy; but—freed from artificial social restraints—praxis is free to determine itself in man's creative activity in all forms of human life. Appearing as popular sovereignty, as citizenship, and as constituting the political constitution, praxis—free creative activity—realizes itself. This is what Rousseau called "moral liberty." For Marx, it requires a free and open expression of ideas in the public sphere, as well as a free press.

> The free press is the ubiquitous vigilant eye of the people's soul, the embodiment of the people's faith in itself, the eloquent link that connects the individual with the state and the world, the embodiment of culture that transforms material struggles into intellectual struggles and idealizes their crude material form. It is a people's frank confession to itself, and the redeeming power of confession is well known. It is the spiritual mirror in which a people can see itself, and self-examination is the first condition of wisdom. It is the spirit of the state, which can be delivered into every cottage, cheaper than coal gas. It is all-sided, ubiquitous, omniscient. It is the ideal world which always wells up out of the real world and flows back into it with ever greater spiritual riches and renews its soul.[59]

To exercise its legislative and executive functions, popular democracy must involve an open public discussion of all social and economic issues; and it is in this process that citizen education and maturation take place. Aristotle and Marx are the founders of a *Diskursethik* (ethic of public discourse), though it is much more implicit in the latter's writings. "All substantive pronouncements on the validity of single norms must originate in *real discourse* or, alternatively, in discourses undertaken in an advocacy way. The outcome of these discourses cannot be anticipated by philosophers."[60] Though neither one of the two social theorists has a pure consensus theory of truth or pure political theory of discursive rationality, a *Diskursethik* is essential to an understanding of both. As the list comparing the relationships between Marx and Aristotle indicates, their *Diskursethik* is supplemented by a substantive ethics grounded in their philosophy of man and belief in self-realization—that is, in their theory of social needs and happiness.

EPISTEMOLOGY, PRAXIS, AND DEMOCRACY: A CRITIQUE OF HABERMAS'S INTERPRETATION OF MARX

Jürgen Habermas—recognizing the structural transformations within advanced capitalist society—has felt the need to revise Marx's social theory. Habermas has called into question Marx's theory of value, while relying more on the economic theory of Joan Robinson and the Cambridge School of neo-Ricardians.[61] He has also criticized Marx's theory of praxis as being based on a too limited and instrumental concept of technical rationality. Habermas recognizes the epistemological importance of praxis as the objective activity of the individual in both the material and life worlds: That is, it is both an economic activity and a meaning-creation activity (symbolic action). Praxis is thus a transcendental category, for it creates the social conditions necessary for human life. "The materialist study of history is directed toward societal categories that determine both the real process of life and the transcendental conditions of the constitution of life worlds."[62]

However, with the primacy of labor in historical materialism, Marx has reduced the two social categories and social worlds into one. By reducing the world of culture, tradition, and symbolic interchange to work, these areas become social reflexes of instrumental activity, with the result that the social arena—in which individual and public self-reflection proceed—is lost. The world becomes depoliticized and disenchanted when meaning is reduced to the administrative directives of large corporations and the modern state, on the one hand, and to the imperatives of positivism, on the other. Marx interprets "species' self-reflection through work"[63] to mean that the instrumental activity at the heart of the logic of capital accumulation becomes not only the dominant theme within society, but the dominant conceptual framework from which self-reflection takes place.[64] The logic of domination and control built into the concepts of technological rationality limits the range and types of questions that can be raised regarding the nature of an emancipated and rational society. Social praxis represses the possibilities of meaning that exist in the social world of interpersonal interaction; it reduces the conceptual frame of language itself. Just as positivism limits the scope of questions about the nature of knowledge, so too administrative and instrumental rationality limit the range of social and economic issues; validation of a particular theory is then limited to technical success. With the technological evolution of advanced capitalism, with the development of the modern state (whose chief administrative functions are capital formation and crisis avoidance), with the rise of modern science and positivism and the loss of hermeneutics and epistemology, the public realm of criticial reflection disappears—and with it, the very possibility for understanding, deliberation, and judgment.

> Because this sort of rationality extends to the correct choice among strategies, the appropriate application of technologies, and the efficient establishment of systems (with *presupposed* aims in a *given* situation), it removes the total social framework of interests in which strategies are chosen, technologies applied, and systems established, from the scope of reflection and rational reconstruction.[65]

By reducing reflective knowledge (*Reflexionswissen*) to productive knowledge (*Produktionswissen*), and communicative interaction to the logic of the machine, phenomenological self-reflection disappears—and with it, the ability of the species to reflect on its own historical past and the possibilities of its own future liberation. "Habermas must eliminate the social relations of production from production or make them independent over against the productive forces in order to eliminate the material basis for the process of history [*unbegreiflich zu machen*] and to justify his own dualism."[66] By separating social and class relations from the productive forces and the domination of nature, Habermas—in effect—replaces an objective social theory with a subjective theory of knowledge, which abstracts from the social and historical context within which science and technology evolve.[67] This represents a return to the transcendental subject of Kant, while losing the social dialectic of Hegel. The dialectic between the social relations and the technological imperatives of modern science is replaced by interaction and work. They constitute the transcendental conditions for species development. This represents a fetishism of technology.

Seeing oneself in the other, the social creation of meaning, the ethics of public discourse, the moral totality of ethical life, and the communal basis of society in its creation of public meanings and symbols are repressed in the social unconscious of work and *techne*. Relying on the works of Arendt and Gadamer, Habermas builds his theory of communicative action and critique of Marx on the bedrock of Aristotle's distinction between *praxis* and *poiesis*, *phronesis* and *techne*.[68] Habermas argues that Marx defines *praxis* in terms of both *poiesis* and *techne*, while the theoretical and institutional aspects of Aristotle's *phronesis* and *praxis* are lost. The argument developed in this work, however, has made the exact opposite claim that the concepts of *praxis* and *phronesis* used by both Marx and Aristotle are very similar. Habermas has conflated technical control and practical activity and, in general, has misunderstood Marx's use of the term "social praxis." He has also falsely characterized Marx's critique of political economy as being a positivistic example of natural science. There is abundant secondary literature on these issues that seem to justify and further Habermas's position, however. Tradition appears to be on the side of Habermas.

"Praxis" does refer to the activity of work in the production process, but is not limited to this one meaning of the term. In the *Paris Manuscripts*, Marx argues that religion, the family, the state, law, morality, science, and art are "particular forms of production."[69] Just as Hegel had included the Objective and Absolute Spirit as self-manifestations of the work of the pure Mind, so too Marx includes them within his overall understanding of the nature of social praxis.

> However, it is important to remember that productivity is seen by Marx as a general human trait, characterizing economic, social, artistic, and even scientific activity. He clearly regarded the latter as proper human activities. They actually have priority over economic labor, which was to assume less and less importance with the progress of technology.[70]

To be fair to Habermas, Marx did emphasize the economic connotations of productive activity, but it would be incorrect to characterize him as limiting himself to such a narrow definition. Praxis went beyond labor to include a wide variety of political, scientific, and aesthetic activities.[71] In modern society, the worker has been reduced to an appendage of the machine; and alienation is the process in which he or she is reduced to simply mechanical labor. We must not confuse Marx's critique of ideology and alienation with his own ideas about philosophical anthropology. Throughout the *Grundrisse* and *Capital*, he stresses the diversification of human powers and activities as the means for realization of species being and the critique of irrational and repressive limits placed on individual development by the structures of capital. "Yet an almost Aristotelian notion of activities

carried on for their own sakes reverberates throughout Marx's indict-
ment of capitalist exploitation."[72]

This is actually the reverse of the problem we have seen with his
ethics. Marx's critique of bourgeois morality does not represent a
critique of all moral values, while his critique of political economy
should not be interpreted as limiting social categories to economic
ones. The criticisms of Habermas on these issues are extensive. Some
have said that he fails to consider the relationship between the
production forces and the social relations of production—that the
process of "interaction is de-materialized."[73] Habermas sees interaction and work as transcendental categories of species constitution and
has removed them from the actual process of the making of history.
The irony here is that the central concern for Habermas was the loss
of self-consciousness, rationality, and the public sphere by the modern reduction of social communication to instrumental rationality.

> When Habermas interprets Marx's production paradigm with its con-
> cept of work, which means merely technical, instrumental activity, he is
> actually guilty of a technological reductionism, which Marx never started
> either at the level of concrete analysis or at the conceptual level. . . . It is
> not true that the production paradigm necessarily reduces historical
> development to the dimension of the development of technical control
> of nature. . . . Markus enlarges: "Actually Marx connects both character-
> istics of the process of historical development (in the sense of 'universal-
> ization' and 'emancipation' of men): the domination of men over nature
> and the manner of social communication."[74]

However, by replacing Marx's dialectic and social theory with Kantian
logic and a theory of knowledge, Habermas has reduced the public
sphere and political discourse to pure transcendental and epistemological categories. The latter have lost their historical, politicoecon-
omic, and dialectical content. As we have already seen, Marx's theory
of value, exchange value and abstract labor are not economic categories, but rather historical and sociological ones.[75] With the rise of
modernity, there is also a corresponding depletion of the opportunities for symbolic exchange; there is a closing-off of the avenues for
self- and species-reflection. With the primacy of positivism and the
loss of epistemology, with the reduction of the public realm to the
logic of the private sphere, and with the technological rationality of
the economy and the state, the opportunities for communicative
interaction have been curtailed, and their need repressed.

This is a description of the actual reduction of interaction to work; but it certainly does not represent Marx's view, especially when we consider his positions on democratic control, popular sovereignty, and emancipated self-consciousness. Habermas has mistaken Marx's critique of alienation and fetishism, the classical labor theory of value, the anthropological assumptions of political philosophy and economics (possessive individualism), and the positivism of political economy for the latter's views. Habermas's own theoretical priorities of reformulating moral universalism on the securer foundations of a neo-Kantian transcendentalism, his abstract and ahistorical juxtapositioning of interaction and labor, his unquestioning attitude toward scientific and technological rationality, his rejection of political economy and Marx's theory of value all direct him away from an historical and materialist position.

These comments about Habermas's theory of communicative interaction have been an introduction to the key points that are central to the issues discussed in this book. They are mentioned by Ferrara in his essay "A Critique of Habermas' *Diskursethik*." Ferrara criticizes Habermas for not having a theory of the good life, for having reduced *phronesis* to a psychological category, and for having fallen back behind both Marx and Hegel while "immunizing Kant's case from Hegel's critique."[76] Once the theoretical foundations for separating interaction and work had been laid, Habermas was in a position to develop his theory of the ideal speech situation, which is a social and linguistic variation on Kantian themes. Though Habermas certainly rejects positivism as explaining symbolic interaction and democratic consensus, he does unconsciously recreate some of the real problems associated with positivist theories of democracy. The evaluation of moral judgments takes place within an ideal speech situation according to the universalistic criteria established by the *Diskursethik*. Ferrara argues that Habermas fails to consider two aspects of this situation. In the first place, there is no reflective backup to check the results coming out of the ideal speech situation. That is, Habermas cannot presuppose the validity of any a priori moral values by introducing an extraneous theory of the good life. Habermas tries to overcome the epistemological problems associated with foundationalism by setting up the universal and necessary conditions for valid truth claims. However, there is a second problem here that is similar to the one found in contemporary political science and the positivist redefinition of classical democracy as a "democratic method" for choosing leaders from within a circulation of elites. Bachrach writes:

On the other hand, to insist that democracy is simply a political method, devoid of a dominant purpose, is to leave the theorist in the position of saying that democracy is that political system which actually exists in various countries, such as the United States, Britain, Canada, and the like. The fundamental disadvantage of this criterion is that it gives the theorist no basis for judging whether the system is becoming more democratic or more elitist in nature.[77]

In order to explain his reservations about Habermas's theory, Ferrara uses the hypothetical example of a jury trial in which someone accused of infanticide is under prosecution. During the jury deliberation (and approximating Habermas's ideal speech situation), Kant—acting as defense attorney—argues eloquently for acquittal. Swaying the rest of the jury with his logic and rationality, Ferrara asks the question of whether, in fact, there is not another level to this sequence of logical events. "There is no way of saying, within the framework of the *Diskursethik*, that the jury's decision was wrong or unjust at the time it was made."[78] There is no objective criterion other than the mechanism of the ideal speech situation itself, which—like the positivist interpretation of democracy as a political method (*techne*)—reduces consensus formation to a purely technical process. In effect, *phronesis* is reduced to *techne* even against the expressed wishes of Habermas himself. Ferrara also says that this problem is further complicated by the fact that Habermas's understanding of *phronesis* is reduced to a psychological category. By misinterpreting Marx's notion of work, by separating work from communicative interaction, by separating political economy from philosophy, and by establishing a neo-Kantian transcendental argument (which intensifies these other dichotomies even further), Habermas has developed a theory of society separated from the real historical institutions of modernity. By not developing a theory of the good life that would include an ethical, political, and economic theory, Habermas has lost the ability to judge the substantive nature of the ideal speech situation itself.

Neither Aristotle nor Marx develop theories of deliberation and democratic consensus.[79] But the component parts for the development of a true *Diskursethik* are found in both their theories in the form of their substantive ethics, metaethics, and social theory. It is important to realize that both individuals tied their notion of the validation of truth claims to their understanding of the realities of political and economic life and did not attempt to develop purely theoretical ideals about communication, social interaction, or truth.

For Marx, democracy was understood as a synthesis of the universal and particular—form and content—in a society that would make possible "a fully developed human identity on the basis of non-restricted mutual recognition."[80] The strengths of Marx's and Aristotle's theories lie in the fact that both include an analysis of the structural parameters within which moral judgments and virtuous activity take place (structures of social praxis) and also a critique of the political and economic forms that would undermine community interaction and a just society (metaethics). The structures of social praxis and the metaethics provide the institutional and structural preconditions for the speech situation within which praxis operates. These views of practical wisdom have an institutional component firmly rooted in the materialist structures of political economy, and not in a philosophy of language. There is to be no objective, historical inevitability to the social revolution—only the moral necessity demanded by the societal contradictions between what could be and what is.

From his earliest writings on freedom of the press, defense of peasant rights, and critique of Hegel's *Philosophy of Right*, Marx's central focus was on the issues of freedom and democracy.[81] Though his concept of democracy evolves over time and incorporates what in liberalism are both the private and public spheres and though he is critical of liberalism and its natural rights theory, Marx has always maintained the primacy of democratic participation and citizen self-determination. His views are more concrete in his analysis of the Paris Commune, which acts as a model for social change in which workers begin to organize themselves into economic democracies and participate in the executive and legislative decisions of the community. "Drawing on an Aristotelian conception of political participation as an intrinsic good, Marx recognized that the Commune's worker-officials carried out their political activity for its own sake and not for money."[82] In the context of the Paris Commune, the numerous calls by Marx for members of the working class to take responsibility and control over their lives receive institutional support. This is an outgrowth of his earlier critiques of idolatry and natural laws; it constitutes the realization of his idea from the *Contribution to the Critique of Hegel's Philosophy of Law* that politics is participation. "Deliberating and deciding means *giving effect* to the state as an actual affair."[83] The Commune represents the structural framework within which political and economic decisions in the popular democracy of cooperative production would be publicly articulated, discussed, and voted on.

Through public deliberation, the values become clearer, and the goals more real. In the same vein as Aristotle's critique of ethical and political science—but with more rhetorical flourish and political venom—Marx attacks "the didactic patronage of well-wishing bourgeois-doctrinaires, pouring forth their ignorant platitudes and sectarian crotchets in the oracular tone of scientific infallibility."[84] These are the positivists who claim universal knowledge outside of political activity, deliberation, and public discourse. With Aristotle, Marx stands on the side of those who argue that knowledge and truth are part of the acquisition of wisdom in the process of creating the social world. Just as the empirical world is never a pure immediacy resulting from scientific facts, knowledge can never be obtained through pure theory. Cöster also recognizes that a consensus theory of truth is implicit in historical materialism.

> Marx's way of conceptualizing these issues is different from the manner in which Habermas begins his analysis. What Habermas develops as a pure transcendental communicative action: the practical-emancipatory idea of rational development in the sense of a free intersubjectivity of goals, lets itself just as easily be deduced from the basic structure of the social relations of production.[85]

Cöster believes that "the practical-emancipatory aspects of universalization of the goals of social action are immanent . . . in Marx's theory of the activity of the species-being."[86] Marx's social theory has those very aspects necessary for a developed consensus theory of truth and an ethics of public discourse. Psychopedis argues that there is a "consensus theory dimension" in Marx's concept of the developing political awareness and social action of the proletariat.[87] The institutional dynamics of modern society provides the framework for consensus with the development of science (*Standpunkt der Wissenschaft*), the modern workplace and its division of labor and class relationships (*Standpunkt der Objektivität*), and the growing class consciousness of the proletariat (*Standpunkt der proletarischen Akteure*).[88] As we have seen in Chapter Five, the theory of value is an historical theory of social institutions and of the social and power relationships that underlie their structures. Marx's whole social theory is one that balances economics and sociology, economic structures and consciousness formation. What appear to be objective economic facts and natural laws are in essence only social relationships that have been fetishized. The notion of fetishism in *Capital* gives us a direct indication of how we should interpret the rest of his analysis as a critique of the method, concepts, and theories of political economy. It also directs us elsewhere in the search for ethical certainty. Once the myth of science, objectivity, and prediction are negated, the configuration of Marx's later works take on new meaning and purpose.

For Marx, not only is the general social framework for deliberation, judgment, and consensus formation outlined in his theory of democracy, needs, distributive justice, freedom, and human emancipation, but also he has developed economic and political theories critiquing any deviations that would undermine or distort communicative interaction—such as fetishism, ideology, alienated workplace, distorted development of the self, exploitative class structures, economic inefficiency and inequality, irrational technological development, destruction of the community, and loss of the public sphere. This certainly mirrors Aristotle's similar pattern of analysis where he outlines those social forms that have a tendency to undermine the community, the just political constitution, and the education of the virtuous citizen. Such detrimental structures include the false forms of constitutions—such as dictatorships, oligarchies, and false democracies—unlimited economic exchange, interest on loans, commercial profits, and a life of pure utilitarian pleasure.

Habermas could question Marx and Aristotle by saying that their social ethics presupposed a theory of democracy and deliberation, a philosophical anthropology, and—finally—a social telos that could not be justified through consensus. This is a similar criticism to the one leveled against John Rawls. In response, however, the nature of *phronesis* must be kept in mind. This is not a strict measuring standard, but a flexible, imprecise, and fragile guideline that adjusts to the conditions of the particular situation—as does Aristotle's relating of the practice of medicine, the telling of jokes, and the measurement of Lesbian columns.

> Aristotle tells us that a person who attempts to make every decision by appeal to some antecedent principle held firm and inflexible for the occasion is like an architect who tries to use a straight ruler on the intricate curves of a fluted column. . . . Good deliberation, like this rule [the flexible ruler of Lesbos], accommodates itself to what it finds, responsively and with respect for complexity. It does not assume that the form of the rule *governs* the appearances; it allows the appearances to govern themselves and to be normative for correctness of rule.[89]

The aspect of both Aristotle's and Marx's theories that has infuriated modern readers is their unwillingness to be precise about the very things modern interpreters have reduced to technical issues. Though they do define the nature of man, democracy, and rationality, they do so in a fashion that sets the parameters of rational discourse without interfering in any way with a public consensus about the nature of the future institutions themselves. Marx has joined together an "historical science" and critique of modernity with the healthy epistemological skepticism and love for participatory citizenship within a community of friends from the Greeks. Truth is not a thing or commodity to be possessed or to be technically manipulated as a *Herrschaftswissen*.[90] It is an ongoing ethical activity of social praxis, which presupposes the existence of a "brotherhood and nobility of man"[91] and whose ultimate goal is the realization of this same brotherhood. Discussion about the nature of knowledge turns into discussion about the nature of society; epistemology turns into social theory and praxis. Knowledge is part of the process by which the individual regains his freedom, dignity, and moral autonomy in a complex industrial democratic society. With the instrumentalization of reason and the repressive reduction of knowledge to modern science and positivism—all for the purposes of maintaining class stability and profit maximization—modernity has been divorced from the Ancients. Critical social theory must capture their inner connectedness in order to transcend both pure scholasticism and technical rationality. Through this reading of the nineteenth-century German tradition, the most forceful opponent of modernity—Karl Marx—becomes the first postmodern critic.

Notes

INTRODUCTION

1. George McCarthy, *Marx' Critique of Science and Positivism: The Methodological Foundations of Political Economy* (Dordrecht, Netherlands: Kluwer Academic Publishers, 1988).

2. Patrick Murray, *Marx's Theory of Scientific Knowledge* (Atlantic Highlands, N.J.: Humanities International Press, 1988).

3. Norman D. Livergood, *Activity in Marx's Philosophy* (The Hague, Netherlands: Martinus Nijhoff, 1967), p. 4.

4. Throughout this work social justice will be interpreted as part of the more comprehensive theory of social ethics, while political economy (historical and structural analyses of capitalism) will be viewed as part of the broader perspective of social theory (analysis of community, interaction, consciousness formation, social and political values, the possibilities of self-realization and human emancipation, and democracy).

5. Karl Marx, "Toward the Critique of Hegel's Philosophy of Law: Introduction," in *Writings of the Young Marx on Philosophy and Society*, ed. and trans. by Loyd Easton and Kurt Guddat (Garden City, N.Y.: Doubleday, 1967), pp. 257–58.

6. The Old Testament Mosaic codes of Deuteronomy and Leviticus, along with the prophetic tradition, are also an important part of the classical ethical tradition. Marx is certainly integrating the classics of the Hellenes, Hebrews, and modern Germans. However, an examination of Marx's indebtedness to this tradition will be examined in a separate work.

7. Drucilla Cornell, "Should a Marxist Believe in Rights?" *Praxis International* 4, 1 (April 1984), p. 50.

8. Richard Rorty, *Philosophy and the Mirror of Nature* (Princeton, N.J.: Princeton University Press, 1979).

9. The relationship between Marx and the Greeks should be understood carefully and with sensitivity. The connections are not always immediate and the borrowings are not always direct, and they are certainly mediated by the philosophical and historical distances between them. The emphasis in this work is on the similarity of their formal approaches to common theoretical questions.

CHAPTER ONE: MARX AND EPICURUS

1. Rolf Sannwald, *Marx und die Antike*, Stattswissenschaftliche Studien, ed. by Edgar Salin and V. F. Wagner (Zurich, Switzerland: Polygraphischer Verlag, 1957), p. 35. See also Chapter One in S. S. Prawer, *Karl Marx and World Literature* (Oxford, U.K.: Clarendon Press, 1976).

2. Ibid.

3. Laurence Baronovitch, "German Idealism, Greek Materialism, and the Young Marx," *International Philosophical Quarterly* (September 1984), p. 266—referred to as "Marx and Epicurus" in these notes.

4. Sannwald, *Marx und Antike*, pp. 72–73.

5. Ibid., p. 70.

6. Hannah Arendt, "Tradition and the Modern Age," in *Between Past and Present* (New York: Viking Press, 1961), p. 19, and *On Revolution* (New York: Viking Press, 1963), p. 57; Shlomo Avineri, *Hegel's Theory of the Modern State* (Cambridge, U.K.: Cambridge University Press, 1972), pp. 19–33; Richard Bernstein, *Praxis and Action: Contemporary Philosophies of Human Activity* (Philadelphia: University of Pennsylvania Press, 1971), p. 70; George Brenkert, *Marx's Ethics of Freedom* (London: Routledge and Kegan Paul, 1983), p. 18; Carol Gould, *Marx's Social Ontology: Individuality and Community in Marx's Theory of Social Reality* (Cambridge, Mass.: MIT Press, 1978), pp. 44–46 and 127; Sidney Hook, *From Hegel to Marx: Studies in the Intellectual Development of Karl Marx* (Ann Arbor: University of Michigan Press, 1978), pp. 35–36, and *Marx and the Marxists: The Ambiguous Legacy* (Princeton, N.J.: D. Van Nostrand, 1955), p. 16; Philip Kain, *Schiller, Hegel, and Marx: State, Society, and the Aesthetic Ideal of Ancient Greece* (Kingston, Ont., Canada: McGill-Queen's University Press, 1982), and *Marx' Method, Epistemology, and Humanism: A Study in the Development of His Thought* (Dordrecht, Netherlands: Reidel Publishing, 1986), p. 14; István Mészáros, *Marx's Theory of Alienation* (New York: Harper and Row, 1970), pp. 254–55; Horst Mewes, "On the Concept of Politics in the Early Work of Karl Marx," *Social Research* 43, 2, (Summer 1976); Tom Rockmore, *Fichte, Marx, and the German Philosophical Tradition* (Carbondale: Southern Illinois University Press, 1980), pp. 62–71; Nancy Schwartz, "Distinctions between Public and Private Life: Marx on the *zōon politikon*," *Political Theory* (May 1979); and Patricia Springborg, "Karl Marx on Democracy, Participation, Voting, and Equality," *Political Theory* (November 1984), p. 537ff; and "Marx, Democracy, and the Ancient Polis," *Critical Philosophy* 1, 1 (March 1984).

For a further bibliography, which includes reference to some of the works of Gilbert, Tucker, Action, DiQuattro, Husami, Krader, Arnovitch, Panichas, Whelan, Wolin, Somerville, Lauer, Colletti, Schumpeter, Lichtheim, Wartofsky, Avineri, Kolakowski, Hook, Miller, Nasser, and Castoriadis, see Michael DeGolger, "Science and Society, Justice and Equality: An Historical Approach to Marx," dissertation, University of Michigan microfilm, 1985, pp. 83–84.

7. Karl Marx, "Difference between the Democritean and Epicurean

Philosophy of Nature," dissertation, in *Karl Marx and Friedrich Engels, Collected Works*, vol. 1 (New York: International Publishers, 1975)—referred to as *Dissertation* in the text and these notes, and "Notebooks on Epicurean Philosophy," in *Karl Marx and Friedrich Engels, Collected Works*, vol. 1 (New York: International Publishers, 1975)—referred to as *Notebooks* in the text and these notes.

8. David McLellan, *Karl Marx: His Life and Thought* (New York: Harper and Row, 1973), p. 34.

9. Peter Fenves, "Marx's Doctoral Thesis on Two Greek Atomists and the Post-Kantian Interpretations," *Journal of the History of Ideas* 47, 3 (July–September 1986), p. 433.

10. Joseph Femia, *Gramsci's Political Thought: Hegemony, Consciousness, and the Revolutionary Process* (Oxford, U.K.: Clarendon Press, 1981), pp. 67–72; and Karl Marx, "The Holy Family," in *Karl Marx and Friedrich Engels, Collected Works*, vol. 4 (New York: International Publishers, 1975), pp. 123–33.

11. August Cornu, *The Origins of Marxian Thought* (Springfield, Ill.: C.C. Thomas, 1957); Georg Lukács, *History and Class Consciousness: Studies in Marxist Dialectics*, trans. by Rodney Livingstone, (Cambridge, Mass.: MIT Press, 1971), and *The Young Hegel*, trans. by Rodney Livingstone (Cambridge, Mass.: MIT Press, 1976); Günther Hillmann, *Marx und Hegel: Von der Spekulation zur Dialektik* (Frankfurt/Main, FRG: Europäische Verlagsanstalt, 1966); Franz Mehring, *Karl Marx: The Story of His Life*, trans. by Edward Fitzgerald (Ann Arbor: University of Michigan Press, 1962); and Sannwald, *Marx und Antike*.

12. Sannwald, *Marx und Antike*, p. 7.

13. Marx, *Dissertation*, p. 30.

14. Baronovitch, "Marx and Epicurus," p. 254; and Georg Friedrich Hegel, *Hegel's Lectures on the History of Philosophy*, vol. 2, trans. by E. S. Haldane and Frances Simon (London: Routledge and Kegan Paul, 1974), p. 292.

15. Hillmann, *Marx und Hegel*, p. 354; Dick Howard, *The Development of the Marxian Dialectic* (Carbondale: Southern Illinois University Press, 1972), p. 18; McLellan, *Karl Marx*, p. 35; and Nicholas Lobkowicz, *Theory and Practice: History of a Concept from Aristotle to Marx* (Notre Dame, Ind.: University of Notre Dame Press, 1967), p. 240.

16. Hillman, *Marx und Hegel*, p. 335.

17. Marx, *Dissertation*, p. 30.

18. Cyril Bailey, "Karl Marx on Greek Atomism," *Classical Quarterly* 22 (July 1928), p. 205. For praise of Marx's Greek scholarship by a noted British classicist, read Bailey's review of Marx's dissertation.

19. Marx, *Dissertation*, p. 38.

20. Ibid., p. 39.

21. Georg Friedrich Hegel, *Science of Logic*, vol. 2, trans. by W. H. Johnston and L. G. Struthers (London: Allen and Unwin, 1966), ch. 1 of the "Doctrine of Essence," pp. 19–34.

22. Marx, *Dissertation*, p. 41.

23. Georg Friedrich Hegel, *Philosophy of Right*, trans. by T. M. Knox (Oxford, U.K.: Oxford University Press, 1967), p. 90.

24. Marx, *Dissertation*, p. 43.

25. Ibid., p. 41.

26. Howard, *Development of Dialectic*, p. 15.

27. Fenves, "Marx's Doctoral Thesis," p. 438.

28. Herbert Marcuse, *Reason and Revolution: Hegel and the Rise of Social Theory* (Boston: Beacon Press, 1960), p. 23.

29. G. W. Smith, "Sinful Science? Marx's Theory of Freedom from Thesis to Theses," *History of Political Thought* 2 (Spring 1981), pp. 148–51; and Karl Marx, "The Critical Battle against French Materialism," from "The Holy Family," in *Karl Marx and Friedrich Engels, Collected Works*, vol. 4 (New York: International Publishers, 1975), pp. 124–34.

30. Wolfdietrich Schmied-Kowarzik has written extensively on the radical nature of Marx's view of natural science, his break with positivism, his alternative view of materialism, and his indebtedness to Schelling in *Die Dialektik der gesellschaftlichen Praxis. Zur Genesis und Kernstruktur der Marxschen Theorie* (FRG: ·Verlag Karl Alber, 1981), and *Das dialektische Verhältnis des Menschen zur Natur. Philosophiegeschichte Studien zur Naturproblematik bei Karl Marx* (Freiburg, FRG: Verlag Karl Alber, 1984), and *Bruchstücke zur Dialektik der Philosophie. Studien zur Hegel-Kritik und zum Problem von Theorie und Praxis* (Ratingen, FRG: A. Henn-Verlag, 1974); Wolfdietrich Schmied-Kowarzik and Hans Immler, *Marx und die Naturfrage. Ein Wissenschaftsstreit* (Hamburg, FRG: VSA-Verlag, 1984); Mészáros, *Marx's Theory of Alienation*, pp. 101–4; Manfred Frank and Gerhard Kurz, eds., *Materialien zu Schellings philosophischen Anfängen* (Frankfurt/Main, FRG: Suhrkamp Verlag, 1975); Sannwald, *Marx und Antike*, pp. 101–4; Ernst Bloch, *Das Materialismusproblem, seine Geschichte, und Substanz* (Frankfurt/Main, FRG: Suhrkamp Verlag, 1985); Maurice Merleau-Ponty, "The Concept of Nature," in *Themes from the Lectures at the College de France 1952–1960*, trans. by John O'Neill (Evanston, Ill.: Northwestern University Press, 1970), pp. 62–87; and George McCarthy, *Marx' Critique of Science and Positivism: The Methodological Foundations of Political Economy* (Dordrecht, Netherlands: Kluwer Academic Publishers, 1988), ch. 3.

31. Karl Marx, "Private Property and Communism," in *Karl Marx: Early Writings*, trans. by T. B. Bottomore (New York: McGraw-Hill, 1963), pp. 163–65.

32. Sannwald, *Marx und Antike*, p. 102.

33. Alvin Gouldner, *The Two Marxisms: Contradictions and Anomalies in the Development of Theory* (New York: Oxford University Press, 1980).

34. Marx, *Dissertation*, p. 52.

35. Lucretius, "On the Nature of Things," quoted in Marx, *Notebooks*, p. 474.

36. Marx, *Dissertation*, p. 50.

37. Ibid., p. 52.

38. Ibid., p. 61.

39. Ibid., p. 59.

40. Ibid., p. 62.

41. Ibid.

42. McCarthy, *Marx' Critique of Science*, pp. 70ff. Hillmann in his *Marx und Hegel*, p. 331, also makes reference to Hegel's use of the term *Gleichgültigkeit* in his *History of Philosophy*; Hillmann views it as meaning flight to the inner self and sees it as a translation of the Epicurean notion of freedom.

43. Marx, *Dissertation*, p. 62.

44. Marx, *Notebooks*, p. 420.

45. Karl Popper, *The Logic of Scientific Discovery* (New York: Harper and Row, 1968), pp. 40–43.

46. Marx, *Dissertation*, pp. 64–65.

47. Ibid., p. 65.

48. Karl Marx, "The Economic and Philosophical Manuscripts," in *Karl Marx: Early Writings*, trans. by T. B. Bottomore (New York: McGraw-Hill, 1963), pp. 159–60.

49. Marx, *Dissertation*, p. 65.

50. McCarthy, *Marx' Critique*, pp. 69–77.

51. Smith, "Sinful Science?" pp. 141ff; Norman D. Livergood, *Activity in Marx's Philosophy* (The Hague: Martinus Nijhoff, 1967), p. 1; and James O'Rourke, *The Problem of Freedom in Marxist Thought: An Analysis of the Treatment of Human Freedom by Marx, Engels, Lenin, and Contemporary Soviet Philosophy* (Dordrecht, Netherlands: Reidel Publishing, 1974), p. 14.

52. Marx, *Notebooks*, p. 437.

53. Marx, *Dissertation*, p. 45, and *Notebooks*, p. 421.

54. Marx, *Dissertation*, p. 45.

55. Marx, "Private Property and Communism," pp. 163–67.

56. Marx, *Dissertation*, p. 69.

57. Ibid., p. 70.

58. Ibid., p. 71.

59. Fenves, "Marx's Doctoral Thesis," p. 446.

60. Marx, *Dissertation*, pp. 72–73.

61. Ibid., p. 62.

62. Manfred Hülsewede, *Die Universellen Individuen: Entmystifikation und Universalität bei Marx* (Kastellaun, FRG: Aloys Henn Verlag, 1977), p. 36.

63. Hillmann, *Marx und Hegel*, p. 225; Baronovitch, "Marx and Epicurus," p. 248; and Fenves, "Marx's Doctoral Thesis," p. 449.

64. Marx, *Dissertation*, p. 85.

65. Ibid., p. 71.

66. Karl Marx, "The German Ideology," in *Karl Marx and Friedrich Engels, Collected Works*, vol. 5 (New York: International Publishers, 1976), p. 66.

67. Sannwald, *Marx und Antike*, p. 110.

68. Hülsewede, *Universellen Individuen*, pp. 38–39.

69. Ibid., p. 37.
70. Marx, *Dissertation*, p. 52.
71. Marx, *Notebooks*, p. 472.
72. Ibid., p. 64.
73. Ibid., p. 65.
74. Hülsewede, *Universellen Individuen*, pp. 31–32.
75. Ibid., p. 33.
76. Sannwald, *Marx und Antike*, p. 150.
77. Marx, *Notebooks*, p. 431.
78. Ibid., p. 432.
79. Hillmann, *Marx und Hegel*, pp. 127–28.
80. Marx, *Notebooks*, pp. 432–41.
81. Georg Friedrich Hegel, *Philosophy of History*, trans. by James Sibree (New York: Dover Publications, 1956), pp. 318–36.
82. Marx, *Notebooks*, pp. 436–37.
83. Ibid., p. 437.
84. Ibid., p. 438.
85. Ibid., p. 439.
86. Ibid., p. 449.
87. Marx, *Dissertation*, notes to appendix, p. 104.
88. Laurence Baronovitch, "Two Appendices to a Doctoral Dissertation: Some New Light on the Origin of Karl Marx' Dissociation from Bruno Bauer and the Young Hegelians," *Philosophical Forum* 8 (1978), p. 234.
89. McLellan, *Karl Marx*, pp. 40–41.
90. Baronovitch, "Two Appendices," p. 234.
91. Marx, *Dissertation*, p. 105.
92. Baronovitch, "Marx and Epicurus," p. 253.
93. For an understanding of the broader intellectual and philosophical influences on Marx during this crucial period of his development, see Lobkowicz, *Theory and Practice*; David McLellan, *The Young Hegelians and Karl Marx* (London: Macmillan, 1978); Mehring, *Karl Marx*; Hook, *From Hegel to Marx*; W. Brazill, *The Young Hegelians* (New Haven, Conn.: Yale University Press, 1970); Karl Löwith, *From Hegel to Nietzsche: The Revolution in Nineteenth-century Thought*, trans. by David Green (Garden City, N.Y.: Doubleday, 1967); and Zvi Rosen, *Bruno Bauer and Karl Marx* (The Hague, Netherlands: Martinus Nijhoff, 1977).
94. Patrick Murray, *Marx's Theory of Scientific Knowledge* (Atlantic Highlands, N.J.: Humanities International Press, 1988), p. 12.
95. For Marx's critique of the Left-Hegelian Max Stirner and the latter's interpretation of the history of Greek philosophy, see Marx, "German Ideology," pp. 136–44.

CHAPTER TWO: MARX AND ARISTOTLE

1. Hannah Arendt, *The Human Condition* (Chicago: University of Chicago, 1974); Nicholas Lobkowicz, *Theory and Practice: History of a Concept from*

Aristotle to Marx (Notre Dame, Ind.: University of Notre Dame, 1967); Jürgen Habermas, *Theory and Practice*, trans. by John Viertel (Boston: Beacon Press, 1974); and Albrecht Wellmer, *Critical Theory of Society*, trans. by John Cumming (New York: Herder and Herder, 1971).

2. Carol Gould, *Marx's Social Ontology: Individuality and Community in Marx's Theory of Social Reality* (Cambridge, Mass.: MIT Press, 1978), pp. 77–79; Philip Kain, *Schiller, Hegel, and Marx: State, Society, and the Aesthetic Ideal of Ancient Greece* (Kingston, Ont., Canada: McGill-Queen's University Press, 1982), pp. 74–158; and David Meyers, "The Young Marx and Kantian Ethics," *Studies in Soviet Thought* 31 (May 1986), pp. 278–79 and 297; Richard Bernstein, *Praxis and Action: Contemporary Philosophies of Human Activity* (Philadelphia: University of Pennsylvania Press, 1971), p. 70; Tom Rockmore, *Fichte, Marx, and the German Philosophical Tradition* (Carbondale: Southern Illinois University Press, 1980), pp. 66–71; George Brenkert, *Marx's Ethics of Freedom* (London: Routledge and Kegan Paul, 1983), p. 19; Horst Mewes, "On the Concept of Politics in the Early Work of Karl Marx," *Social Research* 43, 2 (Summer 1976), p. 278; Sidney Hook, *Revolution, Reform, and Social Justice: Studies in the Theory and Practice of Marxism* (New York: New York University Press, 1975), pp. 82–83, and *Marx and the Marxists: The Ambiguous Legacy* (Princeton, N.J.: D. Van Nostrand, 1955), p. 16; Arendt, *Human Condition*, p. 131, and *On Revolution* (Harmondsworth, U.K.: Penguin Books, 1965), p. 63; Nancy Schwartz, "Distinction between Public and Private Life: Marx on the *zōon politikon*," *Political Theory* (May 1979), pp. 253–54; István Mészáros, *Marx's Theory of Alienation* (New York: Harper and Row, 1970), p. 255; David Rouse, "Marx's Materialist Concept of Democracy," *Philosophy Research Archives* (1976), pp. 437ff.; David Depew, "Aristotle's *De Anima* and Marx's Theory of Man," *Graduate Faculty Philosophy Journal*, New School for Social Research, 8 (Spring 1982), p. 134; Alan Gilbert, "Historical Theory and the Structure of Moral Argument in Marx," *Political Theory* 9 (May 1981), p. 178, and "Marx's Moral Realism: Eudaimonism and Moral Progress," in *After Marx*, ed. by Terence Ball and James Farr (Cambridge, U.K.: Cambridge University Press, 1984), pp. 154ff.; William McBride, "Marxism and Natural Law," *American Journal of Jurisprudence* 15 (1970), p. 135; Norman Levine, *The Tragic Deception: Marx contra Engels* (Oxford, U.K.: Clio Books, 1975), p. 24; Patricia Springborg, "Aristotle and the Problem of Needs," *History of Political Thought* 5 (Winter 1984), pp. 408–9 and 419, and "Marx, Democracy, and the Ancient Polis," *Critical Philosophy* 1, 1 (1984); Helmut Seidel, "Das Verhältnis von Karl Marx zu Aristoteles," *Deutsche Zeitschrift für Philosophie* 27 (1979), p. 668; Andrew Collier, "Aristotelian Marx," *Inquiry* 29, 4 (1986); Martha Nussbaum, "Nature, Function, and Capability: Aristotle on Political Distribution," in *Oxford Studies in Ancient Philosophy*, suppl. vol., ed. by Julia Annas and Robert Grimm (Oxford, U.K.: Clarendon Press, 1988), pp. 183–84; Richard Miller, "Marx and Aristotle: A Kind of Consequentialism," in *Marx and Morality*, ed. by Kai Nielsen and Steven Patten (Guelf, Ont.: Canadian Association for

Publishing in Philosophy, 1981), p. 326; and G. E. M. de Sainte Croix, *The Class Struggle in the Ancient Greek World: From the Archaic Age to the Arab Conquests* (Ithaca, N.Y.: Cornell University Press, 1981), pp. 69ff. See also Robert Padgug, "Selected Bibliography on Marxism and the Study of Antiquity," *Arethusa* 8, 1, (Spring 1975), pp. 203–10. For a further general overview of the relationship between Aristotle and Marx see Marcel Reding. *Thomas von Aquin und Karl Marx* (Graz: Akademische Druck und Verlagsanstalt, 1953); and the work of one of his students Thomas Ehleiter, *Die Kategorie des Bonum Commune bei Karl Marx in Bezeihung zu Aristoteles und Thomas von Aquin* (Berlin: Dissertation from the Free University of Berlin, 1971). Throughout this essay I will be stressing the commonality of perspectives for it seems quite clear that—as Saul Padover in *Karl Marx: An Intimate Biography* (New York: McGraw-Hill, 1978), has said—Marx's intellectual debt rests in the old natural law tradition, and not the modern natural right tradition.

3. Aristotle, "Nicomachean Ethics," in *Introduction to Aristotle*, trans. by W. D. Ross (New York: Random House, 1947), sec. 1099a8, pp. 321ff.—referred to as *Nicomachean Ethics* in these notes.

4. Ibid., sec. 1098a1, p. 318.

5. Ibid., sec. 1098a11–17, pp. 318–19.

6. Leo Strauss, *Natural Right and History* (Chicago: University of Chicago, 1953), p. 136; and Henry Veatch, *Aristotle: A Contemporary Appreciation* (Bloomington: Indiana University Press, 1974), p. 120. See also Henry Veatch, *Rational Man: A Modern Interpretation of Aristotelian Ethics* (Bloomington: Indiana University Press, 1964), p. 55.

7. Aristotle, *Nicomachean Ethics*, secs. 1129b1–1131a8, pp. 398–402.

8. For an overview of the debate about the nature of particular and universal justice, see Max Hamburger, *Morals and Law: The Growth of Aristotle's Legal Theory* (New Haven, Conn.: Yale University Press, 1951), pp. 45–53; D. G. Ritchie, "Aristotle's Subdivisions of 'Particular Justice,'" *Classical Review* (May 1894), pp. 186ff.; and Josef Soudek, "Aristotle's Theory of Exchange: An Inquiry into the Origin of Economic Analysis," *Proceedings of the American Philosophical Society* 96, 1 (1952), p. 53.

9. Aristotle, *Nicomachean Ethics*, sec. 1134a26–30, p. 411.

10. Ibid., sec. 1129a35, p. 398.

11. Ibid., sec. 1130a10, p. 400.

12. Ibid., sec. 1130b25–26, p. 402.

13. Cornelius Castoriadis, "Value, Equality, Justice, Politics: From Marx to Aristotle and from Aristotle to Ourselves," in *Crossroads in the Labyrinth*, trans. by Kate Soper and Martin Ryle (Cambridge, Mass.: MIT Press, 1984), p. 287.

14. M. I. Finley, "Aristotle and Economic Analysis," in *Articles on Aristotle*, vol. 2: *Ethics and Politics*, ed. by J. Barnes, M. Schofield, and R. Sorabji (New York: St. Martin's Press, 1977), p. 144.

15. Delba Winthrop, "Aristotle and Theories of Justice," *American Political Science Review* 72 (1978), p. 1201.

16. John Cooper, "Aristotle on the Forms of Friendship," *Review of Metaphysics* 30 (June 1977). The *Nicomachean Ethics* was compiled from different student lecture notes over a period of many years, and there is no guarantee

that the ideas or organization are what Aristotle originally intended. Many times, the various beginnings and endings of issues do not fit into a comprehensive flow of ideas. Questions are raised and never directly answered. See also John Burnet's introduction to *The Ethics of Aristotle* (New York: Arno Press, 1973); Castoriadis, "Value, Equality, Justice, Politics," p. 284; and Winthrop, "Aristotle and Justice," p. 1204.

17. Veatch, *Aristotle*, p. 98.

18. Aristotle, *Nicomachean Ethics*, sec. 1132a32–33, p. 406.

19. Ibid., sec. 1131a25–29, p. 403.

20. Karl Polanyi, "Aristotle Discovers the Economy," in *Primitive, Archaic, and Modern Economics: Essays of Karl Polanyi*, ed. by George Dalton (Boston: Beacon Press, 1971), p. 108–11.

21. Finley, "Aristotle and Economic Analysis," p. 144.

22. Ritchie, "Aristotle's 'Particular Justice,' " pp. 191–92; F. Rosen, "The Political Context of Aristotle's Categories of Justice," *Phronesis* 20 (1975), p. 237; and Soudek, "Aristotle's Theory of Exchange," pp. 49–54. Though on page 186 Ritchie states that commutative or reciprocal justice is a third kind, on page 192 he qualifies this by maintaining that "Catallactic Justice is not a species of Particular Justice alongside of the other two." Ritchie implies that the third form of particular justice is the economic foundation for the other two—what I will call metaethics or political economy.

23. Aristotle, *Nicomachean Ethics*, sec. 1133a1, p. 408.

24. Scott Meikle, "Aristotle and the Political Economy of the Polis," *Journal of Hellenic Studies* 99 (1979), pp. 57–73.

25. For an overview of the contemporary literature on Marx and his theory of need, see Michael DeGolyer, "Science and Society, Justice and Equality: An Historical Approach to Marx," dissertation, University of Michigan microfilm, 1985, ch. 5.

26. Aristotle, *Nicomachean Ethics*, sec. 1133b15–19, p. 410.

27. Ibid., sec. 1133a30, p. 409.

28. Karl Marx, *Capital: A Critique of Political Economy*, vol. 1: *A Critical Analysis of Capitalist Production*, trans. by Samuel Moore and Edward Aveling (New York: International Publishers, 1968), pp. 59–60.

29. Soudek, "Aristotle's Theory of Exchange," p. 57.

30. DeGolyer, "Science and Society," p. 264.

31. Finley, "Aristotle and Economic Analysis," p. 149.

32. E. Barker, *The Political Thought of Plato and Aristotle* (New York: G.P. Putnam's Sons, 1906), p. 338.

33. Polanyi, "Aristotle Discovers Economy," p. 97.

34. Aristotle, *The Politics*, trans. by H. Rackham (London: William Heinemann, 1932), sec. 1253a9, p. 13.

35. Castoriadis, "Value, Equality, Justice, Politics," p. 293.

36. Lobkowicz, *Theory and Practice*, p. 30.

37. Polanyi, "Aristotle Discovers Economy," p. 113. See also Odd Langh-

olm, *Wealth and Money in the Aristotelian Tradition* (Bergen, Norway: Universitetsforlaget, 1983), pp. 52–53.

38. Polanyi, "Aristotle Discovers Economy," p. 101.

39. Finley, "Aristotle and Economic Analysis," p. 152.

40. Aristotle, *Politics*, sec. 1257a17, p. 41.

41. Meikle, "Aristotle and Political Economy," p. 62.

42. Aristotle, *Politics*, secs. 1258a37–1258b3, p. 51. For an analysis of how Marx develops these historical and sociological ideas of Aristotle, see the examination of Marx's *Ethnological Notebooks* in Springborg, "Marx, Democracy, and Ancient Polis," pp. 47–66.

43. Aristotle, *Politics*, sec. 1259b17–21, p. 59.

44. Cooper, "Aristotle on Friendship," p. 624.

45. Aristotle, *Nicomachean Ethics*, sec. 1155a23–27, pp. 471–72.

46. Cooper, "Aristotle on Friendship," p. 629.

47. Aristotle, *Nicomachean Ethics*, sec. 1161a23–28, p. 488.

48. Aristotle, *Politics*, sec. 1279a25–39, pp. 205–7.

49. Strauss, *Natural Right and History*, p. 136.

50. Aristotle, *Politics*, sec. 1280b39–42, p. 219.

51. Barker, *Political Thought of Plato and Aristotle*, pp. 294–95.

52. Jean Jacques Rousseau, *The Social Contract and Discourses*, trans. by G. D. H. Cole (New York: E.P. Dutton, 1950), pp. 94–95; James Miller, *Rousseau: Dreamer of Democracy* (New Haven, Conn.: Yale University Press, 1986); and Lucio Colletti, *From Rousseau to Lenin*, trans. by J. Merrington and J. White (New York: Monthly Review Press, 1972), pp. 142–93.

53. Winthrop, "Aristotle and Justice," p. 1206.

54. Aristotle, *Nicomachean Ethics*, bk. 6, ch. 3.

55. Lobkowicz, *Theory and Practice*, pp. 3–4. For a comprehensive analysis of the confusion between these various forms of knowledge within Greek philosophy, see Arendt, *Human Condition*, pp. 195–96 and 222–30.

56. Martha Nussbaum, *The Fragility of Goodness: Luck and Ethics in Greek Tragedy and Philosophy* (Cambridge, U.K.: Cambridge University Press, 1986), p. 299. See also Roger Sullivan, *Morality and the Good Life: A Commentary on Aristotle's Nicomachean Ethics* (Memphis: Memphis State University Press, 1980), pp. 83–84.

57. Nussbaum, *Fragility of Goodness*, p. 305.

58. Max Horkheimer and Theodor Adorno, *The Dialectic of the Enlightenment*, trans. by John Cumming (New York: Herder and Herder, 1972); and William Leiss, *The Domination of Nature* (Boston: Beacon Press, 1974).

59. Sullivan, *Morality and Good Life*, pp. 66 and 103; Hans-Georg Gadamer, *Idea of the Good in Platonic-Aristotelian Philosophy*, trans. by P. Christopher Smith (New Haven, Conn.: Yale University Press, 1986), pp. 111, 165, and 171; and W. F. R. Hardie, *Aristotle's Ethical Theory* (Oxford, U.K.: Clarendon Press, 1980), pp. 248ff.

60. Hans-Georg Gadamer, *Truth and Method* (New York: Seabury Press, 1975), pp. 287–88.

61. Henry Liddell and Robert Scott, *A Greek–English Lexicon* (Oxford, U.K.: Clarendon Press, 1968), pp. 324–25; Castoriadis, "Value, Equality, Justice, Politics," p. 282; Otfried Höffe, *Ethik und Politik: Grundmodelle und probleme der praktischen Philosophie* (Frankfurt/Main, FRG: Suhrkamp Verlag, 1979), p. 51; and J. A. Stewart, *Notes on the Nicomachean Ethics of Aristotle*, vol. 2 (Oxford, U.K.: Clarendon Press, 1892), p. 44.

62. Larry Arnhart, *Aristotle on Political Reasoning: A Commentary on the "Rhetoric"* (DeKalb: Northern Illinois University Press, 1981), pp. 4–5.

63. Aristotle, *Nicomachean Ethics*, sec. 1094b23, p. 310.

64. Gadamer, *Truth and Method*, p. 283.

65. Ibid., p. 280.

66. Aristotle, *Nicomachean Ethics*, sec. 1141b13–18, pp. 431–32.

67. Sullivan, *Morality and Good Life*, pp. 108–11.

68. Aristotle, *Nicomachean Ethics*, sec. 1142b10–15, pp. 434–35.

69. Gadamer, *Truth and Method*, p. 284; and Aristotle, *Nicomachean Ethics*, secs. 1137a31–1137b35, pp. 420–21. See also John Cooper, *Reason and Human Good in Aristotle* (Cambridge, Mass.: Harvard University Press, 1975), pp. 24ff.; and Hardie, *Aristotle's Ethical Theory*, pp. 230ff.

70. Gadamer, *Truth and Method*, p. 288; Ronald Beiner, *Political Judgment* (Chicago: University of Chicago Press, 1983), pp. 73–74; and Hardie, *Aristotle's Ethical Theory*, p. 221.

71. Gadamer, *Truth and Method*, p. 288.

72. Beiner, *Political Judgment*, p. 76.

73. Winthrop, "Aristotle and Justice," pp. 1211–12.

74. George McCarthy, *Marx' Critique of Science and Positivism: The Methodological Foundations of Political Economy* (Dordrecht, Netherlands: Kluwer Academic Publishers, 1988), pp. 139ff.

75. Winthrop, "Aristotle and Justice," p. 1204; Alasdair MacIntyre, *A Short History of Ethics* (New York: Macmillan, 1971), p. 99; and Aristotle, *Nicomachean Ethics*, bk. 6.

76. Aristotle, *Nicomachean Ethics*, sec. 1094b12–29, pp. 309–10, and secs. 1140a33–1140b4, p. 428. Contemporary philosophers interested in questions of hermeneutics, moral and political judgment, consensus theory and democracy, and so forth have relied on Aristotle to justify their critiques of modern epistemology and Cartesianism—especially Cartesian objectivity, scientific method, and universal truth. See Gadamer, *Truth and Method*, p. 246; Beiner, *Political Judgment*, p. 85; and Benjamin Barber, *Strong Democracy: Participatory Politics for a New Age* (Berkeley: University of California Press, 1984), pp. 55–56. See also Gerald Galgan, "Maturation of the Scientific Method," in *The Logic of Modernity* (New York: New York University Press, 1982), pp. 50–73.

77. Nussbaum, *Fragility of Goodness*, p. 300.

78. Aristotle, *Politics*, bk. 3, ch. 11.

79. Beiner, *Political Judgment*, p. 141.

80. Ibid.

81. Aristotle, *Politics*, sec. 1281b1–8, pp. 221–23.

82. Jürgen Habermas, *Communication and the Evolution of Society*, trans. by Thomas McCarthy (Boston: Beacon Press, 1979), pp. 1–68; Paul Feyerabend, *Science in a Free Society* (London: NLB, 1978); Barber, *Strong Democracy*; J. S. Mill, *On Liberty* (Indianapolis: Bobbs-Merrill, 1976); and Rousseau, *Social Contract*.

83. Veatch, *Aristotle*, pp. 119–20.

84. Aristotle quoted in W. von Leyden, *Aristotle on Equality and Justice: His Political Argument* (New York: St. Martin's Press, 1985), p. 45.

85. Ibid. See the analysis of the institutional mechanics of Aristotle's ideal democratic society at ibid., pp. 44–105.

86. Karl Marx, "The Critique of the Gotha Program," in *Marx and Engels: Basic Writings on Politics and Philosophy*, ed. by Louis Feuer (Garden City, N.Y.: Doubleday, 1959), p. 120.

87. Karl Marx, "Introduction," in *Grundrisse: Foundations of the Critique of Political Economy*, trans. by Martin Nicolaus (New York: Vintage Books, 1973), p. 91.

88. Marx, "Critique of Gotha Program," p. 118.

89. Ibid.

90. Ibid., pp. 118–19.

91. Jean Baudrillard, *The Mirror of Production*, trans. by Mark Poster (St. Louis: Telos Press, 1975), p. 31; and Arendt, *Human Condition*, p. 89.

92. Marx, "Critique of Gotha Program," p. 119, and *Grundrisse*, p. 488.

93. Norman Geras, "The Controversy about Marx and Justice," *Philosophica* 33 (1984), p. 74; and Kai Nielsen, "Marx, Engels, and Lenin on Justice: The Critique of the Gotha Program," *Studies in Soviet Thought* 32 (1986), p. 31.

94. Castoriadis, "Value, Equality, Justice, Politics," p. 311.

95. Aristotle, *Nicomachean Ethics*, sec. 1163a 36–b4, p. 494.

96. Geras, "Controversy about Marx and Justice," pp. 72–73.

97. Agnes Heller, "Marx, Justice, Freedom: The Libertarian Prophet," *Philosophica* 33 (1984), p. 91.

98. Donald van de Veer, "Marx's View of Justice," *Philosophy and Phenomenological Research* 33 (March 1973), p. 373.

99. Marx, "Critique of Gotha Program," p. 119.

100. Karl Marx, "Private Property and Communism," in *Karl Marx: Early Writings*, trans. by T. B. Bottomore (New York: McGraw-Hill, 1963), p. 153.

101. Ibid.

102. Marx, "Private Property and Communism," p. 152.

103. Marx, "On the Jewish Question," in *Karl Marx: Early Writings*, trans. by T. B. Bottomore (New York: McGraw-Hill, 1963), p. 13.

104. Ziyad Husami, "Marx on Distributive Justice," in *Marx, Justice, and History*, ed. by Marshall Cohen, Thomas Nagel, and Thomas Scanlon (Princeton, N.J.: Princeton University, 1980), p. 60.

105. Karl Marx, *Civil War in France: The Paris Commune* (New York: International Publishers, 1972), p. 62.

106. Alvin Gouldner, *The Two Marxisms: Contradictions and Anomalies in the Development of Theory* (Oxford, U.K.: Oxford University Press, 1980).

107. Karl Marx, "Theses on Feuerbach," in *Marx and Engels: Basic Writings on Politics and Philosophy*, ed. by Louis Feuer (Garden City, N.Y.: Doubleday, 1959), p. 241.

108. Ibid.

109. Max Horkeimer, "Traditional and Critical Theory," in *Critical Sociology*, ed. by Paul Connerton (Harmondsworth, U.K.: Penguin, 1976), p. 213.

110. Marx, "Theses on Feuerbach," p. 241.

111. Czeslaw Prokopczyk, *Truth and Reality in Marx and Hegel* (Amherst: University of Massachusetts, 1980), pp. 65–66.

112. Shlomo Avineri, *The Social and Political Thought of Karl Marx* (Cambridge, U.K.: Cambridge University Press, 1975), pp. 134–49.

113. Prokopczyk, *Truth and Reality*, p. 72.

114. Marx, *Grundrisse*, p. 101.

115. Ibid., p. 257.

116. Jindřich Zelený, *The Logic of Marx*, ed. by Terrell Carver (Oxford, U.K.: Oxford University Press, 1980), p. 61.

117. Avineri, *Social and Political Thought of Marx*, p. 131.

118. Lobkowicz, *Theory and Practice*, p. 36.

119. Aristotle, *Nicomachean Ethics*, sec. 1094b11–24, pp. 309–10. Emphasis added.

120. Arendt, *Human Condition*, p. 229.

121. Avineri, *Social and Political Thought of Marx*, p. 131.

122. Lobkowicz, *Theory and Practice*, pp. 14 and 42–44.

123. Marx, *Grundrisse*, p. 106.

124. See McCarthy, *Marx' Critique of Science*, ch. 1, pp. 20ff, on development of the notion of "critique" in eighteenth- and nineteenth-century German philosophy—from Kant's critique of pure and practical reason, to Hegel's phenomenological critique, to Marx's critique of political economy.

125. Lobkowicz, *Theory and Practice*, p. 36.

126. Marx, *Grundrisse*, p. 84.

127. Karl Marx, "The German Ideology," in *Karl Marx and Friedrich Engels, Collected Works*, vol. 5 (New York: International Publishers, 1976), p. 93.

128. Marx, *Grundrisse*, p. 87.

129. Levine, *Tragic Deception*, p. 37.

130. Barker, *Political Thought of Plato and Aristotle*, p. 283.

131. Marx, Karl "Alienated Labour," in *Karl Marx: Early Writings*, trans. by T. B. Bottomore (New York: McGraw-Hill, 1963), p. 127.

132. Lobkowicz, *Theory and Practice*, p. 22.

133. Marx, "Private Property and Communism," p. 160.

134. Ibid., p. 167.

135. Karl Marx, "For a Ruthless Criticism of Everything Existing," in *Marx–Engels Reader*, ed. by R. Tucker (New York: W.W. Norton, 1978), p. 13.

136. Helmut Peukert, *Science, Action, and Fundamental Theology: Toward a Theology of Communicative Action*, trans. by James Bohman (Cambridge, Mass.: MIT Press, 1984), pp. 202–10.

137. Mewes, "On the Concept of Politics in Early Marx"; and Schwartz, "Distinction between Public and Private."

138. Schwartz, "Distinction between Public and Private," p. 261.

139. Barker, *Political Thought of Plato and Aristotle*, p. 220.

140. Marx, *Grundrisse*, p. 300. See also Gould, *Marx's Social Ontology*, pp. 77–80.

CHAPTER THREE: KANT AND HEGEL

1. Paul Edwards, ed., *The Encyclopedia of Philosophy*, vol. 3 (New York: Macmillan and Free Press, 1972), p. 81–82.

2. Joachim Ritter, *Hegel and the French Revolution*, trans. by Richard Winfield (Cambridge, Mass.: MIT Press, 1984), pp. 159–60.

3. Ibid., p. 163.

4. Ibid., p. 165.

5. Robert Solomon, *In the Spirit of Hegel: A Study of G. W. F. Hegel's "Phenomenology of Spirit"* (New York: Oxford University Press, 1983), p. 482.

6. Charles Taylor, "Marxism and Empiricism," in *British Analytic Philosophy*, ed. by Bernard Williams and Alan Montefiore (London: Routledge and Kegan Paul, 1966).

7. Ritter, *Hegel and French Revolution*, p. 17.

8. For a more comprehensive analysis of the distinctions between *Moralität* and *Sittlichkeit*, see Walter Kaufmann, *Hegel: Reinterpretation, Texts, and Commentary* (Garden City, N.Y.: Doubleday, 1965).

9. Georg Friedrich Hegel, "The Positivity of the Christian Religion," in *On Christianity: Early Theological Writings*, trans. by T. M. Knox (New York: Harper and Brothers, 1961), p. 145.

10. Ibid., p. 211.

11. Trent Schroyer, *The Critique of Domination: The Origins and Development of Critical Theory* (New York: George Braziller, 1973), pp. 61–65.

12. Georg Friedrich Hegel, *Natural Law: The Scientific Ways of Treating Natural Law, Its Place in Moral Philosophy, and Its Relations to the Positive Sciences of Law*, trans. by T. M. Knox (Philadelphia: University of Pennsylvania Press, 1975), pp. 75–76.

13. Immanuel Kant, *Critique of Pure Reason*, trans. by Norman K. Smith (New York: St. Martin's Press, 1965), p. 48.

14. Hegel, *Natural Law*, p. 76.

15. Ibid., p. 78.

16. Ibid., p. 79.

17. Ibid., p. 94.

18. Immanuel Kant, *Fundamental Principles of the Metaphysics of Morals*, trans. by Thomas Abbott (Indianapolis: Bobbs-Merrill, 1949), p. 39.

19. Georg Friedrich Hegel, *Philosophy of Right*, trans. by T. M. Knox (London: Oxford University Press, 1967), p. 90.

20. David Hume, "A Treatise of Human Nature," bk. 2, in Hume's *Moral and Political Philosophy*, ed. by Henry Aiken (New York: Hafner Press, 1948), p. 25.

21. Herbert Marcuse, *Reason and Revolution: Hegel and the Rise of Social Theory* (Boston: Beacon Press, 1960), pp. 19ff.

22. Louis Dupré, *The Philosophical Foundations of Marxism* (New York: Harcourt, Brace, and World, 1966), p. 20.

23. Alasdair MacIntyre, *A Short History of Ethics* (New York: Macmillan, 1971), p. 198. See also Joseph Maier, *On Hegel's Critique of Kant* (New York: Columbia University Press, 1939), pp. 51–52.

24. Dupré, *Philosophical Foundations of Marxism*, p. 21.

25. Georg Lukács, *History and Class Consciousness: Studies in Marxist Dialectics*, trans. by Rodney Livingstone (Cambridge, Mass.: MIT Press, 1971); Marcuse, *Reason and Revolution*; Lucio Colletti, *Marxism and Hegel*, trans. by L. Garner (London: Verso, 1979); Charles Taylor, *Hegel and Modern Society* (Cambridge, Mass.: Cambridge University Press, 1979); Dupré, *Philosophical Foundations of Marxism*; and Leo Kofler, *Geschichte und Dialektik* (Darmstadt, FRG: Luchterhand Verlag, 1972).

26. W. H. Walsh, *Hegelian Ethics* (New York: St. Martin's Press, 1969), p. 17.

27. Hegel, *Philosophy of Right*, pp. 10–11.

28. Georg Friedrich Hegel, *Phenomenology of Spirit*, trans. by A. V. Miller (Oxford, U.K.: Oxford University Press, 1977), pp. 252–62; and Solomon, *Spirit of Hegel*, pp. 522–34.

29. Iring Fetscher, *Marx and Marxism* (New York: Herder and Herder, 1971), p. 58.

30. Hegel, "Absolute Freedom and Terror," in *Phenomenology of Spirit*, pp. 355–66; Hegel, *Philosophy of Right*, pp. 22 and 227; Judith Shklar, *Freedom and Independence: A Study of the Political Ideas of Hegel's "Phenomenology of Mind"* (Cambridge, U.K.: Cambridge University Press, 1976), pp. 178–81; and George Kelly, *Hegel's Retreat from Eleusis: Studies in Political Thought* (Princeton, N.J.: Princeton University Press, 1978), p. 128, and *Idealism, Politics and History: Sources of Hegelian Thought* (Cambridge, U.K.: Cambridge University Press, 1978), pp. 307–9.

31. Steven Smith, "Hegel and the French Revolution: An Epitaph for Republicanism," *Social Research* 56, 1 (Spring 1989).

32. Hegel, *Philosophy of Right*, p. 22.

33. For an analysis of Marx's critique of morality and its relationship to the French Revolution and the Terror, see Patrick Murray, *Marx's Theory of*

Scientific Knowledge (Atlantic Highlands, N.J.: Humanities International Press, 1988), pp. 88–84 and 206–7.

34. Shklar, *Freedom and Independence*, p. 180.

35. Ibid., p. 28.

36. Jonathan Robinson, *Duty and Hypocrisy in Hegel's "Phenomenology of Mind": An Essay in the Real and Ideal* (Toronto: University of Toronto Press, 1977), pp. 56–62.

37. Hegel, *Phenomenology*, pp. 372–73.

38. Ibid., p. 373.

39. Robinson, *Duty and Hypocrisy in Hegel*, p. 65.

40. Jean Hyppolite, *Genesis and Structure of Hegel's "Phenomenology of Spirit"* (Evanston: Illinois University Press, 1974), pp. 474–90.

41. Hegel, *Phenomenology*, p. 370.

42. Walsh, *Hegelian Ethics*, p. 30.

43. Robinson, *Duty and Hypocrisy in Hegel*, p. 35.

44. Shklar, *Freedom and Independence*, p. 184.

45. Joseph Flay, *Hegel's Quest for Certainty* (Albany: State University of New York Press, 1984), p. 210.

46. Ibid., p. 216.

47. Ibid., p. 223.

48. Kaufmann, *Hegel*, p. 105.

49. Manfred Riedel, *Between Tradition and Revolution: The Hegelian Transformation of Political Philosophy*, trans. by Walter Wright (Cambridge, U.K.: Cambridge University Press, 1984), pp. 108ff.; and Ritter, *Hegel and French Revolution*, p. 70.

50. Ritter, *Hegel and French Revolution*, p. 165.

51. Philip Kain, *Schiller, Hegel, and Marx: State, Society, and the Aesthetic Ideal of Ancient Greece* (Kingston, Ont., Canada: McGill-Queen's University Press, 1982).

52. Georg Lukács, *Goethe and His Age: A Major Critical Evaluation of Germany's Great Poet*, trans. by Robert Anchor (New York: Grosset and Dunlap, 1969), p. 105.

53. E. M. Butler, *The Tyranny of Greece over Germany* (Boston: Beacon Press, 1958); and Kelly, "Social Understanding and Social Therapy in Schiller and Hegel," in *Hegel's Retreat from Eleusis*. For a review of the literature analyzing the relationships between Marx and Schiller, see Kain, *Schiller, Hegel, and Marx*, pp. 86–87; Kaufmann, *Hegel*, pp. 46–58; Lukács, *Goethe and His Age*, pp. 68–135. The relationship between Schiller and Kant is outlined in R. D. Miller, *Schiller and the Ideal of Freedom: A Study of Schiller's Philosophical Works with Chapters on Kant* (Oxford, U.K.: Clarendon Press, 1970), p. 20.

The idea of moral freedom, fundamental in Kant, is scarcely less important to his disciple Schiller; and the group of associated ideas which cluster round this main idea—freedom of will, the power of reason to liberate man from his own senuous nature, man as an end in himself, the principle of autonomy, and the supreme importance of the human personality—all of these Kantian ideas are wholeheart-edly accepted by Schiller and became, so to speak, part of his flesh and blood.

54. Kelly, *Hegel's Retreat from Eleusis*, pp. 59ff.
55. Friedrich Schiller, *On the Aesthetic Education of Man in A Series of Letters*, trans. by Reginald Snell (New York: Ungar Publishers, 1965), p. 38.
56. Ibid., p. 40.
57. Kelly, *Hegel's Retreat from Eleusis*, p. 89.
58. There is a debate about the extent of influence of the Greek vision on Hegel's thought. Though there is general consensus about its influence on his earlier writings, the extent of its importance for the *Phenomenology* and *Philosophy of Right* is debated. The list of those who argue that there is a break in Hegel toward Christianity and modernity and away from the Greek ethos includes: Kain, *Schiller, Hegel, and Marx*, p. 70; Kelly, *Hegel's Retreat From Eleusis*, pp. 86–89; Bernard Cullen, *Hegel's Social and Political Thought: An Introduction* (New York: St. Martin's Press, 1979), p. 97; Shlomo Avineri, *Hegel's Theory of the Modern State* (Cambridge, U.K.: Cambridge University Press, 1972), p. 22; and Riedel, *Tradition and Revolution*, p. 126. Those who argue that the Greek ideal continued to play an important part in Hegel's later writings include: Rudolf Haym, *Hegel und seine Zeit* (Hildesheim, FRG: Georg Olms Verlag, 1974), pp. 245ff.; Taylor, *Hegel*, p. 378; Z. A. Pelczynski, "Hegel's Political Philosophy: Its Relevance Today," in *Hegel's Political Philosophy: Problems and Perspectives*, ed. by Z. A. Pelczynski (Cambridge, U.K.: Cambridge University Press, 1976), p. 241; Judith Shklar, "Hegel's *Phenomenology*: An Elegy for Hellas," in Pelczynski, *Hegel's Political Philosophy*, and her *Freedom and Independence*; Solomon, *Spirit of Hegel*, p. 487; H. S. Harris, "Hegel's System of Ethical Life: An Interpretation," in *Hegel's System of Ethical Life and First Philosophy of Spirit*, ed. by H. S. Harris and T. M. Knox (Albany: State University of New York Press, 1979), p. 75; Ritter, *Hegel and French Revolution*, p. 63; and Kaufmann, *Hegel*, p. 105.
59. Taylor, *Hegel and Modern Society*, pp. 82–83.
60. Ibid., p. 94.
61. J. Glenn Gray, *Hegel and Greek Thought* (New York: Harper and Row, 1968), pp. 66–67.
62. Hegel, *Natural Law*, pp. 104ff. See also Georg Lukács, *The Young Hegel*, trans. by Rodney Livingstone (Cambridge, Mass.: MIT Press, 1976), p. 403.
63. Hegel, "Positivity of Christian Religion," p. 154.
64. Ibid., p. 116.
65. Ibid., p. 156.
66. Ibid., p. 157.
67. Avineri, *Hegel's Modern State*, p. 26.
68. Hegel, "Positivity of Christian Religion," p. 163.
69. Ibid., p. 197.
70. Georg Friedrich Hegel, "The Spirit of Christianity and Its Fate," in *On

Christianity: Early Theological Writings, trans. by T. M. Knox (New York: Harper and Brothers, 1961), p. 204.

71. H. S. Harris, *Hegel's Development: Night Thoughts (Jena 1801–1806)* (Oxford, U.K.: Clarendon Press, 1983), pp. 150–52.

72. Hegel, "Positivity of Christian Religion," p. 69.

73. Ibid., p. 143.

74. MacIntyre, *Short History of Ethics*, p. 200.

75. Hegel, *Phenomenology*, pp. 119ff.

76. Georg Friedrich Hegel, *System of Ethical Life and First Philosophy of Spirit*, trans. by H. S. Harris and T. M. Knox (Albany: State University of New York Press, 1979), pp. 104–7. See also the discussion of absolute indifference from the ontological level at the end of volume 1 of Hegel's *Science of Logic*, trans. by W. H. Johnston and L. G. Struthers (London: Allen and Unwin, 1966), pp. 394ff.

77. Fetscher, *Marx and Marxism*, p. 59, calls this "spiritualized democracy."

78. Hegel, *Ethical Life*, p. 167.

79. Cullen, *Hegel's Social and Political Thought*, pp. 32–37; and Lukács, *Young Hegel*, pp. 170ff.

80. Hegel, *Ethical Life*, p. 168.

81. Ibid., p. 171.

82. Ibid.

83. Ibid., p. 176; and Aristotle, *The Politics*, trans. by H. Rackham (London: William Heinemann, 1932), bk. 3, ch. 7.

84. Cullen, *Hegel's Social and Political Thought*, p. 68.

85. Ibid.

86. Hegel, *Philosophy of Right*, p. 124.

87. Ibid., p. 129.

88. Ibid., pp. 129–30.

89. Hegel, *Science of Logic*, vol. 1, pp. 138–49.

90. Hegel, *Philosophy of Right*, p. 170.

91. As to whether Hegel's theory of the state represents a defense of Prussian authoritarianism, or its critique and a defense of representative government, see the debate in Walter Kaufmann, ed., *Hegel's Political Philosophy* (New York: Atherton Press, 1970). Those who have defended Hegel in the past include Ritter, Marcuse, Kaufmann, Avineri, Knox, and Pelczynski, while those who have severely criticized him include Haym, Hook, and Popper.

92. Hegel, *Philosophy of Right*, p. 178.

93. Ibid., p. 191.

94. Shklar, *Freedom and Independence*, p. 190; and Kelly, *Hegel's Retreat from Eleusis*, pp. 62 and 128.

95. Shlomo Avineri, *The Social and Political Thought of Karl Marx* (Cambridge, U.K.: Cambridge University Press, 1975), p. 33.

96. James O'Rourke, *The Problem of Freedom in Marxist Thought: An Analysis of the Treatment of Human Freedom by Marx, Engels, Lenin, and Contemporary Soviet Philosophy* (Dordrecht, Netherlands: Reidel Publishing, 1974), pp. 15ff.

97. Ibid., p. 12.

98. Karl Marx, "Alienated Labour," in *Karl Marx: Early Writings*, trans. by T. B. Bottomore (New York: McGraw-Hill, 1963), p. 129.

99. Ibid., pp. 127–28.

100. Karl Marx, "Private Property and Communism," in *Karl Marx: Early Writings*, trans. by T. B. Bottomore (New York: McGraw-Hill, 1963), p. 157.

101. Nathan Rotenstreich, *From Substance to Subject: Studies in Hegel* (The Hague: Martinus Nijhoff, 1974), p. 119.

102. Ibid.

103. Karl Marx, "The Holy Family," in *Karl Marx and Friedrich Engels, Collected Works*, vol. 4 (New York: International Publishers, 1975), pp. 39 and 53, and "The German Ideology," in *Karl Marx and Friedrich Engels, Collected Works*, vol. 5 (New York: International Publishers, 1976), pp. 455–83.

104. Georg Lukács, "What Is Orthodox Marxism?" in *History and Class Consciousness: Studies in Marxist Dialectics*, trans. by Rodney Livingstone (Cambridge, Mass.: MIT Press, 1971), p. 14.

105. Agnes Heller, *The Theory of Need in Marx* (New York: St. Martin's Press, 1976), p. 23.

106. Marx, "Private Property and Communism," pp. 164–65.

107. Marx, "Alienated Labour," p. 125.

108. Karl Marx, "Needs, Production, and Division of Labour," in *Karl Marx: Early Writings*, trans. by T. B. Bottomore (New York: McGraw-Hill, 1963), p. 159.

109. Ibid., p. 168.

110. Ibid., p. 169.

111. Ibid., p. 170.

112. Ibid., p. 176.

113. István Mészáros, *Marx's Theory of Alienation* (New York: Harper and Row, 1970), p. 184.

114. Ibid., p. 178.

115. Agnes Heller, "Towards a Marxist Theory of Value," trans. by Andrew Arato, *Kinesis*, Graduate Journal in Philosophy, Southern Illinois University, 5, 1 (Fall 1972), pp. 20–21, and her *Theory of Need*, p. 104.

116. Karl Marx, *Grundrisse*, trans. by Martin Nicolaus (New York: Vintage Books, 1973), p. 488.

117. Ibid., p. 706.

118. Ibid., p. 708.

119. Martha Nussbaum, "Nature, Function and Capability: Aristotle on Political Distribution," *Oxford Studies in Ancient Philosophy*, suppl. vol., ed. by Julia Annas and Robert Grimm (Oxford, U.K.: Clarendon Press, 1988), p. 184.

CHAPTER FOUR: CRITIQUE OF CLASSICAL LIBERALISM

1. Alfred Schmidt, *The Concept of Nature in Marx* (London: NLB, 1971), Georg Lukács, "What is Orthodox Marxism?" in *History and Class Consciousness: Studies in Marxist Dialectics*, trans. by Rodney Livingstone (Cambridge,

Mass.: MIT Press, 1971); and Iring Fetscher, *Marx and Marxism* (New York: Herder and Herder, 1971), pp. 3–25.

2. George McCarthy, *Marx' Critique of Science and Positivism: The Methodological Foundations of Political Economy* (Dordrecht, Netherlands: Kluwer Academic Publishers, 1988).

3. Lucio Colletti, "Rousseau as Critic of 'Civil Society,' " *From Rousseau to Lenin: Studies in Ideology and Society*, trans. by John Merrington (New York: Monthly Review Press, 1972), pp. 143–93; Graeme Duncan, *Marx and Mill: Two Views of Social Conflict and Social Harmony* (Cambridge, U.K.: Cambridge University Press, 1973); Philip Kain, *Marx' Method, Epistemology, and Humanism: A Study in the Development of His Thought* (Dordrecht, Netherlands: Reidel Publishing, 1986), pp. 28–57; and Lucien Goldmann, *Immanuel Kant*, trans. by Robert Black (London: NLB, 1971).

4. For a critique of the epistemological and social-psychological foundations of liberalism, see Thomas Spragens, *The Irony of Liberal Reason* (Chicago: University of Chicago Press, 1981), esp. ch. 2.

5. Karl Marx, "Private Property and Communism," in *Karl Marx: Early Writings*, trans. by T. B. Bottomore (New York: McGraw-Hill, 1963), p. 163.

6. For a discussion about positive and negative freedoms and their intellectual context, see Isaiah Berlin, "Two Concepts of Liberty," in *From Essays on Liberty* (New York: Oxford University Press, 1970), pp. 118–72.

7. See Graeme Duncan, *Marx and Mill*; and C. B. MacPherson, *The Life and Times of Liberal Democracy* (Oxford, U.K.: Oxford University Press, 1977), for a comparison of the different assumptions of liberal political theory and their implications for social structures.

8. Marx, "Private Property and Communism," p. 162.

9. Steven Lukes, *Marxism and Morality* (Oxford, U.K.: Clarendon Press, 1985), p. 30. Though much of Lukes's analysis of Marx's critique of natural rights theory and a theory of bourgeois justice is correct, the conclusions he draws from it are questionable. For valuable studies of Hegel's critique of liberalism and natural rights theory see Steven Smith, *Hegel's Critique of Liberalism: Rights in Context* (Chicago: University of Chicago Press, 1989), pp. 57–97; and William Maker, *Hegel on Economics and Freedom* (Macon, Georgia: Mercer University Press, 1987).

10. Ibid.

11. Ibid., pp. 29–30.

12. Karl Marx, "Needs, Production, and Division of Labour," in *Karl Marx: Early Writings*, trans. by T. B. Bottomore (New York: McGraw-Hill, 1961), p. 173.

13. Ibid., p. 174.

14. Ibid., p. 171.

15. Ibid., p. 169.

16. Ibid., p. 171.

17. William Ophuls, *Ecology and the Politics of Scarcity* (San Francisco: W.H. Freeman, 1977), pp. 146–51; Kai Nielsen, *Equality and Liberty: A Defense of Radical Egalitarianism* (Totowa, N.J.: Rowman and Allanheld Publishers, 1985), pp. 228ff; Peter Singer, "Rights in the Market" in *Justice and Economic Distribution*, edited by John Arthur and William Shaw (Englewood Cliffs, N.J.:

Prentice-Hall, 1978), pp. 215–18; and Robert Holsworth and J. Harry Wray, *American Politics and Everyday Life* (New York: John Wiley and Sons, 1982), pp. 21ff.

18. Marx, *Capital: A Critique of Political Economy*, vol. 3: *The Process of Capitalist Production as a Whole* (New York: International Publishers, 1968), p. 820.

19. Eugene Kamenka, *The Ethical Foundations of Marxism* (London: Routledge and Kegan Paul, 1972), pp. 26ff.

20. Marx, "Needs, Production and Division of Labour," p. 171.

21. Ibid., p. 174.

22. Karl Marx, "On the Jewish Question," in *Karl Marx: Early Writings*, trans. by T. B. Bottomore (New York: McGraw-Hill, 1963), p. 15.

23. Radoslav Selucký, *Marxism, Socialism, Freedom: Towards a General Democratic Theory of Labour-managed Systems* (New York: St. Martin's Press, 1979), p. 63.

24. Marx, "On the Jewish Question," p. 23.

25. Ibid., p. 11.

26. MacPherson, *Liberal Democracy*, pp. 33 and 51.

27. "Declaration of the Rights of Man and Citizen," from John Stewart, *A Documentary Survey of the French Revolution* (New York: Macmillan, 1951), arts. 1–35, pp. 455–58.

28. Joseph Femia, "Marxism and Radical Democracy," *Inquiry* 28 (1985), p. 306.

29. Lukes, *Marxism and Morality*, p. 77.

30. "Declaration of Rights," art. 7, p. 456. Emphasis added.

31. Selucký, *Marxism, Socialism, Freedom*, p. 81.

32. Marx, "On the Jewish Question," p. 25.

33. Ibid., p. 27.

34. Ibid., p. 26.

35. Ibid., p. 27.

36. Karl Marx, "Contribution to the Critique of Hegel's Philosophy of Law," in *Karl Marx and Friedrich Engels, Collected Works*, vol. 3 (New York: International Publishers, 1975), p. 16.

37. Ibid., p. 62. Werner Maihofer in *Demokratie in Sozialismus* (Frankfurt/Main, FRG: Vittoria Klostermann, 1968), p. 15, states that Marx replaced the concept of the state with terms such as *Gemeinwesen*, Commune, and republic.

38. Dick Howard, *The Development of the Marxian Dialectic* (Carbondale: Southern Illinois University Press, 1972), p. 62.

39. Marx, "Contribution to Critique of Hegel," pp. 31–32.

40. Howard, *Development of Dialectic*, p. 71.

41. Marx, "Contribution to Critique of Hegel," p. 118.

42. Karl Marx, *Writings of the Young Marx on Philosophy and Society*, trans. by L. Easton and K. Guddat (Garden City, N.Y.: Doubleday, 1967), p. 206.

43. Marx, "Contribution to Critique of Hegel," p. 63.

44. Ibid., p. 8.

45. Ibid., pp. 14–15 and 19.

46. Ibid., p. 27.

47. Ibid., p. 29.

48. Ibid.

49. Ibid.

50. David Rouse, "Marx's Materialist Concept of Democracy," *Philosophy Research Archives* 2, 1064 (1976), p. 431.

51. Marx, "Contribution to Critique of Hegel," p. 30.

52. Ibid., p. 104.

53. Ibid., p. 31.

54. Ibid., p. 62.

55. Ibid., p. 30.

56. Patricia Springborg, "Karl Marx on Democracy, Participation, Voting, and Equality," *Political Theory* 12 (November 1984), pp. 542–43.

57. Marx, "Contribution to Critique of Hegel," p. 30.

58. Ibid.

59. Ibid., p. 57; and Richard Matthews, *The Radical Politics of Thomas Jefferson: A Revisionist View* (Lawrence: University of Kansas Press, 1986), p. 23.

60. Marx, "Contribution to Critique of Hegel," p. 105.

61. Ibid., p. 116.

62. Norman Fischer, "Marx's Early Concept of Democracy and the Ethical Bases of Socialism," in *Marxism and the Good Society*, ed. by John Burke, L. Crocker, and L. Legters (Cambridge, U.K.: Cambridge University Press, 1981), p. 63.

63. Marx, "Contribution to Critique of Hegel," p. 121.

64. Ibid., p. 107.

65. David McLellan, "Marx and Engels on the Future Communist Society," in *Marxism and the Good Society*, ed. by John Burke, L. Crocker, and L. Legters (Cambridge, U.K.: Cambridge University Press, 1981), p. 111.

66. Ibid., p. 73.

67. Marx, "Contribution to Critique of Hegel," p. 41.

68. Ibid., p. 98.

69. Ibid., p. 108.

70. Ibid., p. 119. Emphasis added.

71. The importance of Spinoza's works should be mentioned here, since he was so influential on Marx's early development of a theory of democracy. Of special interest to Marx was the former's theory of democracy, tolerance, freedom, political ideology, and critique of religion. See Fred Schrader, "Substanz und Begriff: Zur Spinoza-Rezeption Marxens," in *Marx und Spinoza*, ed. by P. F. Moreau (Hamburg, FRG: VSA Verlag, 1978); Maximilien Rubel, "Notes on Marx's Conception of Democracy," *New Politics* (1962), pp. 81–82; Ronald Commers, "Marx's Concept of Justice and the Two Traditions in

European Political Thought," *Philosophica* 33 (1984), pp. 113–14; Joel Schwartz, "Liberalism and the Jewish Connection: A Study of Spinoza and the Young Marx," *Political Theory* (February 1985); Shlomo Avineri, *Moses Hess: Prophet of Communism and Zionism* (New York: New York University Press, 1985), ch. 2 and pp. 210–14; and Sigmund Krancberg, "Karl Marx and Democracy," *Studies in Soviet Thought* 24 (July 1982), pp. 27–28.

72. Karl Marx, *The Eighteenth Brumaire of Louis Bonaparte* (New York: International Publishers, 1975), pp. 65–67.

73. Ibid., p. 65.

74. Ibid., p. 67.

75. Karl Marx, *Civil War in France: The Paris Commune* (New York: International Publishers, 1972), p. 58.

76. Ibid., p. 58–59.

77. Shlomo Avineri, *The Social and Political Thought of Karl Marx* (Cambridge, U.K.: Cambridge University Press, 1975), p. 240; Richard Hunt, *The Political Ideas of Marx and Engels: Marxism and Totalitarian Democracy 1818–1850* (Pittsburgh: University of Pittsburgh Press, 1974), ch. 9, pp. 284–336; and Sidney Hook, *Marx and the Marxists: The Ambiguous Legacy* (Princeton, N.J.: D. Van Nostrand, 1955), p. 33.

78. For a critique of the idea that the withering away of the state is synonymous with the withering away of the public sphere—held by Hannah Arendt, *The Human Condition* (Chicago: University of Chicago, 1958), p. 60; and Sheldon Wolin, *Politics and Vision* (London: Allen and Unwin, 1961), pp. 130–31 and 360–61—see Nancy Schwartz, "Distinction between Public and Private Life: Marx on the *zōon politikon*," *Political Theory* 7, 2 (May 1979), pp. 245ff; and Paul Thomas, "Alien Politics: A Marxian Perspective on Citizenship and Democracy," in *After Marx*, ed. by Terence Ball and James Farr (Cambridge, U.K.: Cambridge University Press, 1984), pp. 125–26.

79. Peter Bachrach, *The Theory of Democratic Elitism* (Boston: Little, Brown, 1967). See also Wolfgang Mommsen, *The Political and Social Theory of Max Weber* (Chicago: University of Chicago Press, 1989), pp. 30–43.

80. Alan Gilbert, "Historical Theory and the Structure of Moral Argument in Marx," *Political Theory* 9 (May 1981), p. 193.

81. Marx, *Civil War in France*, p. 60.

82. Ibid., p. 61.

83. Ibid., p. 65.

84. Marx, "Private Property and Communism," p. 158.

85. Engels quoted in Hunt, *Political Ideas of Marx and Engels*, p. 136.

86. Aristotle quoted in R. K. Sinclair, *Democracy and Participation in Athens* (Cambridge, U.K.: Cambridge University Press, 1988) p. 21.

CHAPTER FIVE: MARX AND RICARDO

1. Norman Geras, "The Controversy about Marx and Justice," *Philosophica* 33 (1984).

2. Karl Marx, *Capital: A Critique of Political Economy*, vol. 4: *Theories of*

Surplus Value, trans. and ed. by S. Ryanzanskaya (Moscow: Progress Publishers, 1968), pt. 2, p. 169.

3. David Ricardo, *The Principles of Political Economy and Taxation* (London: J.M. Dent and Sons, 1973), ch. 1.

4. Marx, *Theories of Surplus Value*, pt. 2, p. 164.

5. Ibid., p. 166.

6. Karl Marx, *The Poverty of Philosophy* (New York: International Publishers, 1969), p. 69. See also Robert Lekachman, *A History of Economic Ideas* (New York: McGraw-Hill, 1976), pp. 172–76. For a critique of utopian socialism, see Marx's critique of the socialist time-chitters in the *Grundrisse: Foundations of the Critique of Political Economy*, trans. by Martin Nicolaus (New York: Vintage Books, 1973), pp. 137–39.

7. Marx, *Theories of Surplus Value*, pt. 2, p. 169.

8. Marx, *Theories of Surplus Value*, pp. 373ff. See also Bhikhu Parekh, *Marx's Theory of Ideology* (Baltimore: Johns Hopkins University Press, 1983), pp. 100–35; and Geoffrey Pilling, *Marx's "Capital": Philosophy and Political Economy* (London: Routledge and Kegan Paul, 1980), pp. 9–66.

9. Donald Winch, "Introduction," in David Ricardo's *The Principles of Political Economy and Taxation*, (London: J.M. Dent and Sons, 1973), p. xvi; and Marx, *Grundrisse*, pp. 401–13.

10. Geoffrey Pilling, "The Law of Value in Ricardo and Marx," *Economy and Society* 1 (1972), p. 284.

11. Alfred Medio, "Profits and Surplus Value: Appearance and Reality in Capitalist Production," in *Critique of Economic Theory*, ed. E. K. Hunt (Harmondsworth, U.K.: Penguin Books, 1972), p. 321.

12. Marx, *Theories of Surplus Value*, p. 164.

13. Ibid., p. 172.

14. Maximilien Rubel, *Rubel on Marx: Five Essays*, ed. by Joseph O'Malley and Keith Algozin (Cambridge, U.K.: Cambridge University Press, 1981), p. 11.

15. Marx, *Theories of Surplus Value*, p. 408.

16. A. Cutler, B. Hindess, P. Hirst, and A. Hussain, *Marx's "Capital" and Capitalism Today*, vol. 1 (London: Routledge and Kegan Paul, 1977), p. 43. For an interpretation of Marx's view of labor as an ontological category or substance, see Cornelius Castoriadis, "Value, Equality, Justice, Politics: From Marx to Aristotle and from Aristotle to Ourselves," in *Crossroads in the Labyrinth*, trans. by Kate Soper and Martin Ryle (Cambridge, Mass.: MIT Press, 1984), pp. 261ff; Hans-Georg Backhaus, "Materialien zur Rekonstruktion der Marxschen Werttheorie," *Gesellschaft Beiträge zur Marxschen Theorie*, vol. 1 (Frankfurt, FRG: Suhrkamp Verlag, 1974), p. 216; and Marc Linder, *Reification and the Consciousness of the Critics of Political Economy: Studies in the Development of Marx's Theory of Value* (Copenhagen: Rhodos International Science and Art Publishers, 1975), p. 70.

17. Pilling, "Law of Value in Ricardo and Marx," and *Marx's "Capital."*

18. Karl Marx, *A Contribution to the Critique of Political Economy*, trans. by S. W. Ryazanskaya (New York: International Publishers, 1970), ch. 1 on the nature of the commodity. This is the key insight Marx reached in his analysis of the law of value and exchange value in the *Grundrisse* and *Capital*. See Karl Marx, *Capital: A Critique of Political Economy*, vol. 1: *A Critical Analysis of Capitalist Production*, trans. by Samuel Moore and Edward Aveling, (New York: International Publishers, 1968), pp. 71–83; and I. I. Rubin, *Essays on Marx's Theory of Value*, trans. by Milos Samardzija and Fredy Perlman (Detroit: Black and Red, 1972), pt. 1, chs. 1–7.

19. Karl Korsch, *Karl Marx* (Frankfurt/Main, FRG: Europäische Verlagsanstalt, 1975), p. 104.

20. Marx, *Grundrisse*, p. 240.

21. Ibid., pp. 244–45, and see also pp. 163, 458, and 509.

22. Ibid., p. 243.

23. Ibid., p. 245.

24. Immanuel Kant, *The Fundamental Principles of the Metaphysics of Morals*, trans. by Thomas Abbott (Indianapolis: Bobbs-Merrill, 1949), p. 50.

25. Marx, *Grundrisse*, p. 245.

26. Ibid., pp. 247–48.

27. Marx, *Poverty of Philosophy*, pp. 69–79 and *Grundrisse*, p. 48. See also Norman Levine, *The Tragic Deception: Marx contra Engels* (Oxford, U.K.: Clio Books, 1975), pp. 16–27.

28. Marx, *Grundrisse*, p. 249.

29. For a survey of those who stress a social theory of production—with its emphasis on labor rather than price, and history and social organization rather than the transformation of values into prices, surplus value into profits—see Rudolf Hilferding, "Boehm-Bawerk's Criticism of Marx," in *Karl Marx and the Close of His System*, ed. by Paul Sweezy (New York: Augustus M. Kelly, 1949); Franz Petry, *Der soziale Gehalt der Marxschen Werttheorie* (Bonn: Willi Hammer Verlag, 1984); Rubin, *Essays on Marx*, and *A History of Economic Thought* (London: INK Links, 1979); Pilling, "Law of Value in Ricardo and Marx," and *Marx's "Capital"*; Frank Roosevelt, "Cambridge Economics as Commodity Fetishism," *Review of Radical Political Economics* (1975); E. K. Hunt, "Marx's Concept of Human Nature and the Labor Theory of Value," *Review of Radical Political Economics* 14, 2 (Summer 1982); Backhaus, "Materialien zur Rekonstruktion," vol. 1, and "Materialien zur Rekonstruktion der Marxschen Werttheorie," in *Gesellschaft Beiträge zur Marxschen Theorie*, vol. 3 (Frankfurt/Main, FRG: Suhrkamp Verlag, 1975); and Paul Mattick, *Marx and Keynes: The Limits of the Mixed Economy* (Boston: Porter Sargent Publisher, 1969), chs. 3 and 4.

For an overview of the "Transformation debate" that began with an exchange between Boehm-Bawerk and Hilferding, there are a few important readers in the area: E. K. Hunt, *Critique of Economic Theory* (Harmondsworth, U.K.: Penguin Books, 1972); Ian Steedman, ed., *Value Controversy* (London: New Left Books, 1981); "Modern Approaches to the Theory of Value," *Review of Radical Political Economics* 14, 2 (Summer 1982); and Ben Fine, ed., *The Value Dimension: Marx versus Ricardo and Sraffa* (London: Routledge and Kegan Paul, 1986).

30. Korsch, *Karl Marx*, p. 110.

31. M. I. Finley, "Aristotle and Economic Analysis," in *Articles on Aristotle*, vol. 2: *Ethics and Politics*, ed. by J. Barnes, M. Schofield, and R. Sorabji (New York: St. Martin's Press, 1977), p. 152.

32. Medio, "Profits and Surplus Value," p. 317.

33. Marx, *Grundrisse*, p. 140.

34. Pilling, *Marx's "Capital,"* ch. 5; and Parekh, *Marx's Theory of Ideology*, pp. 136–63.

35. Korsch, *Karl Marx*, pp. 95–121.

36. Petry, *Der soziale Gehalt der Marxschen Werttheorie*, pp. 16–17.

37. Ibid., p. 15; and Pilling, "Law of Value in Ricardo and Marx," pp. 289–90.

38. Petry, *Der soziale Gehalt der Marxschen Werttheorie*, p. 23.

39. Korsch, *Karl Marx*, p. 117.

40. For an attempt to critique the metaphysical laws of value in Marx and to reinterpret him as a price theorist, see Piero Sraffa, *Production of Commodities by Means of Commodities: Prelude to a Critique of Economic Theory* (Cambridge, Mass.: Cambridge University Press, 1960), pp. 29ff.

41. Petry, *Der soziale Gehalt der Marxschen Werttheorie*, pp. 5 and 17.

42. Ibid., p. 6.

43. Korsch, *Karl Marx*, p. 112.

44. Ibid.

45. Petry, *Der soziale Gehalt der Marxschen Werttheorie*, p. 22.

46. Ibid., pp. 33–35.

47. Ibid., p. 32.

48. Ian Hunt, "The Labors of Steedman on Marx," *Review of Radical Political Economics* (Winter 1982); Medio, "Profits and Surplus Value," p. 316; and "Modern Approaches to Theory of Value."

49. Pilling, "Law of Value in Ricardo and Marx," p. 301.

50. Petry, *Der soziale Gehalt der Marxschen Werttheorie*, p. 35.

51. Jon Elster, *Making Sense of Marx* (Cambridge, U.K.: Cambridge University Press, 1985); and Richard Miller, *Analyzing Marx: Morality, Power and History* (Princeton, N.J.: Princeton University Press, 1984), p. 214.

52. This is the thesis developed by Korsch, Petry, and Pilling.

53. For a critique of Marx's theory of value from the neo-Ricardian Cambridge school of economics, see Joan Robinson, *An Essay on Marxian Economics* (London: Macmillan, 1966); Sraffa, *Production of Commodities*; Luigi Pasinetti, *Lectures on the Theory of Production* (New York: Columbia University

Press, 1977); Ian Steedman, *Marx after Sraffa* (London: New Left Books, 1977); and Geoff Hodgson, "Marx without the Labor Theory of Value," *Review of Radical Political Economics* 14, 2 (Summer 1982), pp. 59–65.

Other Marxists who reject Marx's labor theory of value include: Cutler, Hindness, Hirst, and Hussain, *"Capital" and Capitalism Today*, vol. 1. Those who are critical of Marx's labor theory of value and wish to reconcile Marx and Sraffa include: Maurice Dobb, *Political Economy and Capitalism: Some Essays in Economic Tradition* (New York: International Publishers, 1940); and Ronald Meek, *Studies in the Labour Theory of Value* (New York: Monthly Review Press, 1956).

An interesting response to this approach is offered by Backhaus, "Materialien zur Rekonstruktion," vol. 1, pp. 213–17. For a critique of the Cambridge school of thought and Robinson, Sraffa, Sweezy, Dobb, and Lange's appropriation of Marx, see Linder, *Reification and the Consciousness of the Critics*, pp. 86–88 and 121–24.

54. Agnes Heller, *Beyond Justice* (Oxford, U.K.: Basil Blackwell, 1987), pp. 106–7; and my review of her book in *Contemporary Sociology* 17, 3 (July 1988). Unfortunately, Heller separates freedom and justice, and denies that Marx can and does develop the latter.

55. Marx, *Capital*, vol. 1, p. 59.

56. Castoriadis, "Value, Equality, Justice, Politics." For a more sensitive interpretation of Marx, but a similar reduction of value to a metaphysical category of labor see Robinson, *Essay on Marxian Economics*, pp. 1–22.

57. Marx, *Grundrisse*, pp. 251–52.

58. Ibid., p. 144.

59. For a nice summary of the nature of abstract value and its relation to alienation, see Claudio Napoleoni's *Ricardo und Marx* (Frankfurt/Main, FRG: Suhrkamp Verlag, 1974), pp. 204 and 213–27. This book is an analysis of the famous "unpublished" chapter 6 of the first book of *Capital*, which is now available separately: *Resultate des unmittelbaren Produktionsprozesses* (Frankfurt/Main, FRG: Verlag Neue Kritik, 1969).

60. Marx, *Grundrisse*, p. 144.

61. Rubin, *Essays on Marx*, p. 63.

62. Marx, *Contribution to Critique of Political Economy*, p. 36.

63. Marx, *Grundrisse*, p. 143.

64. Ibid., p. 157.

65. Ibid., p. 158.

66. Here is a summary of the seven notebooks of Marx, *Grundrisse*:

1. Analysis of simple exchange
2. Examination of equality and freedom in exchange; transition from circulation and simple exchange to production; analysis of exchange value and capital, labor and capital
3. Theory of surplus value and profits

4. Discussion of the realization problem, economic crises, and over-production
5. History; analysis of noncapitalist and precapitalist social systems
6. Critique of classical political economy and their emphasis on a theory of circulation
7. History of the development of labor in England; study of labor, machinery, and science
Appendix. Fall of the rate of profit, and discussion of the nature of profit in classical political economy

67. Marx, *Grundrisse*, p. 156.
68. Karl Polanyi, *The Great Transformation: The Political and Economic Origins of Our Time* (Boston: Beacon Press, 1957).
69. Marx, *Grundrisse*, p. 171.
70. Ibid., p. 172.
71. Ibid., p. 289.
72. Ibid., p. 297.
73. Ibid., p. 308.
74. Ibid., p. 471.
75. Ibid., p. 506.
76. Ibid., p. 507.
77. Ibid., pp. 509–10.
78. Ibid., p. 324.
79. Ibid., p. 334.
80. Ibid., p. 364.
81. Ibid., p. 365.
82. Edward Nell, "Value and Capital in Marxian Economics," in *The Crisis in Economic Theory* (New York: Basic Books, 1981), pp. 179–80 and 190; Petry, *Der soziale Gehalt der Marxschen Werttheorie*, pp. 50–51; and Korsch, *Karl Marx*, p. 110.
83. Marx, *Grundrisse*, p. 411.
84. Ibid., p. 410.
85. Ibid., p. 412.
86. Ibid., p. 415. See also Elster, *Making Sense*.
87. Marx, *Grundrisse*, p. 415.
88. Ibid., p. 416.
89. Ibid., p. 420.
90. Ibid., p. 421.
91. Ibid., p. 652.
92. Levine, *Tragic Deception*, p. 26.
93. Marx, *Grundrisse*, p. 706.
94. Albrecht Wellmer, *Critical Theory of Society*, trans. by John Cumming (New York: Herder and Herder, 1971), p. 82.
95. Marx, *Capital*, vol. 1, p. 57.

96. "Modern Approaches to Theory of Value."
97. Marx, *Capital*, vol. 1, p. 751.

CHAPTER SIX: THEORY OF ETHICS AND SOCIAL JUSTICE

1. Philip Grier, *Marxist Ethical Theory in the Soviet Union* (Dordrecht, Netherlands: Reidel Publishing, 1978), pp. 15–18; Thomas Willey, *Back to Kant: The Revival of Kantianism in German Social and Historical Thought, 1860–1914* (Detroit: Wayne State University Press, 1978), pp. 32–33; Leszek Kolakowski, *Main Currents of Marxism: Its Rise, Growth, and Dissolution*, vol. 2: *The Golden Age*, trans. by P. S. Falla (Oxford, U.K.: Clarendon Press, 1978), pp. 249–50; David Lipton, *Ernst Cassirer: The Dilemma of a Liberal Intellectual in Germany 1914–1933* (Toronto: University of Toronto Press, 1978), pp. 19–23; Karl Vorländer, *Kant und der Sozialismus. Unter besonderer Berücksichtigung der neuesten theoretischen Bewegung innerhalb des Marxismus* (Berlin: Reuther und Reichard Verlag, 1900); Hermann Cohen, *Kants Begründung der Ethik* (Berlin: Bruno Cassirer Verlag, 1910); and Theodor Steinbüchel, "Zur Kritik des marxistischen Sozialismus," in *Sozialismus* (Tübingen, FRG: J.C.B. Mohr Verlag (Paul Siebeck), 1950).

2. Karl Vorländer, *Kant und Marx: Ein Beitrag Zur Philosophie des Sozialismus* (Tübingen, FRG: J.C.B. Mohr Verlag (Paul Siebeck), 1926), p. 129.

3. Allan Wood, *Karl Marx* (London: Routledge and Kegan Paul, 1981); and Marshall Cohen, Thomas Nagel, and Thomas Scanlon, eds., *Marx, Justice, and History* (Princeton, N.J.: Princeton University Press, 1980). See also George Brenkert, *Marx's Ethics of Freedom* (London: Routledge and Kegan Paul, 1983); and Allen Buchanan, *Marx and Justice* (Totowa, N.J.: Rowman and Littlefield, 1982).

4. Robert Tucker, *The Marxian Revolutionary Idea* (New York: W.W. Norton, 1969), p. 37.

5. See the discussion between Alan Wood, "The Marxian Critique of Justice," and Ziyad Husami, "Marx on Distributive Justice," in Cohen, Nagel, and Scanlon, *Marx, Justice, and History*. Also see the response of Carol Gould to the limited nature of the discussion about distributive justice in *Marx's Social Ontology: Individuality and Community in Marx's Theory of Social Reality* (Cambridge, Mass.: MIT Press, 1978), p. 159.

6. Norman Geras, "The Controversy about Marx and Justice," *Philosophica* 33 (1984), pp. 35–50. Geras organizes a list of the literature surrounding this debate. Among those listed who do not critique capitalism for being unjust are Tucker, Wood, Brenkert, Buchanan, Lukes, Allen, Crocker, and Miller. Those listed who do see the use of justice in Marx's writings include Arneson, G. A. Cohen, Elster, Green, Husami, Riley, Ryan, van der Linden, van de Veer, and Young. For another overview of the debate, see Steven Lukes, *Marxism and Morality* (Oxford, U.K.: Clarendon Press, 1985), pp. 48–70.

7. Wood, *Karl Marx*, pp. 126–27.

8. George McCarthy, *Marx' Critique of Science and Positivism: The Methodological Foundations of Political Economy* (Dordrecht, Netherlands: Kluwer Academic Publishers, 1988), ch. 4, pp. 98ff.

9. Seyla Benhabib, *Critique, Norm, and Utopia: A Study of the Foundations of Critical Theory* (New York: Columbia University Press, 1987), pp. 105–33; and Jean Cohen, *Class and Civil Society: The Limits of Marxian Critical Theory* (Amherst: University of Massachusetts Press, 1982), pp. 29–52.

10. Karl Marx, *Capital: A Critique of Political Economy*, vol. 1: *A Critical Analysis of Capitalist Production*, trans. by Samuel Moore and Edward Aveling (New York: International Publishers, 1968).

11. Jon Elster, *Making Sense of Marx* (Cambridge, U.K.: Cambridge University Press, 1985), pp. 157ff.

12. Karl Marx, *Grundrisse: Foundations of the Critique of Political Economy*, trans. by Martin Nicolaus (New York: Vintage Books, 1973), p. 488.

13. Michael DeGolyer, "Science and Society, Justice and Equality: An Historical Approach to Marx," dissertation, University of Michigan microfilm, 1985, p. 267.

14. Ibid., p. 265.

15. Marx, *Grundrisse*, p. 245.

16. McCarthy, *Marx' Critique of Science*, pt. 1, pp. 20ff.

17. There is a tendency to overemphasize the Hegelian critiques of Kant and to miss the strong component of Kantian ethics in Marx's works. See David Meyers, "The Young Marx and Kantian Ethics," *Studies in Soviet Thought* 33 (May 1986), and "Marx and Transcendence of Ethical Humanism," *Studies in Soviet Thought* 21 (November 1980); Franz von Magnis, *Normative Voraussetzungen im Denken des jungen Marx* (Freiberg, FRG: Verlag Karl Alber, 1975), p. 205; and Philip Kant, *Marx and Ethics* (Oxford, U.K.: Clarendon Press, 1988), pp. 15–82. In distinction to the neo-Kantians from the Marburg School, they argue that Kantian ethics is internally part of Marx's social theory.

18. Jürgen Habermas, *Communication and the Evolution of Society*, trans. by Thomas McCarthy (Boston: Beacon Press, 1979).

19. James O'Rourke, *The Problem of Freedom in Marxist Thought: An Analysis of the Treatment of Human Freedom by Marx, Engels, Lenin, and Contemporary Soviet Philosophy* (Dordrecht, Netherlands: Reidel Publishing, 1974), p. 14.

20. Ulrich Erckenbrecht, *Das Geheimnis des Fetishismus. Grundmotive der Marxschen Erkenntniskritik* (Frankfurt/Main, FRG: Europäische Verlagsanstalt, 1976), p. 20; Karl Nachfolgn, "Grundlagentheoretische Erörterung des philosophischen Begriffs des Problem der Produktion, zum Verhältnis von Selfskonstitution und Erfahrung bei Kant, Hegel und Marx," dissertation, University of Köln, 1984, p. 122; and Herbert Marcuse, *Reason and Revolution: Hegel and the Rise of Social Theory* (Boston: Beacon Press, 1960), p. 316.

21. Paul Mattick, *Marx and Keynes: The Limits of the Mixed Economy* (Boston: Porter Sargent Publishers, 1969), pp. 28–29.

22. Lukes, *Marxism and Morality*; and Brenkert, *Marx's Ethics of Freedom*. For an article very critical of recent analytical philosophers' readings of

Marx—including Wood, Brenkert, M. Cohen, and Buchanan—see Anton Leist, "Mit Marx von Gerechtigkeit zu Freiheit und zurück," in *Philosophische Rundschau*, ed. by R. Bubner and B. Waldenfels (Tübingen, FRG: J.S.B. Mohr, 1985). Leist believes that the U.S. philosophical tradition has failed to consider adequately the role of German philosophy—especially Kant and Hegel—in its analyses of Marx.

23. Driscilla Cornell, "Should a Marxist Believe in Rights?" *Praxis International* 4, 1 (April 1984), p. 54.

24. Alan Gilbert, "Historical Theory and the Structure of Moral Argument in Marx," *Political Theory* 9 (May 1981), p. 193. See also Gilbert's "Marx's Moral Realism: Eudaimonism and Moral Progress," in *After Marx*, ed. by Terence Ball and James Farr (Cambridge, U.K.: Cambridge University Press, 1984).

25. Joachim Ritter, *Metaphysik und Politik. Studien zu Aristoteles und Hegel* (Frankfurt/Main, FRG: Suhrkamp Verlag, 1969), p. 145; Heinz Krumpel, *Zur Moralphilosophie Hegels* (Berlin: VEB Deutscher Verlag der Wissenschaften, 1972), p. 57; and Otfried Höffe, et al., eds. *Lexikon der Ethik* (Munich: Verlag C.H. Beck, 1986), p. 54.

26. Philip Kain, *Schiller, Hegel, and Marx: State, Society, and the Aesthetic Ideal of Ancient Greece* (Kingston, Ont., Canada: McGill-Queen's University Press, 1982).

27. Cornell, "Should a Marxist Believe in Rights?" p. 52.

28. Karl Marx, "Letters from the *Deutsch-Französische Jahrbücher*, Sept. 1843," in *Karl Marx and Friedrich Engels, Collected Works*, vol.3 (New York: International Publishers, 1975), p. 144.

29. Karl Marx, "The German Ideology," in *Karl Marx and Friedrich Engels, Collected Works*, vol.5 (New York: International Publishers, 1976), p. 49.

30. Joseph Femia, "Marxism and Radical Democracy," *Inquiry* 28 (1985), p. 299; and John O'Neill, "Scientific Socialism and Democracy: A Response to Femia," *Inquiry* 29, 3 (September 1986), pp. 345–53.

31. McCarthy, *Marx' Critique of Science*, pp. 44–66; Herbert Marcuse, *Hegel's Ontology and the Theory of Historicity*, trans. by S. Benhabib (Cambridge, Mass.: MIT Press, 1987), pp. 80–88; Shlomo Avineri, *The Social and Political Thought of Karl Marx* (Cambridge, U.K.: Cambridge University Press, 1975), pp. 221–22; Walter Kaufmann, *Hegel: Reinterpretation, Texts, and Commentary* (Garden City, N.Y.: Doubleday, 1965), p. 175; Geoffrey Pilling, "The Law of Value in Ricardo and Marx," *Economy and Society* 1 (1972), pp. 289–90; Richard Bernstein, *Praxis and Action: Contemporary Philosophies of Human Action* (Philadelphia: University of Pennsylvania Press, 1971), p. 34. Though he accepts the idea that Marx was using the method of the natural sciences, Femia in "Marxism and Radical Democracy," p. 300, recognizes that Marx's critique of utopian socialism represents a critique of making social blueprints about the future.

32. Donald van de Veer, "Marx's View of Justice," *Philosophy and Phenomenological Research* 33, 3 (March 1973), p. 385.

33. Jürgen Habermas, *Knowledge and Human Interests*, trans. by Jeremy Shapiro (Boston: Beacon Press, 1971). Similar themes found in different philosophical schools of thought are analyzed in Richard Rorty, *Philosophy and the Mirror of Nature* (Princeton, N.J.: Princeton University Press, 1979), pp. 131–212; and Benjamin Barber, *Strong Democracy: Participatory Politics for a New Age* (Berkeley: University of California Press, 1984), pp. 146–66.

34. Roger Garaudy, *Marxism in the Twentieth Century*, trans. by Rene Hague (New York: Charles Scribner's Sons, 1970), p. 78. Garaudy recognizes the dilemma of morality and the solution in social interaction and communication, but he does not develop this beyond an analysis of Existentialism and Fichte.

> In this Marxist attitude to man and his history, the moral problem cannot be shelved: it cannot be replaced by the scientific and technical problem of truth, of the search for and discovery of a *true* order of things and of nature which would give to moral conduct a foundation external to man.

35. Tom Goff, *Marx and Mead: Contributions to a Sociology of Knowledge* (London: Routledge and Kegan Paul, 1980), p. 35; Alan Swingewood, *Marx and Modern Social Theory* (New York: John Wiley and Sons, 1975), pp. 58–86; David-Hillel Ruben, *Marx and Materialism: A Study in Marxist Theory of Knowledge* (Sussex: Harvester Press, 1977); Michael Schwalbe, *The Psychosocial Consequences of Natural and Alienated Labor* (Albany: State University of New York Press, 1986), pp. 7–56; Eugene Kamenka, *The Ethical Foundations of Marxism* (London: Routledge and Kegan Paul, 1972), pp. 122–31; and Georg Lukács, *History and Class Consciousness: Studies in Marxist Dialectics*, trans. by Rodney Livingstone (Cambridge, Mass.: MIT Press, 1971).

36. Adolfo Sánchez Vázquez, "The Philosophy of Praxis, trans. by Mike Gonzalez (London: Merlin Press, 1977), pp. 116ff., defends the expansive role of praxis; while Bhikhu Parekh, *Marx's Theory of Ideology* (Baltimore: Johns Hopkins University Press, 1982), p. 195, narrows the role to the constitution of the objects of experience, and finally ends by supporting a modified correspondence theory of truth, p. 203.

37. Kolakowski quoted in Goff, *Marx and Mead*, p. 33.

38. John Plamenatz, *Karl Marx's Philosophy of Man* (Oxford, U.K.: Clarendon Press, 1975), p. 346.

39. Sánchez Vázquez, *Philosophy of Praxis*, p. 121.

40. David Campbell, "Rationality, Democracy, and Freedom in Marxist Critiques of Hegel's *Philosophy of Right*," *Inquiry* 28, 1 (March 1985), p. 69.

41. Marcuse, *Reason and Revolution*, pp. 6–27.

42. Barber, *Strong Democracy*, pp. 64–65. Sidney Hook holds a similar view in *Revolution, Reform, and Social Justice: Studies in the Theory and Practice of Marxism* (New York: New York University Press, 1975), p. 80.

43. There have been works that attempt to make the connection between Marx and pragmatism. See Norman D. Livergood, *Activity in Marx's Philosophy*

(The Hague, Netherlands: Martinus Nijhoff, 1967); Bernstein, *Praxis and Action*, pp. 80–81; Jim Cork, "John Dewey, Karl Marx, and Democratic Socialism," *Antioch Review* 9, 4 (December 1949), Goff, *Marx and Mead*, pp. 33–34; Leszek Kolakowski, "Karl Marx and the Classical Definition of Truth," in *Marxism and Beyond*, trans. by Jane Peel (London: Paul Mall Press, 1968); and Ruben, *Marx and Materialism*, pp. 113ff. The popular notion of pragmatism—that truth is what works—is antithetical to Marx's idea of truth, since the former reduces truth to *techne*.

44. Georg Friedrich Hegel, *Philosophy of Right*, trans. by T. M. Knox (London: Oxford University Press, 1967), p. 13.

45. Richard Hunt, *The Political Ideas of Marx and Engels: Marxism and Totalitarian Democracy 1818–1850* (Pittsburgh: University of Pittsburgh Press, 1974), p. 5.

46. Barber, *Strong Democracy*, p. 65.

47. Aristotle, *The Politics*, trans. by H. Rackham (London: William Heinemann, 1932), sec. 1286a26–30, p. 257.

48. Karl Marx, "Theses on Feuerbach," in *Marx and Engels: Basic Writings on Politics and Philosophy*, ed. by Lewis Feuer (Garden City, N.Y.: Doubleday, 1959), p. 243.

49. Lukács, *History and Class Consciousness*, p. 2.

50. Karl Marx, "Contribution to the Critique of Hegel's Philosophy of Law: An Introduction," in *Karl Marx and Friedrich Engels, Collected Works*, vol. 3 (New York: International Publishers, 1975), p. 182.

51. Alan Gilbert, *Marx's Politics: Communists and Citizens* (New Brunswick, N.J.: Rutgers University Press, 1981), pp. 30ff.

52. Karl Marx, *Civil War in France: The Paris Commune* (New York: International Publishers, 1972), pp. 58 and 65.

53. Ibid., pp. 57–58.

54. Gilbert, *Marx's Politics*, pp. 122–24; Hunt, *Political Ideas of Marx and Engels*, pp. 167–70; and Thomas Sowell, "Karl Marx and the Freedom of the Individual," *Ethics* 73 (January 1963), pp. 122–23.

55. Karl Marx, "Needs, Production, and Division of Labour," in *Karl Marx: Early Writings*, trans. by T. B. Bottomore (New York: McGraw-Hill, 1963), p. 176; Hunt, *Political Ideas of Marx and Engels*, pp. 90–91, 167, and 229; and Hal Draper, *Karl Marx's Theory of Revolution*, volume 2: *The Politics of Social Classes* (New York: Monthly Review Press, 1978), pp. 52–56.

56. Marx, "The German Ideology," pp. 77–78.

57. Gilbert, *Marx's Politics*, p. 39.

58. Jean Jacques Rousseau, *The Social Contract and Discourses*, trans. by G. D. H. Cole (New York: E.P. Dutton, 1950), pp. 18–19, 26–27, and 94–95. For a further positive analysis of the relationships between Marx and Rousseau and Marx and the Jacobins, see Gilbert, *Marx's Politics*; Plamenatz, *Marx's Philosophy of Man*, pp. 322–96; Erica Sherover-Marcuse, *Emancipation and Consciousness: Dogmatic and Dialectic Perspectives in the Early Marx* (Oxford,

U.K.: Basil Blackwell, 1986), pp. 36–43; George Lichtheim, *The Origins of Socialism* (New York: Praeger Publishers, 1969); and Norman Levine, *The Tragic Deception: Marx contra Engels* (Oxford, U.K.: Clio Books, 1975). For a critical approach, see Hunt, *Political Ideas of Marx and Engels*, p. 84; István Mészáros, *Marx's Theory of Alienation* (New York: Harper and Row, 1970), pp. 48–65; Patricia Springborg, *The Problem of Human Needs and the Critique of Civilization* (London: Allen and Unwin, 1981), pp. 35–52 and 94–117; and John Maguire, *Marx's Theory of Politics* (Cambridge, U.K.: Cambridge University Press, 1978), pp. 10–11.

59. Karl Marx, "Debates on Freedom of the Press and Publication of the Proceedings of the Assembly of the Estates," in *Karl Marx and Friedrich Engels, Collected Works*, vol. 1 (New York: International Publishers, 1975), p. 165.

60. Alessandro Ferrara, "A Critique of Habermas' *Diskursethik*," *Telos* (Winter 1986).

61. Wolfgang Müller, "Habermas und die Anwendbarkeit der Arbeitswerttheorie," *Sozialistische Politik* (1969), pp. 45–49.

62. Habermas, *Knowledge and Human Interests*, p. 30.

63. Ibid., p. 42.

64. Cohen, *Class and Civil Society*, pp. 80–81.

65. Habermas, *Knowledge and Human Interests*, p. 82.

66. Erich Hahn, "Die theoretischen Grundlagen der Soziologie von Jürgen Habermas," in *Theoretische Probleme der marxistischen Soziologie* (Köln, FRG: Pahl-Rugenstein Verlag, 1974), p. 215. The same essay also appears in *Die "Frankfurter Schule" im Lichte des Marxismus* (Frankfurt/Main, FRG: Verlag Marxistische Blätter GmbH, 1970), pp. 70–89.

67. Hahn, "Theoretischen Grundlagen der Soziologie von Habermas," p. 222.

68. Eberhard Rüddenklau, *Gesellschaftliche Arbeit oder Arbeit und Interaktion? Zum Stellenwert des Arbeitsbegriffs bei Habermas, Marx, und Hegel* (Frankfurt/Main, FRG: Peter Lang Verlag, 1982), p. 156.

69. Karl Marx, "Private Property and Communism," in *Karl Marx: Early Writings*, trans. by T. B. Bottomore (New York: McGraw-Hill, 1963), p. 156.

70. O'Rourke, *Problem of Freedom in Marxist Thought*, p. 23.

71. For a broader interpretation of Marx's notion of practical activity, see Avineri, *Social and Political Thought of Marx*, pp. 138–39; Bernstein, *Praxis and Action*, pt. 1; Gajo Petrović, *Marx in the Mid-Twentieth Century* (Garden City, N.Y.: Doubleday, 1967), pp. 77–80; William McBride, "Marxism and Natural Law," *American Journal of Jurisprudence* 15 (1970), p. 146; Lawrence Crocker, "Marx, Liberty, and Democracy," in *Marxism and the Good Society*, ed. by John Burke, L. Crocker, and L. Legters (Cambridge, U.K.: Cambridge University Press, 1981); Sánchez Vázquez, *Philosophy of Praxis*, p. 155. Jean Cohen—who in her *Class and Civil Society*, p. 47, accepts Habermas's interpretation—recognizes a range of different meanings attached to the concept by Marx, beyond labor.

72. Gilbert, *Marx's Politics*, p. 111.

73. Gerhard Steege, *Gesellschaftliche Werte und Ziele—Ihre inhaltlich—quali-tative Bestimmung und ihre Entstehung—zum philosophisch-anthropologischen Grun-dlegung einer materialistischen soziologischen Werttheorie* (Frankfurt/Main, FRG: Peter Lang Verlag, 1986), p. 170.

74. Oskar Cöster, *Hegel und Marx. Struktur und Moralität ihrer Begriffe politische-sozialer Vernunft* (Bonn: Bouvier Verlag, 1983), p. 676.

75. Franz Petry, *Der soziale Gehalt der Marxschen Werttheorie* (Bonn: Willi Hammer Verlag, 1984), p. 28.

76. Ferrara, "Critique of *Diskursethik*," p. 67.

77. Peter Bachrach, *The Theory of Democratic Elitism: A Critique* (Boston: Little, Brown, 1967), p. 24. See also Thomas Spragens, *The Irony of Liberal Reason* (Chicago: University of Chicago Press, 1981), p. 290. For an analysis of this problem in relation to Hegel, see Steven Smith, "Hegel and the French Revolution: An Epitaph for Republicanism," *Social Research* 56, 1 (Spring 1989), p. 250.

78. Ferrara, "Critique of *Diskursethik*," p. 64.

79. Martha Nussbaum, *The Fragility of Goodness: Luck and Ethics in Greek Tragedy and Philosophy* (Cambridge, U.K.: Cambridge University Press, 1986), p. 312.

80. David Depew, "Aristotle's *De Anima* and Marx's Theory of Man," *Graduate Faculty Philosophy Journal*, New School for Social Research, 8 (Spring 1982), p. 138. For a discussion that connects Marx's concept of praxis to symbolic interaction, see Mary Ellen Batiuk and Howard Sacks, "George Herbert Mead and Karl Marx: Exploring Consciousness and Community," *Symbolic Interaction* 4, 2 (1981). For a further development of these ideas, see the analysis of Gramsci's position that the world is "not cognitively innocent" and that reality "exists and is intelligible only in relation with human activ-ity"—resulting in an objectivity that "is identical (or closely associated) with intersubjective consensus"—in Joseph Femia, *Gramsci's Political Thought: He-gemony, Consciousness, and the Revolutionary Process* (Oxford, U.K.: Clarendon Press, 1981), pp. 102–3.

81. The primacy of individual freedom has been recognized by a variety of authors including: Mihailo Marković, *From Affluence to Praxis: Philosophy and Social Criticism* (Ann Arbor: University of Michigan Press, 1974), pp. 62 and 182; Petrović, *Marx in Mid-Twentieth Century*, pp. 125–27; O'Rourke, *Problem of Freedom in Marxist Thought*, p. 15; Radoslav Selucký, *Marxism, Socialism, Freedom: Towards a General Democratic Theory of Labour-managed Systems* (New York: St. Martin's Press, 1979), p. 82; Jim Cork, "Dewey, Marx, and Democratic Socialism," p. 448; Gould, *Marx's Social Ontology*, ch. 4; Brenkert, *Marx's Ethics of Freedom*, ch. 4; Bertell Ollman, *Alienation: Marx's Conception of Man in Capitalist Society* (Cambridge: Cambridge University Press, 1971), pp. 116–20; Erich Fromm, *Marx's Concept of Man* (New York: Frederick Ungar Publishing, 1969), p. 61; and Sidney Hook, *Marx and the Marxists: The*

Ambiguous Legacy (Princeton, N.J.: D. Van Nostrand, 1955), p. 16. Lukes in *Marxism and Morality* theorizes that Marx's concept of freedom falls into the tradition of Spinoza, Rousseau, Kant, and Hegel and is a "category of wider, more complex, or richer views of freedom." Steven Smith provides a fuller philosophical context for an understanding of these issues in his work *Hegel's Critique of Liberalism: Rights in Context* (Chicago: University of Chicago Press, 1989). He argues that Hegel's rejection of natural rights rests on liberalism's inadequate view of reason, creativity, rights, community, human nature, freedom, and the common good. In the end it leads to false consciousness, a faulty conception of civic virtue, moral abstractionism, and ultimately to political terror.

82. Alan Gilbert, "The Storming of Heaven: Politics and Marx's *Capital*," in *Marxism*, Nomos Series, no. 26, ed. by J. Roland Pennock and John Chapman (New York: New York University Press, 1983), p. 150.

83. Karl Marx, "Contribution to the Critique of Hegel's Philosophy of Law," in *Karl Marx and Friedrich Engels, Collected Works*, vol. 3 (New York: International Publishers, 1975), p. 117.

84. Marx, *Civil War in France*, p. 62.

85. Cöster, *Hegel und Marx*, p. 554.

86. Ibid., p. 556.

87. Kosmas Psychopedis, *Geschichte und Methode. Begründungstypen und Interpretationskriterien der Gesellschaftstheorie—Kant, Hegel, Marx, und Weber* (Frankfurt/Main, FRG: Compus Verlag, 1984), p. 214.

88. Ibid.

89. Nussbaum, *Fragility of Goodness*, p. 301.

90. William Leiss, *The Domination of Nature* (Boston: Beacon Press, 1974), pp. 101–14.

91. Marx, "Needs, Production, and Division of Labour," p. 176.

About the Author

GEORGE E. MCCARTHY is Associate Professor of Sociology at Kenyon College, Gambier, Ohio. He received an M.A. and Ph.D. in philosophy from Boston College and an M.A. and Ph.D. in sociology from the Graduate Faculty, New School for Social Research in New York. He has been a research fellow at the University of Frankfurt/Main and a guest professor at the University of Munich, West Germany. He is the author of *Marx' Critique of Science and Positivism* (Dordrecht, Netherlands: Kluwer Academic Publishers, 1988) and *Social Justice and the Economy*, with Royal Rhodes (Maryknoll, N.Y.: Orbis Books, forthcoming).

Index

335